Merriam-Webster's
Manual for
Writers and Editors

Merriam-Webster's
Manual for
Writers and Editors

Merriam-Webster, Incorporated
Springfield, Massachusetts

A GENUINE MERRIAM-WEBSTER

The name *Webster* alone is no guarantee of excellence. It is used by a number of publishers and may serve mainly to mislead an unwary buyer.

Merriam-Webster™ is the name you should look for when you consider the purchase of dictionaries and other fine reference books. It carries the reputation of a company that has been publishing since 1831 and is your assurance of quality and authority.

Copyright © 1998 by Merriam-Webster, Incorporated

Library of Congress Cataloging-in-Publication Data

Merriam-Webster's manual for writers and editors
        p.   cm.
    Rev. ed. of: Webster's standard American style manual. 1985.
    Includes bibliographical references and index.
    ISBN 0–87779–622–X
    1. Authorship—Style manuals.   I. Merriam-Webster, Inc.
    II. Webster's standard American style manual.
    PN147.M49   1998
    808′.027—dc21   97–40798
                                                              CIP

Printed and bound in the United States of America

Contents

Preface   xi

1 Punctuation   1

Apostrophe 1
Brackets 3
Colon 4
Comma 6
Dash 16
Ellipsis Points 19
Exclamation Point 21

Hyphen 22
Parentheses 23
Period 26
Question Mark 27
Quotation Marks 28
Semicolon 32
Slash 34

2 Capitals and Italics   36

Beginnings 36
Proper Nouns and Adjectives 38
Other Styling Conventions 54

3 Plurals, Possessives, and Compounds   58

Plurals 58
Possessives 63
Compounds 67

4 Abbreviations   79

Punctuation 79
Capitalization 81
Plurals, Possessives, and Compounds 81
Specific Styling Conventions 83

5 Numbers   91

Numbers as Words or Figures 91
Punctuation 95
Specific Styling Conventions 98

6 Mathematics and Science   108

Mathematics 108
Physical Sciences 119
Biology and Medicine 127
Computer Terminology 133
Signs and Symbols 134

7 Quotations 139

Styling Block Quotations 139
Alterations and Omissions 141
Epigraphs and Blurbs 144
Quoting Verse 145

8 Foreign Languages 148

General Guidelines 148
German 150
Dutch 153
Danish, Norwegian, Swedish 153
Spanish 155
French 156
Italian 159
Portuguese 160

Latin 161
Polish 161
Czech 162
Classical Greek 163
Russian 165
Arabic and Hebrew 168
Chinese and Japanese 169

9 Tables and Illustrations 172

Tables and Graphs 172
Art 193

10 Notes and Bibliographies 207

Footnotes and Endnotes 210
Parenthetical References 217
Other Systems 220
Bibliographies 223
Special Types of References 231

11 Indexes 238

Index Types and Formats 239
The Elements of an Index Entry 240
Preparing the Index 246
Special Problems 259
Producing the Final Copy 266
Index Design and Typesetting 268

12 Production Editing, Copyediting, and Proofreading 272

Overview 272
The Manuscript 274
Copyediting the Manuscript 275
Proofs and Proofreading 301
Parts of a Book 313
Copyright and Permissions 319

13 Design and Typography   323

Letters, Type Styles, and Typefaces 323
Page-Design Elements 336
Writing the Design Specifications 343

14 Typesetting, Printing, and Binding   348

Typesetting 348
Typesetting Codes and Generic Markup 350
Platemaking and Printing 355
Paper 358
Binding 361

Grammar Glossary   365

Bibliography   383

Index   393

Preface

This manual is one of a very few guides that attempt to address a broad range of topics normally encountered by working writers and editors for all kinds of publications and in all subjects. Though the book writer and editor are the obvious audience for several chapters, most of the text should prove as valid and useful for the desktop-publishing specialist, the undergraduate or graduate student, the business writer, the freelance journalist, or the newspaper editor.

The fundamentals of standard English style—punctuation, capitalization, etc.—are presented in Chapters 1–5. Style issues peculiar to mathematics and the sciences are discussed in Chapter 6. Chapter 7 deals with conventions for the treatment of quotations. Chapter 8 discusses the editorial problems presented by eighteen foreign languages. Creating tables and incorporating art into a text are the subjects of Chapter 9. Chapter 10 introduces the various standard styles of source documentation. Chapter 11 is a thorough guide to basic indexing. Chapter 12 takes up the many duties of the production editor and the special tasks of the copy editor and the proofreader. Typography and design are the subjects of Chapter 13. Chapter 14 describes the essentials of typesetting, printing, and binding technology. A grammar glossary provides definitions and examples for the standard grammatical terms and discusses common grammar problems, and a bibliography lists further authorial and editorial resources.

This is the second edition of the work originally titled *Webster's Standard American Style Manual* and represents a thoroughgoing revision of that text. Every sentence has been reviewed and reconsidered, and most of the examples have been replaced. Chapter 8, "Foreign Languages," is entirely new. The discussion of art in Chapter 9 has been significantly expanded. Chapter 10 introduces two modes of source documentation not described in the previous edition. Chapter 12 now includes a discussion of the standard parts of a book and an expanded treatment of copyright and permissions. In Chapter 13 the discussion of design has been enlarged. Chapter 14 now treats the subjects of typesetting codes and generic tagging and discusses printing papers. The grammar glossary is another new addition to the text.

The revision naturally reflects, among other things, the continuing progress of technology. When the first edition appeared thirteen years ago, for example, it was still unusual for authors to submit manuscripts on diskette; today it is the almost invariable practice. This edition describes the revolutionary advances these years have seen, particularly as they have affected manuscript creation, design, illustration, typesetting and coding, and platemaking.

Style manuals have historically been written by editors working for particular publications or publishing houses, and have described the particular style rules they follow, usually taking unequivocal stands on issues about which there is in fact considerable diversity of opinion. By contrast, this manual—like the Merriam-Webster dictionaries—attempts to reflect the actual practice of American writers and editors. Its first edition was perhaps the first commercial attempt to develop a major style manual by means of the methods of descriptive lexicography that are the hallmark of this company's dictionaries. Like the current edition, it was based on Merriam-Webster's continuous study of the ways that Americans use their language, and drew on our extensive citation files, which now include 15 million examples of English words used in context, gathered from books, newspapers, magazines, journals, and other publications.

The treatment of style in this volume—as comprehensive a treatment as any now available—thus attempts to reflect both the consensus and the variety of style in American published writing. In the style chapters, the usage consensus is recorded with simple descriptive sentences. When a statement must be qualified, the term *usually, generally,* or *normally* indicates that a significant minority of writers and editors follow another practice; *sometimes* is used when describing such an alternative practice. *Often* or *frequently* indicates that a convention is commonly but not universally followed; it does not necessarily identify a majority practice. Whenever a practice raises questions that require further explanation, a brief note is provided. Conventions restricted to journalism or specialized fields are labeled as such.

No single manual can attempt to discuss the entire range of the writer's and editor's craft and skills. Most of the diverse challenges of prose composition—those that go beyond the "mechanics" of writing—are not addressed here, nor are such important editorial subjects as acquisition, development, agents, packagers, and marketing. Instead, we have tried to fit into an optimally concise text a wealth of the most useful reference information, representing the accumulated knowledge of many editors and writers, which we hope may prove of practical use to a large number of practitioners.

The first edition, *Webster's Standard American Style Manual,* was prepared under the editorship of John M. Morse, with assistance from Julie A. Collier, Kathleen M. Doherty, James G. Lowe, Madeline L. Novak, Stephen J. Perrault, and Coleen K. Withgott, and especially from E. Ward Gilman and Frederick C. Mish.

The present edition, like most Merriam-Webster publications, is likewise indebted to the work of numerous editors and specialists. First, James L. Rader wrote the new chapter on foreign languages. Roger W. Pease and Michael D. Roundy reviewed and updated the material on mathematics and science style. Lynn Stowe Tomb amended and enlarged sections of the text dealing with illustrations, design, typesetting, and printing. Eileen M. Haraty and Amy Lyon each reviewed individual chapters. Robert D. Copeland contributed a new section to Chapter 14. Pete Alaimo, E. Ward Gilman, John B. Hughes, Kara L. Noble, Stephen J. Perrault, Judith G. Recke, Michael Shally-Jensen, and Amy

West provided essential assistance of various kinds. From outside the company, Robie Grant reviewed Chapter 11 and prepared the book's index, Arthur Maisel of Penguin Putnam contributed material for use in Chapter 12, and Stephen Perkins of Pagesetters Incorporated corrected and clarified a number of points in the final chapter. Proofreading and cross-referencing was carried out by Daniel B. Brandon, Rebecca R. Bryer, Deanna Chiasson, Kathleen M. Doherty, Sarah E. LeSure, Donna L. Rickerby, Michael Roundy, Maria A. Sansalone, and Adrienne M. Scholz. John Morse, now President and Publisher, offered numerous suggestions and welcome support. Finally, Jocelyn White Franklin undertook a wide range of editorial, research, and production tasks and guided the long metamorphosis of the first edition into the second.

Mark A. Stevens
Editor

Merriam-Webster's
Manual for
Writers and Editors

1 Punctuation

Apostrophe   1
Brackets   3
Colon   4
Comma 6
Dash   16
Ellipsis Points   19
Exclamation Point   21
Hyphen 22
Parentheses   23
Period   26
Question Mark   27
Quotation Marks   28
Semicolon   32
Slash   34

Punctuation marks are used to help clarify the structure and meaning of sentences. They separate groups of words for meaning and emphasis; they convey an idea of the variations in pitch, volume, pauses, and intonation of the spoken language; and they help avoid ambiguity. The choice of what punctuation to use, if any, will often be clear and unambiguous. In other cases, a sentence may allow for several punctuation patterns. In cases like these, varying notions of correctness have developed, and two writers might, with equal correctness, punctuate the same sentence quite differently, relying on their individual judgment and taste.

Apostrophe

The apostrophe is used to form most possessives and contractions as well as some plurals and inflections.

1. The apostrophe is used to indicate the possessive of nouns and indefinite pronouns. (For details, see the section beginning on page 63.)

the girl's shoe
the boys' fathers
Simmons's role
children's laughter
anyone's guess

the Browns' house
Arkansas's capital

2. Apostrophes are sometimes used to form plurals of letters, numerals, abbreviations, symbols, and words referred to as words. (For details, see the section beginning on page 58.)

cross your *t*'s
three 8's   *or*   three 8s
two L.H.D.'s   *or*   two L.H.D.s
used &'s instead of *and*'s

3. Apostrophes mark omissions in contractions made of two or more words and in contractions of single words.

wasn't
they're
she'd rather not
Jake's had it
ass'n
dep't

4. The apostrophe is used to indicate that letters have been intentionally omitted from a word in order to imitate informal speech.

"Singin' in the Rain," the popular song and movie
"Snap 'em up" was his response.

Sometimes such words are so consistently spelled with an apostrophe that the spelling becomes an accepted variant.

rock 'n' roll [*for* rock and roll]
ma'am [*for* madam]
sou'wester [*for* southwester]

5. Apostrophes mark the omission of digits in numerals.

class of '98
fashion in the '90s

If the apostrophe is used when writing the plurals of numerals, either the apostrophe that stands for the missing figures is omitted or the word is spelled out.

90's   *or*   nineties   *but not*   '90's

6. In informal writing, apostrophes are used to produce forms of verbs that are made of individually pronounced letters. An apostrophe or a hyphen is also sometimes used to add an *-er* ending to an abbreviation; if no confusion would result, the apostrophe is usually omitted.

OK'd the budget
X'ing out the mistakes
4-H'er
49er

Brackets

Outside of mathematics and chemistry texts, brackets are primarily used for insertions into carefully handled quoted matter. They are rarely seen in general writing but are common in historical and scholarly contexts.

1. Brackets enclose editorial comments, corrections, and clarifications inserted into quoted matter.

> Surely that should have peaked [sic] the curiosity of a serious researcher.
>
> Here they much favour the tiorba [theorbo], the arclute [archlute], and the cittarone [chitarrone], while we at home must content ourselves with the lute alone.
>
> In Blaine's words, "All the vocal aristocracy showed up—Nat [Cole], Billy [Eckstine], Ella [Fitzgerald], Mabel Mercer—'cause nobody wanted to miss that date."

2. Brackets enclose insertions that take the place of words or phrases.

> And on the next page: "Their assumption is plainly that [Durocher] would be the agent in any such negotiation."

3. Brackets enclose insertions that supply missing letters.

> A postscript to a December 17 letter to Waugh notes, "If D[eutsch] won't take the manuscript, perhaps someone at Faber will."

4. Brackets enclose insertions that alter the form of a word used in an original text.

> He dryly observes (p. 78) that the Gravely investors had bought stocks because "they want[ed] to see themselves getting richer."

5. Brackets are used to indicate that capitalization has been altered. This is generally optional; it is standard practice only where meticulous handling of original source material is crucial (particularly legal and scholarly contexts).

> As Chief Justice Warren held for the Court, "[T]he Attorney General may bring an injunctive action . . ."
>
> *or in general contexts*
>
> "The Attorney General may bring . . ."

Brackets also enclose editorial notes when text has been italicized for emphasis.

> But tucked away on page 11 we find this fascinating note: "In addition, we anticipate that *siting these new plants in marginal neighborhoods will decrease the risk of organized community opposition*" [italics added].

6. Brackets function as parentheses within parentheses, especially where two sets of parentheses could be confusing.

> Posner's recent essays (including the earlier *Law and Literature* [1988]) bear this out.

7. In mathematical copy, brackets are used with parentheses to indicate units contained within larger units. They are also used with various meanings in chemical names and formulas.

$$x + 5[(x + y)(2x - y)]$$
$$Ag[Pt(NO_2)_4]$$

With Other Punctuation

8. Punctuation that marks the end of a phrase, clause, item in a series, or sentence follows any bracketed material appended to that passage.

> The report stated, "if we fail to find additional sources of supply [of oil and gas], our long-term growth will be limited."

When brackets enclose a complete sentence, closing punctuation is placed within the brackets.

> [Since this article was written, new archival evidence of document falsification has come to light.]

Colon

The colon is usually a mark of introduction, indicating that what follows it— generally a clause, a phrase, or a list—has been pointed to or described in what precedes it. (For the use of capitals following a colon, see paragraphs 7–8 on page 37.)

With Phrases and Clauses

1. A colon introduces a clause or phrase that explains, illustrates, amplifies, or restates what has gone before.

> An umbrella is a foolish extravagance: if you don't leave it in the first restaurant, a gust of wind will destroy it on the way home.
> Dawn was breaking: the distant peaks were already glowing with the sun's first rays.

2. A colon introduces an amplifying word, phrase, or clause that acts as an appositive. (For details on appositives, see the section on page 9.)

> That year Handley's old obsession was replaced with a new one: jazz.
> The issue comes down to this: Will we offer a reduced curriculum, or will we simply cancel the program?

3. A colon introduces a list or series, often following a phrase such as *the following* or *as follows*.

> She has trial experience on three judicial levels: county, state, and federal.
> Anyone planning to participate should be prepared to do the following: hike five miles with a backpack, sleep on the ground without a tent, and paddle a canoe through rough water.

It is occasionally used like a dash to introduce a summary statement following a series.

> Baseball, soccer, skiing, track: he excelled in every sport he took up.

4. Although the colon usually follows a full independent clause, it also often interrupts a sentence before the clause is complete.

> The nine proposed program topics are: offshore supply, vessel traffic, ferry services, ship repair, . . .
>
> Information on each participant includes: name, date of birth, mailing address, . . .
>
> For example: 58 percent of union members voted, but only 44 percent of blue-collar workers as a whole.
>
> The association will:
>> Act with trust, integrity, and professionalism.
>> Operate in an open and effective manner.
>> Take the initiative in seeking diversity.

With Quotations

5. A colon usually introduces lengthy quoted material that is set off from the rest of a text by indentation but not by quotation marks.

> The *Rumpole* series has been nicely encapsulated as follows:
>> Rumpled, disreputable, curmudgeonly barrister Horace Rumpole often wins cases despite the disdain of his more aristocratic colleagues. Fond of cheap wine ("Château Thames Embankment") and Keats's poetry, he refers to his wife as "She Who Must Be Obeyed" (an allusion to the title character of H. Rider Haggard's *She*).

6. A colon is often used before a quotation in running text, especially when (1) the quotation is lengthy, (2) the quotation is a formal statement or is being given special emphasis, or (3) a full independent clause precedes the colon.

> Said Murdoch: "The key to the success of this project is good planning. We need to know precisely what steps we will need to take, what kind of staff we will require, what the project will cost, and when we can expect completion."
>
> The inscription reads: "Here lies one whose name was writ in water."
>
> This was his verbatim response: "At this time Mr. Wilentz is still in the company's employ, and no change in his status is anticipated imminently."

Other Uses

7. A colon separates elements in bibliographic publication data and page references, in biblical citations, and in formulas used to express time and ratios. No space precedes or follows a colon between numerals.

> Stendhal, *Love* (New York: Penguin, 1975)
> *Paleobiology* 3:121
> John 4:10
> 8:30 a.m.

a winning time of 3:43:02
a ratio of 3:5

8. A colon separates titles and subtitles.

Southwest Stories: Tales from the Desert

9. A colon follows the salutation in formal correspondence.

Dear Judge Wright:
Dear Laurence:
Dear Product Manager:
Ladies and Gentlemen:

10. A colon follows headings in memorandums, government correspondence, and general business letters.

TO:
SUBJECT:
VIA:
REFERENCE:

11. An unspaced colon separates the writer's and typist's initials in the identification lines of business letters.

WAL:jml

A colon also separates copy abbreviations from the initials of copy recipients. (The abbreviation *cc* stands for *carbon* or *courtesy copy; bcc* stands for *blind carbon* or *courtesy copy.*) A space follows a colon used with the fuller name of a recipient.

cc:RSP
   JES
bcc:MWK
bcc: Mr. Jones

With Other Punctuation

12. A colon is placed outside quotation marks and parentheses that punctuate the larger sentence.

The problem becomes most acute in "Black Rose and Destroying Angel": plot simply ceases to exist.
Wilson and Hölldobler remark on the same phenomenon in *The Ants* (1990):

Comma

The comma is the most frequently used punctuation mark in English and the one that provides the most difficulties to writers. Its most common uses are to separate items in a series and to set off or distinguish grammatical elements within sentences.

Between Main Clauses

1. A comma separates main clauses joined by a coordinating conjunction, such as *and, but, or, nor,* or *so.*

> She knew very little about the new system, and he volunteered nothing.
> The trial lasted for nine months, but the jury took only four hours to reach its verdict.
> We will not respond to any more questions on that topic this afternoon, nor will we respond to similar questions in the future.
> All the first-floor windows were barred, so he had clambered up onto the fire escape.

2. When one or both of the clauses are short or closely related in meaning, the comma is often omitted.

> They said good-bye and everyone hugged.

If commas set off another phrase that modifies the whole sentence, the comma between main clauses is often omitted.

> Six thousand years ago, the top of the volcano blew off in a series of powerful eruptions and the sides collapsed into the middle.

3. Commas are sometimes used to separate short and obviously parallel main clauses that are not joined by conjunctions.

> One day you're a successful corporate lawyer, the next day you're out of work.

Use of a comma to join clauses that are neither short nor obviously parallel, called *comma fault* or *comma splice,* is avoided. Clauses not joined by conjunctions are normally separated by semicolons. For details, see paragraph 1 on page 32.

4. If a sentence is composed of three or more clauses that are short and free of commas, the clauses are occasionally all separated by commas even if the last two are not joined by a conjunction. If the clauses are long or punctuated, they are separated with semicolons; the last two clauses are sometimes separated by a comma if they are joined by a conjunction. (For more details, see paragraph 5 on page 33.)

> Small fish fed among the marsh weed, ducks paddled along the surface, an occasional muskrat ate greens along the bank.
> The kids were tired and whiny; Napoleon, usually so calm, was edgy; Tabitha seemed to be going into heat, and even the guinea pigs were agitated.

With Compound Predicates

5. Commas are not normally used to separate the parts of a compound predicate.

> The firefighter tried to enter the burning building but was turned back by the thick smoke.

However, they are often used if the predicate is long and complicated, if one part is being stressed, or if the absence of a comma could cause a momentary misreading.

> The board helps to develop the financing and marketing strategies for new corporate divisions, and issues periodic reports on expenditures, revenues, and personnel appointments.
>
> This is an unworkable plan, and has been from the start.
>
> I try to explain to him what I want him to do, and get nowhere.

With Subordinate Clauses and Phrases

6. Adverbial clauses and phrases that begin a sentence are usually set off with commas.

> Having made that decision, we turned our attention to other matters.
>
> In order to receive a high school diploma, a student must earn 16 credits from public or private secondary schools.
>
> In addition, staff members respond to queries, take new orders, and initiate billing.

If the sentence can be easily read without a comma, the comma may be omitted. The phrase will usually be short—four words or less—but even after a longer phrase the comma is often omitted.

> As cars age, they depreciate.   *or*   As cars age they depreciate.
>
> In January the firm will introduce a new line of investigative services.
>
> On the map the town appeared as a small dot in the midst of vast emptiness.
>
> If nobody comes forward by Friday I will have to take further steps.

7. Adverbial clauses and phrases that introduce a main clause other than the first main clause are usually set off with commas. If the clause or phrase follows a conjunction, one comma often precedes the conjunction and one follows the clause or phrase. Alternatively, one comma precedes the conjunction and two more enclose the clause or phrase, or a single comma precedes the conjunction. Short phrases, and phrases in short sentences, tend not to be enclosed in commas.

> They have redecorated the entire store, but[,] to the delight of their customers, it retains much of its original flavor.
>
> We haven't left Springfield yet, but when we get to Boston we'll call you.

8. A comma is not used after an introductory phrase if the phrase immediately precedes the main verb.

> From the next room came a loud expletive.

9. A subordinate clause or phrase that modifies a noun is not set off by commas if it is *restrictive* (or *essential*)—that is, if its removal would alter the noun's meaning.

> The man who wrote this obviously had no firsthand knowledge of the situation.
>
> They entered through the first door that wasn't locked.

If the meaning would not be altered by its removal, the clause or phrase is considered *nonrestrictive* (or *nonessential*) and usually is set off by commas.

> The new approach, which was based on team teaching, was well received.
> Wechsler, who has done solid reporting from other battlefronts, is simply out of his depth here.
> They tried the first door, which led nowhere.

10. Commas set off an adverbial clause or phrase that falls between the subject and the verb.

> The Clapsaddle sisters, to keep up appearances, rode to the park every Sunday in their rented carriage.

11. Commas set off modifying phrases that do not immediately precede the word or phrase they modify.

> Scarbo, intent as usual on his next meal, was snuffling around the butcher's bins.
> The negotiators, tired and discouraged, headed back to the hotel.
> We could see the importance, both long-term and short-term, of her proposal.

12. An absolute phrase (a participial phrase with its own subject that is grammatically independent of the rest of the sentence) is set off with commas.

> Our business being concluded, we adjourned for refreshments.
> We headed southward, the wind freshening behind us, to meet the rest of the fleet in the morning.
> I'm afraid of his reaction, his temper being what it is.

With Appositives

13. Commas set off a word, phrase, or clause that is in apposition to (that is, equivalent to) a preceding or following noun and that is nonrestrictive.

> It sat nursing its front paw, the injured one.
> Aleister Crowley, Britain's most infamous satanist, is the subject of a remarkable new biography.
> A cherished landmark in the city, the Hotel Sandburg has managed once again to escape the wrecking ball.
> The committee cochairs were a lawyer, John Larson, and an educator, Mary Conway.

14. Restrictive appositives are not set off by commas.

> He next had a walk-on role in the movie *The Firm*.
> Longfellow's poem *Evangeline* was a favorite of my grandmother's.
> The committee cochairs were the lawyer John Larson and the educator Mary Conway.
> Lord Castlereagh was that strange anomaly[,] a Labor-voting peer.

With Introductory and Interrupting Elements

15. Commas set off transitional words and phrases.

> Indeed, close coordination will be essential.
> Defeat may be inevitable; however, disgrace is not.
> The second report, on the other hand, shows a strong bias.

When such words and phrases fall in the middle of a clause, commas are sometimes unnecessary.

> They thus have no chips left to bargain with.
> The materials had indeed arrived.
> She would in fact see them that afternoon.

16. Commas set off parenthetic elements, such as authorial asides.

> All of us, to tell the truth, were completely amazed.
> It was, I should add, not the first time I'd seen him in this condition.

17. Commas are often used to set off words or phrases that introduce examples or explanations, such as *namely, for example,* and *that is.*

> He expects to visit three countries, namely, France, Spain, and Germany.
> I would like to develop a good, workable plan, that is, one that would outline our goals and set a timetable for accomplishing them.

Such introductory words and phrases may also often be preceded by a dash, parenthesis, or semicolon. Regardless of the punctuation that precedes the word or phrase, a comma usually follows it.

> Sports develop two valuable traits—namely, self-control and the ability to make quick decisions.
> In writing to the manufacturer, be as specific as possible (i.e., list the missing or defective parts, describe the malfunction, and identify the store where the unit was purchased).
> Most had traveled great distances to participate; for example, three had come from Australia, one from Japan, and two from China.

18. Commas set off words in direct address.

> This is our third and final notice, Mr. Sutton.
> The facts, my fellow Americans, are very different.

19. Commas set off mild interjections or exclamations.

> Ah, the mosaics in Ravenna are matchless.
> Uh-oh, His Eminence seems to be on the warpath this morning.

With Contrasting Expressions

20. A comma is sometimes used to set off contrasting expressions within a sentence.

> This project will take six months, not six weeks.

21. When two or more contrasting modifiers or prepositions, one of which is introduced by a conjunction or adverb, apply to a noun that follows immediately, the second is set off by two commas or a single comma, or not set off at all.

> A solid, if overly wordy, assessment
>   *or* a solid, if overly wordy assessment

or   a solid if overly wordy assessment

This street takes you away from, not toward, the capitol.

   or   This street takes you away from, not toward the capitol.

grounds for a civil, and maybe a criminal, case

   or   grounds for a civil, and maybe a criminal case

   or   grounds for a civil and maybe a criminal case

Dashes or parentheses are often used instead of commas in such sentences.

grounds for a civil (and maybe a criminal) case

22. A comma does not usually separate elements that are contrasted through the use of a pair of correlative conjunctions such as *either . . . or, neither . . . nor,* and *not only . . . but also.*

Neither my brother nor I noticed the error.

He was given the post not only because of his diplomatic connections but also because of his great tact and charm.

When correlative conjunctions join main clauses, a comma usually separates the clauses unless they are short.

Not only did she have to see three salesmen and a visiting reporter, but she also had to prepare for next day's meeting.

Either you do it my way or we don't do it at all.

23. Long parallel contrasting and comparing clauses are separated by commas; short parallel phrases are not.

The more that comes to light about him, the less savory he seems.

The less said the better.

With Items in a Series

24. Words, phrases, and clauses joined in a series are separated by commas.

Men, women, and children crowded aboard the train.

Her job required her to pack quickly, to travel often, and to have no personal life.

He responded patiently while reporters shouted questions, flashbulbs popped, and the crowd pushed closer.

When the last two items in a series are joined by a conjunction, the final comma is often omitted, especially where this would not result in ambiguity. In individual publications, the final comma is usually consistently used, consistently omitted, or used only where a given sentence would otherwise be ambiguous or hard to read. It is consistently used in most nonfiction books; elsewhere it tends to be used or generally omitted equally often.

We are looking for a house with a big yard, a view of the harbor[,] and beach and docking privileges.

25. A comma is not generally used to separate items in a series all of which are joined with conjunctions.

> I don't understand what this policy covers or doesn't cover or only partially covers.
> They left behind the fogs and the wood storks and the lonesome soughing of the wind.

26. When the elements in a series are long or complex or consist of clauses that themselves contain commas, the elements are usually separated by semicolons, not commas. See paragraph 7 on page 33.

With Coordinate Modifiers

27. A comma is generally used to separate two or more adjectives, adverbs, or phrases that modify the same word or phrase.

> She spoke in a calm, reflective manner.
> They set to their work again grimly, intently.

The comma is often omitted when the adjectives are short.

> one long thin strand
> a small white stone
> little nervous giggles
> skinny young waiters
> in this harsh new light

The comma is generally omitted where it is ambiguous whether the last modifier and the noun—or two of the modifiers—constitute a unit.

> the story's stark dramatic power
> a pink stucco nightclub

In some writing, especially works of fiction, commas may be omitted from most series of coordinate modifiers as a matter of style.

28. A comma is not used between two adjectives when the first modifies the combination of the second plus the noun it modifies.

> the last good man
> a good used car
> his protruding lower lip
> the only fresh water
> the only freshwater lake
> their black pickup truck

A comma is also not used to separate an adverb from the adjective or adverb that it modifies.

> this formidably difficult task

In Quotations

29. A comma usually separates a direct quotation from a phrase identifying its source or speaker. If the quotation is a question or an exclamation and the identifying phrase follows the quotation, the comma is replaced by a question mark or an exclamation point.

> She answered, "I'm afraid it's all we've got."
> "The comedy is over," he muttered.
> "How about another round?" Elaine piped up.
> "I suspect," said Mrs. Horowitz, "we haven't seen the last of her."
> "You can sink the lousy thing for all I care!" Trumbull shouted back.
> "And yet . . . [,]" she mused.
> "We can't get the door op—" Captain Hunt is heard shouting before the tape goes dead.

In some cases, a colon can replace a comma preceding a quotation; see paragraph 6 on page 5.

30. When short or fragmentary quotations are used in a sentence that is not primarily dialogue, they are usually not set off by commas.

> He glad-handed his way through the small crowd with a "Looking good, Joe" or "How's the wife" for every beaming face.
> Just because he said he was "about to leave this minute" doesn't mean he actually left.

Sentences that fall within sentences and do not constitute actual dialogue are not usually set off with commas. These may be mottoes or maxims, unspoken or imaginary dialogue, or sentences referred to as sentences; and they may or may not be enclosed in quotation marks. Where quotation marks are not used, a comma is often inserted to mark the beginning of the shorter sentence clearly. (For the use of quotation marks with such sentences, see paragraph 6 on page 29.)

> "The computer is down" was the response she dreaded.
> He spoke with a candor that seemed to insist, This actually happened to me and in just this way.
> The first rule is, When in doubt, spell it out.

When the shorter sentence functions as an appositive (the equivalent to an adjacent noun), it is set off with commas when nonrestrictive and not when restrictive.

> We had the association's motto, "We make waves," printed on our T-shirts.
> He was fond of the slogan "Every man a king, but no man wears a crown."

31. A comma introduces a directly stated question, regardless of whether it is enclosed in quotation marks or if its first word is capitalized. It also introduces a tag question.

> I wondered, what is going on here?
> The question is, How do we get out of this situation?
> That's obvious, isn't it?

A comma is not used to set off indirect discourse or indirect questions introduced by a conjunction (such as *that* or *what*).

> Margot replied quietly that she'd never been happier.
> I wondered what was going on here.
> The question is how do we get out of this situation.

32. The comma is usually omitted before quotations that are very short exclamations or representations of sounds.

> He jumped up suddenly and cried "I've got it!"

Replacing Omitted Words

33. A comma may indicate the omission of a word or phrase in parallel constructions where the omitted word or phrase appears earlier in the sentence. In short sentences, the comma is usually omitted.

> The larger towns were peopled primarily by shopkeepers, artisans, and traders; the small villages, by peasant farmers.
> Seven voted for the proposal, three against.
> He critiqued my presentation and I his.

34. A comma sometimes replaces the conjunction *that.*

> The smoke was so thick, they were forced to crawl.
> Chances are, there are still some tickets left.

With Addresses, Dates, and Numbers

35. Commas set off the elements of an address except for zip codes.

> Write to Bureau of the Census, Washington, DC 20233.
> In Needles, California, their luck ran out.

When a city name and state (province, country, etc.) name are used together to modify a noun that follows, the second comma may be omitted but is more often retained.

> We visited their Enid, Oklahoma plant.
> *but more commonly*
> We visited their Enid, Oklahoma, plant.

36. Commas set off the year in a full date.

> On July 26, 1992, the court issued its opinion.
> Construction for the project began on April 30, 1995.

When only the month and year are given, the first comma is usually omitted.

> In December 1903, the Wright brothers finally succeeded in keeping an airplane aloft for a few seconds.
> October 1929 brought an end to all that.

37. A comma groups numerals into units of three to separate thousands, millions, and so on.

> 2,000 case histories
> 15,000 units

a population of 3,450,000
a fee of $12,500

Certain types of numbers do not contain commas, including decimal fractions, street addresses, and page numbers. (For more on the use of the comma with numbers, see paragraphs 1–3 on page 95.)

2.5544
12537 Wilshire Blvd.
page 1415

With Names, Degrees, and Titles

38. A comma separates a surname from a following professional, academic, honorary, or religious degree or title, or an abbreviation for a branch of the armed forces.

Amelia P. Artandi, M.D.
Robert Hynes Menard, Ph.D., L.H.D.
John L. Farber, Esq.
Sister Mary Catherine, S.C.
Admiral Herman Washington, USN

39. A comma is often used between a surname and the abbreviations *Jr.* and *Sr.*

Douglas Fairbanks, Sr.   *or*   Douglas Fairbanks Sr.
Dr. Martin Luther King, Jr.   *or*   Dr. Martin Luther King Jr.

40. A comma is often used to set off corporate identifiers such as *Incorporated, Inc., Ltd., P.C.,* and *L.P.* However, many company names omit this comma.

StarStage Productions, Incorporated
Hart International Inc.
Walsh, Brandon & Kaiser, P.C.
The sales manager from Doyle Southern, Inc., spoke at Tuesday's meeting.

Other Uses

41. A comma follows the salutation in informal correspondence and usually follows the complimentary close in both informal and formal correspondence.

Dear Rachel,
Affectionately,
Very truly yours,

42. The comma is used to avoid ambiguity when the juxtaposition of two words or expressions could cause confusion.

Under Mr. Thomas, Jefferson High School has flourished.
He scanned the landscape that opened out before him, and guided the horse gently down.

43. When normal sentence order is inverted, a comma often precedes the subject and verb. If the structure is clear without it, it is often omitted.

> That we would succeed, no one doubted.
> And a splendid occasion it was.

With Other Punctuation

44. Commas are used next to brackets, ellipsis points, parentheses, and quotation marks. Commas are not used next to colons, dashes, exclamation points, question marks, or semicolons. If one of the latter falls at the same point where a comma would fall, the comma is dropped. (For more on the use of commas with other punctuation, see the sections for each individual mark.)

> "If they find new sources [of oil and gas], their earnings will obviously rebound. . . ."
> "This book takes its place among the most serious, . . . comprehensive, and enlightened treatments of its great subject."
> There are only six small files (at least in this format), which take up very little disk space.
> According to Hartmann, the people are "savage," their dwellings are "squalid," and the landscape is "a pestilential swamp."

Dash

The dash can function like a comma, a colon, or a parenthesis. Like commas and parentheses, dashes set off parenthetic material such as examples, supplemental facts, and explanatory or descriptive phrases. Like a colon, a dash introduces clauses that explain or expand upon something that precedes them. Though sometimes considered a less formal equivalent of the colon and parenthesis, the dash may be found in all kinds of writing, including the most formal, and the choice of which mark to use is often a matter of personal preference.

The common dash (also called the *em dash,* since it is approximately the width of a capital M in typeset material) is usually represented by two hyphens in typed and keyboarded material. (Word-processing programs make it available as a special character.)

Spacing around the dash varies. Most newspapers insert a space before and after the dash; many popular magazines do the same; but most books and journals omit spacing.

The *en dash* and the *two-* and *three-em dashes* have more limited uses, which are explained in paragraphs 13–15 on page 19.

Abrupt Change or Suspension

1. The dash marks an abrupt change or break in the structure of a sentence.

> The students seemed happy enough with the new plan, but the alumni—there was the problem.

2. A dash is used to indicate interrupted speech or a speaker's confusion or hesitation.

> "The next point I'd like to bring up—" the speaker started to say.
> "Yes," he went on, "yes—that is—I guess I agree."

Parenthetic and Amplifying Elements

3. Dashes are used in place of commas or parentheses to emphasize or draw attention to parenthetic or amplifying material.

> With three expert witnesses in agreement, the defense can be expected to modify its strategy—somewhat.
> This amendment will finally prevent corporations—large and small—from buying influence through exorbitant campaign contributions.

When dashes are used to set off parenthetic elements, they often indicate that the material is more digressive than elements set off with commas but less digressive than elements set off by parentheses. For examples, see paragraph 16 on page 10 and paragraph 1 on page 23.

4. Dashes set off or introduce defining phrases and lists.

> The fund sought to acquire controlling positions—a minimum of 25% of outstanding voting securities—in other companies.
> Davis was a leading innovator in at least three styles—bebop, cool jazz, and jazz-rock fusion.

5. A dash is often used in place of a colon or semicolon to link clauses, especially when the clause that follows the dash explains, summarizes, or expands upon the preceding clause in a somewhat dramatic way.

> The results were in—it had been a triumphant success.

6. A dash or a pair of dashes often sets off illustrative or amplifying material introduced by such phrases as *for example, namely,* and *that is,* when the break in continuity is greater than that shown by a comma, or when the dash would clarify the sentence structure better than a comma. (For more details, see paragraph 17 on page 10.)

> After some discussion the motion was tabled—that is, it was removed indefinitely from the board's consideration.
> Lawyers should generally—in pleadings, for example—attempt to be as specific as possible.

7. A dash may introduce a summary statement that follows a series of words or phrases.

> Crafts, food booths, children's activities, cider-making demonstrations—there was something for everyone.
> Once into bankruptcy, the company would have to pay cash for its supplies, defer maintenance, and lay off workers—moves that could threaten its future.

8. A dash often precedes the name of an author or source at the end of a quoted passage—such as an epigraph, extract, or book or film blurb—that is not part of the main text. The attribution may appear immediately after the quotation or on the next line.

> Only the sign is for sale.
> —Søren Kierkegaard

> "I return to her stories with more pleasure, and await them with more anticipation, than those of any of her contemporaries."—William Logan, *Chicago Tribune*

With Other Punctuation

9. If a dash appears at a point where a comma could also appear, the comma is omitted.

> Our lawyer has read the transcript—all 1,200 pages of it—and he has decided that an appeal would not be useful.

> If we don't succeed—and the critics say we won't—then the whole project is in jeopardy.

In a series, dashes that would force a comma to be dropped are often replaced by parentheses.

> The holiday movie crowds were being entertained by street performers: break dancers, a juggler (who doubled as a sword swallower), a steel-drummer, even a three-card-monte dealer.

10. If the second of a pair of dashes would fall where a period should also appear, the dash is omitted.

> Instead, he hired his mother—an odd choice by any standard.

Much less frequently, the second dash will be dropped in favor of a colon or semicolon.

> Valley Health announced general improvements to its practice—two to start this week: evening office hours and a voice-mail message system.

> His conduct has always been exemplary—near-perfect attendance, excellent productivity, a good attitude; nevertheless, his termination cannot be avoided.

11. When a pair of dashes sets off material ending with an exclamation point or a question mark, the mark is placed inside the dashes.

> His hobby was getting on people's nerves—especially mine!—and he was extremely good at it.

> There would be a "distinguished guest speaker"—was there ever any other kind?—and plenty of wine afterwards.

12. Dashes are used inside parentheses, and vice versa, to indicate parenthetic material within parenthetic material. The second dash is omitted if it would immediately precede the closing parenthesis; a closing parenthesis is never omitted.

> We were looking for a narrator (or narrators—sometimes a script calls for more than one) who could handle a variety of assignments.

The wall of the Old City contains several gates—particularly Herod's Gate, the Golden Gate, and Zion Gate (or "David's Gate")—with rich histories.

En Dash and Long Dashes

13. The *en dash* generally appears only in typeset material; in typed or keyboarded material the simple hyphen is usually used instead. (Word-processing programs provide the en dash as a special character.) Newspapers similarly use the hyphen in place of the en dash. The en dash is shorter than the em dash but longer than the hyphen. It is most frequently used between numbers, dates, or other notations to signify "(up) to and including."

> pages 128–34
> 1995–97
> September 24–October 5
> 8:30 a.m.–4:30 p.m.

The en dash replaces a hyphen in compound adjectives when at least one of the elements is a two-word compound. It replaces the word *to* between capitalized names, and is used to indicate linkages such as boundaries, treaties, and oppositions.

> post–Cold War era
> Boston–Washington train
> New Jersey–Pennsylvania border
> male–female differences   *or*   male-female differences

14. A *two-em dash* is used to indicate missing letters in a word and, less frequently, to indicate a missing word.

> The nearly illegible letter is addressed to a Mr. P—— of Baltimore.

15. A *three-em dash* indicates that a word has been left out or that an unknown word or figure is to be supplied.

> The study was carried out in ———, a fast-growing Sunbelt city.

Ellipsis Points

Ellipsis points (also known as *ellipses, points of ellipsis,* and *suspension points*) are periods, usually in groups of three, that signal an omission from quoted material or indicate a pause or trailing off of speech. A space usually precedes and follows each ellipsis point. (In newspaper style, spaces are usually omitted.)

1. Ellipsis points indicate the omission of one or more words within a quoted sentence.

> We the People of the United States . . . do ordain and establish this Constitution for the United States of America.

2. Ellipsis points are usually not used to indicate the omission of words that precede the quoted portion. However, in some formal contexts, especially when the quotation is introduced by a colon, ellipsis points are used.

> He ends with a stirring call for national resolve that "government of the people, by the people, for the people shall not perish from the earth."
>
> Its final words define the war's purpose in democratic terms: ". . . that government of the people, by the people, for the people shall not perish from the earth."

Ellipsis points following quoted material are omitted when it forms an integral part of a larger sentence.

> She maintained that it was inconsistent with "government of the people, by the people, for the people."

3. Punctuation used in the original that falls on either side of the ellipsis points is often omitted; however, it may be retained, especially if this helps clarify the sentence structure.

> Now we are engaged in a great civil war, testing whether that nation . . . can long endure.
>
> We the People of the United States, in Order to . . . establish Justice, . . . and secure the Blessings of Liberty . . . , do ordain and establish this Constitution for the United States of America.

For details on punctuating omissions within block quotations, see Chapter 7, "Quotations."

4. If the last words of a quoted sentence are omitted and the original sentence ends with punctuation other than a period, the end punctuation often follows the ellipsis points, especially if it helps clarify the quotation.

> He always ends his harangues with some variation on the question, "What could you have been thinking when you . . . ?"

5. When ellipsis points are used to indicate that a quotation has been intentionally left unfinished, the terminal period is omitted. No space separates the last ellipsis point and the quotation mark.

> The paragraph beginning "Recent developments suggest . . ." should be deleted.

6. A line of ellipsis points indicates that one or more lines have been omitted from a poem. Its length usually matches the length of the line above. (For more details on quoting verse, see the section beginning on page 145.)

> When I heard the learned astronomer,
> . . . .
> How soon unaccountable I became tired and sick,
> Til rising and gliding out I wandered off by myself,
> In the mystical moist night-air, and from time to time,
> Looked up in perfect silence at the stars.

7. Ellipsis points are used to indicate faltering speech, especially if the faltering involves a long pause or a sentence that trails off or is intentionally left unfinished. Generally no other terminal punctuation is used.

> The speaker seemed uncertain. "Well, that's true . . . but even so . . . I think we can do better."
> "Despite these uncertainties, we believe we can do it, but . . ."
> "I mean . . ." he said, "like . . . How?"

8. Ellipsis points are sometimes used informally as a stylistic device to catch a reader's attention, often replacing a dash or colon.

> They think that nothing can go wrong . . . but it does.

9. In newspaper and magazine columns consisting of social notes, local events listings, or short items of celebrity news, ellipsis points often take the place of paragraphing to separate the items. (Ellipsis points are also often used in informal personal correspondence in place of periods or paragraphing.)

> Congratulations to Debra Morricone, our up-and-coming singing star, for her full scholarship to the Juilliard School this fall! . . . And kudos to Paul Chartier for his winning All-State trumpet performance last Friday in Baltimore! . . . Look for wit and sparkling melody when the Lions mount their annual Gilbert & Sullivan show at Syms Auditorium. This year it's . . .

Exclamation Point

The exclamation point is used to mark a forceful comment or exclamation.

1. An exclamation point can punctuate a sentence, phrase, or interjection.

> There is no alternative!
> Without a trace!
> My God! It's monstrous!

2. The exclamation point may replace the question mark when an ironic, angry, or emphatic tone is more important than the actual question.

> Aren't you finished yet!
> Do you realize what you've done!
> Why me!

Occasionally it is used *with* the question mark to indicate a very forceful question.

> How much did you say?!
> You did what!?

3. The exclamation point falls within brackets, dashes, parentheses, and quotation marks when it punctuates only the enclosed material. It is placed outside them when it punctuates the entire sentence.

All of this proves—at long last!—that we were right from the start.

Somehow the dog got the gate open (for the third time!) and ran into the street.

He sprang to his feet and shouted "Point of order!"

At this rate the national anthem will soon be replaced by "You Are My Sunshine"!

4. If an exclamation point falls where a comma could also go, the comma is dropped.

"Absolutely not!" he snapped.

They wouldn't dare! she told herself over and over.

If the exclamation point is part of a title, it may be followed by a comma. If the title falls at the end of a sentence, no period follows it.

Hello Dolly!, which opened in 1964, would become one of the ten longest-running shows in Broadway history.

His favorite management book is still *Up the Organization!*

Hyphen

Hyphens have a variety of uses, the most significant of which is to join the elements of compound nouns and modifiers.

1. Hyphens are used to link elements in compound words. (For more on compound words, see the section beginning on page 67.)

secretary-treasurer
cost-effective
fund-raiser
spin-off

2. In some words, a hyphen separates a prefix, suffix, or medial element from the rest of the word. Consult a dictionary in doubtful cases. (For details on using a hyphen with a prefix or a suffix, see the section beginning on page 75.)

anti-inflation
umbrella-like
jack-o'-lantern

3. In typed and keyboarded material, a hyphen is generally used between numbers and dates with the meaning "(up) to and including." In typeset material it is replaced by an en dash. (For details on the en dash, see paragraph 13 on page 19.)

pages 128–34
the years 1995–97

4. A hyphen marks an end-of-line division of a word.

In 1975 smallpox, formerly a great scourge, was declared totally eradicated by the World Health Organization.

5. A hyphen divides letters or syllables to give the effect of stuttering, sobbing, or halting speech.

"S-s-sammy, it's my t-toy!"

6. Hyphens indicate a word spelled out letter by letter.

l-i-a-i-s-o-n

7. Hyphens are sometimes used to produce inflected forms of verbs made of individually pronounced letters or to add an *-er* ending to an abbreviation. However, apostrophes are more commonly used for these purposes. (For details on these uses of the apostrophe, see paragraph 6 on page 2.)

DH-ing for the White Sox   *or*   DH'ing for the White Sox
a dedicated UFO-er   *or*   a dedicated UFO'er

Parentheses

Parentheses generally enclose material that is inserted into a main statement but is not intended to be an essential part of it. For some of the cases described below, commas or dashes are frequently used instead. (For examples, see paragraph 16 on page 10 and paragraph 3 on page 17.) Parentheses are particularly used when the inserted material is only incidental. Unlike commas and dashes, an opening parenthesis is always followed by a closing one. Because parentheses are almost always used in pairs, and their shapes indicate their relative functions, they often clarify a sentence's structure better than commas or dashes.

Parenthetic Elements

1. Parentheses enclose phrases and clauses that provide examples, explanations, or supplementary facts or numerical data.

Nominations for principal officers (president, vice president, treasurer, and secretary) were heard and approved.
Four computers (all outdated models) will be replaced.
Although we liked the restaurant (their Italian food was the best), we seldom had time for the long trip into the city.
First-quarter sales figures were good (up 8%), but total revenues showed a slight decline (down 1%).

2. Parentheses sometimes enclose phrases and clauses introduced by expressions such as *namely, that is, e.g.,* and *i.e.,* particularly where parentheses would clarify the sentence's structure better than commas. (For more details, see paragraph 17 on page 10.)

In writing to the manufacturer, be as specific as possible (i.e., list the defective parts, describe the malfunction, and identify the store where the unit was purchased), but also as concise.

3. Parentheses enclose definitions or translations in the main part of a sentence.

> The company announced plans to sell off its housewares (small-appliances) business.
> The *grand monde* (literally, "great world") of prewar Parisian society consisted largely of titled aristocracy.

4. Parentheses enclose abbreviations that follow their spelled-out forms, or spelled-out forms that follow abbreviations.

> She cited a study by the Food and Drug Administration (FDA).
> They attended last year's convention of the ABA (American Booksellers Association).

5. Parentheses often enclose cross-references and bibliographic references.

> Specialized services are also available (see list of stores at end of brochure).
> The diagram (Fig. 3) illustrates the action of the pump.
> Subsequent studies (Braxton 1990; Roh and Weinglass 1993) have confirmed these findings.

6. Parentheses enclose numerals that confirm a spelled-out number in a business or legal context.

> Delivery will be made in thirty (30) days.
> The fee is Four Thousand Dollars ($4,000), payable to UNCO, Inc.

7. Parentheses enclose the name of a state that is inserted into a proper name for identification.

> the Kalispell (Mont.) Regional Hospital
> the *Sacramento* (Calif.) *Bee*

8. Parentheses may be used to enclose personal asides.

> Claims were made of its proven efficacy (some of us were skeptical).
> *or*
> Claims were made of its proven efficacy. (Some of us were skeptical.)

9. Parentheses are used to enclose quotations that illustrate or support a statement made in the main text.

> After he had a few brushes with the police, his stepfather had him sent to jail as an incorrigible ("It will do him good").

Other Uses

10. Parentheses enclose unpunctuated numbers or letters indicating individual elements or items in a series within a sentence.

> Sentences can be classified as (1) simple, (2) multiple or compound, and (3) complex.

11. Parentheses indicate alternative terms.

> Please sign and return the enclosed form(s).

12. Parentheses may be used to indicate losses in accounting.

Operating Profits (in millions)	
Cosmetics	26.2
Food products	47.7
Food services	54.3
Transportation	(17.7)
Sporting goods	(11.2)
Total	99.3

With Other Punctuation

13. When an independent sentence is enclosed in parentheses, its first word is capitalized and a period (or other closing punctuation) is placed inside the parentheses.

> The discussion was held in the boardroom. (The results are still confidential.)

A parenthetic expression that occurs within a sentence—even if it could stand alone as a separate sentence—does not end with a period but may end with an exclamation point, a question mark, or quotation marks.

> Although several trade organizations opposed the legislation (there were at least three paid lobbyists working on Capitol Hill), the bill passed easily.
> The conference was held in Portland (Me., not Ore.).
> After waiting in line for an hour (why do we do these things?), we finally left.

A parenthetic expression within a sentence does not require capitalization unless it is a quoted sentence.

> He was totally confused ("What can we do?") and refused to see anyone.

14. If a parenthetic expression within a sentence is composed of two independent clauses, a semicolon rather than a period usually separates them. Independent sentences enclosed together in parentheses employ normal sentence capitalization and punctuation.

> We visited several showrooms, looked at the prices (it wasn't a pleasant experience; prices in this area have not gone down), and asked all the questions we could think of.
> We visited several showrooms and looked at the prices. (It wasn't a pleasant experience. Prices in this area have not gone down.)

Entire paragraphs are rarely enclosed in parentheses; instead, paragraphs of incidental material often appear as footnotes or endnotes.

15. No punctuation (other than a period after an abbreviation) is placed immediately before an opening parenthesis within a sentence; if punctuation is required, it follows the final parenthesis.

> I'll get back to you tomorrow (Friday), when I have more details.
> Tickets cost $14 in advance ($12 for seniors); the price at the door is $18.
> The relevant figures are shown below (in millions of dollars):

16. Parentheses sometimes appear within parentheses when no confusion would result; alternatively, the inner parentheses are replaced with brackets.

> Checks must be drawn in U.S. dollars. (*Please note:* We cannot accept checks drawn on Canadian banks for amounts less than four U.S. dollars ($4.00). The same regulation applies to Canadian money orders.)

17. Dashes and parentheses may be used together to set off parenthetic material. (For details, see paragraph 12 on page 18.)

> The orchestra is spirited, and the cast—an expert and enthusiastic crew of Savoyards (some of them British imports)—comes through famously.

Period

Periods almost always serve to mark the end of a sentence or abbreviation.

1. A period ends a sentence or a sentence fragment that is neither a question nor an exclamation.

> From the Format menu, choose Style.
> Robert decided to bring champagne.
> Unlikely. In fact, inconceivable.

Only one period ends a sentence.

> The jellied gasoline was traced to the Trenton-based Quality Products, Inc.
> Miss Toklas states categorically that "This is the best way to cook frogs' legs."

2. A period punctuates some abbreviations. No space follows an internal period within an abbreviation. (For details on punctuating abbreviations, see the section beginning on page 79.)

> Assn.   e.g.
> Ph.D.   p.m.
> Dr.   etc.

3. Periods are used with a person's initials, each followed by a space. (Newspaper style omits the space.) If the initials replace the name, they are unspaced and may also be written without periods.

> J. B. S. Haldane
> L.B.J.   *or*   LBJ

4. A period follows numerals and letters when they are used without parentheses in outlines and vertical lists.

> I. Objectives
>   A. Economy
>   1. Low initial cost
>   2. Low maintenance cost
>   B. Ease of operation

Required skills are:
1. Shorthand
2. Typing
3. Transcription

5. A period is placed within quotation marks, even when it did not punctuate the original quoted material. (In British practice, the period goes outside the quotation marks whenever it does not belong to the original quoted material.)

The founder was known to his employees as "the old man."

"I said I wanted to fire him," Henry went on, "but she said, 'I don't think you have the contractual privilege to do that.'"

6. When brackets or parentheses enclose an independent sentence, the period is placed inside them. When brackets or parentheses enclose a sentence that is part of a larger sentence, the period for the enclosed sentence is omitted.

Arturo finally arrived on the 23rd with the terrible news that Katrina had been detained by the police. [This later proved to be false; see letter 255.]

I took a good look at her (she was standing quite close to me).

Question Mark

The question mark always indicates a question or doubt.

1. A question mark ends a direct question.

What went wrong?

"When do they arrive?" she asked.

A question mark follows a period only when the period punctuates an abbreviation. No period follows a question mark.

Is he even an M.D.?

"Will you arrive by 10 p.m.?"

A local professor would be giving a paper with the title "Economic Stagnation or Equilibrium?"

2. Polite requests that are worded as questions usually take periods, because they are not really questions. Conversely, a sentence that is intended as a question but whose word order is that of a statement is punctuated with a question mark.

Could you please send the necessary forms.

They flew in yesterday?

3. The question mark ends a question that forms part of a sentence. An indirect question is not followed by a question mark.

What was her motive? you may be asking.
I naturally wondered, Will it really work?
I naturally wondered whether it would really work.
He asked when the report was due.

4. The question mark punctuates each element of a series of questions that share a single beginning and are neither numbered nor lettered. When the series is numbered or lettered, only one question mark is generally used.

Can you give us a reasonable forecast? Back up your predictions? Compare them with last year's earnings?
Can you (1) give us a reasonable forecast, (2) back up your predictions, and (3) compare them with last year's earnings?

5. The question mark indicates uncertainty about a fact or the accuracy of a transcription.

Homer, Greek epic poet (9th–8th? cent. B.C.)
He would have it that Farjeon[?] is the onlie man for us.

6. The question mark is placed inside brackets, dashes, parentheses, or quotation marks when it punctuates only the material enclosed by them and not the sentence as a whole. It is placed outside them when it punctuates the entire sentence.

I took a vacation in 1992 (was it really that long ago?), but I haven't had time for one since.
What did Andrew mean when he called the project "a fiasco from the start"?
Williams then asks, "Do you realize the extent of the problem [the housing shortage]?"

Quotation Marks

The following paragraphs describe the use of quotation marks to enclose quoted matter in regular text, and for other, less frequent uses. For the use of quotation marks to enclose titles, see paragraph 70 on page 53.

Basic Uses

1. Quotation marks enclose direct quotations but not indirect quotations or paraphrases.

Dr. Mee added, "We'd be grateful for anything you could do."
"We just got the lab results," he crowed, "and the blood types match!"
"I'm leaving," she whispered. "This meeting could go on forever."
"Mom, we *tried* that already!" they whined in unison.
"Ssshh!" she hissed.
She said she was leaving.
Algren once said something like, Don't ever play poker with anyone named Doc, and never eat at a diner called Mom's.

2. Quotation marks enclose fragments of quoted matter.

> The agreement makes it clear that he "will be paid only upon receipt of an acceptable manuscript."
> As late as 1754, documents refer to him as "yeoman" and "husbandman."

3. Quotation marks enclose words or phrases borrowed from others, and words of obvious informality introduced into formal writing. Words introduced as specialized terminology are sometimes enclosed in quotation marks but more often italicized.

> Be sure to send a copy of your résumé—or as some folks would say, your "biodata summary."
> They were afraid the patient had "stroked out"—had had a cerebrovascular accident.
> New Hampshire's only "green" B&B
> referred to as "closed" or "privately held" corporations
> *but more frequently*
> referred to as *closed* or *privately held* corporations

4. Quotation marks are sometimes used to enclose words referred to as words. Italics are also frequently used for this purpose.

> changed every "he" to "she"
> *or*
> changed every *he* to *she*

5. Quotation marks may enclose representations of sounds, though these are also frequently italicized.

> If it sounds like "quank, quank" [*or* like *quank, quank*], it may be the green treefrog.

6. Quotation marks often enclose short sentences that fall within longer sentences, especially when the shorter sentence is meant to suggest spoken dialogue. Mottoes and maxims, unspoken or imaginary dialogue, and sentences referred to as sentences may all be treated in this way.

> On the gate was the inscription "Arbeit macht frei" [or *Arbeit macht frei*]—"Work will make you free."
> The fact was, the poor kid didn't know "C'mere" from "Sic 'em."
> In effect, the voters were saying "You blew it, and you don't get another chance."
> Their reaction could only be described as "Kill the messenger."
> She never got used to their "That's the way it goes" attitude.
> *or*
> She never got used to their that's-the-way-it-goes attitude.

Quotation marks are often omitted in sentences of this kind when the structure is clear without them. (For the use of commas in such sentences, see paragraphs 29–30 on pages 12–13.)

> The first rule is, When in doubt, spell it out.

7. Direct questions are enclosed in quotation marks when they represent quoted dialogue, but usually not otherwise.

> She asked, "What went wrong?"
> The question is, What went wrong?
> We couldn't help wondering, Where's the plan?
> *or*
> We couldn't help wondering, "Where's the plan?"

8. Quotation marks enclose translations of foreign or borrowed terms.

> This is followed by the Dies Irae ("Day of Wrath"), a climactic movement in many settings of the Requiem.
> The term comes from the Latin *sesquipedalis,* meaning "a foot and a half long."

They also frequently enclose definitions.

> *Concupiscent* simply means "lustful."
> *or*
> *Concupiscent* simply means lustful.

9. Quotation marks sometimes enclose letters referred to as letters.

> The letter "m" is wider than the letter "i."
> Put an "x" in the right spot.

However, such letters are more frequently italicized (or underlined), or left undifferentiated from the surrounding text where no confusion would result.

> How many *e*'s are in her name?
> a V-shaped blade
> He was happy to get a B in the course.

With Longer Quotations

10. Quotation marks are not used with longer passages of prose or poetry that are indented as separate paragraphs, called *block quotations* or *extracts.* For a thorough discussion of quotations, see Chapter 7.

11. Quotation marks enclose lines of poetry run in with the text. A spaced slash separates the lines. (For details on poetry set as an extract, see the section beginning on page 145.)

> When Gerard Manley Hopkins wrote that "Nothing is so beautiful as spring— / When weeds, in wheels, shoot long and lovely and lush," he probably had my yard in mind.

12. Quotation marks are not used with epigraphs. However, they are generally used with advertising blurbs. (For details on epigraphs and blurbs, see the section beginning on page 144.)

> The whole of science is nothing more than a refinement of everyday thinking.
> > —Albert Einstein
>
> "A brutal irony, a slam-bang humor and a style of writing as balefully direct as a death sentence."—*Time*

With Other Punctuation

13. When a period or comma follows text enclosed in quotation marks, it is placed within the quotation marks, even if the original language quoted was not followed by a period or comma.

> He smiled and said, "I'm happy for you."
> But perhaps Pound's most perfect poem was "The Return."
> The cameras were described as "waterproof," but "moisture-resistant" would have been a better description.

In British usage, the period or comma goes outside the quoted matter whenever the original text did not include the punctuation.

14. When a colon or semicolon follows text enclosed in quotation marks, the colon or semicolon is placed outside the quotation marks.

> But they all chimed in on "O Sole Mio": raw adolescents, stately matrons, decrepit old pensioners, their voices soaring in passion together.
> She spoke of her "little cottage in the country"; she might better have called it a mansion.

15. The dash, question mark, and exclamation point are placed inside quotation marks when they punctuate the quoted matter only, but outside the quotation marks when they punctuate the whole sentence.

> "I can't see how—" he started to say.
> He thought he knew where he was going—he remembered her saying, "Take two lefts, then stay to the right"—but the streets didn't look familiar.
> He asked, "When did they leave?"
> What is the meaning of "the open door"?
> She collapsed in her seat with a stunned "Good God!"
> Save us from his "mercy"!

Single Quotation Marks

16. Single quotation marks replace double quotation marks when the quoted material occurs within quoted material.

> The witness said, "I distinctly heard him say, 'Don't be late,' and then I heard the door close."
> "We'd like to close tonight with that great Harold Arlen wee-hours standard, 'One for My Baby.'"
> This analysis is indebted to Del Banco's "Elizabeth Bishop's 'Insomnia': An Inverted View."

When both single and double quotation marks occur at the end of a sentence, the period falls within both sets of marks.

> The witness said, "I distinctly heard him say, 'Don't be late.'"

British usage often reverses American usage, enclosing quoted material in single quotation marks, and enclosing quotations within quotations in double quotation marks. In British usage, commas and periods following quoted material go inside only those quotation marks that enclose material that originally included the period or comma.

17. A quotation within a quotation within a quotation is usually enclosed in double quotation marks. (Such constructions are usually avoided by rewriting.)

> As the *Post* reported it, "Van Houten's voice can be clearly heard saying, 'She said "You wouldn't dare" and I said "I just did."'"
>
> *or*
>
> The *Post* reported that Van Houten's voice was clearly heard saying, "She said 'You wouldn't dare' and I said 'I just did.'"

Semicolon

The semicolon may be used much like the comma, period, or colon, depending on the context. Like a comma, it may separate elements in a series. Like a period or colon, it frequently marks the end of a complete clause, and like a colon it signals that the remainder of the sentence is closely related to the first part. However, in each case the semicolon is normally used in a distinctive way. It serves as a higher-level comma; it connects clauses, as a period does not; and it does not imply any following exemplification, amplification, or description, as a colon generally does.

Between Clauses

1. A semicolon separates related independent clauses joined without a coordinating conjunction.

> Cream the shortening and sugar; add the eggs and beat well.
> The river rose and overflowed its banks; roads became flooded and impassable; freshly plowed fields disappeared from sight.

2. A scmicolon often replaces a comma between two clauses joined by a coordinating conjunction if the sentence might otherwise be confusing—for example, because of particularly long clauses or the presence of other commas.

> In a society that seeks to promote social goals, government will play a powerful role; and taxation, once simply a means of raising money, becomes, in addition, a way of furthering those goals.

3. A semicolon joins two clauses when the second includes a conjunctive adverb such as *accordingly, however, indeed,* or *thus,* or a phrase that acts like a conjunctive adverb such as *in that case, as a result,* or *on the other hand.*

> Most people are covered by insurance of some kind; indeed, many don't even see their medical bills.
> It won't be easy to sort out the facts; a decision must be made, however.
> The case could take years to work its way through the courts; as a result, many plaintiffs will accept settlements.

When *so* and *yet* are treated as conjunctive adverbs, they are often preceded by a semicolon and followed by a comma. When treated as coordinating conjunctions, as they usually are, they are generally only preceded by a comma.

> The new recruits were bright, diligent, and even enthusiastic; yet[,] the same problems persisted.
> His grades improved sharply, yet the high honor roll still eluded him.

4. A semicolon may join two statements when the second clause is elliptical, omitting essential words that are supplied by the first. In short sentences, a comma often replaces the semicolon.

> The conference sessions, designed to allow for full discussions, were much too long; the breaks between them, much too short.
> The aged Scotch was haunting, the Asiago piquant.

5. When a series of clauses are separated by semicolons and a coordinating conjunction precedes the final clause, the final semicolon is sometimes replaced with a comma.

> The bars had all closed hours ago; a couple of coffee shops were open but deserted[; *or* ,] and only a few lighted upper-story windows gave evidence of other victims of insomnia.

6. A semicolon is often used before introductory expressions such as *for example, that is,* and *namely,* in place of a colon, comma, dash, or parenthesis. (For more details, see paragraph 17 on page 10.)

> On one point only did everyone agree; namely, too much money had been spent already.
> We were fairly successful on that project; that is, we made our deadlines and met our budget.

In a Series

7. A semicolon is used in place of a comma to separate phrases or items in a series when the phrases or items themselves contain commas. A comma may replace the semicolon before a conjunction that precedes the last item in a series.

> The assets in question include $22 million in land, buildings, and equipment; $34 million in cash, investments, and accounts receivable; and $8 million in inventory.
> The votes against were: Precinct 1, 418; Precinct 2, 332; Precinct 3, 256.
> The debate about the nature of syntactic variation continues to this day (Labov 1991; Dines 1991, 1993; Romaine 1995).
> The Pissarro exhibition will travel to Washington, D.C.; Manchester, N.H.; Portland, Ore., and Oakland, Calif.

When the items in a series are long or are sentences themselves, they are usually separated by semicolons even if they lack internal commas.

> Among the committee's recommendations were the following: more hospital beds in urban areas where there are waiting lines for elective surgery; smaller

staff size in half-empty rural hospitals; and review procedures for all major purchases.

With Other Punctuation

8. A semicolon that punctuates the larger sentence is placed outside quotation marks and parentheses.

> I heard the senator on yesterday's "All Things Considered"; his views on Medicare are encouraging.
>
> She found him urbane and entertaining (if somewhat overbearing); he found her charmingly ingenuous.

Slash

The slash (also known as the *virgule, diagonal, solidus, oblique,* and *slant*) is most commonly used in place of a short word or a hyphen or en dash, or to separate numbers or text elements. There is generally no space on either side of the slash.

1. A slash represents the words *per* or *to* when used between units of measure or the terms of a ratio.

> 40,000 tons/year
> 29 mi/gal
> price/earnings ratio   *or*   price–earnings ratio
> cost/benefit analysis   *or*   cost–benefit analysis
> a 50/50 split   *or*   a 50-50 split
> 20/20 vision

2. A slash separates alternatives, usually representing the words *or* or *and/or.*

> alumni/ae
> his/her
> the *affect/effect* problem   *or*   the *affect-effect* problem

3. A slash replaces the word *and* in some compound terms.

> air/sea cruise   *or*   air-sea cruise
> the May/June issue   *or*   the May-June issue
> 1996/97   *or*   1996–97
> travel/study trip   *or*   travel-study trip

4. A slash is sometimes used to replace certain prepositions such as *at, versus,* and *for.*

> U.C./Berkeley   *or*   U.C.–Berkeley
> parent/child issues   *or*   parent–child issues
> Vice President/Editorial   *or*   Vice President, Editorial

5. A slash punctuates a few abbreviations.

> w/o [*for* without]
> c/o [*for* care of]

I/O [*for* input/output]
d/b/a [*for* doing business as]
w/w [*for* wall-to-wall]
o/a [*for* on or about]

6. The slash separates the elements in a numerical date, and numerators and denominators in fractions.

11/29/95
2 3/16 inches wide   *or* $2\frac{3}{16}$ inches wide

a 7/8-mile course   *or*   a $\frac{7}{8}$-mile course

7. The slash separates lines of poetry that are run in with the text around them. A space is usually inserted before and after the slash.

Alexander Pope once observed: "'Tis with our judgments as our watches, none / Go just alike, yet each believes his own."

2 Capitals and Italics

Beginnings   36
Proper Nouns and Adjectives   38
Other Styling Conventions   54

Words and phrases are capitalized or italicized (underlining takes the place of italics in typed or handwritten text) to indicate that they have a special significance in particular contexts. (Quotation marks sometimes perform the same functions; see paragraphs 69–71 on page 53 and the section on quotation marks beginning on page 28.)

Beginnings

1. The first word of a sentence or sentence fragment is capitalized.

> They make a desert and call it peace.
> So many men, so many opinions.
> O times! O customs!

2. The first word of a sentence contained within parentheses is capitalized. However, a parenthetical sentence occurring inside another sentence is not capitalized unless it is a complete quoted sentence.

> No one answered the telephone. (They were probably on vacation.)
> The road remains almost impassable (the locals don't seem to care), and the journey is only for the intrepid.
> After waiting in line for an hour (what else could we do?), we finally left.
> In the primary election Evans placed third ("My campaign started late").

3. The first word of a direct quotation is capitalized. However, if the quotation is interrupted in mid-sentence, the second part does not begin with a capital.

> The department manager explained, "We have no budget for new computers."
> "We have no budget for new computers," explained the department manager, "but we may next year."

4. When a quotation, whether a sentence fragment or a complete sentence, is syntactically dependent on the sentence in which it occurs, the quotation does not begin with a capital.

> The brochure promised a tour of "the most exotic ancient sites."
> His first response was that "there is absolutely no truth to the reports."

5. The first word of a sentence within a sentence that is not a direct quotation is usually capitalized. Examples include mottoes and rules, unspoken or imaginary dialogue, sentences referred to as sentences, and direct questions. (For the use of commas and quotation marks with such sentences, see paragraphs 30–31 on pages 13–14 and paragraphs 6–7 on pages 29–30.)

> You know the saying "Fools rush in where angels fear to tread."
> The first rule is, When in doubt, spell it out.
> One ballot proposition sought to enforce the sentencing rule of "Three strikes and you're out."
> My question is, When can we go?

6. The first word of a line of poetry is traditionally capitalized. However, in the poetry of this century line beginnings are often lowercased. The poem's original capitalization is always reproduced.

> Death is the mother of beauty, mystical,
> Within whose burning bosom we devise
> Our earthly mothers waiting, sleeplessly.
> —Wallace Stevens

> > If tributes cannot
> be implicit,
> give me diatribes and the fragrance of iodine,
> the cork oak acorn grown in Spain . . .
> —Marianne Moore

7. The first word following a colon is lowercased when it begins a list and usually lowercased when it begins a complete sentence. However, when the sentence introduced is lengthy and distinctly separate from the preceding clause, it is often capitalized.

> In the early morning they broadcast an urgent call for three necessities: bandages, antibiotics, and blood.
> The advantage of this system is clear: it's inexpensive.
> The situation is critical: This company cannot hope to recoup the fourth-quarter losses that were sustained in five operating divisions.

8. If a colon introduces a series of sentences, the first word of each sentence is capitalized.

> Consider the steps we have taken: A subcommittee has been formed to evaluate past performance. New sources of revenue are being explored. Several candidates have been interviewed for the new post of executive director.

9. The first words of items that form complete sentences in run-in lists are usually capitalized, as are the first words of items in vertical lists. However, numbered phrases within a sentence are lowercased. For details, see the section beginning on page 102.

10. The first word in an outline heading is capitalized.

> I. Editorial tasks
> II. Production responsibilities
>   A. Cost estimates
>   B. Bids

11. In minutes and legislation, the introductory words *Whereas* and *Resolved* are capitalized (and *Resolved* is also italicized). The word immediately following is also capitalized.

> Whereas, Substantial benefits . . .
> *Resolved,* That . . .

12. The first word and certain other words of the salutation of a letter and the first word of a complimentary close are capitalized.

> Dear Sir or Madam:
> Ladies and Gentlemen:
> To whom it may concern:
> Sincerely yours,
> Very truly yours,

13. The first word and each subsequent major word following a SUBJECT or TO heading in a memorandum are capitalized.

> SUBJECT: Pension Plans
> TO: All Department Heads and Editors

Proper Nouns and Adjectives

The following paragraphs describe the ways in which a broad range of proper nouns and adjectives are styled. Capitals are always employed, sometimes in conjunction with italics or quotation marks.

Abbreviations

1. Abbreviated forms of proper nouns and adjectives are capitalized, just as the spelled-out forms would be. (For details on capitalizing abbreviations, see the section on page 81.)

> Jan. [*for* January]
> NATO [*for* North Atlantic Treaty Organization]

Abstractions and Personifications

2. Abstract concepts and qualities are sometimes capitalized when the concept or quality is being personified. If the term is simply used in conjunction with other words that allude to human characteristics or qualities, it is not capitalized.

> as Autumn paints each leaf in fiery colors
> the statue of Justice with her scales
> hoping that fate would lend a hand

Academic Degrees

3. The names of academic degrees are capitalized when they follow a person's name. The names of specific degrees used without a person's name are usually lowercased. More general names for degrees are lowercased.

Lawton I. Byrne, Doctor of Laws
earned his associate in science degree
   or   earned his Associate in Science degree
completed course work for his doctorate
working for a master's degree

Abbreviations for academic degrees are always capitalized. (For details, see paragraphs 11–12 on page 85.)

Susan L. Wycliff, M.S.W.
received her Ph.D. in clinical psychology

Animals and Plants

4. The common names of animals and plants are not capitalized unless they contain a proper noun, in which case the proper noun is usually capitalized and any name element preceding (but not following) it is often capitalized. When in doubt, consult a dictionary. (For scientific names, see the section beginning on page 50.)

the springer spaniel	Queen Anne's lace
Holstein cows	black-eyed Susan
California condor	mayflower
a Great Dane	jack-in-the-pulpit

Awards and Prizes

5. Names of awards and prizes are capitalized. Words and phrases that are not actually part of the award's name are lowercased.

Academy Award
Emmy
Rhodes Scholarship
Rhodes scholar
Pulitzer Prize–winning novelist
Nobel Prize winner
Nobel Prize in medicine
   but
Nobel Peace Prize

Derivatives of Proper Names

6. Derivatives of proper names are capitalized when used in their primary sense. If the derived term has taken on a specialized meaning, it is often lowercased. Consult a dictionary when in doubt.

Roman sculpture
Viennese culture
Victorian prudery
a Britishism
Hodgkin's disease
chinaware
pasteurized milk

french fries
but
American cheese
Dutch door

Geographical and Topographical References

7. Terms that identify divisions of the earth's surface and distinct areas, regions, places, or districts are capitalized, as are derivative nouns and adjectives.

the Pacific Rim	Burgundy
the Great Lakes	Burgundians
Arnhem Land	the Highlands
the Golan Heights	Highland attitudes

8. Popular names of localities are capitalized.

Little Italy	the Sunbelt
the Left Bank	the Big Easy

9. Compass points are capitalized when they refer to a geographical region or form part of a place-name or street name. They are lowercased when they refer to a simple direction.

the Southwest	North Pole
West Coast	north of the Rio Grande
North Atlantic	born in the East
East Pleasant Street	driving east on I-90

10. Nouns and adjectives that are derived from compass points and that designate or refer to a specific geographical region are usually capitalized.

Southern hospitality
Easterners
Southwestern recipes
Northern Europeans

11. Words designating global, national, regional, and local political divisions are capitalized when they are essential elements of specific names. They are usually lowercased when they precede a proper name or are not part of a specific name.

the Roman Empire
British Commonwealth nations
New York State
the state of New York
the Third Precinct
voters in three precincts

In legal documents, such words are often capitalized regardless of position.

the State of New York

12. Generic geographical terms (such as *lake, mountain, river,* or *valley*) are capitalized if they are part of a proper name.

Lake Tanganyika	Cape of Good Hope
Great Salt Lake	Massachusetts Bay
Atlas Mountains	Cayman Islands
Mount Everest	Yosemite Valley

When a place-name is subsequently referred to by its generic term, the term is lowercased.

> They went water-skiing on Lake Michigan that afternoon; the lake was calm and the weather beautiful.

When *the* precedes the generic term, the term is lowercased.

> the river Nile

13. Generic geographical terms preceding two or more names are usually capitalized.

> Lakes Huron and Erie
> Mounts McKinley, Whitney, and Shasta

14. Generic geographical terms that are not used as part of a single proper name are not capitalized. These include plural terms that follow two or more proper names, and terms that are used descriptively or alone.

> the Indian and South Pacific oceans
> the Mississippi and Missouri rivers
> the Pacific coast of Mexico
> Caribbean islands
> the river delta

15. The names of streets, monuments, parks, landmarks, well-known buildings, and other public places are capitalized. However, common terms that are part of these names (such as *street, park,* or *bridge*) are lowercased when they occur after multiple names or are used alone.

State Street	Golden Gate Bridge
the Lincoln Memorial	Empire State Building
Statue of Liberty	Beverly Hills Hotel
the Pyramids	back to the hotel
Grant Park	Main and Oak streets

Well-known shortened forms of place-names are capitalized.

> the Hill [*for* Capitol Hill]
> the Channel [*for* English Channel]
> the Street [*for* Wall Street]

Governmental, Judicial, and Political Bodies

16. Full names of legislative, deliberative, executive, and administrative bodies are capitalized, as are easily recognizable short forms of these names. However, nonspecific noun and adjective references to them are usually lower-cased.

> United States Congress
> Congress
> the House
> the Fed
> congressional hearings
> a federal agency

When words such as *department, committee,* or *agency* are used in place of a full name, they are most often capitalized when the department or agency is referring to itself, but otherwise usually lowercased.

> This Department welcomes constructive criticism . . .
> The department claimed to welcome such criticism . . .

When such a word is used in the plural to describe more than one specific body, it is usually capitalized when it precedes the names and lowercased when it follows them.

> involving the Departments of State and Justice
> a briefing from the State and Justice departments

17. Full names of high courts are capitalized. Short forms of such names are often capitalized in legal documents but lowercased otherwise.

> . . . in the U.S. Court of Appeals for the Ninth Circuit
> International Court of Justice
> The court of appeals [*or* Court of Appeals] held . . .
> the Virginia Supreme Court
> a federal district court
> the state supreme court

However, both the full and short names of the U.S. Supreme Court are capitalized.

> the Supreme Court of the United States
> the Supreme Court
> the Court

18. Names of city and county courts are usually lowercased.

> the Springfield municipal court
> small-claims court
> the county court
> juvenile court

19. The noun *court,* when it applies to a specific judge or presiding officer, is capitalized in legal documents.

> It is the opinion of this Court that . . .
> The Court found that . . .

20. The terms *federal* and *national* are capitalized only when they are essential elements of a name or title. (*Federal* is also capitalized when it refers to a historical architectural style, to members of the original Federalist party, or to adherents of the Union in the Civil War.)

> Federal Election Commission
> a federal commission
> Federalist principles
> National Security Council
> national security

21. The word *administration* is sometimes capitalized when it refers to the administration of a specific U.S. president, but is more commonly lowercased. Otherwise, it is lowercased except when it is a part of the official name of a government agency.

> the Reagan administration   *or*   the Reagan Administration
> the administration   *or*   the Administration
> from one administration to the next
> the Social Security Administration

22. Names of political organizations and their adherents are capitalized, but the word *party* is often lowercased.

> the Democratic National Committee
> the Republican platform
> the Christian Coalition
> most Republicans
> the Democratic party   *or*   the Democratic Party
> party politics

Names of less-distinct political groupings are usually lowercased, as are their derivative forms.

> the right wing
> the liberals
> the conservative agenda
>   *but often*
> the Left
> the Right

23. Terms describing political and economic philosophies are usually lowercased; if derived from proper names, they are usually capitalized. Consult a dictionary for doubtful cases.

> authoritarianism   nationalism
> democracy   social Darwinist
> fascism   *or*   Fascism   Marxist

Historical Periods and Events

24. The names of some historical and cultural periods and movements are capitalized. When in doubt, consult a dictionary or encyclopedia.

> Bronze Age   Third Reich
> Middle Ages   the atomic age

Prohibition	Victorian era
the Renaissance	age of Pericles
New Deal	the baby boom
Fifth Republic	

25. Century and decade designations are normally lowercased.

the nineteenth century
the twenties
the turn of the century
a 12th-century manuscript
> *but*
Gay Nineties
Roaring Twenties

26. The names of conferences, councils, expositions, and specific sporting, cultural, and historical events are capitalized.

Fourth World Conference on Women
Council of Trent
New York World's Fair
Super Bowl
Cannes Film Festival
Miss America Contest
San Francisco Earthquake
Johnstown Flood

27. Full names of specific treaties, laws, and acts are capitalized.

Treaty of Versailles
the Nineteenth Amendment
the Bill of Rights
Clean Air Act of 1990
> *but*
gun-control laws
an equal-rights amendment

28. The words *war, revolution,* and *battle* are capitalized when they are part of a full name. Official names of actions are capitalized. Descriptive terms such as *assault* and *siege* are usually lowercased even when used in conjunction with a place-name.

War of the Roses
World War II
the French Revolution
Battle of Gettysburg
Operation Desert Storm
between the two world wars
the American and French revolutions
the siege of Leningrad
Washington's winter campaign

Hyphenated Compounds

29. The second (third, etc.) element of a hyphenated compound is generally capitalized only if it is itself a proper noun or adjective. (For hyphenated titles, see paragraph 65 below.)

> Arab-Israeli negotiations *or* Arab–Israeli negotiations
> East-West trade agreements *or* East–West trade agreements
> French-speaking peoples
> Forty-second street
> twentieth-century architecture

30. When joined to a proper noun or adjective, common prefixes (such as *pre-* or *anti-*) are usually lowercased, but geographical and ethnic combining forms (such as *Anglo-* or *Sino-*) are capitalized. (For details, see paragraphs 45 and 52 on pages 76–77.)

> anti-Soviet forces
> Sino-Japanese relations

Legal Material

31. The names of the plaintiff and defendant in legal case titles are italicized. The *v.* (for *versus*) may be roman or italic. Cases that do not involve two opposing parties are also italicized. When the party involved rather than the case itself is being discussed, the reference is not italicized. In running text, a case name involving two opposing parties may be shortened.

> *Jones* v. *Massachusetts*
> *Smith et al. v. Jones*
> *In re Jones*
> She covered the Jones trial for the newspaper.
> The judge based his ruling on a precedent set in the *Jones* decision.

Medical Terms

32. Proper names that are elements in terms designating diseases, symptoms, syndromes, and tests are capitalized. Common nouns are lowercased; however, abbreviations of such nouns are all-capitalized.

> Alzheimer's disease   black lung disease
> Tourette's syndrome   mumps
> Schick test   AIDS

33. Scientific names of disease-causing organisms follow the rules discussed in paragraph 58 on page 50. The names of diseases or conditions derived from scientific names of organisms are lowercased and not italicized.

> a neurotoxin produced by *Clostridium botulinum*
> nearly died of botulism

34. Generic names of drugs are lowercased; trade names should be capitalized.

retinoic acid
Retin-A

Military Terms

35. The full titles of branches of the U.S. armed forces are capitalized, as are standard short forms.

U.S. Marine Corps	the Marines
the Marine Corps	the Corps

Those of other countries are capitalized when the precise title is used; otherwise they are usually lowercased. The plurals of *army, navy, air force,* and *coast guard* are lowercased.

Royal Air Force
the Guatemalan army
the tiny armies of both countries

The modifiers *army, navy, marine, coast guard,* and *air force* are usually lowercased; *naval* is lowercased unless it is part of an official name. The noun *marine* is usually lowercased.

an army helicopter	the first naval engagement
a career navy man	the Naval Reserves
the marine barracks	a former marine

Full or shortened names of specific units of a branch are usually capitalized.

U.S. Army Corps of Engineers
the Third Army
the Eighty-second [*or* 82nd] Airborne
the U.S. Special Forces, or Green Berets
. . . of the First Battalion. The battalion commander . . .

36. Military ranks are capitalized when they precede the names of their holders, or replace the name in direct address. Otherwise they are lowercased.

Major General Smedley Butler
Please be seated, Admiral.
The major arrived precisely on time.

37. The names of decorations, citations, and medals are capitalized.

Medal of Honor
Purple Heart

Numerical Designations

38. A noun introducing a reference number is usually capitalized. The abbreviation *No.* is usually omitted.

Order 704	Form 2E
Flight 409	Policy 118-4-Y

39. Nouns used with numbers or letters to refer to major reference entities or actual captions in books or periodicals are usually capitalized. Nouns that designate minor reference entities and do not appear in captions are lowercased.

Book II	Figure D.4
Volume 5	page 101
Chapter 2	line 8
Table 3	paragraph 6.1
Example 16.2	question 21

Organizations

40. Names of organizations, corporations, and institutions, and terms derived from those names to designate their members, are capitalized.

> the League of Women Voters
> General Motors Corporation
> the Smithsonian Institution
> the University of the South
> the Rotary Club
> all Rotarians

Common nouns used descriptively or occurring after the names of two or more organizations are lowercased.

> enrolled at the university
> Yale and Harvard universities
> *but*
> the Universities of Utah and Nevada

41. Words such as *agency, department, division, group,* or *office* that designate corporate and organizational units are capitalized only when used as part of a specific proper name. (For governmental units, see paragraph 16 on pages 41–42.)

> head of the Sales Division of K2 Outfitters
> a memo to the sales divisions of both companies

42. Nicknames for organizations are capitalized.

> the Big Six accounting firms
> referred to IBM as Big Blue
> trading on the Big Board

People

43. The names and initials of persons are capitalized. If a name is hyphenated, both elements are capitalized. Particles forming the initial elements of surnames (such as *de, della, der, du, l', la, le, ten, ter, van,* and *von*) may or may not be capitalized, depending on the practice of the family or individual. However, the particle is always capitalized at the beginning of a sentence. The prefixes *Mac, Mc,* and *O'* are always capitalized.

Cecil Day-Lewis
Agnes de Mille
Cecil B. DeMille
Walter de la Mare
Mark deW. Howe
Martin Van Buren
. . . of van Gogh's life. Van Gogh's technique is . . .

44. A nickname or epithet that either is added to or replaces the name of a person or thing is capitalized.

Babe Ruth	the Sun King
Stonewall Jackson	Deep Throat
Billy the Kid	Big Mama Thornton

A nickname or epithet placed between a person's first and last name is enclosed in quotation marks or parentheses or both. If it precedes the first name, it is sometimes enclosed in quotation marks but more often not.

Charlie "Bird" [*or* ("Bird") *or* (Bird)] Parker
Mother Maybelle Carter

45. Words of family relationship preceding or used in place of a person's name are capitalized; otherwise, they are lowercased.

Uncle Fred	her uncle's book
Mother's birthday	my mother's legacy

46. Words designating languages, nationalities, peoples, races, religious groups, and tribes are capitalized. Designations based on color are usually lowercased.

Spanish	Muslims
Spaniards	Assiniboin
Chinese	both blacks and whites
Asians	white, black, and Hispanic jurors

47. Corporate, professional, and governmental titles are capitalized when they immediately precede a person's name, unless the name is being used as an appositive.

President John Tyler
Professor Wendy Doniger of the University of Chicago
Senator William Fulbright of Arkansas
Arkansas's late former senator, William Fulbright

48. When corporate or governmental titles are used as part of a descriptive phrase to identify a person rather than as part of the name itself, the title is lowercased.

Marcia Ramirez, president of Logex Corp.
the president of Logex Corp., Marcia Ramirez

but

Logex Corp.'s prospects for the coming year were outlined by President Marcia Ramirez.

49. High governmental titles may be capitalized when used in place of individuals' names. In minutes and official records of proceedings, corporate or organizational titles are capitalized when used in place of individuals' names.

> The Secretary of State objected.
> The Judge will respond to questions in her chambers.
> The Treasurer then stated his misgivings about the project.
> *but*
> The report reached the senator's desk yesterday.
> The judge's rulings were widely criticized.
> The co-op's treasurer, it turned out, had twice been convicted of embezzlement.

50. The word *president* may be capitalized whenever it refers to the U.S. presidency, but more commonly is capitalized only when it refers to a specific U.S. president.

> It is the duty of the president [*or* President] to submit a budget to Congress.
> The President's budget, due out on Wednesday, is being eagerly awaited.

51. Titles are capitalized when they are used in direct address.

> Is it very contagious, Doctor?
> You may call your next witness, Counselor.

Religious Terms

52. Words designating the supreme being are capitalized. Plural forms such as *gods, goddesses,* and *deities* are not.

Allah	the Almighty
Brahma	the Trinity
Jehovah	in the eyes of God
Yahweh	the angry gods

53. Personal pronouns referring to the supreme being are often capitalized, especially in religious writing. Relative pronouns (such as *who, whom,* and *whose*) usually are not.

> God gave His [*or* his] Son
> Allah, whose Prophet, Muhammad . . .

54. Traditional designations of apostles, prophets, and saints are capitalized.

the Madonna	the Twelve
the Prophet	St. John of the Cross
Moses the Lawgiver	John the Baptist

55. Names of religions, denominations, creeds and confessions, and religious orders are capitalized, as are adjectives and nouns derived from these names.

Judaism	Eastern Orthodox
Church of England	Islamic
Apostles' Creed	Jesuit teachers
Society of Jesus	a Buddhist

Full names of specific places of worship are capitalized, but terms such as *church, synagogue,* and *mosque* are lowercased when used alone. The word *church* is sometimes capitalized when it refers to the worldwide Catholic Church.

Hunt Memorial Church
the local Baptist church
Beth Israel Synagogue
services at the synagogue

56. Names of the Bible and other sacred works, their books and parts, and versions or editions of them are capitalized but not italicized. Adjectives derived from the names of sacred books are capitalized, except for the words *biblical* and *scriptural.*

Bible	biblical
the Scriptures	Talmud
Revised Standard Version	Talmudic
Old Testament	Koran *or* Qur'an
Book of Revelation	Koranic *or* Qur'anic

57. The names of prayers and well-known passages of the Bible are capitalized.

the Ave Maria	Ten Commandments
Lord's Prayer	Sermon on the Mount
the Our Father	the Beatitudes

Scientific Terms

58. Genus names in biological binomial nomenclature are capitalized; species names are lowercased, even when derived from a proper name. Both names are italicized.

Both the wolf and the domestic dog are included in the genus *Canis.*
The California condor *(Gymnogyps californianus)* is facing extinction.

The names of races, varieties, or subspecies are lowercased and italicized.

Hyla versicolor chrysoscelis
Otis asio naevius

59. The New Latin names of classes, families, and all groups above the genus level in zoology and botany are capitalized but not italicized. Their derivative nouns and adjectives are lowercased.

Gastropoda	gastropod
Thallophyta	thallophytic

60. The names, both scientific and informal, of planets and their satellites, stars, constellations, and other specific celestial objects are capitalized. However, except in technical writing, the words *sun, earth,* and *moon* are usually lowercased unless they occur with other astronomical names. A generic term that follows the name of a celestial object is usually lowercased.

Jupiter	Mars, Venus, and Earth
the North Star	life on earth
Andromeda	a voyage to the moon
Ursa Major	Halley's comet
the Little Dipper	

Names of meteorological phenomena are lowercased.

aurora australis
northern lights
parhelic circle

61. Terms that identify geological eons, eras, periods, systems, epochs, and strata are capitalized. The generic terms that follow them are lowercased.

Mesozoic era
Upper Cretaceous epoch
Quaternary period
in the Middle Ordovician
the Age of Reptiles

62. Proper names that are elements of the names of scientific laws, theorems, and principles are capitalized, but the common nouns *law, theorem, theory,* and the like are lowercased. In the names of popular or fanciful theories or observations, such words are usually capitalized as well.

Mendel's law
the Pythagorean theorem
Occam's razor
Einstein's theory of relativity
Murphy's Law
the Peter Principle

63. The names of computer services and databases are capitalized. Some names of computer languages are written with an initial capital letter, some with all letters capitalized, and some commonly both ways. When in doubt, consult a dictionary.

America Online
World Wide Web
CompuServe
Microsoft Word

Pascal   *or*   PASCAL
BASIC
Internet   *or*   internet

Time Periods and Dates

64. The names of the days of the week, months of the year, and holidays and holy days are capitalized. Names of the seasons are lowercased.

Tuesday   Ramadan
June   Holy Week
Yom Kippur   last winter's storm
Veterans Day

Titles of Works

65. Words in titles of books, magazines, newspapers, plays, movies, long poems, and works of art such as paintings and sculpture are capitalized except for internal articles, coordinating conjunctions, prepositions, and the *to* of infinitives. Prepositions of four or more letters are often capitalized. The entire title is italicized. For sacred works, see paragraph 56 on page 50.

Far from [or *From*] *the Madding Crowd*
Wolfe's *Of Time and the River*
Publishers Weekly
USA Today
the original play *A Streetcar Named Desire*
All about [or *About*] *Eve*, with Bette Davis
Monet's *Water-Lily Pool*, in the Louvre
Rodin's *Thinker*

The elements of hyphenated compounds in titles are usually capitalized, but articles, coordinating conjunctions, and prepositions are lowercased.

Knock-offs and Ready-to-Wear: The Low End of Fashion
Politics in Early Seventeenth-Century England

66. The first word following a colon in a title is capitalized.

Jane Austen: A Literary Life

67. An initial article that is part of a title is capitalized and italicized. It is often omitted if it would be awkward in context.

The Oxford English Dictionary
the 20-volume *Oxford English Dictionary*

68. In the titles of newspapers, the city or local name is usually italicized, but the preceding *the* is usually not italicized or capitalized. (In newspaper writing, any *the* is generally capitalized.)

reported in the *New York Times*
last Thursday's *Atlanta Constitution*

69. Many periodicals, especially newspapers, do not use italics for titles, but instead either simply capitalize the important words of the title or, more commonly, capitalize the words and enclose the title in quotation marks.

> the NB. column in The Times Literary Supplement
> The Nobel committee singled out Walcott's book-length epic "Omeros."

70. The titles of articles in periodicals, short poems, short stories, essays, lectures, dissertations, chapters of books, radio and television programs, and novellas published in a collection are capitalized and enclosed in quotation marks. The capitalization of articles, conjunctions, and prepositions follows the rules explained in paragraph 65 above.

> an article on Rwanda, "After the Genocide," in the *New Yorker*
> Robert Frost's "Death of the Hired Man"
> O'Connor's story "Good Country People"
> "The Literature of Exhaustion," John Barth's seminal essay
> last Friday's lecture, "Labor's Task: A View for the Nineties"
> *The Jungle Book*'s ninth chapter is the well-known "Rikki-tikki-tavi."
> listening to "All Things Considered"
> watched "Good Morning America"

71. The titles of long musical compositions are generally capitalized and italicized; the titles of songs and other short compositions are capitalized and enclosed in quotation marks, as are the popular names of longer works. The titles of compositions identified primarily by their musical forms (such as *quartet, sonata,* or *mass*) are capitalized only, as are movements identified by their tempo markings.

> Mozart's *The Magic Flute*
> Frank Loesser's *Guys and Dolls*
> "The Lady Is a Tramp"
> Beethoven's "Für Elise"
> the Piano Sonata in C-sharp minor, Op. 27, No. 2, or "Moonlight" Sonata
> Symphony No. 104 in D major
> Brahms's Violin Concerto in D
> the Adagietto movement from Mahler's Fifth Symphony

72. Common titles of book sections (such as *preface, introduction,* or *index*) are usually capitalized when they refer to a section of the same book in which the reference is made. Otherwise, they are usually lowercased. (For numbered sections of books, see paragraph 39 on page 47.)

> See the Appendix for further information.
> In the introduction to her book, the author explains her goals.

Trademarks

73. Registered trademarks, service marks, collective marks, and brand names are capitalized. They do not normally require any further acknowledgment of thir special status.

Frisbee	Jacuzzi	Levi's
Coke	Kleenex	Vaseline
College Board	Velcro	Dumpster
Realtor	Xerox	Scotch tape
Walkman	Band-Aid	Teflon

Transportation

74. The names of individual ships, submarines, airplanes, satellites, and space vehicles are capitalized and italicized. The designations *U.S.S., S.S., M.V.,* and *H.M.S.* are not italicized.

> *Challenger*
> *Enola Gay*
> H.M.S. *Bounty*

The names of train lines, types of aircraft, and space programs are not italicized.

> Metroliner
> Boeing 727
> Pathfinder Program

Other Styling Conventions

1. Foreign words and phrases that have not been fully adopted into English are italicized. In general, any word that appears in the main section of *Merriam-Webster's Collegiate Dictionary* does not need to be italicized.

> These accomplishments will serve as a monument, *aere perennius,* to the group's skill and dedication.
> "The cooking here is *wunderbar!*"
> The prix fixe lunch was $20.
> The committee meets on an ad hoc basis.

A complete foreign-language sentence (such as a motto) can also be italicized. However, long sentences are usually treated as quotations; that is, they are set in roman type and enclosed in quotation marks. (For details, see paragraph 6 on page 29.)

> The inscription *Honi soit qui mal y pense* encircles the seal.

2. In nonfiction writing, unfamiliar words or words that have a specialized meaning are set in italics on their first appearance, especially when accompanied by a short definition. Once these words have been introduced and defined, they are not italicized in subsequent references.

> *Vitiligo* is a condition in which skin pigment cells stop making pigment. Vitiligo usually affects . . .
> Another method is the *direct-to-consumer* transaction, in which the publisher markets directly to the individual by mail or door-to-door.

3. Italics are often used to indicate words referred to as words. However, if the word was actually spoken, it is usually enclosed in quotation marks instead.

> Purists still insist that *data* is a plural noun.
> *Only* can also be an adverb, as in "I *only* tried to help."
> We heard his warning, but we weren't sure what "repercussions" meant in that context.

4. Italics are often used for letters referred to as letters, particularly when they are shown in lowercase.

> You should dot your *i*'s and cross your *t*'s.

If the letter is being used to refer to its sound and not its printed form, slashes or brackets are used instead of italics in technical contexts.

> The pure /p/ sound is rarely heard in the mountain dialect.

A letter used to indicate a shape is capitalized but not italicized. Such letters are often set in sans-serif type.

> an A-frame house
> the I beam
> Churchill's famous V sign
> forming a giant X

5. Italics are often used to show numerals referred to as numerals. However, if there is no chance of confusion, they are usually not italicized.

> The first *2* and the last *1* are barely legible.
> Anyone whose ticket number ends in 4 or 6 will win a door prize.

6. Italics are used to emphasize or draw attention to words in a sentence.

> Students must notify the dean's office *in writing* of any added or dropped courses.
> It was not *the* model for the project, but merely *a* model.

7. Italics are used to indicate a word created to suggest a sound.

> Its call is a harsh, drawn-out *kreee-awww.*

8. Individual letters are sometimes italicized when used for lists within sentences or for identifying elements in an illustration.

> providing information about *(a)* typing, *(b)* transcribing, *(c)* formatting, and *(d)* graphics
> located at point A on the diagram

9. Commas, colons, and semicolons that follow italicized words are usually italicized.

> the Rabbit tetralogy *(Rabbit Run, Rabbit Redux, Rabbit Is Rich,* and *Rabbit at Rest); Bech: A Book; S;* and others

However, question marks, exclamation points, quotation marks, and apostrophes are not italicized unless they are part of an italicized title.

> Did you see the latest issue of *Newsweek*?
> Despite the greater success of *Oklahoma!* and *South Pacific*, Rodgers was fondest of *Carousel*.
> "Over Christmas vacation he finished *War and Peace*."
> Students always mistake the old script *s*'s for *f*'s.

Parentheses and brackets may be italicized if most of the words they enclose are also italicized, or if both the first and last words are italicized.

> *(see also Limited Partnership)*
> [German, *Dasein*]
> *(and* is replaced throughout by *&)*

10. Full capitalization is occasionally used for emphasis or to indicate that a speaker is talking very loudly. It is avoided in formal writing, where italics are far more often used for emphasis.

> Term papers received after Friday, May 18, WILL BE RETURNED UNREAD.
> Scalpers mingled in the noisy crowd yelling "SIXTY DOLLARS!"

11. The text of signs, labels, and inscriptions may be reproduced in various ways.

> a poster reading SPECIAL THRILLS COMING SOON
> a gate bearing the infamous motto "Arbeit macht frei"
> a Do Not Disturb sign
> a barn with an old CHEW MAIL POUCH ad on the side
> the stop sign

12. *Small capitals,* identical to large capitals but usually about the height of a lowercase *x*, are commonly used for era designations and computer commands. They may also be used for cross-references, for headings in constitutions and bylaws, and for speakers in a dramatic dialogue.

> The dwellings date from A.D. 200 or earlier.
> Press ALT+CTRL+PLUS SIGN on the numeric keyboard.
> (See LETTERS AS LETTERS, page 162.)
> SECTION IV. The authority for parliamentary procedure in meetings of the Board . . .
> LADY WISHFORT. O dear, has my Nephew made his Addresses to Millamant? I order'd him.
> FOIBLE. Sir Wilfull is set in to drinking, Madam, in the Parlour.

13. *Underlining* indicates italics in typed material. It is almost never seen in typeset text.

14. *Boldface* type has traditionally been used primarily for headings and captions. It is sometimes also used in place of italics for terminology introduced in the text, especially for terms that are accompanied by definitions;

for cross-references; for headwords in listings such as glossaries, gazetteers, and bibliographies; and for page references in indexes that locate a specific kind of material, such as illustrations, tables, or the main discussions of a given topic. (In mathematical texts, arrays, tensors, vectors, and matrix notation are standardly set bold as well.)

> **Application Forms and Tests**   Many offices require applicants to fill out an employment form. Bring a copy . . .
>
> **Figure 4.2: The Electromagnetic Spectrum**
>
> The two axes intersect at a point called the **origin**.
>
> See **Medical Records**, page 123.
>
> **antecedent:** the noun to which a pronoun refers
> **appositive:** a word, phrase, or clause that is equivalent to a preceding noun
>
> Records, medical, **123–37**, 178, 243
> Referrals, **38–40**, 139

Punctuation that follows boldface type is set bold when it is part of a heading or heading-like text; otherwise it is generally set roman.

> **Table 9:** Metric Conversion
>
> **Warning:** This and similar medications . . .
>
> Excellent fourth-quarter earnings were reported by the pharmaceutical giants **Abbott Laboratories, Glaxo Wellcome,** and **Merck**.

3 Plurals, Possessives, and Compounds

Plurals 58
Possessives 63
Compounds 67

This chapter describes the ways in which plurals, possessives, and compounds are most commonly formed.

In regard to plurals and compounds, consulting a dictionary will solve many of the problems discussed in this chapter. A good college dictionary, such as *Merriam-Webster's Collegiate Dictionary*, will provide plural forms for any common word, as well as a large number of permanent compounds. Any dictionary much smaller than the *Collegiate* will often be more frustrating in what it fails to show than helpful in what it shows.

Plurals

The basic rules for writing plurals of English words, stated in paragraph 1, apply in the vast majority of cases. The succeeding paragraphs treat the categories of words whose plurals are most apt to raise questions.

Most good dictionaries give thorough coverage to irregular and variant plurals, and many of the rules provided here are reflected in the dictionary entries.

The symbol → is used here to link the singular and plural forms.

1. The plurals of most English words are formed by adding *-s* to the singular. If the noun ends in *-s, -x, -z, -ch,* or *-sh,* so that an extra syllable must be added in order to pronounce the plural, *-es* is added. If the noun ends in a *-y* preceded by a consonant, the *-y* is changed to *-i* and *-es* is added.

   > voter → voters
   > anticlimax → anticlimaxes
   > blitz → blitzes
   > blowtorch → blowtorches
   > calabash → calabashes
   > allegory → allegories

Abbreviations

2. The plurals of abbreviations are commonly formed by adding *-s* or *-'s;* however, there are some significant exceptions. (For details, see paragraphs 1–5 on pages 81–82.)

yr. → yrs.

TV → TVs

M.B.A. → M.B.A.'s

p. → pp.

Animals

3. The names of many fishes, birds, and mammals have both a plural formed with a suffix and one that is identical with the singular. Some have only one or the other.

bass → bass   *or*   basses

partridge → partridge   *or*   partridges

sable → sables   *or*   sable

lion → lions

sheep → sheep

Many of the animals that have both plural forms are ones that are hunted, fished, or trapped; those who hunt, fish for, and trap them are most likely to use the unchanged form. The *-s* form is often used to emphasize diversity of kinds.

caught three bass

  but

basses of the Atlantic Ocean

a place where antelope feed

  but

antelopes of Africa and southwest Asia

Compounds and Phrases

4. Most compounds made up of two nouns—whether they appear as one word, two words, or a hyphenated word—form their plurals by pluralizing the final element only.

courthouse → courthouses

judge advocate → judge advocates

player-manager → player-managers

5. The plural form of a compound consisting of an *-er* noun and an adverb is made by pluralizing the noun element only.

runner-up → runners-up

onlooker → onlookers

diner-out → diners-out

passerby → passersby

6. Nouns made up of words that are not nouns form their plurals on the last element.

show-off → show-offs

pushover → pushovers

tie-in → tie-ins

lineup → lineups

7. Plurals of compounds that consist of two nouns separated by a preposition are normally formed by pluralizing the first noun.

> sister-in-law → sisters-in-law
> attorney-at-law → attorneys-at-law
> power of attorney → powers of attorney
> chief of staff → chiefs of staff
> grant-in-aid → grants-in-aid

8. Compounds that consist of two nouns separated by a preposition and a modifier form their plurals in various ways.

> snake in the grass → snakes in the grass
> justice of the peace → justices of the peace
> jack-in-the-box → jack-in-the-boxes *or* jacks-in-the-box
> will-o'-the wisp → will-o'-the-wisps

9. Compounds consisting of a noun followed by an adjective are usually pluralized by adding -*s* to the noun. If the adjective tends to be understood as a noun, the compound may have more than one plural form.

> attorney general → attorneys general *or* attorney generals
> sergeant major → sergeants major *or* sergeant majors
> poet laureate → poets laureate *or* poet laureates
> heir apparent → heirs apparent
> knight-errant → knights-errant

Foreign Words and Phrases

10. Many nouns of foreign origin retain the foreign plural. However, most also have a regular English plural.

> alumnus → alumni
> genus → genera
> crisis → crises
> criterion → criteria
> appendix → appendixes *or* appendices
> concerto → concerti *or* concertos
> symposium → symposia *or* symposiums

11. Phrases of foreign origin may have a foreign plural, an English plural, or both.

> pièce de résistance → pièces de résistance
> hors d'oeuvre → hors d'oeuvres
> beau monde → beau mondes *or* beaux mondes

Irregular Plurals

12. A few English nouns form their plurals by changing one or more of their vowels, or by adding -*en* or -*ren*.

> foot → feet   woman → women
> goose → geese   tooth → teeth

louse → lice	ox → oxen
man → men	child → children
mouse → mice	

13. Some nouns do not change form in the plural. (See also paragraph 3 above.)

series → series	corps → corps
politics → politics	species → species

14. Some nouns ending in *-f, -fe,* and *-ff* have plurals that end in *-ves.* Some of these also have regularly formed plurals.

elf → elves
loaf → loaves
scarf → scarves   *or*   scarfs
wife → wives
staff → staffs   *or*   staves

Italic Elements

15. Italicized words, phrases, abbreviations, and letters are usually pluralized by adding *-s* or *-'s* in roman type. (See also paragraphs 16, 21, and 26 below.)

three *Fortune*s missing from the stack
a couple of *Gravity's Rainbow*s in stock
used too many *etc.*'s in the report
a row of *x*'s

Letters

16. The plurals of letters are usually formed by adding *-'s,* although capital letters are often pluralized by adding *-s* alone.

p's and q's
V's of migrating geese   *or*   Vs of migrating geese
dot your *i*'s
straight As   *or*   straight A's

Numbers

17. Numerals are pluralized by adding *-s* or, less commonly, *-'s.*

two par 5s   *or*   two par 5's
1990s   *or*   1990's
in the 80s   *or*   in the 80's   *or*   in the '80s
the mid-$20,000s   *or*   the mid-$20,000's

18. Written-out numbers are pluralized by adding *-s.*

all the fours and eights
scored three tens

Proper Nouns

19. The plurals of proper nouns are usually formed with -*s* or -*es*.

> Clarence → Clarences
> Jones → Joneses
> Fernandez → Fernandezes

20. Plurals of proper nouns ending in -*y* usually retain the -*y* and add -*s*.

> Sunday → Sundays
> Timothy → Timothys
> Camry → Camrys

Words ending in -*y* that were originally proper nouns are usually pluralized by changing -*y* to -*i* and adding -*es*, but a few retain the -*y*.

> bobby → bobbies
> johnny → johnnies
> Tommy → Tommies
> Bloody Mary → Bloody Marys

Quoted Elements

21. The plural of words in quotation marks are formed by adding -*s* or -'*s* within the quotation marks, or -*s* outside the quotation marks. (See also paragraph 26 below.)

> too many "probably's" [*or* "probablys"] in the statement
> one "you" among millions of "you"s
> a record number of "I can't recall"s

Symbols

22. When symbols are referred to as physical characters, the plural is formed by adding either -*s* or -'*s*.

> printed three *s
> used &'s instead of *and*'s
> his π's are hard to read

Words Ending in *-ay, -ey,* and *-oy*

23. Words that end in -*ay*, -*ey*, or -*oy*, unlike other words ending in -*y*, are pluralized by simply adding -*s*.

> castaways
> donkeys
> envoys

Words Ending in *-ful*

24. Any noun ending in *-ful* can be pluralized by adding -*s*, but most also have an alternative plural with -*s* preceding the suffix.

handful → handfuls
teaspoonful → teaspoonfuls
armful → armfuls *or* armsful
bucketful → bucketfuls *or* bucketsful

Words Ending in *-o*

25. Most words ending in *-o* are normally pluralized by adding *-s*. However, some words ending in *-o* preceded by a consonant take *-es* plurals.

solo → solos
photo → photos
tomato → tomatoes
potato → potatoes
hobo → hoboes
hero → heroes
cargo → cargoes *or* cargos
proviso → provisos *or* provisoes
halo → haloes *or* halos
echo → echoes
motto → mottoes

Words Used as Words

26. Words referred to as words and italicized usually form their plurals by adding *-'s* in roman type. (See also paragraph 21 above.)

five *and*'s in one sentence
all those *wherefore*'s and *howsoever*'s

When a word referred to as a word has become part of a fixed phrase, the plural is usually formed by adding *-s* without the apostrophe.

oohs and aahs
dos and don'ts *or* do's and don'ts

Possessives

Common Nouns

1. The possessive of singular and plural common nouns that do not end in an *s* or *z* sound is formed by adding *-'s* to the end of the word.

the child's skates
women's voices
the cat's dish
this patois's range
people's opinions
the criteria's common theme

2. The possessive of singular nouns ending in an *s* or *z* sound is usually formed by adding *-'s*. A less common alternative is to add *-'s* only when it is easily pronounced; if it would create a word that is difficult to pronounce, only an apostrophe is added.

> the witness's testimony
> the disease's course
> the race's sponsors
> the prize's recipient
> rickets's symptoms   *or*   rickets' symptoms

A multisyllabic singular noun that ends in an *s* or *z* sound drops the *-s* if it is followed by a word beginning with an *s* or *z* sound.

> for appearance' sake
> for goodness' sake

3. The possessive of plural nouns ending in an *s* or *z* sound is formed by adding only an apostrophe. However, the possessive of one-syllable irregular plurals is usually formed by adding *-'s*.

> dogs' leashes
> birds' migrations
> buyers' guarantees
> lice's lifespans

Proper Names

4. The possessives of proper names are generally formed in the same way as those of common nouns. The possessive of singular proper names is formed by adding *-'s*.

> Jane's rules of behavior
> three books of Carla's
> Tom White's presentation
> Paris's cafes

The possessive of plural proper names, and of some singular proper names ending in an *s* or *z* sound, is made by adding just an apostrophe.

> the Stevenses' reception
> the Browns' driveway
> Massachusetts' capital
> New Orleans' annual festival
> the United States' trade deficit
> Protosystems' president

5. The possessive of singular proper names ending in an *s* or *z* sound may be formed by adding either *-'s* or just an apostrophe. Adding *-'s* to all such names, without regard for the pronunciation of the resulting word, is more common than adding just the apostrophe. (For exceptions see paragraph 6 below.)

Jones's car   *or*   Jones' car
Bliss's statue   *or*   Bliss' statue
Dickens's novels   *or*   Dickens' novels

6. The possessive form of classical and biblical names of two or more syllables ending in -*s* or -*es* is usually made by adding just an apostrophe. If the name has only one syllable, the possessive form is made by adding -'s.

Socrates' students
Claudius' reign
Ramses' kingdom

Elias' prophecy
Zeus's warnings
Cis's sons

The possessives of the names *Jesus* and *Moses* are always formed with just an apostrophe.

Jesus' disciples
Moses' law

7. The possessive of names ending in a silent -*s*, -*z*, or -*x* are usually formed with -'s.

Des Moines's recreation department
Josquin des Prez's music
Delacroix's painting

8. When the possessive ending is added to an italicized name, it is not italicized.

East of Eden's main characters
the *Spirit of St. Louis*'s historic flight
Brief Encounter's memorable ending

Pronouns

9. The possessive of indefinite pronouns is formed by adding -'s.

anyone's rights
everybody's money
someone's coat
somebody's wedding
one's own
either's preference

Some indefinite pronouns usually require an *of* phrase to indicate possession.

the rights of each
the inclination of many
the satisfaction of all

10. Possessive pronouns do not include apostrophes.

mine
ours

hers
his

yours   theirs
its

Miscellaneous Styling Conventions

11. No apostrophe is generally used today with plural nouns that are more descriptive than possessive.

weapons systems   steelworkers union
managers meeting   awards banquet
singles bar

12. The possessive form of a phrase is made by adding an apostrophe or -'s to the last word in the phrase.

his father-in-law's assistance
board of directors' meeting
from the student of politics' point of view
after a moment or so's thought

Constructions such as these are often rephrased.

from the point of view of the student of politics
after thinking for a moment or so

13. The possessive form of words in quotation marks can be formed in two ways, with -'s placed either inside the quotation marks or outside them.

the "Marseillaise"'s [*or* "Marseillaise's"] stirring melody

Since both arrangements look awkward, this construction is usually avoided.

the stirring melody of the "Marseillaise"

14. Possessives of abbreviations are formed like those of nouns that are spelled out. The singular possessive is formed by adding -'s; the plural possessive, by adding an apostrophe only.

the IRS's ruling
AT&T's long-distance service
IBM Corp.'s annual report
Eli Lilly & Co.'s chairman
the HMOs' lobbyists

15. The possessive of nouns composed of numerals is formed in the same way as for other nouns. The possessive of singular nouns is formed by adding -'s; the possessive of plural nouns is formed by adding an apostrophe only.

1996's commencement speaker
the 1920s' greatest jazz musicians

16. Individual possession is indicated by adding -'s to each noun in a sequence. Joint possession may be indicated in the same way, but is most commonly indicated by adding an apostrophe or -'s to the last noun in the sequence.

Joan's and Emily's friends
Jim's, Ed's, and Susan's reports
her mother and father's anniversary
Peter and Jan's trip   *or*   Peter's and Jan's trip

Compounds

A compound is a word or word group that consists of two or more parts that work together as a unit to express a specific concept. Compounds can be formed by combining two or more words (as in *double-check, cost-effective, farmhouse, graphic equalizer, park bench, around-the-clock,* or *son of a gun*), by combining prefixes or suffixes with words (as in *ex-president, shoeless, presorted,* or *uninterruptedly*), or by combining two or more word elements (as in *macrophage* or *photochromism*). Compounds are written in one of three ways: solid (as in *cottonmouth*), hyphenated (*screenwriter-director*), or open (*health care*). Because of the variety of standard practice, the choice among these styles for a given compound represents one of the most common and vexing of all style issues that writers encounter.

A good dictionary will list many *permanent compounds,* compounds so commonly used that they have become permanent parts of the language. It will not list *temporary compounds,* those created to meet a writer's need at a particular moment. Most compounds whose meanings are self-evident from the meanings of their component words will not be listed, even if they are permanent and quite widely used. Writers thus cannot rely wholly on dictionaries to guide them in writing compounds.

One approach is to hyphenate all compounds not in the dictionary, since hyphenation immediately identifies them as compounds. But hyphenating all such compounds runs counter to some well-established American practice and can therefore call too much attention to the compound and momentarily distract the reader. Another approach (which applies only to compounds whose elements are complete words) is to leave open any compound not in the dictionary. Though this is widely done, it can result in the reader's failing to recognize a compound for what it is. A third approach is to pattern the compound after other similar ones. Though this approach is likely to be more complicated, it can make the compound look more familiar and thus less distracting or confusing. The paragraphs that follow are intended to help you use this approach.

As a general rule, writing meant for readers in specialized fields usually does not hyphenate compounds, especially technical terminology.

Compound Nouns

Compound nouns are combinations of words that function in a sentence as nouns. They may consist of two or more nouns, a noun and a modifier, or two or more elements that are not nouns.

Short compounds consisting of two nouns often begin as open compounds but tend to close up as they become familiar.

1. **noun + noun** Compounds composed of two nouns that are short and commonly used, of which the first is accented, are usually written solid.

farmhouse	paycheck
hairbrush	football
lifeboat	workplace

2. When a noun + noun compound is short and common but pronounced with nearly equal stress on both nouns, it is more likely to be open.

fuel oil	health care
park bench	desk lamp

3. Noun + noun compounds that consist of longer nouns and are self-evident or temporary are usually written open.

   costume designer
   computer terminal
   billiard table

4. When a noun + noun compound describes a double title or double function, the compound is hyphenated.

   hunter-gatherer
   secretary-treasurer
   bar-restaurant

   Sometimes a slash is used in place of the hyphen.

   bar/restaurant

5. Compounds formed from a noun or adjective followed by *man, woman, person,* or *people* and denoting an occupation are normally solid.

anchorman	spokesperson
congresswoman	salespeople

6. Compounds that are units of measurement are hyphenated.

foot-pound	column-inch
kilowatt-hour	light-year

7. **adjective + noun** Most adjective + noun compounds are written open.

municipal court	minor league
genetic code	nuclear medicine
hazardous waste	basic training

8. Adjective + noun compounds consisting of two short words are often written solid when the first word is accented. However, some are usually written open, and a few are hyphenated.

notebook	dry cleaner
bluebird	steel mill
shortcut	two-step

9. participle + noun Most participle + noun compounds are written open.

landing craft	barbed wire
frying pan	preferred stock
sounding board	informed consent

10. noun's + noun Compounds consisting of a possessive noun followed by another noun are usually written open; a few are hyphenated. Compounds of this type that have become solid have lost the apostrophe.

fool's gold	cat's-paw
hornet's nest	bull's-eye
seller's market	foolscap
Queen Anne's lace	menswear

11. noun + verb + -er or -ing Compounds in which the first noun is the object of the verb are most often written open but sometimes hyphenated. Permanent compounds like these are sometimes written solid.

problem solver	fund-raiser
deal making	gene-splicing
air conditioner	lifesaving

12. object + verb Noun compounds consisting of a verb preceded by a noun that is its object are written in various ways.

fish fry	bodyguard
eye-opener	roadblock

13. verb + object A few, mostly older compounds are formed from a verb followed by a noun that is its object; they are written solid.

cutthroat	carryall
breakwater	pickpocket

14. noun + adjective Compounds composed of a noun followed by an adjective are written open or hyphenated.

sum total	president-elect
consul general	secretary-general

15. particle + noun Compounds consisting of a particle (usually a preposition or adverb) and a noun are usually written solid, especially when they are short and the first syllable is accented.

downturn	undertone
outfield	upswing
input	afterthought
outpatient	onrush

A few particle + noun compounds, especially when composed of longer elements or having equal stress on both elements, are hyphenated or open.

on-ramp	off year
cross-reference	cross fire

16. verb + particle; verb + adverb These compounds may be hyphenated or solid. Compounds with particles such as *to, in,* and *on* are often hyphenated. Compounds with particles such as *up, off,* and *out* are hyphenated or solid with about equal frequency. Those with longer particles or adverbs are usually solid.

lean-to	spin-off
trade-in	payoff
add-on	time-out
start-up	turnout
backup	hideaway

17. verb + -er + particle; verb + -ing + particle Except for *passerby,* these compounds are hyphenated.

runner-up	carrying-on
diners-out	talking-to
listener-in	falling-out

18. letter + noun Compounds formed from a single letter (or sometimes a combination of them) followed by a noun are either open or hyphenated.

T square	T-shirt
B vitamin	f-stop
V neck	H-bomb
Rh factor	A-frame
D major	E-mail *or* e-mail

19. Compounds of three or four elements Compounds of three or four words may be either hyphenated or open. Those incorporating prepositional phrases are more often open; others are usually hyphenated.

editor in chief	right-of-way
power of attorney	jack-of-all-trades
flash in the pan	give-and-take
base on balls	rough-and-tumble

20. Reduplication compounds Compounds that are formed by reduplication and so consist of two similar-sounding elements are hyphenated if each element has more than one syllable. If each element has only one syllable, the compound is often written solid. Very short words and newly coined words are more often hyphenated.

namby-pamby	singsong
razzle-dazzle	sci-fi
crisscross	hip-hop

Compound Adjectives

Compound adjectives are combinations of words that work together to modify a noun—that is, they work as *unit modifiers.* As unit modifiers they can be distinguished from other strings of adjectives that may also precede a noun.

For instance, in "a low, level tract of land" the two adjectives each modify the noun separately; the tract is both low and level. These are *coordinate* (i.e., equal) *modifiers.* In "a low monthly fee" the first adjective modifies the noun plus the second adjective; the phrase denotes a monthly fee that is low. It could not be revised to "a monthly and low fee" without altering or confusing its meaning. Thus, these are *noncoordinate modifiers.* However, "low-level radiation" does not mean radiation that is low and level or level radiation that is low, but rather radiation that is at a low level. Both words work as a unit to modify the noun.

Unit modifiers are usually hyphenated, in order to help readers grasp the relationship of the words and to avoid confusion. The hyphen in "a call for more-specialized controls" removes any ambiguity as to which word *more* modifies. By contrast, the lack of a hyphen in a phrase like "graphic arts exhibition" may give it an undesirable ambiguity.

21. Before the noun (attributive position) Most two-word compound adjectives are hyphenated when placed before the noun.

>   the fresh-cut grass
>   its longer-lasting effects
>   her lace-trimmed dress
>   a made-up excuse
>   his best-selling novel
>   projected health-care costs

22. Compounds whose first word is an adverb ending in *-ly* are usually left open.

>   a privately chartered boat
>   politically correct opinions
>   its weirdly skewed perspective
>   a tumultuously cascading torrent

23. Compounds formed of an adverb not ending in *-ly* followed by a participle (or sometimes an adjective) are usually hyphenated when placed before a noun.

>   the well-worded statement
>   more-stringent measures
>   his less-exciting prospects
>   their still-awaited assignments
>   her once-famous uncle

24. The combination of *very* + adjective is not a unit modifier. (See also paragraph 33 below.)

>   a very happy baby

25. When a compound adjective is formed by using a compound noun to modify another noun, it is usually hyphenated.

>   a hazardous-waste site
>   the basic-training period

> a minor-league pitcher
> a roll-call vote
> their problem-solving abilities

Some familiar open compound nouns are frequently left open when used as adjectives.

> a high school diploma   *or*   a high-school diploma
> a real estate license   *or*   a real-estate license
> an income tax refund   *or*   an income-tax refund

26. A proper name used as a modifier is not hyphenated. A word that modifies the proper name is attached by a hyphen (or an en dash in typeset material).

> the Civil War era
> a New England tradition
> a *New York Times* article
> the Supreme Court decision
> the splendid *Gone with the Wind* premiere
> a Los Angeles-based company
> a Pulitzer Prize–winning author
> pre–Bull Run skirmishes

27. Compound adjectives composed of foreign words are not hyphenated when placed before a noun unless they are hyphenated in the foreign language itself.

> per diem expenses
> an ad hoc committee
> her *faux-naïf* style
> a comme il faut arrangement
> the a cappella chorus
> a ci-devant professor

28. Compounds that are quoted, capitalized, or italicized are not hyphenated.

> a "Springtime in Paris" theme
> the book's "I'm OK, you're OK" tone
> his AMERICA FIRST sign
> the *No smoking* notice

29. Chemical names and most medical names used as modifiers are not hyphenated.

> a sodium hypochlorite bleach
> the amino acid sequence
> a new Parkinson's disease medication

30. Compound adjectives of three or more words are hyphenated when they precede the noun.

> step-by-step instructions
> state-of-the-art equipment

a wait-and-see attitude
a longer-than-expected list
turn-of-the-century medicine

31. **Following the noun** When a compound adjective follows the noun it modifies, it usually ceases to be a unit modifier and is therefore no longer hyphenated.

> instructions that guide you step by step
> a list that was longer than expected

However, a compound that follows the noun it modifies often keeps its hyphen if it continues to function as a unit modifier, especially if its first element is a noun.

> hikers who were ill-advised to cross the glacier
> an actor too high-strung to relax
> industries that could be called low-tech
> metals that are corrosion-resistant
> tends to be accident-prone

32. Permanent compound adjectives are usually written as they appear in the dictionary even when they follow the noun they modify.

> for reasons that are well-known
> a plan we regarded as half-baked
> The problems are mind-boggling.

However, compound adjectives of three or more words are normally not hyphenated when they follow the noun they modify, since they usually cease to function as adjectives.

> These remarks are off the record.
> medical practice of the turn of the century

When compounds of three or more words appear as hyphenated adjectives in dictionaries, the hyphens are retained as long as the phrase is being used as a unit modifier.

> The candidate's position was middle-of-the-road.

33. When an adverb modifies another adverb that is the first element of a compound modifier, the compound may lose its hyphen. If the first adverb modifies the whole compound, however, the hyphen is retained.

> a very well developed idea
> *but*
> a delightfully well-written book
> a most ill-timed event

34. Adjective compounds that are color names in which each element can function as a noun are almost always hyphenated.

> red-orange fabric
> The fabric was red-orange.

Color names in which the first element can only be an adjective are often unhyphenated before a noun and usually unhyphenated after.

a bright red tie
the pale yellow-green chair
reddish orange fabric   *or*   reddish-orange fabric
The fabric was reddish orange.

35. Compound modifiers that include a number followed by a noun (except for the noun *percent*) are hyphenated when they precede the noun they modify, but usually not when they follow it. (For details on measurement, see paragraph 42 on pages 106–7.)

the four-color press
a 12-foot-high fence
a fence 12 feet high
a 300-square-mile area
an area of 300 square miles
but
a 10 percent raise

If a currency symbol precedes the number, the hyphen is omitted.

an $8.5 million deficit

36. An adjective composed of a number followed by a noun in the possessive is not hyphenated.

a nine days' wonder
a two weeks' wait
but
a two-week wait

Compound Adverbs

37. Adverb compounds consisting of preposition + noun are almost always written solid. However, there are a few important exceptions.

downstairs
uphill
offshore
overnight
but
in-house
off-key
on-line

38. Compound adverbs of more than two words are usually written open, and they usually follow the words they modify.

here and there
more or less
head and shoulders
hand in hand

every which way
once and for all
but
a more-or-less certain result

A few three-word adverbs are usually hyphenated, but many are written open even if the corresponding adjective is hyphenated.

placed back-to-back
met face-to-face
but
a word-for-word quotation
quoted word for word
software bought off the shelf

Compound Verbs

39. Two-word verbs consisting of a verb followed by an adverb or a preposition are written open.

follow up	take on
roll back	run across
strike out	set back

40. A compound composed of a particle followed by a verb is written solid.

overlook	undercut
outfit	download

41. A verb derived from an open or hyphenated compound noun is hyphenated.

double-space	water-ski
rubber-stamp	field-test

42. A verb derived from a solid noun is written solid.

mastermind	brainstorm
highlight	sideline

Compounds Formed with Word Elements

Many new and temporary compounds are formed by adding word elements to existing words or by combining word elements. There are three basic kinds of word elements: prefixes (such as *anti-, non-, pre-, post-, re-, super-*), suffixes (such as *-er, -fold, -ism, -ist, -less, -ness*), and combining forms (such as *mini-, macro-, pseudo-, -graphy, -logy*). Prefixes and suffixes are usually attached to existing words; combining forms are usually combined to form new words.

43. prefix + word Except as specified in the paragraphs below, compounds formed from a prefix and a word are usually written solid.

anticrime	subzero
nonaligned	superheroine

premedical   transnational
reorchestration   postdoctoral

44. If the prefix ends with a vowel and the word it is attached to begins with the same vowel, the compound is usually hyphenated.

anti-incumbent   semi-independent
de-escalate   intra-arterial
co-organizer   pre-engineered

However, there are many exceptions.

reelect
preestablished
cooperate

45. If the base word or compound to which a prefix is added is capitalized, the resulting compound is almost always hyphenated.

pre-Victorian
anti-Western
post-Darwinian
non-English-speaking
    but
transatlantic
transalpine

If the prefix and the base word together form a new proper name, the compound may be solid with the prefix capitalized.

Postimpressionists
Precambrian
    but
Pre-Raphaelite

46. Compounds made with *ex-*, in its "former" sense, and *self-* are hyphenated.

ex-mayor   self-control
ex-husband   self-sustaining

Compounds formed from *vice-* are usually hyphenated. Some permanent compounds are open.

vice-chair   vice president
vice-consul   vice admiral

A temporary compound with *quasi(-)* or *pseudo(-)* may be written open (if *quasi* or *pseudo* is being treated as a modifier) or hyphenated (if it is being treated as a combining form).

quasi intellectual   *or*   quasi-intellectual
pseudo liberal   *or*   pseudo-liberal

47. If a prefix is added to a hyphenated compound, it may be either followed by a hyphen or closed up solid to the next element. Permanent compounds of this kind should be checked in a dictionary.

unair-conditioned
ultra-up-to-date
non-self-governing
unself-confident

48. If a prefix is added to an open compound, the hyphen is often replaced by an en dash in typeset material.

ex–campaign treasurer
post–World War I era

49. A compound that would be identical with another word if written solid is usually hyphenated to prevent misreading.

a re-creation of the setting
shopped at the co-op
multi-ply fabric

50. Compounds that might otherwise be solid are often hyphenated in order to clarify their formation, meaning, or pronunciation.

tri-city	non-news
de-iced	anti-fur
re-oil	pro-choice

51. When prefixes are attached to numerals, the compounds are hyphenated.

pre-1995 models
post-1945 economy
non-19th-century architecture

52. Compounds created from proper ethnic or national combining forms are hyphenated when the second element is an independent word, but solid when it is a combining form.

Anglo-Saxon	Anglophile
Judeo-Christian	Francophone
Sino-Japanese	Sinophobe

53. Prefixes that are repeated in the same compound are separated by a hyphen.

re-refried
post-postmodern

54. Compounds consisting of different prefixes or adjectives with the same base word which are joined by *and* or *or* are shortened by pruning the first compound back to a hyphenated prefix.

pre- and postoperative care
anti- or pro-Revolutionary sympathies
over- and underachievers
early- and mid-20th-century painters
4-, 6-, and 8-foot lengths

55. word + suffix Except as noted in the paragraphs below, compounds formed by adding a suffix to a word are written solid.

Fourierism	characterless
benightedness	custodianship
yellowish	easternmost

56. Compounds made with a suffix or a terminal combining form are often hyphenated if the base word is more than two syllables long, if it ends with the same letter the suffix begins with, or if it is a proper name.

industry-wide	jewel-like
recession-proof	Hollywood-ish
American-ness	Europe-wide

57. Compounds made from a number + -*odd* are hyphenated. A number + -*fold* is written solid if the number is spelled out but hyphenated if it is in numerals.

fifty-odd	tenfold
50-odd	10-fold

58. Most compounds formed from an open or hyphenated compound + a suffix do not separate the suffix with a hyphen. But combining forms that also exist as independent words, such as -*like*, -*wide*, -*worthy*, and -*proof*, are attached by a hyphen.

self-righteousness
middle-of-the-roadism
bobby-soxer
a Red Cross-like approach
a New York-wide policy

Open compounds often become hyphenated when a suffix is added unless they are proper nouns.

flat-taxer
Ivy Leaguer
World Federalist

59. combining forms New terms in technical fields created with one or more combining forms are normally written solid.

cyberworld
macrographic

4 Abbreviations

Punctuation 79
Capitalization 81
Plurals, Possessives, and Compounds 81
Specific Styling Conventions 83

Abbreviations may be used to save space and time, to avoid repetition of long words and phrases, or simply to conform to conventional usage.

The contemporary styling of abbreviations is inconsistent and arbitrary, and no set of rules can hope to cover all the possible variations, exceptions, and peculiarities encountered in print. The form abbreviations take—capitalized vs. lowercased, punctuated vs. unpunctuated—often depends on a writer's preference or a publisher's or organization's policy. However, the following paragraphs provide a number of useful guidelines to contemporary practice. In doubtful cases, a good general dictionary or a dictionary of abbreviations will usually show standard forms for common abbreviations.

The present discussion deals largely with general, nontechnical writing. In scientific writing, abbreviations are almost never punctuated.

An abbreviation is not divided at the end of a line.

Abbreviations are almost never italicized. An abbreviation consisting of single initial letters, whether punctuated or not, never standardly has spacing between the letters. (Initials of personal names, however, normally are separated by spaces.)

The first reference to any frequently abbreviated term or name that could be confusing or unfamiliar is commonly spelled out, often followed immediately by its abbreviation in parentheses. Later references employ the abbreviation alone.

Punctuation

1. A period follows most abbreviations that are formed by omitting all but the first few letters of a word.

> cont. [*for* continued]
> enc. [*for* enclosure]
> Oct. [*for* October]
> univ. [*for* university]

Former abbreviations that are now considered words do not need a period.

lab   photo
gym   ad

2. A period follows most abbreviations that are formed by omitting letters from the middle of a word.

> govt. [*for* government]
> atty. [*for* attorney]
> bros. [*for* brothers]
> Dr. [*for* Doctor]

Some abbreviations, usually called *contractions,* replace the omitted letters with an apostrophe. Such contractions do not end with a period. (In American usage, very few contractions other than two-word contractions involving verbs are in standard use.)

> ass'n   *or*   assn. [*for* association]
> dep't   *or*   dept. [*for* department]
> nat'l   *or*   natl. [*for* national]
> can't [*for* cannot]

3. Periods are usually omitted from abbreviations made up of single initial letters. However, for some of these abbreviations, especially uncapitalized ones, the periods are usually retained. No space follows an internal period.

> GOP [*for* Grand Old Party]
> PR [*for* public relations]
> CEO   *or*   C.E.O. [*for* chief executive officer]
> a.m. [*for* ante meridiem]

4. A few abbreviations are punctuated with one or more slashes in place of periods. (For details on the slash, see the section beginning on page 34.)

> c/o [*for* care of]
> d/b/a   *or*   d.b.a. [*for* doing business as]
> w/o [*for* without]
> w/w [*for* wall-to-wall]

5. Terms in which a suffix is added to a numeral are not genuine abbreviations and do not require a period. (For details on ordinal numbers, see the section beginning on page 93.)

> 1st   3d
> 2nd   8vo

6. Isolated letters of the alphabet used to designate a shape or position in a sequence are not abbreviations and are not punctuated.

> T square
> A1
> F minor

7. When a punctuated abbreviation ends a sentence, its period becomes the terminal period.

> For years she claimed she was "the oldest living fossil at Briggs & Co."

Capitalization

1. Abbreviations are capitalized if the words they represent are proper nouns or adjectives.

>F [*for* Fahrenheit]
>IMF [*for* International Monetary Fund]
>Jan. [*for* January]
>Amer. [*for* American]
>LWV [*for* League of Women Voters]

2. Abbreviations are usually all-capitalized when they represent initial letters of lowercased words. However, some common abbreviations formed in this way are often lowercased.

>IQ [*for* intelligence quotient]
>U.S. [*for* United States]
>COLA [*for* cost-of-living allowance]
>FYI [*for* for your information]
>f.o.b.   *or*   FOB [*for* free on board]
>c/o [*for* care of]

3. Most abbreviations formed from single initial letters that are pronounced as words, rather than as a series of letters, are capitalized. Those that are not proper nouns and have been assimilated into the language as words in their own right are most often lowercased.

>OSHA   snafu
>NATO   laser
>CARE   sonar
>NAFTA   scuba

4. Abbreviations that are ordinarily capitalized are commonly used to begin sentences, but abbreviations that are ordinarily uncapitalized are not.

>Dr. Smith strongly disagrees.
>OSHA regulations require these new measures.
>Page 22 [*not* P. 22] was missing.

Plurals, Possessives, and Compounds

1. Punctuated abbreviations of single words are pluralized by adding -*s* before the period.

>yrs. [*for* years]
>hwys. [*for* highways]
>figs. [*for* figures]

2. Punctuated abbreviations that stand for phrases or compounds are usually pluralized by adding -'*s* after the last period.

M.D.'s *or* M.D.s
Ph.D.'s *or* Ph.D.s
LL.B.'s *or* LL.B.s
v.p.'s

3. All-capitalized, unpunctuated abbreviations are usually pluralized by adding a lowercase -*s*.

IRAs	CPAs
PCs	SATs

4. The plural form of a few lowercase one-letter abbreviations is made by repeating the letter.

ll. [*for* lines]
pp. [*for* pages]
nn. [*for* notes]
vv. [*for* verses]
ff. *or* ff [*for* and the following ones *or* folios]

5. The plural form of abbreviations of units of measurement (including one-letter abbreviations) is the same as the singular form. (For more on units of measurement, see the section beginning on page 106.)

10 cc *or* cc. [*for* cubic centimeters]
30 m *or* m. [*for* meters]
15 mm *or* mm. [*for* millimeters]
24 h. [*for* hours]
10 min. [*for* minutes]
45 mi. [*for* miles]

However, in informal nontechnical text several such abbreviations are pluralized like other single-word abbreviations.

lbs.	qts.
gals.	hrs.

6. Possessives of abbreviations are formed like those of spelled-out nouns: the singular possessive is formed by adding -'*s*, the plural possessive simply by adding an apostrophe.

the CEO's speech
Apex Co.'s profits
the PACs' influence
Brown Bros.' ads

7. Compounds that consist of an abbreviation added to another word are formed in the same way as compounds that consist of spelled-out nouns.

an FDA-approved drug
an R&D-driven company
the Eau Claire, Wisc.–based publisher

Compounds formed by adding a prefix or suffix to an abbreviation are usually hyphenated.

pre-CD recordings
non-IRA deductions
a CIA-like operation
a PCB-free product

Specific Styling Conventions

A and *An*

1. The choice of the article *a* or *an* before abbreviations depends on the sound, rather than the actual letter, with which the abbreviation begins. If it begins with a consonant sound, *a* is normally used; if with a vowel sound, *an* is used.

> a CD-ROM version
> a YAF member
> a U.S. Senator
> an FDA-approved drug
> an M.D. degree
> an ABA convention

A.D. and B.C.

2. The abbreviations A.D. and B.C. and other abbreviated era designations usually appear in books and journals as small capitals; in newspapers and in typed or keyboarded material, they usually appear as full capitals. The abbreviation B.C. follows the date; A.D. usually precedes the date, though in many publications A.D. follows the date as well. In references to whole centuries, A.D. follows the century. (For more on era designations, see paragraph 12 on page 100.)

> A.D. 185   *but also*   185 A.D.
> 41 B.C.
> the fourth century A.D.

Agencies, Associations, Organizations, and Companies

3. The names of agencies, associations, and organizations are usually abbreviated after being spelled out on their first occurrence in a text. If a company is easily recognizable from its initials, the abbreviation is likewise usually employed after the first mention. The abbreviations are usually all-capitalized and unpunctuated. (In contexts where the abbreviation will be recognized, it often replaces the full name throughout.)

> Next, the president of the Pioneer Valley Transit Authority presented the annual PVTA award.
> . . . at the American Bar Association (ABA) meeting in June. The ABA's new officers . . .

International Business Machines released its first-quarter earnings figures to-day. An IBM spokesperson . . .

4. The words *Company, Corporation, Incorporated,* and *Limited* in company names are commonly abbreviated even at their first appearance, except in quite formal writing.

Procter & Gamble Company   *or*   Procter & Gamble Co.
Brandywine Corporation   *or*   Brandywine Corp.

Ampersand

5. The ampersand (&), representing the word *and,* is often used in the names of companies.

H&R Block
Standard & Poor's
Ogilvy & Mather

It is not used in the names of federal agencies.

U.S. Fish and Wildlife Service
Office of Management and Budget

Even when a spelled-out *and* appears in a company's official name, it is often replaced by an ampersand in writing referring to the company, whether for the sake of consistency or because of the writer's inability to verify the official styling.

6. When an ampersand is used in an abbreviation, there is usually no space on either side of the ampersand.

The Barkers welcome all guests to their B&B at 54 West Street.
The S&P 500 showed gains in technology stocks.
The Texas A&M Aggies prevailed again on Sunday.

7. When an ampersand is used between the last two elements in a series, the comma is omitted.

Jones, Kuhn & Malloy, Attorneys at Law

Books of the Bible

8. Books of the Bible are spelled out in running text but generally abbreviated in references to chapter and verse.

The minister based his first Advent sermon on Matthew.
Ye cannot serve God and mammon.—Matt. 6:24

Compass Points

9. Compass points are normally abbreviated when they follow street names; these abbreviations may be punctuated and are usually preceded by a comma.

1600 Pennsylvania Avenue[,] NW [N.W.]

When a compass point precedes the word *Street, Avenue,* etc., or when it follows the word but forms an integral part of the street name, it is usually spelled out.

> 230 West 43rd Street
> 50 Park Avenue South

Dates

10. The names of days and months are spelled out in running text.

> at the Monday editorial meeting
> the December issue of *Scientific American*
> a meeting held on August 1, 1995

The names of months usually are not abbreviated in datelines of business letters, but they are often abbreviated in government and military correspondence.

> *business dateline:*   November 1, 1995
> *military dateline:*   1 Nov 95

Degrees and Professional Ratings

11. Abbreviations of academic degrees are usually punctuated; abbreviations of professional ratings are slightly more commonly unpunctuated.

> Ph.D.
> B.Sc.
> M.B.A.
> PLS   *or*   P.L.S. [*for* Professional Legal Secretary]
> CMA   *or*   C.M.A. [*for* Certified Medical Assistant]
> FACP   *or*   F.A.C.P. [*for* Fellow of the American College of Physicians]

12. Only the first letter of each element in abbreviations of degrees and professional ratings is generally capitalized.

> D.Ch.E. [*for* Doctor of Chemical Engineering]
> Litt.D. [*for* Doctor of Letters]
> D.Th. [*for* Doctor of Theology]
> *but*
> LL.B. [*for* Bachelor of Laws]
> LL.M. [*for* Master of Laws]
> LL.D. [*for* Doctor of Laws]

Geographical Names

13. When abbreviations of state names are used in running text immediately following the name of a city or county, the traditional state abbreviations are often used.

> Ellen White of 49 Lyman St., Saginaw, Mich., has been chosen . . .
> the Dade County, Fla., public schools

but
Grand Rapids, in western Michigan, . . .

Official postal service abbreviations for states are used in mailing addresses.

6 Bay Rd.
Gibson Island, MD 21056

14. Terms such as *Street, Road,* and *Boulevard* are often written as punctuated abbreviations in running text when they form part of a proper name.

an accident on Windward Road [*or* Rd.]
our office at 1234 Cross Blvd. [*or* Boulevard]

15. Names of countries are usually spelled in full in running text.

South Africa's president urged the United States to impose meaningful sanctions.

Abbreviations for country names (in tables, for example), are usually punctuated. When formed from the single initial letters of two or more individual words, they are sometimes unpunctuated.

Mex.	Scot.
Can.	U.K. *or* UK
Ger.	U.S. *or* US

16. *United States* is normally abbreviated when used as an adjective or attributive. When used as a noun, it is generally spelled out.

the U.S. Department of Justice
U.S. foreign policy
The United States has declined to participate.

17. *Saint* is usually abbreviated when it is part of a geographical or topographical name. *Mount, Point,* and *Fort* may be either spelled out or abbreviated. (For the abbreviation of *Saint* with personal names, see paragraph 25 below.)

St. Paul, Minnesota *or* Saint Paul, Minnesota
St. Thomas, U.S.V.I. *or* Saint Thomas
Mount Vernon *or* Mt. Vernon
Point Reyes *or* Pt. Reyes
Fort Worth *or* Ft. Worth
Mt. Kilimanjaro *or* Mount Kilimanjaro

Latin Words and Phrases

18. Several Latin words and phrases are almost always abbreviated. They are punctuated, lowercased, and usually not italicized.

etc.	ibid.
i.e.	op. cit.

e.g.	q.v.
cf.	c. *or* ca.
viz.	fl.
et al.	et seq.

Versus is usually abbreviated *v.* in legal writing, *vs.* otherwise.

> *Da Costa* v. *United States*
> good vs. evil
>   *or* good versus evil

Latitude and *Longitude*

19. The words *latitude* and *longitude* are abbreviated in tables and in technical contexts but often written out in running text.

> *in a table:* lat. 10°20′N *or* lat. 10-20N
> *in text:* from 10°20′ north latitude to 10°30′ south latitude
>   *or* from lat. 10°20′N to lat. 10°30′S

Military Ranks and Units

20. Official abbreviations for military ranks follow specific unpunctuated styles for each branch of the armed forces. Nonmilitary writing usually employs a punctuated and less concise style.

> *in the military:* BG Carter R. Stokes, USA
>   LCDR Dawn Wills-Craig, USN
>   Col S. J. Smith, USMC
>   LTJG Carlos Ramos, USCG
>   Sgt Bernard P. Brodkey, USAF
> *outside the military:* Brig. Gen. Carter R. Stokes
>   Lt. Comdr. Dawn Wills-Craig
>   Col. S. J. Smith
>   Lt. (j.g.) Carlos Ramos
>   Sgt. Bernard P. Brodkey

21. Outside the military, military ranks are usually given in full when used with a surname only but abbreviated when used with a full name.

> Major Mosby
> Maj. John S. Mosby

Number

22. The word *number,* when followed by a numeral, is usually abbreviated to *No.* or *no.*

> The No. 1 priority is to promote profitability.
> We recommend no. 6 thread.
> Policy No. 123-5-X
> Publ. Nos. 12 and 13

Personal Names

23. When initials are used with a surname, they are spaced and punctuated. Unspaced initials of a few famous persons, which may or may not be punctuated, are sometimes used in place of their full names.

> E. M. Forster
> C. P. E. Bach
> JFK   *or*   J.F.K.

24. The abbreviations *Jr.* and *Sr.* may or may not be preceded by a comma.

> Martin Luther King Jr.
>   *or*   Martin Luther King, Jr.

Saint

25. The word *Saint* is often abbreviated when used before the name of a saint. When it forms part of a surname or an institution's name, it follows the style used by the person or institution. (For the styling of *Saint* in geographical names, see paragraph 17 on page 86.)

> St. [*or* Saint] Teresa of Avila
> Augustus Saint-Gaudens
> Ruth St. Denis
> St. Martin's Press
> St. John's College

Scientific Terms

26. In binomial nomenclature, a genus name may be abbreviated to its initial letter after the first reference. The abbreviation is always capitalized, punctuated, and italicized.

> . . . its better-known relative *Atropa belladonna* (deadly nightshade).
> Only *A. belladonna* is commonly found in . . .

27. Abbreviations for the names of chemical compounds and the symbols for chemical elements and formulas are unpunctuated.

> MSG   O
> PCB   NaCl
> Pb   FeS

28. Abbreviations in computer terms are usually unpunctuated.

> PC   Esc
> RAM   Alt
> CD-ROM   Ctrl
> I/O   ASCII
> DOS   EBCDIC

Time

29. When time is expressed in figures, the abbreviations *a.m. (ante meridiem)* and *p.m. (post meridiem)* are most often written as punctuated lowercase letters, sometimes as punctuated small capital letters. In newspapers, they usually appear in full-size capitals. (For more on *a.m.* and *p.m.*, see paragraph 39 on page 106.)

> 8:30 a.m.   *or*   8:30 A.M.   *or*   8:30 A.M.
> 10:00 p.m.   *or*   10:00 P.M.   *or*   10:00 P.M.

Time-zone designations are usually capitalized and unpunctuated.

> 9:22 a.m. EST [*for* eastern standard time]
> 4:45 p.m. CDT [*for* central daylight time]

Titles and Degrees

30. The courtesy titles *Mr., Ms., Mrs.,* and *Messrs.* occur only as abbreviations today. The professional titles *Doctor, Professor, Representative,* and *Senator* are often abbreviated.

> Ms. Lee A. Downs
> Messrs. Lake, Mason, and Nambeth
> Doctor Howe   *or*   Dr. Howe

31. Despite some traditional objections, the honorific titles *Honorable* and *Reverend* are often abbreviated, with and without *the* preceding the titles.

> the Honorable Samuel I. O'Leary
>   *or*   [the] Hon. Samuel I. O'Leary
> the Reverend Samuel I. O'Leary
>   *or*   [the] Rev. Samuel I. O'Leary

32. When an abbreviation for an academic degree, professional certification, or association membership follows a name, no courtesy or professional title precedes it.

> Dr. Jesse Smith   *or*   Jesse Smith, M.D.
>   *but not*   Dr. Jesse Smith, M.D.
> Katherine Fox Derwinski, CLU
> Carol W. Manning, M.D., FACPS
> Michael B. Jones II, J.D.
> Peter D. Cohn, Jr., CPA

33. The abbreviation *Esq.* (for *Esquire*) often follows attorneys' names in correspondence and in formal listings, and less often follows the names of certain other professionals, including architects, consuls, clerks of court, and justices of the peace. It is not used if a degree or professional rating follows the name, or if a courtesy title or honorific (*Mr., Ms., Hon., Dr.,* etc.) precedes the name.

Carolyn B. West, Esq.
not   Ms. Carolyn B. West, Esq.
and not   Carolyn B. West, J.D., Esq.

Units of Measurement

34. A unit of measurement that follows a figure is often abbreviated, especially in technical writing. The figure and abbreviation are separated by a space. If the numeral is written out, the unit should also be written out.

15 cu. ft.   *but*   fifteen cubic feet
What is its capacity in cubic feet?

35. Abbreviations for metric units are usually unpunctuated; those for traditional units are usually punctuated in nonscientific writing. (For more on units of measurement, see the section beginning on page 106.)

14 ml	8 ft.
12 km	4 sec.
50 m	20 min.

5 Numbers

Numbers as Words or Figures   91
Punctuation   95
Specific Styling Conventions   98

The treatment of numbers presents special difficulties because there are so many conventions to follow, some of which may conflict in a particular passage. The major issue is whether to spell out numbers or to express them in figures, and usage varies considerably on this point.

Numbers as Words or Figures

At one style extreme—usually limited to proclamations, legal documents, and some other types of very formal writing—all numbers (sometimes even including dates) are written out. At the other extreme, some types of technical writing may contain no written-out numbers. Figures are generally easier to read than spelled-out numbers; however, the spelled-out forms are helpful in certain circumstances, and are often felt to be less jarring than figures in nontechnical writing.

Basic Conventions

1. Two alternative basic conventions are in common use. The first and more widely used system requires that numbers up through nine be spelled out, and that figures be used for exact numbers greater than nine. (In a variation of this system, the number ten is spelled out.) Round numbers that consist of a whole number between one and nine followed by *hundred, thousand, million,* etc., may either be spelled out or expressed in figures.

    > The museum includes four rooms of early American tools and implements, 345 pieces in all.
    > He spoke for almost three hours, inspiring his audience of 19,000 devoted followers.
    > They sold more than 700 [*or* seven hundred] TVs during the 10-day sale.
    > She'd told him so a thousand times.

2. The second system requires that numbers from one through ninety-nine be spelled out, and that figures be used for all exact numbers above ninety-nine. (In a variation of this system, the number one hundred is spelled out.) Numbers that consist of a whole number between one and ninety-nine followed by *hundred, thousand, million,* etc., are also spelled out.

Audubon's engraver spent nearly twelve years completing these four volumes, which comprise 435 hand-colored plates.
In the course of four hours, she signed twenty-five hundred copies of her book.

3. Written-out numbers only use hyphens following words ending in *-ty*. The word *and* before such words is usually omitted.

twenty-two
five hundred ninety-seven
two thousand one hundred forty-nine

Sentence Beginnings

4. Numbers that begin a sentence are written out. An exception is occasionally made for dates. Spelled-out numbers that are lengthy and awkward are usually avoided by restructuring the sentence.

Sixty-two new bills will be brought before the committee.
or There will be 62 new bills brought before the committee.
Nineteen ninety-five was our best earnings year so far.
or occasionally 1995 was our best earnings year so far.
One hundred fifty-seven illustrations, including 86 color plates, are contained in the book.
or The book contains 157 illustrations, including 86 color plates.

Adjacent Numbers and Numbers in Series

5. Two separate figures are generally not written adjacent to one another in running text unless they form a series. Instead, either the sentence is rephrased or one of the figures is spelled out—usually the figure with the shorter written form.

sixteen ½-inch dowels
worked five 9-hour days in a row
won twenty 100-point games
lost 15 fifty-point matches
By 1997, thirty schools . . .

6. Numbers paired at the beginning of a sentence are usually written alike. If the first word of the sentence is a spelled-out number, the second number is also spelled out. However, each number may instead be styled independently, even if that results in an inconsistent pairing.

Sixty to seventy-five copies will be required.
or Sixty to 75 copies will be required.

7. Numbers that form a pair or a series within a sentence or a paragraph are often treated identically even when they would otherwise be styled differently. The style of the largest number usually determines that of the others. If one number is a mixed or simple fraction, figures are used for all the numbers in the series.

She wrote one composition for English and translated twelve [*or* 12] pages for French that night.

His total record sales came to a meager 8 [*or* eight] million; Bing Crosby's, he mused, may have surpassed 250 million.

The three jobs took 5, 12, and 4½ hours, respectively.

Round Numbers

8. Approximate or round numbers, particularly those that can be expressed in one or two words, are often spelled out in general writing. In technical and scientific writing, they are expressed as numerals.

> seven hundred people *or* 700 people
> five thousand years *or* 5,000 years
> four hundred thousand volumes *or* 400,000 volumes
>> *but not* 400 thousand volumes
>>> *but in technical writing*
> 200 species of fish
> 50,000 people per year
> 300,000 years

9. Round (and round-appearing) numbers of one million and above are often expressed as figures followed by the word *million, billion,* and so forth. The figure may include a one- or two-digit decimal fraction; more exact numbers are written entirely in figures.

> the last 600 million years
> about 4.6 billion years old
> 1.2 million metric tons of grain
> $7.25 million
> $3,456,000,000

Ordinal Numbers

10. Ordinal numbers generally follow the styling rules for cardinal numbers. In technical writing, ordinal numbers are usually written as figure-plus-suffix combinations. Certain ordinal numbers—for example, those for percentiles and latitudes—are usually set as figures even in nontechnical contexts.

> entered the seventh grade
> wrote the 9th [*or* ninth] and 12th [*or* twelfth] chapters
> in the 21st [*or* twenty-first] century
> the 7th percentile
> the 38th parallel

11. In figure-plus-suffix combinations where the figure ends in 2 or 3, either a one- or a two-letter suffix may be used. A period does not follow the suffix.

> 2d *or* 2nd
> 33d *or* 33rd
> 102d *or* 102nd

Roman Numerals

12. Roman numerals are traditionally used to differentiate rulers and popes with identical names.

> King George III
> Henri IV
> Innocent X

13. When Roman numerals are used to differentiate related males with the same name, they are used only with the full name. Ordinals are sometimes used instead of Roman numerals. The possessive is formed in the usual way. (For the use of *Jr.* and *Sr.,* see paragraph 24 on page 88.)

> James R. Watson II
> James R. Watson 2nd *or* 2d
> James R. Watson II's [*or* 2nd's *or* 2d's] alumni gift

14. Lowercase Roman numerals are generally used to number book pages that precede the regular Arabic sequence (often including a table of contents, acknowledgments, foreword, or other material).

> on page iv of the preface
> See Introduction, pp. ix–xiii.

15. Roman numerals are used in outlines; see paragraph 23 on page 103.

16. Roman numerals are found as part of a few established scientific and technical terms. Chords in the study of music harmony are designated by capital and lowercase Roman numerals (often followed by small Arabic numbers). Most technical terms that include numbers, however, express them in Arabic form.

> blood-clotting factor VII
> cranial nerves II and IX
> cancer stage III
> Population II stars
> type I error
> vii$_6$ chord
>   *but*
> adenosine 3′,5′-monophosphate
> cesium 137
> HIV-2

17. Miscellaneous uses of Roman numerals include the Articles, and often the Amendments, of the Constitution. Roman numerals are still sometimes used for references to the acts and scenes of plays and occasionally for volume numbers in bibliographic references.

> Article IX
> Act III, Scene ii   *or* Act 3, Scene 2

(III, ii)   *or*   (3, 2)
Vol. XXIII, No. 4   *but usually*   Vol. 23, No. 4

Punctuation

These paragraphs provide general rules for the use of commas, hyphens, and en dashes with compound and large numbers. For specific categories of numbers, such as dates, money, and decimal fractions, see Specific Styling Conventions, beginning on page 98.

Commas in Large Numbers

1. In general writing, figures of four digits may be written with or without a comma; including the comma is more common. If the numerals form part of a tabulation, commas are necessary so that four-digit numerals can align with numerals of five or more digits.

> 2,000 cases   *or less commonly*   2000 cases

2. Whole numbers of five digits or more (but not decimal fractions) use a comma to separate three-digit groups, counting from the right.

> a fee of $12,500
> 15,000 units
> a population of 1,500,000

3. Certain types of numbers of four digits or more do not contain commas. These include decimal fractions and the numbers of policies and contracts, checks, street addresses, rooms and suites, telephones, pages, military hours, and years.

> 2.5544   Room 1206
> Policy 33442   page 145
> check 34567   1650 hours
> 12537 Wilshire Blvd.   in 1929

4. In technical writing, the comma is frequently replaced by a thin space in numerals of five or more digits. Digits to the right of the decimal point are also separated in this way, counting from the decimal point.

> 28 666 203
> 209.775 42

Hyphens

5. Hyphens are used with written-out numbers between 21 and 99.

> forty-one years old
> his forty-first birthday
> Four hundred twenty-two visitors were counted.

6. A hyphen is used in a written-out fraction employed as a modifier. A non-modifying fraction consisting of two words only is usually left open, although it may also be hyphenated. (For details on fractions, see the section beginning on page 101.)

> a one-half share
> three fifths of her paycheck   *or*   three-fifths of her paycheck
> *but*
> four five-hundredths

7. Numbers that form the first part of a modifier expressing measurement are followed by a hyphen. (For units of measurement, see the section beginning on page 106.)

> a 5-foot board
> a 28-mile trip
> an eight-pound baby
> *but*
> a $6 million profit

8. Serial numbers, Social Security numbers, telephone numbers, and extended zip codes often contain hyphens that make lengthy numerals more readable or separate coded information.

> 020-42-1691
> 413-734-3134   *or*   (413) 734-3134
> 01102-2812

9. Numbers are almost never divided at the end of a line. If division is unavoidable, the break occurs only after a comma.

Inclusive Numbers

10. Inclusive numbers—those that express a range—are usually separated either by the word *to* or by a hyphen or en dash, meaning "(up) to and including."

> spanning the years 1915 to 1941
> the fiscal year 1994–95
> the decade 1920–1929
> pages 40 to 98
> pp. 40–98

Inclusive numbers separated by a hyphen or en dash are not used after the words *from* or *between*.

> from page 385 to page 419   *not*   from page 385–419
> from 9:30 to 5:30   *not*   from 9:30–5:30
> between 1997 and 2000   *not*   between 1997–2000
> between 80 and 90 percent   *not*   between 80–90 percent

11. Inclusive page numbers and dates may be either written in full or elided (i.e., shortened) to save space or for ease of reading.

> pages 523–526   *or*   pages 523–26
> 1955–1969   *or*   1955–69

However, inclusive dates that appear in titles and other headings are almost never elided. Dates that appear with era designations are also not elided.

> *England and the French Revolution 1789–1797*
> 1900–1901   *not*   1900–01   *and not*   1900–1
> 872–863 B.C.   *not*   872–63 B.C.

12. The most common style for the elision of inclusive numbers is based on the following rules: Never elide inclusive numbers that have only two digits.

> 24–28   *not*   24–8
> 86–87   *not*   86–7

Never elide inclusive numbers when the first number ends in 00.

> 100–103   *not*   100–03   *and not*   100–3
> 300–329   *not*   300–29

In other numbers, do not omit the tens digit from the higher number. *Exception:* Where the tens digit of both numbers is zero, write only one digit for the higher number.

> 234–37   *not*   234–7
> 3,824–29   *not*   3,824–9
> 605–7   *not*   605–07

13. Units of measurement expressed in words or abbreviations are usually used only after the second element of an inclusive number. Symbols, however, are repeated.

> ten to fifteen dollars
> 30 to 35 degrees Celsius
> an increase in dosage from 200 to 500 mg
>   *but*
> 45° to 48° F
> $50–$60 million
>   *or* $50 million to $60 million

14. Numbers that are part of an inclusive set or range are usually styled alike: figures with figures, spelled-out words with other spelled-out words.

> from 8 to 108 absences
> five to twenty guests
> 300,000,000 to 305,000,000
>   *not*   300 million to 305,000,000

Specific Styling Conventions

The following paragraphs, arranged alphabetically, describe styling practices commonly followed for specific situations involving numbers.

Addresses

1. Numerals are used for all building, house, apartment, room, and suite numbers except for *one*, which is usually written out.

6 Lincoln Road	Room 982
1436 Fremont Street	Suite 2000
Apartment 609	One Bayside Drive

When the address of a building is used as its name, the number in the address is often written out.

the sophisticated elegance of Ten Park Avenue

2. Numbered streets have their numbers written as ordinals. Street names from First through Tenth are usually written out, and numerals are used for all higher-numbered streets. Less commonly, all numbered street names up to and including One Hundredth are spelled out.

167 Second Avenue
19 South 22nd Street
  or less commonly 19 South Twenty-second Street
145 East 145th Street
in the 60s *or* in the Sixties [streets from 60th to 69th]
in the 120s [streets from 120th to 129th]

When a house or building number immediately precedes the number of a street, a spaced hyphen may be inserted between the two numbers, or the street number may be written out, for the sake of clarity.

2018 - 14th Street
2018 Fourteenth Street

3. Arabic numerals are used to designate highways and, in some states, county roads.

Interstate 90 *or* I-90
U.S. Route 1 *or* U.S. 1
Texas 23
County 213

Dates

4. Year numbers are written as figures. If a year number begins a sentence, it may be left as a figure but more often is spelled out; the sentence may also be rewritten to avoid beginning it with a figure.

the 1997 edition
Nineteen thirty-seven marked the opening of the Golden Gate Bridge.
   or The year 1937 marked the opening of the Golden Gate Bridge.
   or The Golden Gate Bridge opened in 1937.

5. A year number may be abbreviated to its last two digits when an event is so well known that it needs no century designation. In these cases an apostrophe precedes the numerals.

the blizzard of '88
class of '91   *or*   class of 1991
the Spirit of '76

6. Full dates are traditionally written in the sequence month-day-year, with the year set off by commas that precede and follow it. An alternative style, used in the military and in U.S. government publications, is the inverted sequence day-month-year, which does not require commas.

traditional: July 8, 1976, was a warm, sunny day in Philadelphia.
              the explosion on July 16, 1945, at Alamogordo
military: the explosion on 16 July 1945 at Alamogordo
              the amendment ratified on 18 August 1920

7. Ordinal numbers are not used in full dates. Ordinals are sometimes used, however, for a date without an accompanying year, and they are always used when preceded in a date by the word *the.*

December 4, 1829
on December 4th   *or*   on December 4
on the 4th of December

8. All-figure dating, such as 6-8-95 or 6/8/95, is usually avoided in formal writing. For some readers, such dates are ambiguous; the examples above generally mean June 8, 1995, in the United States, but in almost all other countries mean August 6, 1995.

9. Commas are usually omitted from dates that include the month and year but not the day. The word *of* is sometimes inserted between the month and year.

in October 1997
back in January of 1981

10. References to specific centuries may be either written out or expressed in figures.

in the nineteenth century   *or*   in the 19th century
a sixteenth-century painting   *or*   a 16th-century painting

11. The name of a specific decade often takes a short form, usually with no apostrophe and uncapitalized. When the short form is part of a set phrase, it is capitalized.

a song from the sixties
>*occasionally* a song from the 'sixties *or* a song from the Sixties
tunes of the Gay Nineties

The name of a decade is often expressed in numerals, in plural form. The figure may be shortened, with an apostrophe to indicate the missing numerals; however, apostrophes enclosing the figure are generally avoided. Any sequence of such numbers is generally styled consistently.

>the 1950s and 1960s *or* the '50s and '60s
>*but not*
>the '50's and '60's
>the 1950s and '60s
>the 1950s and sixties

12. Era designations precede or follow words that specify centuries or numerals that specify years. Era designations are unspaced abbreviations, punctuated with periods. They are usually typed or keyboarded as regular capitals, and typeset in books as small capitals and in newspapers as full-size capitals. The abbreviation B.C. (before Christ) is placed after the date, while A.D. (*anno Domini*, "in the year of our Lord") is usually placed before the date but after a century designation. Any date given without an era designation or context is understood to mean A.D.

>1792–1750 B.C.
>between 600 and 400 B.C.
>from the fifth or fourth millennium to c. 250 B.C.
>between 7 B.C. and A.D. 22
>c. A.D. 100 to 300
>the second century A.D.
>the 17th century

13. Less common era designations include A.H. (*anno Hegirae*, "in the year of [Muhammad's] Hegira," or *anno Hebraico*, "in the Hebrew year"); B.C.E. (before the common era; a synonym for B.C.); C.E. (of the common era; a synonym for A.D.); and B.P. (before the present; often used by geologists and archeologists, with or without the word *year*). The abbreviation A.H. is usually placed before a specific date but after a century designation, while B.C.E., C.E., and B.P. are placed after both a date and a century.

>the tenth of Muharram, A.H. 61 (October 10, A.D. 680)
>the first century A.H.
>from the 1st century B.C.E. to the 4th century C.E.
>63 B.C.E.
>the year 200 C.E.
>5,000 years B.P.
>two million years B.P.

Degrees of Temperature and Arc

14. In technical writing, a quantity expressed in degrees is generally written as a numeral followed by the degree symbol (°). In the Kelvin scale, neither the word *degree* nor the symbol is used with the figure.

a 45° angle
6°40'10"N
32° F
0° C
Absolute zero is zero kelvins or 0 K.

15. In general writing, the quantity expressed in degrees may or may not be written out. A figure may be followed by either the degree symbol or the word *degree;* a spelled-out number is always followed by the word *degree.*

latitude 43°19"N
latitude 43 degrees N
a difference of 43 degrees latitude
The temperature has risen about thirty degrees.

Fractions and Decimal Fractions

16. In nontechnical prose, fractions standing alone are usually written out. Common fractions used as nouns are usually unhyphenated, although the hyphenated form is also common. When fractions are used as modifiers, they are hyphenated.

lost three quarters of its value   *or*   lost three-quarters of its value
had a two-thirds chance of winning

Multiword numerators and denominators are usually hyphenated, or written as figures.

one one-hundredth of an inch   *or*   1/100 of an inch

17. Mixed fractions (fractions with a whole number, such as 3½) and fractions that form part of a modifier are usually expressed in figures in running text.

waiting 2½ hours
a ⅞-mile course
2½-pound weights

Fractions that are not on the keyboard or available as special characters on a computer may be typed in full-sized digits; in mixed fractions, a space is left between the whole number and the fraction.

a 7/8-mile course
waiting 2 3/4 hours

18. Fractions used with units of measurement are usually expressed in figures, but common short words are often written out.

$\frac{1}{10}$ km	half a mile
$\frac{1}{3}$ oz.	a half-mile walk
$\frac{7}{8}$ inch	a sixteenth-inch gap

19. Decimal fractions are always set as figures. In technical writing, a zero is placed to the left of the decimal point when the fraction is less than a whole number; in general writing, the zero is usually omitted. Commas are not used in numbers following a decimal point.

> An example of a pure decimal fraction is 0.375, while 1.402 is classified as a mixed decimal fraction.
> a .22-caliber rifle
> 0.142857

20. Fractions and decimal fractions are usually not mixed in a text.

> weights of 5½ lbs., 3¼ lbs., and ½ oz.
> *or* weights of 5.5 lbs., 3.25 lbs., and .5 oz.
> *not* weights of 5.5 lbs., 3¼ lbs., and ½ oz.

Lists and Outlines

21. Both run-in and vertical lists are often numbered. In run-in numbered lists—that is, numbered lists that form part of a normal-looking sentence—each item is preceded by a number (or, less often, an italicized letter) enclosed in parentheses. The items are separated by commas if they are brief and unpunctuated; if they are complex or punctuated, they are separated by semicolons. The entire list is introduced by a colon if it is preceded by a full clause, and often when it is not.

> Among the fastest animals with measured maximum speeds are (1) the cheetah, clocked at 70 mph; (2) the pronghorn antelope, at 61 mph; (3) the lion, at 50 mph; (4) the quarter horse, at 47 mph; and (5) the elk, at 45 mph.
> The new medical dictionary has several special features: *(a)* common variant spellings; *(b)* examples of words used in context; *(c)* abbreviations, combining forms, prefixes, and suffixes; and *(d)* brand names for drugs and their generic equivalents.

22. In vertical lists, each number is followed by a period; the periods align vertically. Run-over lines usually align under the item's first word. Each item may be capitalized, especially if the items are syntactically independent of the words that introduce them.

> The English peerage consists of five ranks, listed here in descending order:
> 1. Duke (duchess)
> 2. Marquess (marchioness)
> 3. Earl (countess)
> 4. Viscount (viscountess)
> 5. Baron (baroness)

The listed items end with periods (or question marks) when they are complete sentences, and also often when they are not.

> We require answers to the following questions:
> 1. Does the club intend to engage heavy-metal bands to perform in the future?
> 2. Will any such bands be permitted to play past midnight on weekends?
> 3. Are there plans to install proper acoustic insulation?

Items that are syntactically dependent on the words that introduce them often begin with a lowercase letter and end with a comma or semicolon just as in a run-in series in an ordinary sentence.

Among the courts that are limited to special kinds of cases are
1. probate courts, for the estates of deceased persons;
2. commercial courts, for business cases;
3. juvenile courts, for cases involving children under 18; and
4. traffic courts, for minor cases involving highway and motor vehicle violations.

A vertical list may also be unnumbered, or may use bullets (•) in place of numerals, especially where the order of the items is not important.

Chief among the important advances in communication were these 19th-century inventions:
Morse's telegraph
Daguerre's camera
Bell's telephone
Edison's phonograph

This book covers in detail:
• Punctuation
• Capitalization and italicization
• Numbers
• Abbreviations
• Grammar and composition

23. Outlines standardly use Roman numerals, capitalized letters, Arabic numerals, and lowercase letters, in that order. Each numeral or letter is followed by a period, and each item is capitalized.

III. The United States from 1816 to 1850
  A. Era of mixed feelings
    1. Effects of the War of 1812
    2. National disunity
  B. The economy
    1. Transportation revolution
      a. Waterways
      b. Railroads
    2. Beginnings of industrialization
IV. The Civil War and Reconstruction, 1850–77

Money

24. A sum of money that can be expressed in one or two words is usually written out in running text, as is the unit of currency. But if several sums are mentioned in the sentence or paragraph, all are usually expressed as figures and are used with the unspaced currency symbol.

The scalpers were asking eighty dollars.
Grandfather remembered the days of the five-cent cigar.
The shoes on sale are priced at $69 and $89.
Jill wanted to sell the lemonade for 25¢, 35¢, and 45¢.

25. Monetary units of mixed dollars-and-cents amounts are expressed in figures.

$16.75
$307.02

26. Even-dollar amounts are often expressed in figures without a decimal point and zeros. But when even-dollar amounts appear near amounts that include cents, the decimal point and zeros are usually added for consistency. The dollar sign is repeated before each amount in a series or inclusive range.

> They paid $500 for the watercolor.
> The price had risen from $8.00 to $9.95.
> bids of $80, $90, and $100
> in the $80–$100 range

27. Sums of money in the millions or above rounded to no more than one decimal place are usually expressed in a combination of figures and words.

> a $10-million building program
> $4.5 billion

28. In legal documents a sum of money is usually written out fully, often capitalized, with the corresponding figures in parentheses immediately following.

> Twenty-five Thousand Dollars ($25,000)

Organizations and Governmental Entities

29. Ordinal numbers in the names of religious organizations and churches are usually written out.

> Seventh-Day Adventists
> Third Congregational Church

30. Local branches of labor unions and fraternal organizations are generally identified by a numeral, usually placed after the name.

> Motion Picture Studio Mechanics Local 476
> Loyal Order of Moose No. 220
> Local 4277 Communications Workers of America

31. In names of governmental bodies and electoral, judicial, and military units, ordinal numbers of one hundred or below are usually written out but often not.

> Second Continental Congress
> Fifth Republic
> First Congressional District
> Court of Appeals for the Third Circuit
> U.S. Eighth Army
> Twelfth Precinct   *or*   12th Precinct
> Ninety-eighth Congress   *or*   98th Congress

Percentages

32. In technical writing, and often in business and financial writing, percentages are written as a figure followed by an unspaced % symbol. In general writing, the word *percent* normally replaces the symbol, and the number may either be written out (if it does not include a decimal) or expressed as a figure.

 technical: 15%
     13.5%

 general: 15 percent
     87.2 percent
     Fifteen percent of the applicants were accepted.
     a four percent increase *or* a 4% increase

33. In a series or range, the percent sign is usually included with all numbers, even if one of the numbers is zero.

 rates of 8.3%, 8.8%, and 9.1%
 a variation of 0% to 10% *or* a 0%–10% variation

Plurals

34. The plurals of written-out numbers, including fractions, are formed by adding *-s* or *-es.*

 at sixes and sevens
 divided into eighths
 ever since the thirties
 still in her thirties

35. The plurals of figures are formed by adding *-s* or less commonly *-'s,* especially where the apostrophe can prevent a confusing typographic appearance.

 in the '80s
 since the 1980s [*or less commonly* 1980's]
 temperatures in the 80s and 90s [*or* 80's and 90's]
 the *I*'s looked like *l*'s

Ratios

36. Ratios are generally expressed in figures, usually with the word *to;* in technical writing the figures may be joined by a colon or a slash instead. Ratios expressed in words use a hyphen (or en dash) or the word *to.*

 odds of 10 to 1
 a proportion of 1 to 4
 a 3:1 ratio
 29 mi/gal
 a fifty-fifty chance
 a ratio of ten to four

Time of Day

37. In running text, the time of day is usually spelled out when expressed in even, half, or quarter hours or when it is followed by *o'clock.*

around four-thirty
arriving by ten
planned to leave at half past five
now almost a quarter to two
arrived at nine o'clock

38. Figures are generally used when specifying a precise time.

an appointment at 9:30 tomorrow morning
buses at 8:42, 9:12, and 10:03 a.m.

39. Figures are also used when the time of day is followed by *a.m.* and *p.m.* These are usually written as punctuated lowercase letters, sometimes as small capital letters. They are not used with *o'clock* or with other words that specify the time of day.

8:30 a.m.   *or*   8:30 A.M.
10:30 p.m.   *or*   10:30 P.M.
8 a.m.   *or*   8 A.M.
home by nine o'clock
9:15 in the morning
eleven in the evening

With *twelve o'clock* or 12:00, it is helpful to specify *midnight* or *noon* rather than the ambiguous *a.m.* or *p.m.*

The third shift begins at 12:00 (midnight).

40. Even-hour times are generally written with a colon and two zeros when used in a series or pairing with any times not ending in two zeros.

started at 9:15 a.m. and finished at 2:00 p.m.
worked from 8:30 to 5:00

41. The 24-hour clock system—also called *military time*—uses no punctuation and omits *o'clock, a.m., p.m.*, or any other additional indication of the time of day. The word *hours* sometimes replaces them.

from 0930 to 1100
at 1600 hours

Units of Measurement

42. In technical writing, all numbers used with units of measurement are written as numerals. In nontechnical writing, such numbers often simply follow the basic conventions explained on pages 91–92; alternatively, even in nontechnical contexts all such numbers often appear as numerals.

In the control group, only 8 of the 90 plants were affected.
picked nine quarts of berries
chugging along at 9 [*or* nine] miles an hour
a pumpkin 5 [*or* five] feet in diameter
weighing 7 pounds 9 ounces
a journey of 3 hours and 45 minutes

The singular form of units of measurement is used in a modifier before a noun, the plural form in a modifier that follows a noun.

> a 2- by 9-inch board   *or*   a two-inch by nine-inch board   *or*   a two- by nine-inch board
> measured 2 inches by 9 inches   *or*   measured two inches by nine inches
> a 6-foot 2-inch man
> is 6 feet 2 inches tall   *or*   is six feet two inches tall
> is six feet two   *or*   is 6 feet 2

43. When units of measurement are written as abbreviations or symbols, the adjacent numbers are always figures. (For abbreviations with numerals, see the section on page 90.)

> | | |
> |---|---|
> | 6 cm | 67.6 fl. oz. |
> | 1 mm | 4′ |
> | $4.25 | 98.6° |

44. When two or more quantities are expressed, as in ranges or dimensions or series, an accompanying symbol is usually repeated with each figure.

> 4″ × 6″ cards
> temperatures of 30°, 55°, 43°, and 58°
> $450–$500 suits

Other Uses

45. Figures are generally used for precise ages in newspapers and magazines, and often in books as well.

> Taking the helm is Colin Corman, 51, a risk-taking high roller.
> At 9 [*or* nine] she mastered the Mendelssohn Violin Concerto.
> the champion 3[*or* three]-year-old filly
> for anyone aged 62 and over

46. Figures are used to refer to parts of a book, such as volume, chapter, illustration, and table numbers.

> vol. 5, p. 202
> Chapter 8   *or*   Chapter Eight
> Fig. 4

47. Serial, policy, and contract numbers use figures. (For punctuation of these numbers, see paragraph 3 on page 95.)

> Serial No. 5274
> Permit No. 63709

48. Figures are used to express stock-market quotations, mathematical calculations, scores, and tabulations.

> Industrials were up 4.23.
> $3 \times 15 = 45$
> a score of 8 to 2   *or*   a score of 8–2
> the tally: 322 ayes, 80 nays

6 Mathematics and Science

Mathematics   108
Physical Sciences   119
Biology and Medicine   127
Computer Terminology   133
Signs and Symbols   134

This chapter is intended for the nonspecialist who is preparing technical matter for general-interest publications; it is not intended to be an exhaustive explanation of all aspects of mathematical, scientific, and technical style. See the Bibliography for a list of technical style manuals. For the treatment of numbers in most nonspecialist contexts, see Chapter 5, "Numbers."

Mathematics

Setting mathematical material in type can be difficult and time-consuming—and somewhat expensive, since typesetters standardly charge higher rates for setting math. The pitfalls involve issues of page layout, consistency in styling elements, and maintenance of precise accuracy with material that usually cannot be quickly verified intuitively as it is being scanned.

Authors can help maintain accuracy and avoid costly errors by adopting strictly consistent style rules for all technical matter, keyboarding all mathematical material, and careful rechecking and proofreading. The copy editor (who should preferably be a specialist) and in-house editor must ensure that it will be clear to the typesetter which math copy is to be set off (or *displayed*) and which is to be run in with other text, what style is to be used for fractions, where (and how much) space is needed around symbols and operational signs, and how equations and other math copy are to break at the ends of lines and pages. In addition, a consistent policy must be adopted for the use of symbols or abbreviations, on the one hand, and written-out forms, on the other, especially where the form may legitimately vary between the running text and the equations.

Signs and Symbols

Mathematical copy makes heavy use of specialized characters, all of which can be provided by a typesetter who specializes in mathematics. Any nonspecialist typesetter should be sent the complete manuscript before contracting to typeset the text. Commonly used mathematical symbols are found in the section beginning on page 134.

Type Styles

Italics   In mathematical copy, the single English letters that represent unknowns and variables are set in italic type, even when they are used in subscripts and superscripts. (Computer equation programs normally italicize such letters automatically.) Letters used to describe geometric figures are also italicized. The *e* for exponent is italicized (but not the fuller abbreviation "exp"), as is *d* for derivative and *f* for function. The author usually does not need to underline these letters to indicate italics; a blanket instruction to the typesetter, whether written on the first page of equations or included in the equation specs, will ensure that they are typeset properly. (For details on preparing a manuscript for the typesetter, see the section beginning on page 117.)

Roman type   Numerals are set in roman type, as are the abbreviations for units of measurement and abbreviations of two or more letters such as cos (cosine), csc (cosecant), log (logarithm), sec (secant), sin (sine), tan (tangent), tr (trace), and var (variance).

$$\tan t = -\sqrt{15}$$

$$\sin x \, (2 \cos x + 1) = 0$$

$$\log_a(x^y) = y \log_a x$$

Boldface   Boldface type is usually used for vectors and tensors and in matrix notation (though subscripts, superscripts, and signs of operation that are used with vectors are set in lightface type). Boldface type used in a keyboarded manuscript should be reinforced by a wavy underline on the printout. For a fuller discussion of vectors and tensors, see pages 116–117.

Capitals and small capitals   Headings for definitions, theorems, lemmas, and similar statements are usually set in caps and small caps. (The text following such headings is italicized.)

> THEOREM 7.   *Let f(x, y) be of class C^3 on . . .*
> DEFINITION.   *If D is an elementary region in the plane, . . .*

Headings for proofs, examples, demonstrations, and similar statements are also set in caps and small caps. (The text following these headings is set in roman type.)

> PROOF.   Using the existence of . . .
> EXAMPLE 4.   Let *R* be the rectangle . . .

Generating Equations on the Computer

Math and science equations can be created in standard word-processing programs. Such programs (which can be mastered quickly) provide virtually all the symbols and formats normally used even in advanced mathematics. Such standard formatting as italic type for letter symbols and spacing around operational signs is automatically applied as the equation is entered. Authors who do a lot of technical writing usually use extended versions of such programs, with advanced formatting features.

Before receiving a disk with computer-generated equations, the editor may want to discuss with the author the form or program in which the math copy will be submitted, so as to insure that it will make a proper interface with the typesetter's system. (Most typesetting systems use software such as TeX or La-TeX, which generate math and science symbols in response to coded text.) However, computer-generated math copy will often not be readable by a type-setting system. In addition, using a computer for mathematical copy is considerably slower than writing equations by hand. For these reasons, the editor may not object if the author prefers to handwrite all equations. However, it is imperative that handwritten equations be extremely clear, and general instructions or specs to the typesetter must specify such variables as spacing, italics, and alignment, which will usually be clearer in computer-generated copy.

Structure of Equations

Displaying an equation Equations can be either displayed (set on their own lines with extra space above and below them) or placed within the text line. Most publications prefer the displayed form, especially if the equation is too large to fit the regular depth of a line and extra line spacing must be added above and below. A displayed equation is either centered horizontally or indented a fixed amount from the left margin.

Breaking an equation Long equations should be set in displayed form to avoid an awkward break at the end of a line of text. Some complicated equations have to be broken even in the displayed form. If such an equation runs over, the break should occur just before an operational sign such as + or − or, preferably, =. The second line can be (1) set flush right if the right-aligned runover will be long enough to overlap the first line by an inch or so, (2) indented from the right margin if an equation number is used (see page 112), or (3) lined up on the operational signs, as in the example below. The last alternative is preferred for equations that run more than two lines.

$$\begin{aligned}
\rho_3 &= \sqrt{(ad + bc)^2 + (ac - bd)^2} \\
&= \sqrt{a^2d^2 + 2abcd + b^2c^2 + a^2c^2 - 2abcd + b^2d^2} \\
&= \sqrt{a^2d^2 + b^2c^2 + a^2c^2 + b^2d^2} \\
&= \sqrt{a^2(c^2 + d^2) + b^2(c^2 + d^2)} \\
&= \sqrt{(a^2 + b^2)(c^2 + d^2)} = \sqrt{a^2 + b^2} \cdot \sqrt{c^2 + d^2}
\end{aligned}$$

An element (such as ρ_3 in the example above) that is shared by several parts of an equation, or by a series of equations, is usually not repeated.

In contrast to displayed equations, equations run in with the text are broken *after* an operational sign.

If there are no operational signs or signs of relationship ($>$, $\neq$, etc.) within a formula, it should not be divided at all. Units of aggregation within parentheses, brackets, or braces should not be split at the end of a line, nor should fractions or radical expressions.

Punctuation Equations are basically sentences, in which the sign of relationship represents the verb of the sentence. An equation may be used as a clause within another sentence.

If $2ab = xy$, then $xy = 3cd$; therefore $2ab = 3cd$.

The text that precedes a displayed equation is punctuated as required by its own grammatical construction.

The resulting quadratic equation is thus

$$x^2 - 3x - \frac{5}{2} = 0$$

or, after multiplying both sides by 2,

$$2x^2 - 6x - 5 = 0$$

Within the text line, equations at the end of a sentence are followed by a period. After a displayed equation, punctuation is optional. Punctuation can clarify the progression of a displayed equation and indicate the end of a sentence.

$$x(x - 1) = 0,$$
$$x^2 - x = 0,$$
$$x^2 = x,$$
$$x = 1.$$

Though such punctuation is optional, the use or omission of punctuation should be consistent throughout a publication.

Two equations may be displayed on the same line. They are usually separated by a two-em space without punctuation, but sometimes a comma is added between them.

$$PF = a - f \qquad PF' = a + f$$
$$a + 0 = a, \qquad a \cdot 1 = a$$

A two-em space is used on both sides of the words *and* and *or* when they separate two equations on a line. Explanatory words and limiting terms that are used with equations are set off with a space of one or two ems.

$$(a + b) + c = a + (b + c) \qquad \text{and} \qquad ab = ba$$
$$A = (R^2 - r^2) \quad \text{(for } R\text{)}$$

A sign or symbol used as an appositive directly following a descriptive term is not set off by punctuation unless it is necessary to avoid ambiguity.

Two sets A and B are said to be equivalent if there is a one-to-one correspondence between them.

The symbol $\sqrt[n]{\ }$ is called the nth radical.

Words used to link lines of displayed equations are usually set in roman type, flush left on the line above the equation they introduce. A series of linked equations is either centered or aligned according to a sign such as =.

Thus we have the equation
$$3r^2 \cos^2 \theta + 2r^2 \sin^2 \theta = 6$$
or
$$r^2 \cos^2 \theta + 2r^2(\cos^2 \theta + \sin^2 \theta) = 6.$$
Therefore
$$r^2 \cos^2 \theta + 2r^2 = 6$$
or
$$r^2 (\cos^2 \theta + 2) = 6.$$

Thus we have the equation

$$3r^2 \cos^2 \theta + 2r^2 \sin^2 \theta = 6$$

or

$$r^2 \cos^2 \theta + 2r^2(\cos^2 \theta + \sin^2 \theta) = 6.$$

Therefore

$$r^2 \cos^2 \theta + 2r^2 = 6$$

or

$$r^2 (\cos^2 \theta + 2) = 6.$$

Spacing Spaces are inserted into equations in order to clarify the parts. A word space is usually left before and after operational signs and signs of relationship. (However, when a plus or minus sign is used with a number to denote a positive or negative quantity—for example, $+3$ or -5—it is closed up.) A space also follows a comma used to separate mathematical coordinates, and thin spaces are inserted around abbreviations for trigonometric functions such as *sin*. (In computer-generated equations, spacing is inserted automatically.)

Numbering of Equations

Many mathematical publications assign numbers to displayed equations as a handy means of cross-referencing. Double numeration, with the chapter number as the first digit and the equation number as the second, separated by a period, is common. In each chapter the equations begin with number 1. The entire number is enclosed in parentheses and set flush right opposite the displayed equation, which should not extend to within an em space of it. References to these numbers in the text are also enclosed in parentheses.

If both sides are squared, then

$$2x + 5 = x^2 - 10x + 25 \qquad (6.2)$$

The solution given by equation (6.2) is . . .

Short publications such as journal articles may assign single numbers to displayed equations.

We are left with

$$a_1 b_2 - a_2 b_1 = 0 \qquad (17)$$

Sequential numbering is used only with displayed equations, not with equations that appear in the running text. When there are only a few displayed equations, they may not be numbered at all.

When an equation takes up several lines, or when a single number refers to a series of equations displayed together, the number is either centered vertically or set on the last line of the display.

$$\begin{aligned} a_1 x + b_1 y + c_1 z &= d_1 \\ a_2 x + b_2 y + c_2 &= d_2 \\ a_3 x + b_3 y + c_3 z &= d_3 \end{aligned} \qquad (3.2)$$

$$\begin{aligned} (3 - 5j)(4 + 2j) &= 12 - 20j + 6j - 10j^2 \\ &= 12 + 10 - 20j + 6j = 22 - 14j \end{aligned} \qquad (5.7)$$

Subscripts and Superscripts

Single-letter abbreviations used as subscripts and superscripts are set italic. Longer abbreviations, whole words, and numbers used as subscripts or superscripts are set roman.

$$C_v \qquad \Phi_m \qquad A_{ij} \qquad k_{max} \qquad x^3 \qquad P_0 P_2$$

(Note that the 0 in $P_0 P_2$ above is a subscript zero; the letter O would be italicized.)

Complex symbols may have both subscripts and superscripts. These combinations are usually aligned vertically.

$$S_{p-1}^v \qquad \phi_m^k$$

The alternative is to stagger the subscripts and superscripts, with the subscript set before the superscript.

$$H_k^{\ 2} \qquad P_n^{\ m}$$

However, if the superscript symbol is an asterisk or a prime, or if it consists of three or more characters, then the superscript must be placed directly above the subscript.

$$K_p^* \qquad R_n' \qquad R_b^{2n-1}$$

Alignment of subscript and superscript is preferable even when one of them is complex. If both the staggered and aligned formats will be difficult to set, a helpful alternative is to insert parentheses and set the expression in the following manner:

$$(J_{sx+n})^2$$

An expression containing a complicated exponent can often be simplified by converting to an "in-line" form (see "Fractions" on page 114). If the base of the exponent is the number $e = 2.71828183$, the symbol e can be replaced by "exp" followed by the exponent written in parentheses. For any other base than e, a variable can be substituted for the exponent and evaluated later in the line.

e^{4x^2+5}	*becomes*	$\exp(4x^2 + 5)$
$(ky)^{4x^2+5}$	*becomes*	$(ky)^z$ *where* $z = 4x^2 + 5$
$(x + y)^{\frac{a+b}{c+d}}$	*becomes*	$(x + y)^z$ *where* $z = (a + b)/(c + d)$

Signs of Aggregation (Fences)

Parentheses, brackets, and braces (commonly called *fences*) are used in most kinds of mathematical copy to indicate units contained within larger units. The traditional order, beginning with the innermost element, is parentheses within brackets within braces. If more than three aggregations are required, the fences are repeated in larger type.

$$\{[(\{[(\qquad)]\})]\}$$

These symbols should be large enough to enclose the elements they contain.

$$\iint_A \left[\left(\frac{\partial w}{\partial x} \right)^2 + \left(\frac{\partial w}{\partial y} \right)^2 \right] \mathrm{dxdy}$$

Units of aggregation within fences should not be split at the end of a line.

Fractions

Writers should be familiar with the different ways to express fractions and the circumstances in which each is used. Short, uncomplicated fractions can be set within a line of running text by converting them from the standard *built-up* or *vertical* form to the "in-line" form, with both the numerator and denominator aligned on the baseline and separated by a slash /, which mathematicians often call a *solidus*. Fractions in in-line form require no added line spacing above or below.

$$\frac{\sin x}{\cos x} \qquad becomes \qquad \sin x / \cos x$$

When a built-up fraction containing an operational sign is converted to the in-line form, parentheses are usually added to indicate that the symbols are to be considered as a unit.

$$\frac{ad + bc}{bd} \qquad becomes \qquad (ad + bc)/bd$$

$$5 - \frac{x + 4}{y} + 18 \qquad becomes \qquad 5 - (x+4)/y + 18$$

$$or \qquad 5 - [(x + 4)/y] + 18$$

If a built-up fraction is followed by a number or by a letter symbol, fences must be inserted before the fraction can be expressed in in-line form. However, fences are not needed when the built-up fraction is preceded by a number or letter symbol.

$$\frac{a}{b} x \qquad becomes \qquad (a/b)x$$

$$x \frac{a}{b} \qquad becomes \qquad xa/b$$

The slash or solidus can also make fractions used as subscripts and superscripts more compact and easier to set.

$$(p + p')^{\frac{x+y}{z}} \qquad becomes \qquad (p + p')^{(x+y)/z}$$

A typesetter will usually automatically convert simple in-line fractions to the style known as *case, split,* or *piece fractions,* in which the numbers and symbols are set smaller and the numerator is raised above the baseline. This instruction should also be detailed in the type specs sent to the typesetter.

Thus, the quotient is $^{16}/_{81}$ $\left[or \; \frac{16}{81} \right]$.

Radicals Fractions that include a radical sign can be converted to in-line form by substituting a partial radical sign without the overbar or by using a superscript fraction. This is useful in running text, when the overbar could interfere with the line above. Even in displayed form, where the full radical sign can be set without affecting the line above, the simplified form is sometimes preferred.

$$\sqrt{x + y} \quad \textit{becomes} \quad \sqrt{(x + y)} \quad \textit{or} \quad (x + y)^{1/2}$$

$$\frac{1}{\sqrt{ab}} \quad \textit{becomes} \quad 1/\sqrt{(ab)} \quad \textit{or} \quad (ab)^{-1/2}$$

Expressions of Multiplication

Multiplication can be indicated by the multiplication or times sign $\times$, by a centered dot, by fences such as parentheses, or by the simple juxtaposition of characters.

$$14 \times 7$$
$$a \cdot b = c$$
$$4(8) \quad \textit{or} \quad (4)(8) \quad \textit{but not} \quad (4)8$$
$$3xy$$

When one of the multipliers is an expression denoting a power of ten, the multiplication sign is conventionally used.

$$0.595 \times 10^{-2}$$
$$365 \times 3600 = 1.314 \times 10^{6}$$

Factorials, on the other hand, are conventionally multiplied with centered dots.

$$n! \cdot m! \geqq (n)(m!)$$

Ellipsis Points

Material omitted from a mathematical expression is indicated by three spaced ellipsis points. Any commas or operational signs used in an elision within a mathematical expression are placed after each mathematical term as well as after the ellipsis when it is followed by a final term.

$$a_1, a_2, \ldots, a_x$$
$$a_1 + a_2 + \cdots + a_x$$

These ellipsis points are often raised above the baseline, as in the last example above. However, raising the ellipsis points is done purely for appearance' sake, and the points may be set on the baseline in any context. In running text, they *must* be set on the baseline.

Integral, Summation, and Product Signs

The integral, summation, and product signs ($\int$, Σ, Π, respectively) are usually set in larger type than the surrounding equation. The indices to an integral symbol appear to its right. Indices of summation and product limits are normally set above and below the symbols; however, in running text they may be set to the right as superscripts and subscripts to avoid the need for extra line spacing.

$$\int_a^b f(x)\, dx = F(b) - F(a)$$

$$s = \sum_{v=1}^{\infty} u_v$$

$$\sin\pi x = \pi x \prod_{k=1}^{\infty} [1 - (x^2/k^2)]$$

Thus we have $s = \sum_{v=1}^{x} u_v$

Thus we have $\sin\pi x = \pi x \prod_{k=1}^{x} [1 - (x^2/k^2)]$

Arrays

When mathematical elements are arranged in horizontal rows and vertical columns, the arrangement is called an *array*. There are two types of arrays: *determinants* and *matrices*. Determinants are set off by vertical lines, while matrices are enclosed within brackets or parentheses.

In both types of array, the mathematical elements are aligned vertically in each column.

$$\begin{vmatrix} x & y & 1 \\ x_1 & y_1 & 1 \\ x_2 & y_2 & 1 \end{vmatrix} = 0 \qquad A = \begin{bmatrix} 1 & 0 & 1 & 0 \\ 1 & 1 & 1 & 1 \\ 2 & 1 & 0 & 1 \\ 1 & 1 & 0 & 2 \end{bmatrix} \qquad \begin{pmatrix} 1 & -2 & 2 & 4 \\ 2 & 5 & -1 & 1 \\ 3 & 6 & -2 & 2 \\ 4 & 2 & 5 & 3 \\ -1 & 3 & 2 & 5 \end{pmatrix}$$

The omission of a column is usually indicated by three horizontal dots in each row. The omission of a row is usually indicated by a series of three vertical dots.

$$A = \begin{bmatrix} a_{11} & a_{12} & \cdots & a_{1n} \\ a_{21} & a_{22} & \cdots & a_{2n} \\ \vdots & \vdots & & \vdots \\ a_{n1} & a_{n2} & \cdots & a_{nn} \end{bmatrix}$$

Arrays are normally set in displayed form, although a one-column matrix can be set in running text preceded by the abbreviation "col.," as shown below.

$$\begin{bmatrix} a \\ b \\ c \end{bmatrix} \quad becomes \quad \text{col. } (a, b, c)$$

Since arrays commonly require several lines, they may pose a problem if they run over a page break. A large array can be set and numbered as a figure, referred to in the text by its figure number, and moved freely by the typesetter.

Vectors and Tensors

A vector is a quantity that has magnitude and direction. It is usually indicated by boldface type, and sometimes by bold italics. Vectors may also be shown by an arrow written above the lightface italic expression, but the more commonly used boldface form is easier to typeset.

$$\mathbf{v} + \mathbf{w} \qquad or \qquad \boldsymbol{v} + \boldsymbol{w} \qquad or \qquad \vec{v} + \vec{w}$$

Subscripts, superscripts, signs of operation, and other components of vectors are set in lightface type.

$$\mathbf{r}_1 - \mathbf{r}_2 = P_2 P_1$$

$$\mathbf{c} = -\frac{\mathbf{i}}{\sqrt{2}} + \frac{\mathbf{k}}{\sqrt{2}}$$

A tensor is a generalized vector with more than three components. It is often indicated by a sans-serif italic typeface to distinguish it from a vector. When vectors are set in boldface roman, bold italics may be used for tensors.

$$r + F\, dV = 0 \qquad or \qquad \mathbf{r} + \boldsymbol{F}\, d\mathbf{V} = 0$$

Greek Letters

Greek letters are frequently used in mathematical copy. When handwriting a letter, the author should write out its name in the margin at its first use to ensure that the typesetter interprets the symbol correctly. The names and forms of the letters of the Greek alphabet are listed in Table 6.1.

Table 6.I   Greek Alphabet

Name	*Capital*	*Lowercase*	*Name*	*Capital*	*Lowercase*
alpha	A	α	nu	N	ν
beta	B	β	xi	Ξ	ξ
gamma	Γ	γ	omicron	O	o
delta	Δ	δ	pi	Π	π
epsilon	E	ε	rho	P	ρ
zeta	Z	ζ	sigma	Σ	σ *or* ς
eta	H	η	tau	T	τ
theta	Θ	θ	upsilon	Y	υ
iota	I	ι	phi	Φ	φ
kappa	K	κ	chi	X	χ
lambda	Λ	λ	psi	Ψ	ψ
mu	M	μ	omega	Ω	ω

Typemarking Mathematical Copy

After the author has submitted the manuscript, the editor reviews the copy carefully and marks it as needed for the typesetter. (For general copyediting and proofreading guidelines, see Chapter 12.)

The typesetter chosen to set a math or science text will almost always be experienced in setting such copy. In addition, copy for math and science equations is generally prepared with one of the specific software programs that can produce all the standard signs and symbols in the appropriate italic, roman, and bold type styles. Therefore, only a minimum amount of markup is normally needed before sending the manuscript to the typesetter.

The copy editor still must scan all equations and formulas and mark any symbols or specialized characters that might be confusing. Since letters in equations are standardly italicized, only letters that should not be italicized should be marked. Parentheses in math copy should also be marked, matching the style of the surrounding text rather than the elements within the parentheses. The design specifications should include a general equation spec such as the one below. (For details on writing type specs, see the section beginning on page 343.)

Equation Specifications
9/10 Times Roman, except as marked for special symbols; set single letters in italic, including superscripts and subscripts; set abbreviations and underlined single letters in roman; follow copy for boldface and other variations. Set in-line fractions in case form; use built-up fractions in displayed eqn. or follow copy. Insert thin space before and after signs of operation and relationship. Indent 1st symbol or word 36 pts. from flush left. Break eqn. only before operational signs; align runover lines on signs or indent 48 pts. from fl. left. Set eqn. nos. in parens fl. right. Allow 2-em space either side of words such as *and* or *or*. Allow 18 pts. b/b from normal text above and 24 pts. to normal text below. Follow separate list of special symbols.

Inverted carets need not be drawn below all superscripts, nor carets over all subscripts, if the copy is clear. However, the author should always insert carets in handwritten or typed copy that is unclear or with any multiple subscript or superscript, as in the following examples.

Subscript carrying a superscript: R_{x^y}

Subscript carrying a subscript: R_{y_w}

Superscript carrying a subscript: R^{v_w}

Superscript carrying a superscript: R^{x^y}

With the author's permission, vectors should be marked for setting in boldface type and any arrow drawn over a vector should be deleted. Centered dots and multiplication signs between two vectors, as well as special brackets or parentheses around vectors, should also be marked for boldface.

Math copy that falls in the running text should normally be small enough to fit the type line. Equations or formulas that contain fractions will be set according to the conventions described earlier in this chapter (see the section beginning on page 114). If an author has typed an equation in the running text that should instead be displayed, the editor simply inserts line-break symbols on both sides of the equation (and may also have to delete a period or otherwise revise the punctuation). To move a displayed equation to the running text, the editor merely draws run-in connecting lines.

Reference notes to math copy generally use the system of asterisks and daggers described on page 211, because superscript numbers could easily be mistaken for mathematical symbols. Wherever possible, footnote reference symbols should be placed next to words instead of numerals or other symbols to prevent misinterpretation; this may require that the expressions be rewritten.

Typeset multiplication signs are different from the letter *x*. Where the letter *x* has been used to indicate multiplication, the copy editor crosses over it, making it larger. For reinforcement, the term "multi" or "times" can be circled in the margin, but usually only at the first appearance of the multiplication sign on each page.

Finally, the copy should be searched for other instances where symbols could be misinterpreted. In equations, for example, the letter *l* is distinguished from the numeral 1 by being italicized; but this may not always be clear. Likewise, there are cases where the capital letter *O* might be mistaken for a zero. In these and similar cases, a circled note of clarification ("ell," "one," "oh," "zero") may prevent a typesetting error.

Physical Sciences

Many of the conventions established for writing mathematical notations apply also to the physical sciences; conventions unique to the physical sciences are discussed in this section. For details on capitalizing scientific terms, see the section beginning on page 50. Commonly used scientific signs and symbols are listed in the section beginning on page 134.

International System of Units (SI)

The system of measurement in general worldwide scientific use is the International System of Units, abbreviated SI (for *Système International d'Unités*), which derives from the metric system of physical units. There are seven base units in the system, plus two supplementary units.

Quantity	*Unit*
length	meter (m)
mass	kilogram (kg)
time	second (s)
electric current	ampere (A)
thermodynamic temperature	kelvin (K)
amount of substance	mole (mol)
luminous intensity	candela (cd)
plane angle	radian (rad)
solid angle	steradian (sr)

In addition to the SI base units, the following non-SI units of measurement are frequently found in scientific writing: minute (min), day (d), hour (h), liter (l or L), and degrees Celsius (°C).

Note that, although all the SI units are lowercased, two of their abbreviations are written as capital letters (since these two units are derived from proper names). The abbreviations are set in roman type, without periods.

Derived units Other units of measurement are derived from these base units by combination or by the addition of a prefix that denotes multiple powers of ten (see Table 6.2). Prefix and base unit are closed up without a hyphen, whether written in full or abbreviated. The unpunctuated abbreviation represents both singular and plural forms. (Note that while the kilogram is the base unit of mass, prefixes are added to the term *gram*.)

m/s	meter(s) per second	km	kilometer(s)
cg	centigram(s)	dl	deciliter(s)
ps	picosecond(s)	mA	milliampere(s)

When an abbreviation is preceded by a number, a space separates the two elements.

43 km/h   2 K   18 cm

Table 6.2   Prefixes Used with SI Units

Factor	Prefix	Symbol	Factor	Prefix	Symbol
10^{24}	yotta	Y	10^{-1}	deci	d
10^{21}	zetta	Z	10^{-2}	centi	c
10^{18}	exa	E	10^{-3}	milli	m
10^{15}	peta	P	10^{-6}	micro	μ
10^{12}	tera	T	10^{-9}	nano	n
10^{9}	giga	G	10^{-12}	pico	p
10^{6}	mega	M	10^{-15}	femto	f
10^{3}	kilo	k	10^{-18}	atto	a
10^{2}	hecto	h	10^{-21}	zepto	z
10	deka	da	10^{-24}	yocto	y

In the International System, only numbers between 0.1 and 1,000 are used with SI units. Larger and smaller quantities are expressed by choosing a different unit of measurement.

11,200 meters   *becomes*   11.2 kilometers (km)
0.005 grams   *becomes*   5 milligrams (mg)

Other SI-derived units include those that are powers of base units and those with separate names, some of which are shown in Table 6.3.

Table 6.3   SI-Derived Units

Quantity	Unit	Symbol
area	square meter	m^2
volume	cubic meter	m^3
acceleration	meter per second squared	m/s^2
density	kilogram per cubic meter	kg/m^3
absorbed dose of ionizing radiation	gray	Gy
activity (of radionuclides)	becquerel	Bq
capacitance	farad	F
effective dose of ionizing radiation	sievert	Sv
energy	joule	J
force	newton	N
frequency	hertz	Hz
power	watt	W
pressure	pascal	Pa
quantity of electricity	coulomb	C

By the use of SI and other special units of measurement, lengthy numbers can be avoided in scientific writing. When it is necessary to write lengthy numbers, they are punctuated by either thin spaces or by commas. (In publications that are intended for a general audience, commas are more likely to be used.) Digits on both sides of a decimal are thus separated, counting from the decimal points.

> 23 400 055   15 076.129 300 77

Numbers with only four digits on either side of a decimal point are usually written without a thin space or a comma.

> 4100
> 235.0614

Some writers follow the European convention of using a decimal comma instead of a decimal point, although this is only appropriate in international journals.

> *American and British standard:*   15 976.129
> *European convention:*   15 976,129

Astronomy

Astronomers use the equatorial system as a way to define the position of a celestial object. In this system the equatorial coordinates *right ascension,* abbreviated RA or α (alpha), and *declination,* abbreviated δ (delta), are analogous to terrestrial longitude and latitude. Right ascension is usually expressed in units of time rather than in degrees of arc, so measurements are given in hours, minutes, and seconds. In general usage, a less precise description is acceptable.

> $14^h6^m7^s$ *or in general usage*   14 h 6 min

Declination is given in degrees, minutes, and seconds of arc. Declination is marked positive (+) north of the celestial equator and negative (−) south of it. A declination number that lacks a positive or negative sign is considered positive.

> 49°8′11″   −87°41′08″

For the capitalization of planets, stars, and other celestial objects, see paragraph 60 on page 51.

Chemistry and Physics

Signs and symbols commonly used in chemistry and physics are listed in the section beginning on page 137. A list of technical manuals that will help with styling problems not covered in this chapter may be found in the Bibliography.

Names of elements, compounds, and particles   The names of chemical elements and compounds are usually written out. Two-word compounds are unhyphenated, even when used as modifiers.

> glyceraldehyde   amino acid sequence
> hydrogen chloride   carbon monoxide poisoning
> sodium sulfate

Chemical symbols are one-, two-, or three-letter abbreviations for the names of the chemical elements. The letters are set in roman type without periods, and the first letter is capitalized. The names of the chemical elements with their symbols are listed in Table 6.4.

Table 6.4   Chemical Elements and Their Symbols

Element	Symbol	Element	Symbol	Element	Symbol
actinium	Ac	hassium	Hs	radium	Ra
aluminum	Al	helium	He	radon	Rn
americium	Am	holmium	Ho	rhenium	Re
antimony	Sb	hydrogen	H	rhodium	Rh
argon	Ar	indium	In	rubidium	Rb
arsenic	As	iodine	I	ruthenium	Ru
astatine	At	iridium	Ir	rutherfordium	Rf
barium	Ba	iron	Fe	samarium	Sm
berkelium	Bk	krypton	Kr	scandium	Sc
beryllium	Be	lanthanum	La	seaborgium	Sg
bismuth	Bi	lawrencium	Lr	selenium	Se
bohrium	Bh	lead	Pb	silicon	Si
boron	B	lithium	Li	silver	Ag
bromine	Br	lutetium	Lu	sodium	Na
cadmium	Cd	magnesium	Mg	strontium	Sr
calcium	Ca	manganese	Mn	sulfur	S
californium	Cf	meitnerium	Mt	tantalum	Ta
carbon	C	mendelevium	Md	technetium	Tc
cerium	Ce	mercury	Hg	tellurium	Te
cesium	Cs	molybdenum	Mo	terbium	Tb
chlorine	Cl	neodymium	Nd	thallium	Tl
chromium	Cr	neon	Ne	thorium	Th
cobalt	Co	neptunium	Np	thulium	Tm
copper	Cu	nickel	Ni	tin	Sn
curium	Cm	niobium	Nb	titanium	Ti
dubnium	Db	nitrogen	N	tungsten	W
dysprosium	Dy	nobelium	No	ununbium	Uub
einsteinium	Es	osmium	Os	ununnilium	Uun
erbium	Er	oxygen	O	unununium	Uuu
europium	Eu	palladium	Pd	uranium	U
fermium	Fm	phosphorus	P	vanadium	V
fluorine	F	platinum	Pt	xenon	Xe
francium	Fr	plutonium	Pu	ytterbium	Yb
gadolinium	Gd	polonium	Po	yttrium	Y
gallium	Ga	potassium	K	zinc	Zn
germanium	Ge	praseodymium	Pr	zirconium	Zr
gold	Au	promethium	Pm		
hafnium	Hf	protactinium	Pa		

Names of subatomic particles and quanta may be written out, or their symbols may be used instead. The symbols are set either roman or italic. The names of subatomic particles and quanta with their symbols are shown in Table 6.5.

Table 6.5 Subatomic Particles and Quanta and Their Symbols

Particle or Quantum	Symbol	Particle or Quantum	Symbol
alpha particle	α	nucleon	N
beta particle	β	omega particle	Ω
deuteron	d	photon	γ
electron	e	pion	π
kaon	κ	proton	p
lambda particle	Λ	sigma particle	Σ
muon	μ	triton	t
neutrino	ν	xi particle	Ξ
neutron	n		

Symbols for chemical elements and subatomic particles have limited use in running text. Even in technical writing, they tend to be used only if the full name of the element, compound, or particle has been written out at the first appearance of the symbol.

Subscripts and superscripts Four numerical indices are used with chemical symbols. The *mass number* is given as a superscript to the left of the symbol, the *ionic charge* as a superscript to the right. The *atomic number* is given as a subscript on the left, the *number of atoms* of an element in a molecule as a subscript on the right. Superscripts and subscripts are usually aligned vertically; indices of two or more digits set on the left align from their rightmost digits. Indices set on the right are sometimes aligned, but usually the subscript is set before the superscript. (For details on use with math equations, see the section on page 113.)

$$Fe^{3+} \qquad {}^{63}_{29}Cu \qquad {}^{1}_{1}H \qquad {}^{228}_{90}Th \qquad S_2O_3{}^{2-}$$

The mass number is sometimes placed as a superscript to the right of a chemical symbol instead of to the left, especially in nontechnical writing. The left position, however, should be used in equations. Thus, in nontechnical writing C^{14} is often found, whereas in equations ^{14}C is the common form.

In running text, an isotope is specified in full. The name of the element, often written out but also frequently abbreviated, is followed by a space or a hyphen and the mass number.

carbon 14   *or*   carbon-14   uranium-235
C-14   *or*   C 14   U-235

The ionic charge, given as a superscript to the right of the chemical symbol, may be either positive (+) or negative (−). A number may precede the charge sign, but the charge sign is never followed by a number.

CN^-

Na^+

S^{2-} ions
Sn^{2+} ions

$CO_3{}^{2-}$ *but not* $CO_3{}^{-2}$
O^{2-} *but not* O^{-2}

In running text, however, the charge sign precedes the number on the line when it is not attached to the chemical symbol.

a -3 charge

Spacing When two or more element symbols are combined to represent a chemical compound, no space appears between the symbols or any subscripts, superscripts, brackets, or parentheses within the compound.

$[Co(NH_3)_6]Cl_3$ $C_3H_8O_4NaN$

$Pt(NH_3)_2Cl_2$ Na_2SiO_3

A number that precedes the compound is usually closed up also, but in some publications a thin space is inserted between the number and the compound symbol, especially if needed for clarity (for example, to keep the symbol for oxygen from being mistaken for a zero).

$2KCl$ *or* $2\ KCl$

$6H_2O$ *or* $6\ H_2O$

$25\ O_2(g)$

In chemical expressions each discrete unit is set off by a space. This space may be as large as a word space, but many publications set smaller spaces. A thin space or larger is also used on both sides of connecting signs such as $+$, $-$, $=$, $\rightarrow$, and $\leftrightharpoons$.

$2C_8H_{18}(l) + 25\ O_2(g) \rightarrow 16CO_2(g) + 18H_2O(l)$

$Mg_3N_2 + 6H_2O \rightarrow 3Mg(OH)_2 + 2NH_3$

$Cu(NH_3)_4^{2+} \leftrightharpoons Cu^{2+} + 4NH_3$

Marks of punctuation and relationship A period is placed at the end of a sentence that ends with a chemical expression; commas and semicolons are also used following chemical expressions if appropriate to the grammatical construction of the sentence. When such expressions are not part of a sentence, they are unpunctuated.

The arrow $\rightarrow$ signifies "reaction" or "yields." Two opposing arrows, each single- or double-barbed ($\rightleftharpoons$ or $\rightleftarrows$), indicate a reversible, equilibrium reaction. An arrow with two heads ($\leftrightarrow$) indicates resonance between two equivalent structures. Spaces are used around all of these arrows. The arrow $\downarrow$ signifying a precipitate and the arrow $\uparrow$ signifying evolution of a gas are preceded by a thin space.

$2\ AgNO_3 + CaCl_2 \rightarrow Ca(NO_3)_2 + 2\ AgCl \downarrow$

$Hemoglobin + O_2 \rightleftharpoons Oxyhemoglobin + H_2O$

A description of the reaction conditions, such as the symbol Δ signifying heat, the chemical symbol for a catalyst, or other description of the reaction, may be set close to the "reaction" arrow. Small type is used for such descriptions.

$$2KClO_3 \xrightarrow{\Delta} 2KCl + 3O_2$$

$$C_6H_6 + Br_2 \underset{50^\circ}{\overset{Fe}{\rightleftharpoons}} C_6H_5Br + HBr$$

$$CH_3CH_2CH_2Cl + 2\ NH_3 \xrightarrow{\text{sealed tube}} CH_3CH_2CH_2NH_2 + NH_4^+Cl^-$$

$$B + H^+ \underset{}{\overset{\text{fast}}{\rightleftharpoons}} BH^+$$

Parentheses The abbreviations used in thermochemistry for phase states (such as *aq* aqueous, *g* gas, *l* liquid, and *s* solid) are enclosed in parentheses and set next to the formula that they follow, without an intervening space. These abbreviations may be consistently roman or italic.

$$BaO_2(s) \rightarrow BaO(s) + \tfrac{1}{2}O_2(g)$$
$$Na(s) < NaCl(s) < Br_2(l) < Br_2(g) < N_2O_4(g)$$

The oxidation number of an element is shown by Roman numerals enclosed in parentheses (the Arabic zero is used for zero), with no space between the element's name or symbol and the opening parenthesis.

> Fe(III)
> iron(III) perchlorate
> tin(IV) chloride

Brackets Brackets are used to designate units of chemical concentration.

$$K_a = \frac{[H_3O^+][CH_3CO_2^-]}{[CH_3CO_2H]}$$

Brackets may also be used to enclose a formula that has an indication of its valence.

> $[M(CN)_4]^{2-}$

Hyphen A hyphen separates prefixes composed of single letters, numerals, or letter-numeral combinations from the rest of a chemical term. In addition, the following italicized prefixes are followed by a hyphen: *cis, trans, para* (or *p*), *meta* (or *m*), *ortho* (or *o*), *tert* (or *t*), *sec* (or *s*), *e* (for electron), *n* (for neutron), and *p* (for proton).

> *z*-butene
> 4*H*-quinoziline
> α-particles   *but*   alpha particles
> β-emitters   *but*   beta emitters
> *cis*-oleic acid

Prefixes normally written lowercase are not capitalized when the attached chemical term begins a sentence or is part of a title.

> *z*-Butene is . . .   *cis*-Oleic Acid

The hyphen is also used to separate units of certain complex terms.

α-amino-β-(*p*-hydroxyphenyl)propionic acid
2-methyl-3-ethylpentane

The hyphen separates locants, which denote the position of an atom or group within a molecule. Locants precede the term they refer to, and they are separated from one another by unspaced commas.

dicyclohexano-18-crown-6
4-pentyn-1-ol
6*H*-1,2,5-thiadiazine

In amino acid sequences, hyphens are used to separate the abbreviations.

Ala-Lys-Pro-Thr-Tyr-Phe-Gly-Arg-Glu-Gly

Segments of amino acid sequences are written with a hyphen at each end of the sequence to indicate that parts are missing.

-Ser-Leu-Tyr-Glu-
|
NH_2

Centered dot A centered dot set close to the symbol that it follows indicates an unshared electron in the formula of a free radical.

$Cl_2 \xrightarrow{\text{UV photon}} 2 \; Cl\cdot$
$CH_3\cdot + HCl$
$CH_3\cdot + Cl\cdot$

The centered dot that is used to show a loosely joined part (such as water of hydration) of a compound is usually set closed up; alternatively, a thin space may be inserted on either side. The dot may be set light or boldface.

$BaCl_2\cdot 2H_2O(s) \rightarrow BaCl_2(s) + 2H_2O(g)$

Asterisk The asterisk may be used as a superscript after the lowercase Greek letters sigma (σ) or pi (π) to indicate high-energy antibonding orbitals, as opposed to lower-energy bonding orbitals, which do not use the asterisk.

σ*1s

The asterisk is also used to indicate an excited state of an atom or molecule.

$n + {}^{235}U \rightarrow {}^{236}U*$

Italics One or more English (but not Greek) letters used as a hyphenated prefix is italicized unless a small capital is indicated in the copy. Number prefixes are not italicized. (For more examples of italicized prefixes, see above under "Hyphen.")

z-butene
4*H*-quinoziline
cis-oleic acid

α-particles
D-arabinose
2,3-dimethylbutane

Letters used in atomic orbitals are italicized.

a 3d orbital
three 2p orbitals

In thermodynamics, italicized letters are used to indicate quantities.

$$dS = \frac{dQ}{T}$$
$$dE = dQ - dW$$
$$T\,dS - dQ = 0$$

Line breaks Chemical symbols, including their subscripts and superscripts, should not be broken at the end of a line. Similarly, arrows that signify precipitate and gas should be kept with the symbols that precede them. When chemical equations must be broken, the equation may be split at a horizontal arrow, which should begin the new line. If necessary, lines may also be broken on a connecting symbol such as $+, -$, or $=$, in which case the connecting symbol usually begins the second line. The second line may be set flush right if it is long enough to overlap the first line by at least an inch, or it may be indented from the right margin. The specific format should be detailed in the type specifications sent to the typesetter.

$$CH_3(CH_2)_5CHCH_2 - CBr_3 + \mathbf{Br} - \mathbf{CBr_3}$$
$$\rightarrow CH_3(CH_2)_5CHCH_2 - \mathbf{CBr_3} + \mathbf{CBr_3} \cdot$$
$$|$$
$$\mathbf{Br}$$

Modifiers Modifying words beneath chemical formulas are set in type smaller than that used for the formulas themselves. The first word is capitalized.

Ethylene   Polyethylene

$$H - C \equiv C - H + H_2O \xrightarrow[HgSO_4]{40\% H_2SO_4} [CH_2 = CHOH] \rightarrow CH_3CHO$$

Vinyl alcohol   Acetaldehyde
(not isolable)

Biology and Medicine

Signs and Symbols

In this section four kinds of symbols—the degree sign, the slash, the percent sign, and diacritical marks—are briefly discussed, because of their special application to biological and medical writing. Other signs and symbols commonly used in biology and medicine are listed on page 138.

Degree sign The degree sign is usually included in expressions of temperature, though not in references to the Kelvin scale. In general nontechnical writing, a space is left between the degree sign and the abbreviation F or C (32° F, 0° C). In technical writing, the notation is either closed up entirely or a space is left between the number and the degree sign.

> 100°F   *or*   100 °F
> 39°C   *or*   39 °C
> 384 K

Slash In formal biological and medical writing, the slash is substituted for the word *per* only when all the following conditions exist: (1) the expression contains units of measurement for time or physical quantities, (2) at least one element in the expression is or is part of a specific numerical quantity, and (3) each element of the pair is either a specific numerical quantity or a specific unit of measurement.

> a hemoglobin level of 16 gm/100 cc
> rats treated with $1W/cm^2$ for 10 min
> amylase test: 60-150 Somogyi units/100 ml

The slash does not replace *per* if a prepositional phrase occurs between two or more segments of the construction, if one segment of the construction contains a series, or if the construction does not contain a specific quantity or amount expressed in numbers.

> 40 units of insulin per day
> 6, 8, and 10 mg per hour
> half a dozen weeks per year

Percent sign When a specific percentage is to be expressed, a numeral is followed by an unspaced % sign. The sign is included with all numerals in a series or range, even if one of the numbers is zero.

> studied 5.2% of the patients
> found in 91% of the slides
> a variation of 0% to 10%   [*or* 0%–10%]

The symbol is not substituted for the word *percent* or *percentage* without an accompanying number. (For use of the percent sign in nontechnical writing, see the section on pages 104–5.)

> a small percent of the test plants
> a greater percentage of the subjects

Diacritics Many scientific writers and publishers omit diacritics whenever possible. For example, the umlaut in terms like *Möckeberg's sclerosis* can be omitted without causing confusion. Acute or grave accent marks, as in *Chédiak-Higashi syndrome* and *Lasègue's sign*, can also be dropped. When in doubt, consult a specialized dictionary for the preferred spelling.

Greek Letters

The letters of the Greek alphabet, several of which are used in biological and medical writing, are listed in Table 6.1. Greek letters appear in units of measure (400 µg), in clinical designations (γ-globulin; hemoglobin α chain deficiency), in statistical data ($\Sigma \times B^2 = 2{,}393.82$), in mathematical expressions (πr^2), and in generic drug names and chemical terms (β-amylase; α-methylphenethylamine sulfate).

In a sentence that begins with a normally lowercase Greek letter, the lowercase form is retained and the first English word is capitalized.

> α, β-Unsaturated carbonyl compounds are . . .

Arabic and Roman Numerals

Roman numerals have many specialized uses in formal biological and medical writing, especially in molecular biology and genetics and in established technical and medical terms, such as blood-clotting factors, ECG leads, cancer stages, and types of allergic reactions.

> factor VII
> lead II
> stage III
> type IV allergies

Arabic numerals are also regularly used in biological and medical terminology, especially for blood platelet factors and heart murmurs (to denote their intensity in grades 1 through 6), in certain obstetrics terms, and in the names of virus and organism types.

> platelet factor 3
> grade 2/6
> para 1
> gravida 3
> HIV-2
> B77 avian sarcoma virus RNA subunits

Taxonomic Nomenclature

Living organisms have been given Latinate names composed of a genus (or *generic*) name followed by a species (or *specific*) name. The combination of the two names is called a *binomial*. Binomials are italicized. The genus name is capitalized; the species name is lowercased, even when derived from a proper name.

> California condor *(Gymnogyps californianus)*
> Lucile's glory of the snow *(Chionodoxa luciliae)*
> Hessel's hairstreak *(Mitoura hesseli)*

In running text, genus and species names may or may not be set off by commas or parentheses, depending on the sentence's structure.

> protozoans of the genus *Plasmodium*
> The giant panda, *Ailuropoda melanoleuca*, is endangered throughout its range.

> The convergent lady beetle *(Hippodamia convergens)* and the mealybug destroyer *(Cryptolaemus montrouzieri)* are beneficial in the garden.

After a binomial has been used once in running text, the genus name may be abbreviated to a capital letter followed by a period, even if used with a different species name.

> The tiger, *Panthera tigris,* does not form lasting family bonds. By contrast the lion, *P. leo,* is a social animal that lives in large permanent family groups.

However, an abbreviation is not used when the reader might confuse it with another genus mentioned in the text that begins with the same initial.

Genus names are sometimes followed by the abbreviation "sp." (plural "spp.") set in roman type, which either refers to some or all of the species within a given genus or indicates that a species cannot be identified below the genus level or has not yet been given a species name.

> The microscope revealed a new microorganism, *Paramecium* sp.
> Monkshoods (*Aconitum* spp.) require a rich but light soil.

Subspecies designations   The species name may be followed by a subspecies (or *subspecific*) name, also called a *variety* or *race* name. Like the species name, this third name is italicized and lowercased. If the genus and species names have already been given in the text, they can both be abbreviated when the subspecies is named.

> The great horned owl, *Bubo virginianus,* is usually thought of as a dark brown bird, but the northern subspecies *B. v. subarcticus* is nearly pure white.

In botany, names of subspecies are often introduced by the abbreviation "var." (for "variety"), set in roman type.

> *Polygonum bistorta* var. *superbum*
> *Dahlia excelsa* var. *anemonaeflora*
> *Juniperus communis* var. *oblongapendula*

In taxonomic material the name of the first person or persons to propose a species or subspecies name may be given when the Latin name is first used, along with the date of naming. The author's name is often abbreviated. Both the author's name and the date are set in roman type.

> *Homo sapiens* Linnaeus [*or* Linn. *or* L.], 1758

If there has been a change in the genus name, as is sometimes the case, the original author's name is added in parentheses.

> *Ocypus olens* (Muller)

In botanical nomenclature and to a lesser extent in zoological nomenclature, the original author's name is followed by the name of the author making the assignment to the new genus. It may be necessary to alter the inflectional ending of the specific name to agree with the gender of the new genus.

> *Antirrhinum spurium* L., 1753   *becomes*   *Kickxia spuria* (L.) Dumort, 1827

When assigned to the genus *Kickxia,* the specific name includes the feminine ending to conform to the gender of *Kickxia.*

The full citation with authors and dates is often used only in the most comprehensive monographs. The most expendable item is the date, then the name(s) of the author(s), and finally the scientific names themselves, which may be sacrificed for widely recognized common names.

Horticultural varieties The names of horticultural varieties or cultivars of plants follow the Latin names. Main words within the name are capitalized, and the names are set in roman and either placed within single quotation marks or preceded by the abbreviation "cv." (for "cultivar").

> *Artemisia schmidtiana nana* 'Silver Mound'
> or *Artemisia schmidtiana nana* cv. Silver Mound
> *Hippeastrum striatum* 'Fulgidum' or *Hippeastrum striatum* cv. Fulgidum

Hybrids Plant hybrids are named by a formula in which the taxonomic names of the parents are written in alphabetical order separated by a multiplication sign (×), meaning "crossed with." If the hybrid has not been assigned a special name, a space appears on either side of the × sign. However, if a new genus or species name (or both) is created for the hybrids, the × appears before the name of the hybrid without a space, as if part of the name.

> *Hybrid genus:*   *Guzmania* × *Vriesea*
> *(with new name):*   ×*Guzvriesea*
> *Hybrid species:*   *Rhododendron molle* × *R. occidentale*
> *(with new name):*   *Rhododendron* ×*albicans*

Animal hybrids are usually expressed as a cross between the two parents, with the male parent listed first:

> *Bernicla canadensis* × *Anser cygnoides*

Divisions larger than genus Taxonomic names of divisions larger than genus—family, order, class, and phylum—are capitalized and set in roman type. They are treated as plurals unless they are accompanied by a designation of category.

> Chordata [phylum]
> Mammalia [class]
> Carnivora [order]
> Canidae [family]
> Many Carnivora eat vegetable matter as well as flesh.
> The order Carnivora contains a wide range of forms.

Vernacular forms Many Latin taxonomic names have English counterparts. These vernacular names are set in roman type and lowercased.

> Chordata   chordate
> Mammalia   mammal
> Carnivora   carnivore
> Canidae   canid

The common names of plants and animals do not follow any one set of guidelines. Many publications devoted to a particular group of plants or animals (such as wildflowers, birds, butterflies, or fish) routinely capitalize all elements of the common names of species belonging to the specialized field of interest. Animal-breed publications tend to capitalize all breed names. In most general-interest publications, the common names of animals and plants are lowercased, though any proper noun as a separate element is capitalized. (For more on this use of capitals, see paragraph 4 on page 39.)

English Springer Spaniel   *or*   English springer spaniel
Texas Longhorn cattle   *or*   Texas longhorn cattle
Greater Black-backed Gull   *or*   greater black-backed gull
Queen Anne's Lace   *or*   Queen Anne's lace

Viruses   Virus names are often given in the vernacular, without a Latin form. They are usually written lowercase, but proper nouns within them are capitalized.

varicella-zoster virus
vesicular stomatitis virus (serotype Indiana)
Ebola virus
hepatitis A virus
tick-borne encephalitis virus
Epstein-Barr virus

Types of viruses are sometimes designated by Arabic numerals, by letters, or by a combination of both.

coxsackievirus B2
adenovirus type 2
reovirus type 3
poliovirus 2

Names of Drugs and Diseases

Generic names of drugs should be used in place of trade names wherever appropriate. (Some medical journals ask authors to include a list showing the generic name and any trade names for any drug referred to in a manuscript.) Like all brand names, proprietary drug names should be capitalized. In technical contexts, the proprietary name should usually appear in parentheses immediately after the first use of its generic name.

tranquilized with chlorpromazine (Thorazine)
the prescription of fluoxetine (Prozac)

The names of diseases, signs, symptoms, syndromes, and other medical categories are written lowercase, with the exception of elements formed from proper names.

dengue   Romberg's sign
foot-and-mouth disease   Baker's cyst
Graves' disease   Tourette's syndrome
rheumatoid arthritis   Wassermann reaction

The names of diseases based on the Latin names of pathological organisms are written lowercase and roman, even though the name of the organism itself may be capitalized and italicized. When in doubt, consult a medical or scientific dictionary (see Bibliography).

> Vaginal candidiasis is caused by yeast fungi of the genus *Candida*.

Computer Terminology

The following section provides general information for the author and editor preparing manuscripts for nontechnical publications. Those writing and editing technical publications will typically follow styling conventions specific to those publications.

Capitalization

The names of many computer languages and programs can take several forms, some with all letters capitalized, some with an initial capital letter, and some both ways (for examples, see paragraph 63 on page 51).

The specific names of computer software, such as programs, systems, packages, and routines, should always observe the form used by the manufacturer.

Acronyms and Abbreviations

Acronyms are widely used in computer texts. These are set in roman type, without periods, and usually all-capitalized. Plurals are formed by adding a roman lowercase *s*.

HTTP	(hypertext transfer [*or* transport] protocol)
RAM	(random access memory)
GUI	(graphical user interface)
CPU	(central processing unit)
TCP/IP	(Terminal Control Protocol/Internet Protocol)
URL	(Uniform Resource Locator)
CD-ROMs	(compact disk–read-only memory)
WYSIWYG	(what you see is what you get)
bps	(bits per second)
dpi	(dots per inch)

The styling of abbreviations varies. For example, when used in running text for the name of a telecommunications protocol, *HTTP* is usually all-capitalized; when it appears as part of an URL (as in http://www.webster.m-w.com), it is lowercased.

Computer Commands

Commands appear in print in software manuals and software packages and on software labels. These use a variety of conventions for distinguishing on-screen elements and elements to be keyboarded from the rest of the text. Though these conventions vary widely, some general principles are observed.

Input Commands that the user is to type in or select from a menu are generally distinguished from the main text by typeface or style or both.

To install, choose Run from the File menu and type **a:\setup**.

To install, choose **Run** from the **File** menu and type A:\SETUP.

Commands that are set off from the main text are distinguished by use of a different typeface.

To install, choose Run from the File menu and type the following:
a:\setup.

Optional or variable elements in a command are further distinguished by additional changes in type style or by the use of brackets or braces.

At the prompt, type [drive]**:\install\[directory]**

Keys are indicated in a distinctive fashion, such as small caps, initial caps, or all caps.

To deselect a menu press ESC.
or
To deselect a menu press Esc.

Keys to be pressed simultaneously are connected by a plus sign.

To reboot the computer press CTRL + ALT + DELETE.

Some key names are spelled out for clarity.

Press Ctrl + Period to activate . . .

Case-sensitive text Typed elements in filenames, passwords, lines of programming code, and the like are sometimes case-sensitive—that is, effective only when the proper letters in the typed words are capitalized and lowercased. Any such elements must be set exactly as they are to be typed.

At the prompt for the password, type **ABCaccess** and press RETURN.

Filenames and directory names Filenames and directory names are usually all-capitalized.

After installing the program, consult the README.TXT file for a description of any late changes to the software.

Drag the file from the LETTERS directory and drop it in the SMITH directory.

Signs and Symbols

Mathematics

+ plus; positive—used also to indicate omitted figures or an approximation

− minus; negative

± plus or minus

× *or* · multiplied by; times

÷ *or* : *or* / divided by

E times 10 raised to an indicated exponent ($4.52E5 = 4.52 \times 10^5$)—used esp. in calculator and computer displays

= equals

$\neq$ or $\pm$ is not equal to

$>$ is greater than

$\gg$ is much greater than

$<$ is less than

$\ll$ is much less than

$\geq$ or $\geqq$ is greater than or equal to

$\leq$ or $\leqq$ is less than or equal to

$\not>$ is not greater than

$\not<$ is not less than

$\approx$ is approximately equal to

$\equiv$ is identical to

$\sim$ is similar to; the negation of; the negative of

$\cong$ is congruent to

$\propto$ varies directly as; is proportional to

$:$ is to; the ratio of

$\therefore$ therefore

∞ infinity

$\angle$ angle; the angle

$\llcorner$ right angle

$\perp$ the perpendicular; is perpendicular to

$\parallel$ parallel; is parallel to

$\odot$ or $\bigcirc$ circle

$\frown$ arc of a circle

$\triangle$ triangle

$\square$ square

$\square$ rectangle

$\sqrt{\ }$ or $\sqrt[\ ]{\ }$ root—used without a figure to indicate a square root ($\sqrt{4} = 2$) or with an index above the sign to indicate another degree $\left(\sqrt[3]{27} = 3, \sqrt[5]{32} = 2\right)$

( )   parentheses ⎫

[ ]   brackets   ⎬ indicate that the quantities enclosed by them are to be taken together

{ }   braces ⎭

—   vinculum, spanning two or more symbols in a mathematical expression (equivalent to parentheses or brackets enclosing such symbols)

Δ the operation of finding the difference between two nearby values of a variable or of a function for two values of its independent variable differing by a small nonzero amount

$\int$ integral; integral of

$\int_b^a$ the integral taken between the values a and b of the variable

$\dfrac{df(x)}{dx}$ the derivative of the function $f(x)$ with respect to x

$\dfrac{\partial f(x,y)}{\partial x}$ the partial derivative of the function $f(x,y)$ with respect to x

$\dfrac{\partial^2 f(x,y)}{\partial x^2}$ the second-order partial derivative of the function $f(x,y)$ with respect to x

$\dfrac{\partial^2 f(x,y)}{\partial y \partial x}$ the second-order partial derivative of the function $f(x,y)$ obtained by differentiating first with respect to x and then with respect to y

δ_j^i Kronecker delta

s standard deviation of a sample taken from a population

σ standard deviation of a population

Σ sum; summation

$\bar{x}$ arithmetic mean of a sample of a variable x

μ micrometer; arithmetic mean of a population

μ_2 or σ^2 variance

χ^2 chi-square

P the probability of obtaining a result as great as or greater than the observed result in a statistical test if the null hypothesis is true

r correlation coefficient

$E(x)$ expected value of the random variable x

π pi; the number 3.14159265+; the ratio of the circumference of a circle to its diameter

Π product

$!$ factorial

e *or* ϵ the number 2.7182818+; the base of the natural system of logarithms; the eccentricity of a conic section

i the positive square root of -1

n an unspecified number (as an exponent) esp. when integral

$°$ degree

$'$ minute; foot—used also to distinguish between different values of the same variable or between different variables (e.g., a', a'', a''')

$''$ second; inch

^{0}, ^{1}, ^{2}, ^{3}, etc. indicate that the expression to the left is raised to a power whose degree is indicated by the figure (thus a^2 means a squared)

$^{-1}$, $^{-2}$, $^{-3}$, etc. indicate that the reciprocal of the expression to the left is raised to the power whose degree is indicated by the figure (thus a^{-2} equals $1/a^2$)

$\sin^{-1}x$ arcsine of x

$\cos^{-1}x$ arccosine of x

$\tan^{-1}x$ arctangent of x

f function

f' derivative of f

f'' second derivative of f

f^n n^{th} derivative of f

f_x the partial derivative of f with respect to x

f_{xx} the second-order partial derivative of f with respect to x

f_{xy} the second-order partial derivative of f obtained by differentiating first with respect to x and then with respect to y

f^{-1} the inverse of the function f

$|z|$ the absolute value of z

$[a_{ij}]$ matrix with element a_{ij} in the ith row and jth column

$|a_{ij}|$ determinant of a square matrix with elements a_{ij}

$\|\mathbf{x}\|$ length or magnitude of the vector $\mathbf{x}$

A^{-1} inverse of the matrix A

A^T transpose of the matrix A

$[x]$ the greatest integer not greater than x

(a,b) the open interval $a < x < b$; ordered pair of coordinates

$[a,b]$ the closed interval $a \leq x \geq b$

$\aleph_0$ aleph-null

$\ni$ *or* $:$ such that

$\exists$ there exists

$\forall$ for every, for all

$\cup$ union of two sets

$\cap$ intersection of two sets

$\subset$ is included in, is a subset of

$\supset$ contains as a subset

$\in$ is an element of

$\notin$ is not an element of

Λ *or* 0 empty set, null set *or* $\varnothing$ *or* $\{\}$

Chemistry and Physics

+ plus, together with—used between the symbols of substances brought together for, or produced by, a reaction; used also to indicate a dextrorotatory compound

$^+$ signifies a unit charge of positive electricity (as in Na^+)

− used to indicate the removal of a part from a compound; also used to indicate a levorotatory compound

$^-$ signifies a unit charge of negative electricity (as in Cl^-)

— signifies a single bond, used between the symbols of elements or groups which unite to form a compound

· used to separate parts of a compound regarded as loosely joined (as in $CuSO_4 \cdot 5H_2O$); also used to denote the presence of a single unpaired electron (as in H·)

◯ or ◎ benzene ring

= indicates a double bond

= signifies two unit charges of negative electricity (as in $SO_4^=$)

≡ signifies a triple bond

: indicates an unshared pair of electrons; sometimes used to indicate a double bond

⫶ indicates a triple bond

( ) marks groups within a compound

⌐ or ⌐ joins attached atoms or groups in structural formulas for cyclic compounds

= gives or forms

→ gives, leads to, or is converted to

↔ resonance

⇋ or ⇌ forms and is formed from, is in equilibrium with

↓ indicates precipitation of the substance

↑ indicates that the substance passes off as a gas

≡ is equivalent—used in statements to show how much of one substance will react with a given quantity of another so as to leave no excess of either

1-, 2-, etc. used initially in names, referring to the positions of substituting groups, attached to the first, etc., of the numbered atoms of the parent compound

′ used to distinguish between different substituents of the same kind (as in R′, R″, R‴ to indicate different organic groups)

△ heat

α alpha particle

β beta particle; beta ray

γ gamma; photon; surface tension

∈ permittivity

η efficiency; viscosity

λ wavelength

μ micro-; permeability; magnetic moment

ν frequency; neutrino

ρ density; resistivity

σ conductivity; cross section; surface tension

Φ luminous flux; magnetic flux

Ω ohm

a acceleration

B magnetic induction; magnetic field

c speed of light

e electron; electronic charge

E electric field; energy; illumination; modulus of elasticity; potential difference

F force

G gravitational constant; conductance; weight

h Planck's constant

$\hbar$ $h/2\pi$

H magnetic field strength; enthalpy

^{2}H *also* H^2 deuterium

^{3}H *also* H^3 tritium

J angular momentum

k Boltzmann constant

L inductance; self-inductance

m mass

M metal

n index of refraction; neutron

p momentum of a particle; proton

Ph phenyl

R organic group; alkyl or aryl group

S entropy

T absolute temperature; period

V electrical potential

W work

X halogen atom; power of magnification; reactance

Y admittance

Z impedance; atomic number (for element symbols, see Table 6.4)

Biology and Medicine

○ an individual, specif. a female—used chiefly in inheritance charts

□ an individual, specif. a male—used chiefly in inheritance charts

♀ female

♂ *or* ☿ male

× crossed with; hybrid

+ wild type

F_1 offspring of the first generation

F_2 offspring of the second generation

F_3, F_4, F_5 offspring of the third, fourth, fifth, etc., generation

$\overline{AA}, \overline{A},$ *or* $\overline{aa}$ ana; of each

℞ take—used on prescriptions; prescription; treatment

☠ poison

7   Quotations

Styling Block Quotations 139
Alterations and Omissions 141
Epigraphs and Blurbs 144
Quoting Verse 145

Writers and editors rely on two common conventions to indicate that a passage of prose or poetry is quoted directly from another source. Short quotations are usually run in with the rest of the text and enclosed by quotation marks. Longer passages are usually set off distinctively as separate paragraphs; these paragraphs, called *block quotations* or *extracts,* are the main subject of this chapter. For the treatment of short run-in quotations, see the sections beginning on page 28 (for punctuation) and page 36 (for capitalization).

For prose quotations, length is generally assessed in terms of either the number of words or the number of lines. Quoted text is usually set as a block when it runs longer than about 50 words or three lines. However, individual requirements of consistency, clarity, or emphasis may alter these limits. A uniform policy should generally be observed throughout a given work.

Running in longer quotations can make a passage read more smoothly; alternatively, setting even short quotations as extracts can make them easier for the reader to locate.

For quotations of poetry, different criteria are used. Even a single line of poetry is usually set as an extract, although it is also common to run one or two lines into the text.

Attribution of quotations to their author and source (other than epigraphs and blurbs) is dealt with in Chapter 10, "Notes and Bibliographies." (The unattributed borrowed quotations in this chapter are from William Shakespeare, the *Congressional Record,* Abraham Lincoln, the U.S. Constitution, Martin Lister, the Song of Songs, William Wordsworth, John Keats, T. S. Eliot, Walt Whitman, Ezra Pound, and Matthew Arnold.)

Styling Block Quotations

Block quotations are generally set off from the text that precedes and follows them by adding extra space above and below the quotation, indenting the quoted matter on the left and often on the right as well, and setting the quotation in smaller type with less leading.

Introductory Punctuation, Capitalization, and Indention

Block quotations are usually preceded by a sentence ending with a colon or a period, and they usually begin with a capitalized first word.

Fielding hides his own opinions on the matter deep in *Tom Jones:*

> Now, in reality, the world have paid too great a compliment to critics, and have imagined them men of much greater profundity than they really are. From this complaisance the critics have been emboldened to assume a dictatorial power, and have so far succeeded that they are now become the masters, and have the assurance to give laws to those authors from whose predecessors they originally received them.

If the quoted passage continues an obviously incomplete (unquoted) sentence that precedes it, a comma may be used instead, or no punctuation at all, depending on the sentence's syntax, and the following extract will usually begin with a lowercase letter.

According to Fielding,

> the critics have been emboldened to assume a dictatorial power, and have so far succeeded that they are now become the masters, and have the assurance to give laws to those authors from whose predecessors they originally received them.

When the beginning of a block quotation is also the beginning of a paragraph in the original, the first line of the quotation is normally indented like a paragraph, and any subsequent paragraph openings in an extract are similarly indented.

Expanding on his theme, his tone veers toward the contemptuous:

> The critic, rightly considered, is no more than the clerk, whose office it is to transcribe the rules and laws laid down by those great judges whose vast strength of genius hath placed them in the light of legislators, in the several sciences over which they presided. This office was all which the critics of old aspired to; nor did they ever dare to advance a sentence without supporting it by the authority of the judge from whence it was borrowed.
>
> But in process of time, and in ages of ignorance, the clerk began to invade the power and assume the dignity of his master. The laws of writing were no longer founded on the practice of the author, but on the dictates of the critic. The clerk became the legislator, and those very peremptorily gave laws whose business it was, at first, only to transcribe them.

Quotations within an Extract

If a block quotation itself contains quoted material, double quotation marks enclose that material. (In a run-in quotation, these would be set as single quotation marks.)

> Davenport reports what may have been the last words Pound ever spoke in public:
>
> > "Tempus loquendi," the frail voice said with its typical rising quaver, "tempus tacendi," quoting Ecclesiastes, Malatesta, and Thomas Jefferson simultaneously, and explaining, in this way, that he had said quite enough.

Dialogue in a block quotation is enclosed in quotation marks, and the beginning of each speech is marked by paragraph indention, just as in the original.

> Next O'Connor's hapless protagonist is collared and grilled by the retired schoolteacher in the second-floor apartment:
>
> > "Florida is not a noble state," Mr. Jerger said, "but it is an important one."
> >
> > "It's important alrighto," Ruby said.

> "Do you know who Ponce de Leon was?"
> "He was the founder of Florida," Ruby said brightly.
> "He was a Spaniard," Mr. Jerger said. "Do you know
> what he was looking for?"
> "Florida," Rudy said.
> "Ponce de Leon was looking for the fountain of youth,"
> Mr. Jerger said, closing his eyes.
> "Oh," Ruby muttered.

If a speech runs to more than one paragraph, open quotation marks appear at the beginning of each paragraph of the extract; closing quotation marks appear only at the end of the final paragraph.

For dialogue from a play or meeting minutes, the speakers' names are set on a small indention, in italics or small capitals, followed by a period or colon. Runover lines generally indent about an em space further.

> This vein of rustic drollery resurfaces in the scene where the transformed Bottom meets the fairies (act 2, scene 1):
>
> *Bottom.* I cry your worships mercy, heartily: I beseech your worship's name.
> *Cobweb.* Cobweb.
> *Bottom.* I shall desire you of more acquaintance, good Master Cobweb: if I cut my finger, I shall make bold with you. Your name, honest gentleman?
> *Peaseblossom.* Peaseblossom.
> *Bottom.* I pray you, commend me to Mistress Squash, your mother, and to Master Peascod, your father.

> SEN. BAUCUS: Mr. President, I suggest the absence of a quorum.
> THE PRESIDING OFFICER: The clerk will call the roll.
> The legislative clerk proceeded to call the roll.
> SEN. WARNER: Madam President, I ask unanimous consent that the order for the quorum call be rescinded.
> THE PRESIDING OFFICER: Without objection, it is so ordered.

Alterations and Omissions

Although absolute accuracy is always of first importance when quoting from another source, there are certain kinds of alterations and omissions that authors and editors are traditionally allowed to make. (The conventions described in this section are illustrated with block quotations; however, the conventions are equally applicable to run-in quotations.)

Obviously, the author must always be careful not to change the essential meaning of a quotation by making deletions or alterations or by putting quotations in contexts that may tend to mislead the reader.

Changing Capital and Lowercase Letters

If the opening words of a quotation act as a sentence within the quotation, the first word is capitalized, even if that word did not begin a sentence in the original version.

> Henry Fielding was already expressing identical sentiments in 1749:
>
> The critics have been emboldened to assume a dictatorial power, and have so far succeeded that they are now become the masters. . . .

In situations in which meticulous handling of original source material is crucial (particularly in legal and scholarly writing), the capital letter would be placed in brackets to indicate that it was not capitalized in the original source.

> [T]he critics have been emboldened to assume a dictatorial power, and have so far succeeded that they are now become the masters. . . .

Even if the quotation's first word was capitalized in the original, it is generally not capitalized when the quoted passage is joined syntactically to the sentence that precedes it.

> Fielding asserts boldly that
>
> the critic, rightly considered, is no more than the clerk, whose office it is to transcribe the rules and laws laid down by those great judges whose vast strength of genius hath placed them in the light of legislators, in the several sciences over which they presided.

Omissions at the Beginning or End of a Quotation

Since it is understood that most quotations are extracted from a larger work, ellipsis points at the beginning and end of the quotation are usually unnecessary. If a quotation ends in the middle of a sentence, however, the period following the omission is closed up to the last word and followed by three ellipsis points. Any punctuation that immediately follows the last quoted word in the original is generally dropped.

> We are met on a great battlefield of that war. We have come to dedicate a portion of that field, as a final resting place for those who here gave their lives. . . .

If the omission in the quoted passage ends with a question mark or an exclamation point, such punctuation follows the three ellipsis points. (Some style guides ask that these marks precede the ellipsis points.)

Omissions within Quotations

Omissions from quoted material that fall within a sentence are indicated by three ellipsis points.

> The Place where it is kept . . . is a very Pit or Hole, in the middle of the Fauxbourg, and belongs to the Great Abbey of that Name.

Punctuation used in the original that falls on either side of the ellipsis points is often omitted; however, it may be retained, especially to help clarify the meaning or structure of the sentence.

> We the People of the United States, in Order to . . . establish Justice, . . . provide for the common defence, . . . and secure the Blessings of Liberty . . . , do ordain and establish this Constitution for the United States of America.

If an omission includes one or more entire sentences, or the beginning or end of a sentence, within a paragraph, the end punctuation preceding or following the omission is retained and followed by three ellipsis points.

> We can not dedicate—we can not consecrate—we can not hallow—this ground. The brave men, living and dead, who struggled here, have consecrated it, far above our

> poor power to add or detract. . . . It is for us the living, rather, to be dedicated here to the unfinished work which they who fought here have thus far so nobly advanced.

If a full paragraph or more is omitted, the omission is indicated by ellipsis points at the end of the paragraph that precedes the omission.

> The words were written in 1915 by Hans Leip (1893–1983), a German soldier on his way to the Russian front parting from his sweetheart. His "Lili Marleen" was really a combination of two girls, his own, Lili, and his buddy's, Marleen. The poem was published in 1937 in a book of Leip's poems entitled *Die kleine Hafenorgel* ("The Little Harbor Organ"). Norbert Schultze (1911–), who would become the prominent composer of such propaganda titles as "The Panzers Are Rolling in Africa," set "Lili Marleen" the next year. . . .
>
> It was Lale Andersen, a singer in literary cabarets in Munich and Berlin, whose record of the song was released in late 1939. It was not initially a success, but on August 18, 1941, a German shortwave radio station in Belgrade broadcast the song to Rommel's troops in North Africa.

If text is omitted from the beginning of any paragraph other than the first, three indented ellipsis points mark the omission. Note that they do not stand in for any omitted text preceding the paragraph.

> We were in Paris at the time of the Fair of St. Germain. It lasts six weeks at least: The Place where it is kept, well bespeaks its Antiquity; for it is a very Pit or Hole, in the middle of the Fauxbourg, and belongs to the Great Abbey of that Name. . . .
>
> . . . Knavery here is in perfection as with us; as dextrous Cut-Purses and Pick-Pockets. A Pick-Pocket came into the Fair at Night, extreamly well Clad, with four Lacqueys with good Liveries attending him: He was caught in the Fact, and more Swords were drawn in his Defence than against him; but yet he was taken, and delivered into the Hands of Justice, which is here sudden and no jest.

Other Minor Alterations

Archaic spellings and styles of type, punctuation, and capitalization should be preserved in direct quotations if they do not interfere with a reader's comprehension.

> Also he shewed us the *Mummy of a Woman* intire. The scent of the Hand was to me not unpleasant; but I could not liken it to any Perfume now in use with us.

If such archaisms occur frequently, the author may wish to modernize them, adding an explanation to this effect in a note or in the preface. (Several passages quoted in this chapter have been tacitly modernized.) Obvious typographical errors in modern works may be corrected without comment. Inserting *sic* in brackets after a misspelling in the original version is not necessary unless there is a specific reason for calling attention to the variant. The same holds for using *sic* for other small apparent errors of fact, grammar, punctuation, or word choice or omission.

Sometimes an author wishes to insert a brief explanation, clarification, summary of omitted material, or correction. These insertions, or *interpolations,* are enclosed in brackets. (For more on this use of brackets, see the section beginning on page 3.)

> For, lo, the winter is past, the rain is over and gone;
> The flowers appear on the earth; the time of the singing of birds is come, and the voice of the turtle [i.e., turtledove] is heard in our land.

Words that were not originally italicized may be italicized in the quoted passage for the sake of emphasis, as long as the author adds a bracketed notation such as "Italics mine," "Italics added," or "Emphasis added" immediately following the italicized portion or (more often) at the end of the passage.

> Both Russell and Ochs had noted the same reference: "Portions of the Feingold collection found their way into the hands of Goering and Hess; others would later surface in Romania, Argentina and Paraguay; and *the still unaccounted-for pieces were rumored to be part of a prominent Alsatian estate,* but no systematic effort was made to recover them." [Italics mine.]

Any footnote or endnote numbers or parenthetical references in the original version are usually omitted from short quotations; in their place authors often insert their own references.

Epigraphs and Blurbs

Thorough documentation is normally required only in scholarly writing, and even in scholarly contexts certain kinds of set-off quotations need not be exhaustively documented. These include quotations from classic sources—which will have been published in a number of different editions, and therefore have various possible publishing data—and casual allusions that are not essential to the author's central argument.

Such quotations may particularly be employed as *epigraphs*—short quotations from another source placed at the beginning of an article, chapter (where they may be placed above the title), or book. Other instances would include examples illustrating grammatical elements or word usage, and dictionaries of quotations.

For such quotations, the attribution is generally set by itself on the line below the quotation. Alternatively (and especially if space is a concern), it is run in on the last line of the quotation. When set on its own line, it is generally preceded by an em dash; somewhat less frequently, it is set without an em dash, often enclosed in parentheses. Whatever its punctuation, it is normally set flush right. When run in with the quotation, it usually follows the latter immediately with no intervening space, separated only by either an em dash or parentheses.

The name of the quotation's author is normally set roman, and the name of the publication in which it originally appeared is normally set italic. Either may instead be set in small caps. If all the attributions consist only of authors' names, they may be set in italics.

> I went to the woods because I wished to live deliberately, to front only the essential fact of life, and see if I could not learn what it had to teach, and not, when I came to die, discover that I had not lived.
> —Henry David Thoreau, *Walden*
> *or*
> (Henry David Thoreau)

Epigraph attributions are often very brief; this one, for example, could have read "H. D. Thoreau," "Thoreau, *Walden,*" or simply "Thoreau."

Advertising *blurbs*—favorable quotations from reviewers or customers that appear on book jackets or advertising materials—are standardly enclosed in quotation marks, and the attribution is never enclosed in parentheses. But the latter's placement may vary, subject to the overall design of the jacket or advertisement. The attribution may appear on its own line or be run in with the blurb; it may be preceded by an em dash or unpunctuated; it may be set flush with the right margin of the quotation, run in with the quotation with no intervening space, centered on its own line, or aligned on a set indention.

> "Ms. Kingston finds the necessary, delicate links between two cultures, two centuries, two sexes. Seldom has the imagination performed a more beautiful feat."—*Washington Post*

When an attribution line follows a passage of poetry, the line may be set flush right, centered on the longest line in the quotation, or indented a standard distance from the right margin.

> Bring me my Bow of burning gold,
> Bring me my Arrows of desire,
> Bring me my Spear; O clouds unfold!
> Bring me my Chariot of fire!
> —William Blake, *Milton*

An attribution line following quoted lines from a play or the Bible may include the act and scene or the book and verse.

> All the world's a stage
> And all the men and women merely players;
> They have their exits and their entrances;
> And one man in his time plays many parts,
> His acts being seven ages.
> (*As You Like It*, 2.7)

> A feast is made for laughter, and wine maketh merry:
> but money answereth all things.
> (Ecclesiastes, 10:19)

(For details on documenting other sources of quotations, see Chapter 10, "Notes and Bibliographies.")

Quoting Verse

The major difference between quotations of prose and poetry is that lines of poetry always keep their identity as separate lines. When run in with the text, the poetic lines are separated by a spaced slash.

> Was it Whistler, Wilde, or Swinburne that Gilbert was mocking in the lines "Though the Philistines may jostle, you will rank as an apostle in the high aesthetic band, / If you walk down Piccadilly with a poppy or a lily in your medieval hand"?

When poetic lines are set as extracts, the lines are divided exactly as in the original.

Dickinson describes this post-traumatic numbness as death in life:

> This is the Hour of Lead—
> Remembered, if outlived,
> As Freezing persons, recollect the Snow—
> First—Chill—then Stupor—then the letting go—

Up to three or four short lines of poetry are occasionally run in if they are closely integrated with the text.

> In the thoroughly miscellaneous stanza that follows—"He has many friends, lay men and clerical, / Old Foss is the name of his cat; / His body is perfectly spherical, / He weareth a runcible hat"—Lear seems to bestow new meaning on his older coinage *runcible.*

However, quotations of as few as one or two lines are usually set off from the text as extracts.

> He experienced the heady exaltation of Revolutionary idealism:
>
> > Bliss was it in that dawn to be alive,
> > But to be young was very Heaven!

The horizontal placement of a poetry excerpt is normally determined by its longest line, which is centered horizontally, all the other lines aligning accordingly.

The relative indentions of an excerpt's lines should always be preserved.

> The famous first stanza may have given the English-speaking world its lasting image of the Romantic poet:
>
> > My heart aches, and a drowsy numbness pains
> > My sense, as though of hemlock I had drunk,
> > Or emptied some dull opiate to the drains
> > One minute past, and Lethe-wards had sunk:
> > 'Tis not through envy of thy happy lot,
> > But being too happy in thine happiness,—
> > That thou, light winged Dryad of the trees,
> > In some melodious plot
> > Of beechen green, and shadows numberless,
> > Singest of summer in full-throated ease.

If the quotation does not start at the beginning of a line, it should be indented accordingly.

> I do not find
> The Hanged Man. Fear death by water.

If the lines of a poem are too long to center, the quotation may be set using a standard indention, with runover lines indented further.

> As it nears its end, the poem's language becomes increasingly evocative:
>
> > The last scud of day holds back for me,
> > It flings my likeness after the rest and true as any on
> >   the shadowed wilds,
> > It coaxes me to vapor and the dusk.

In a speech that extends over several lines, quotation marks are placed at the beginning and end of the speech. If a speech extends beyond one stanza or section, quotation marks are placed at the beginning of each stanza or section within the speech.

> In the cream gilded cabin of his steam yacht
> Mr. Nixon advised me kindly, to advance with fewer
> Dangers of delay. "Consider
>   Carefully the reviewer.
>
> "I was as poor as you are;
> When I began I got, of course,
> Advance on royalties, fifty at first," said Mr. Nixon,

It was formerly common to begin every line within a speech with quotation marks, but these added quotation marks are now standardly removed without comment by modern editors.

When a full line or several consecutive lines of poetry are omitted from an extract, the omission is indicated by a line of ellipsis points extending the length of either the preceding line or the missing line.

> Ah, love, let us be true
> To one another! for the world, which seems
> To lie before us like a land of dreams,
> . . . .
> Hath really neither joy, nor love, nor light,

Poetry extracts that do not end in a period or other terminal punctuation may be followed by ellipsis points; alternatively, the original punctuation (or lack of it) may be left by itself.

> This royal throne of kings, this scepter'd isle,
> This earth of majesty, this seat of Mars,
> This other Eden, demi-paradise, [. . .]

8 Foreign Languages

General Guidelines   148
German   150
Dutch   153
Danish, Norwegian, Swedish   153
Spanish   155
French   156
Italian   159
Portuguese   160
Latin   161
Polish   161
Czech   162
Classical Greek   163
Russian   165
Arabic and Hebrew   168
Chinese and Japanese   169

The purpose of this chapter is to give some guidance to authors and editors who must deal with foreign-language extracts embedded in English texts. European languages written in the Latin alphabet will be considered separately from languages written in non-Roman writing systems.

In other languages, the mechanics of writing—punctuation, capitalization, word division—often differ significantly from English practice. Capitalization is a particularly salient problem because proper names, whether of people, places, publications, or organizations, come up with more frequency than plain foreign-language text in the course of writing and editing English-language text, as, for example, in the compilation of a bibliography. Another issue that must be addressed is typography, namely, the use in foreign languages of diacritics and special alphabetic characters absent from English. (For a discussion of the electronic coding of foreign characters, see pages 354–355.)

General Guidelines

Punctuation   The core of English punctuation—period, comma, colon, semicolon, question mark—also constitute the punctuation of nearly all other modern European languages, and are used in approximately the same way. Notable divergences and modifications will be pointed out in the paragraphs to follow on individual language practices. Largely peculiar to English are the inward-facing commas at the top of the type body (" ") that function as quotation marks. The most common foreign equivalents are the lower- and upper-level inverted quotation marks („") that are especially characteristic of German and the double lowercase angle brackets (« »), called *guillemets,* that are especially characteristic of French. The use of English-style quotation marks in other European languages appears to be spreading, at least in part because the foreign adoption of computer software and keyboards designed primarily for an Anglo-American audience make marks in other styles more cumbersome to produce.

The visually most striking difference between the text of, say, an English short story and a short story in most other European languages is in the rendering of dialogue. Rather than being set off by quotation marks, a line of dialogue is typically introduced on its own line by a dash followed by a space; it may or may not be ended by another dash. Both quotation marks and guillemets may also be used to set off dialogue.

Capitalization Certain features of English practice, such as the use of capitals for personal and geographical names, and to mark the first word of a sentence, are general European practice. In other respects, however, English tends to use capitalization more frequently than other European languages. Aside from German, which capitalizes all nouns, European languages do not generally use uppercase letters for a number of categories of words invariably capitalized in English, such as days of the week, months of the year, or religious faiths. Many languages do not capitalize adjectival derivatives of place-names or adjectives denoting nationality and ethnic group. The first-person singular pronoun is not capitalized in any other European language, and pronouns in general are seldom capitalized except when they signal politeness. Titles, whether of books, periodicals, institutions, or organizations, often have only the initial letter capitalized, though there is much variation within individual languages.

Word Division Word-division rules in European languages tend to be more straightforward than in English. The tradition of consulting a dictionary to find out how a word is to be broken—with dictionaries using complex and slightly different systems—is largely alien to languages other than English. The following paragraphs cover major points of word division in foreign languages but are not meant to be an exhaustive treatment.

A number of languages prescribe obligatory breaks between prefix and base, or between major components of a compound. These breaks may not be recognizable by simply consulting a dictionary, and if absolute correctness is desired there may be no alternative to consulting someone with a reasonable knowledge of the language in question.

Diacritics and Special Characters All European languages that adopted the Latin alphabet had to figure out ways to represent sounds that did not occur in Latin. A device employed by English and other languages was to use combinations of letters, or digraphs—*sh,* for example—to represent non-Latin sounds. (The letter *w* began as a digraph—a fact preserved in its name "double u"—that developed a distinctive form through ligaturing of the two letters.) Another strategy was to find completely new letters. Old English introduced (among others) þ and ð to stand for the sounds we now use *th* to represent, and these symbols are still used in two modern Germanic languages, Icelandic and Faroese. A third strategy was to add small extra marks, or diacritics, above, below, or through the Latin letters.

Aside from foreignisms such as *naïveté* (which can also be written without the diaeresis and accent), modern English dispenses with diacritics, but other European languages use them with abandon, and a long sentence in, say, French or Czech can scarcely be found that does not display a variety of marks over letters that cannot be reproduced by the standard Anglo-American typewriter. The replacement of the typewriter by computerized word processing has largely eliminated the need to write diacritics and special characters into typed manuscripts by hand. However, when a manuscript is to be keyboarded by someone not necessarily familiar with the symbols in question, they should be marked or listed in some way so that they are not simply overlooked.

Languages written in non-Roman scripts fall into two divisions, those that are transliterated and those that are Romanized (though the term *Romanization* is often used broadly to refer to any system for rendering a non-Roman script with Latin letters). Russian, Bulgarian, Hebrew, Arabic, Persian, Sanskrit, Hindi, and Korean are written in non-Roman scripts that are basically phonetic in nature; in other words, the characters of the script can be transliterated into corresponding characters of the Latin alphabet. Semitic scripts such as those used to write Hebrew, Aramaic, Arabic, and Persian do not show most vowels as ordinarily written, though ways of showing all vowels in these writing systems exist and are traditionally used for sacred texts. When transliterated into the Latin alphabet, vowels in these languages are conventionally filled in. Chinese is not written in a phonetic script and must be Romanized rather than transliterated; that is, Chinese words are rendered in a phonetic transcription of spoken Chinese using Latin letters to represent Chinese sounds.

ALA-LC Romanization Tables: Transliteration Schemes for Non-Roman Scripts, 1997 Edition (Washington, D.C.: Library of Congress, 1997) is a useful and very comprehensive guide to systems for transliterating and Romanizing many languages of the world. In some respects, however, such as retaining the Wade-Giles system for Romanizing Chinese, the Library of Congress is conservative, and the user should bear this in mind.

The language discussions below begin with Germanic languages and continue with Scandinavian languages, Romance languages (including Latin), Slavic languages written in the Roman alphabet, Classical Greek, Russian, Arabic and Hebrew, and Chinese and Japanese.

German

Editors dealing with textual material in German should be aware that an orthographic reform of German was initiated in 1996, as a result of an agreement signed on July 1, 1995, by cultural representatives of the three major German-speaking countries (Germany, Austria, Switzerland) and of German-speaking minorities in other countries. According to the timetable set up by this agreement, older orthographic norms will be considered outmoded after August 1, 1998, and incorrect after July 31, 2005. The modified rules of most relevance for English-language editors are detailed in the following paragraphs. Those needing guidance to both the traditional and new spellings and syllable divisions may wish to consult *Die neue deutsche Rechtschreibung,* compiled by Ursula Hermann and Lutz Götze (Bertelsmann Lexikon Verlag, 1996). This orthographic dictionary can be utilized with minimal knowledge of German, and for those with a knowledge of German it contains detailed information on current German spelling and style.

Punctuation Characteristic of German are split-level quotation marks („") that face in a direction opposite those of English quotation marks. Quotations within quotations are set off by single marks (‚'), and all punctuation not part of the quoted matter is put outside the marks:

> Die „ostgermanische" Gruppe hat sich erst später durch Zusammenwanderung herausgebildet und sollte eher „Mittelmeergermanisch" oder „Arianisch-Germanisch" genannt werden.

> „Wir mögen sie eigentlich ganz gern", sagte die Stimme, „sie sind so zutraulich. Sie gehören dem Bauern, noch ein Stück die Straße entlang. Er hat zwei Töchter. Die Mädchen sagen: ‚Wenn ihr die Schweine tötet, dann kein *coucher avec vous.*' Da hast du's."

Although the split-level marks are still general in German-language journalism, guillemets (in German, *französische Anführungszeichen,* or "French quotation marks") are also very widely used, and are the norm in fiction to represent dialogue. The points of German-style guillemets normally point inward (» «) rather than outward as in French. Quotations within quotations are set off by single marks (› ‹). Publishers' styles vary on the setting of dialogue; successive speeches by different characters often begin a new line without indention.

Capitalization A distinctive feature of German that sets it apart from all other European languages is the use of capitals for all nouns, whether common or proper. Adjectives, on the other hand, even when derived from proper nouns, are generally lowercase: hence, *ein Deutscher* ("a German"), but as an adjective *deutsch* ("German") and *Österreich* ("Austria") but *österreichisch* ("Austrian"). In proper names, as of organizations and places, adjectives are normally capitalized (*Deutsche Bank, Bayerischer Wald*), though lowercase is maintained in a few traditional names (*Hochschule für Musik und darstellende Kunst „Mozarteum"*). Proper-name derivatives that end in *-er* (*Berliner, Mecklenburger, Schweizer*) are capitalized even when used adjectivally (*die Berliner Bevölkerung, die Mecklenburger Landschaft, Schweizer Käse*).

The tendency of the 1996 orthographic reform has been to unify the rules regarding capitalization of nouns and lowercasing of adjectives. Adjectives derived from personal names that were formerly capitalized are now to be lowercase (hence *die platonischen Dialoge* rather than *die Platonischen Dialoge*). An exception is made for adjectives formed from the suffix *-sch* when the proper name is separated from the suffix by an apostrophe, so that both *die darwinsche Evolutionstheorie* and *die Darwin'sche Evolutionstheorie* are allowable. Adjectives formed from personal names with other suffixes are to be invariably lowercase (*die darwinistische Evolutionstheorie, eine kafkaeske Stimmung*).

Titles of books, periodicals, works of art, and the like begin with a capital letter but are otherwise capitalized in the same way as normal prose (*Der kaukasische Kreidekreis, Wo warst du, Adam?, Zeitschrift für vergleichende Sprachforschung*).

Forms of the second-person pronoun *Sie,* which is used in polite address, as well as the corresponding possessive pronoun *Ihr* are invariably capitalized. The familiar second-person pronouns *du* and *ihr* and the corresponding possessive adjectives *dein* and *euer* begin with a lowercase letter. Though it was formerly traditional, if not obligatory, to capitalize the familiar forms in correspondence, this usage is proscribed by the 1996 spelling reform.

Word Division Words are divided along what are considered to be natural syllable boundaries as far as possible, that is, after vowels when a single consonant follows and between vowel letters when the division is between different syllables: *Bau-er, steu-ern, eu-ro-pä-i-sche, Fa-mi-li-en.* Groups of two consonants are divided between consonants; when there are more than two consonants, the last consonant is carried over to the next line: *El-tern, ros-ten, leug-nen, sin-gen, Wel-le, ren-nen, Ach-tel, imp-fen, knusp-rig, dunk-le.* The combinations *ch, ck,* and *sch,* as well as *ph, rh, sh,* and *th,* which appear almost exclusively in foreign words, cannot be divided: *la-chen, bli-cken, wa-schen, Deut-sche, Sa-phir, Myr-rhe, Bu-shel, Zi-ther, Goe-the.* In foreign words, combinations of a consonant and a following *l, n,* or *r* can be either divided according to German rules or carried over to the next line: *nob-le* or *no-ble, Mag-net* or *Ma-gnet, Arth-ri-tis* or *Ar-thri-tis.*

Compound words and words formed with prefixes are divided between the major components of the derivative, while the components of the derivatives are divided according to the normal rules as set out above: *Schwimm-meis-ter, ab-fah-ren, emp-fan-gen, a-ty-pisch, in-of-fi-zi-ell.* Words that are compounds from a historical standpoint but no longer felt as such, or foreign words that might not necessarily be recognized as derivatives, may be divided either according to German rules or on an etymological basis: *hi-nauf* or *hin-auf, wa-rum* or *war-um, ei-nan-der* or *ein-an-der, He-li-kop-ter* or *He-li-ko-pter, in-te-res-sant* or *in-ter-es-sant, Pä-da-go-gik* or *Päd-a-go-gik.*

Two features of these rules introduced by the 1996 spelling reform are modifications of earlier practices that were actually carryovers from the typesetting of Fraktur, the German script in use before World War II. The first of these changes concerns the treatment of the cluster *st,* which was formerly unbreakable but now is treated like any consonant group (see *ros-ten* above). The second concerns the treatment of *ck,* which was idiosyncratically broken as *k-k* but now is considered unbreakable (see *bli-cken* above).

Diacritics and Special Characters The black-letter script known as Fraktur, in general use in Germany before World War II, was by decree of the Nazi regime replaced with Latin script in 1941. It was not revived after the war and is now used only for decorative purposes.

German uses an umlaut over the vowel letters *a, o,* and *u* (ä Ä, ö Ö, ü Ü). The only special character is *ß* (German, *Eszett*), an adaptation of a Fraktur character that represents an old ligature of *s* and *z.* This character is pronounced exactly the same as *ss,* and in short textual extracts, such as the titles in a bibliography, it is acceptable and in fact normal for English-language editors to replace *ß* with *ss.* It also has no uppercase form, and in all-caps printing is replaced by *SS*. Note that the spelling of words containing *ß* has been significantly altered by the 1996 orthographic reform, so that *ß* now follows only a long vowel or diphthong and *ss* a short vowel. This affects some quite common words such as the conjunction *daß*, now to be spelled *dass*. This change does not pertain to Switzerland, where most printers had already dropped the use of *ß* entirely.

Dutch

Punctuation Dutch traditionally employs split-level quotation marks (""), as does German, to highlight a word or to enclose the translation of a foreign word. Dutch treatment of fictional dialogue varies. The traditional style is to use single quotation marks at the top of the type body, though split-level quotation marks may be used, and some publishers follow the general European style of introducing speech with dashes and no quotation marks.

Capitalization Dutch, like English, generally capitalizes adjectives denoting ethnic or geographic affiliation, as well as the corresponding nouns (*de Nederlandse taal*, "the Dutch language"; *Nederlander*, "Dutchman"). With other categories of words, such as months and days of the week, Dutch uses lowercase along with other European languages. Book titles usually have initial capitals for all important words; periodical titles nearly always do. Organizational names also usually capitalize all important words (e.g., *de Verenigde Naties*, "the United Nations"; *Vereniging voor Vreemdelingenverkeer*, "Tourism Association"; *Ministerie van Buitenlandse Zaken*, "Ministry of Foreign Affairs").

Word Division The rules for division are basically the same as those for German: words are divided after vowels when a single consonant follows, between vowels when the division is between different syllables, and between clusters of two consonants. In groups of two or more consonants, only the last is carried to the next line. The group *ch* is considered indivisible. Also as in German, compound words and derivatives are divided between major components.

Diacritics and Special Characters Dutch uses a diaeresis over *e* (ë) when this letter marks a distinct syllable (*zoëven, financiën, tweeërlei, België*). An acute accent may occasionally be used over homonyms to avoid confusion (*een*, "a"; *één*, "one"). Note that the combination *ij* is treated as if it were a ligature; if it stands at the beginning of a word that is capitalized, both *i* and *j* are capitalized (e.g., *IJsselmeer*).

Danish, Norwegian, Swedish

The three continental Scandinavian languages (Danish, Norwegian, and Swedish) will be treated together in this section.

Punctuation Traditionally Danish, Swedish, and Norwegian use left-facing apostrophes (' ' or " ") for both opening and closing a word or quoted speech.

Danish publishers also frequently used inward-pointing guillemets (»anførsel-stegn«). Swedish uses guillemets with both marks pointing to the right (»an-föringstecken»). Direct speech in fiction may be shown by either quotation marks or indention and a dash.

Capitalization Neither Danish, Norwegian, nor Swedish capitalizes the names for the months or days of the week.

Danish does not capitalize either adjectives or nouns denoting nationality or affiliation with a place (*en dansker,* "a Dane"; *dansk,* "Danish"). Names of institutions, organizations, government departments, etc., as well as book and periodical titles, have capital letters in all important words (*den Europæiske Union, Ministeriet for Kulturelle Anliggender, Ordbog over det Danske Sprog*). Danish capitalizes the second-person plural informal pronoun *I* and all forms of the polite second-person pronoun (*De, Dem, Deres*).

Swedish likewise does not capitalize either adjectives or nouns denoting nationality or affiliation with a place (*en svensk,* "a Swede"; *svensk,* "Swedish"). Book titles usually capitalize only the first word and any proper nouns (*I havsbandet, Gösta Berlings saga*), though some well-known titles are exceptions (e.g., *Svenska Akademiens Ordbok,* the Swedish equivalent of the *Oxford English Dictionary*). There is fluctuation in the treatment of periodical titles (*Nysvenska studier, Arkiv för Nordisk Filologi*); general-interest magazines and newspapers usually capitalize all prominent words (e.g., *Svenska Dagbladet, Dagens Nyheter, Private Affärer*). Institutional and organizational names traditionally have only the initial letter capitalized (*Röda korset,* "the Red Cross"; *Förenta nationerna,* "the United Nations"), though there is much variation in current usage (e.g., *den Europeiska unionen* or *den Europeiska Unionen*). The only pronoun capitalized in Swedish is the now archaic second-person plural pronoun *I.*

Norwegian capitalization practices follow the same lines as Swedish. Like Swedish, there is fluctuation in capitalizing the names of organizations (e.g., *De forente nasjoner* or *De Forente Nasjoner,* "the United Nations"). Like Danish, Norwegian capitalizes the polite second-person pronouns (*De, Dem, Deres*).

Word Division As in most other European languages, Danish carries a single consonant between vowels to the next line and divides double consonants (*bo-gen, øl-let*). There is some flexibility in dealing with consonant clusters: a consonant group that would normally begin a Danish word may or may not be divided (*bis-pen* or *bi-spen, tas-ke* or *ta-ske*). Compounds and derivatives are divided along boundaries of major components, which usually, but not always, correspond to syllabic boundaries (hence, *bil-fabrik, skole-børn, be-tale, for-stå, far-lig, yng-ling,* but *prins-esse*). An inflectional ending can also be separated from the stem of a word (*bøg-erne, hurtig-ere, student-en, vent-ede*).

The rules regarding division before a single consonant and division of double consonants also apply to Swedish. In Swedish, usually only the last consonant of a group of more than two will be carried to the next line (*barns-lig*). The groups *ck, ng,* and *gn* are not broken and are not carried over (*tryck-e-ri, vagn-ar-na, ko-nung-ar-na*). As in Danish, compounds and derivatives are divided along boundaries of major components (*slös-aktig-het, sam-arbets-man*).

Norwegian follows essentially the same rules as Danish. The groups *gj, kj, sj* and *skj* are not divided, nor is *ng* divided in native words.

Diacritics and Special Characters   Danish employs the special vowel letters æ Æ and ø Ø. The letter *a* also has a form with a small circle above it (å Å), called in Danish *bolle-å*. Rather than being treated as *a* with a diacritic, *å* is regarded as a distinct letter of the alphabet. It officially replaced *aa* in a spelling reform carried through in 1948, though *aa* continues to be used in some place-names and personal names. An acute accent may be used to distinguish homonyms, as, for example, *en*, "a," and *én*, "one."

Swedish has forms of *a* and *o* with umlauts (ä Ä, ö Ö), and, like Danish (which borrowed it), a form of *a* with a small circle over it (å Å). These are treated as separate letters of the alphabet rather than as vowels with diacritics.

Norwegian uses the same special letters as Danish, namely å Å, æ Æ, ø Ø. The letter *å* has been used in Norwegian since the early part of the century, though some names still retain the older form *aa*.

Spanish

Punctuation   The most distinctive feature of Spanish punctuation is the addition of an inverted question mark or exclamation point to the beginning of a question or exclamation, or an interrogative or exclamatory portion of a sentence:

> ¿Quién es el dueño de esa compañía?
> Ah, él es de Cuba, ¿verdad?
> ¿Qué hora es ahí? ¡Uyy!, es muy tarde.

Guillemets (Spanish, *comillas*) traditionally function as quotation marks in Spanish prose, though English-style inward-facing commas at the top of the type body are now used in an increasing number of publications, including major newspapers and magazines in both Latin America and Spain.

In fictional dialogue, the usual practice is to introduce successive speeches by indenting and a dash:

> —¡Demetrio Macías! —exclamó el sargento despavorido, dando unos pasos atrás.
> El teniente se puso de pie y enmudeció, quedóse frío e inmóvil como un estatua.
> —¡Mátalos! —exclamó la mujer con la garganta seca.
> —¡Ah, dispense, amigo!... Yo no sabía... Pero yo respeto a los valientes de veras.
>
> —Oiga —habló un hombre a Pancracio en el zaguán—, ¿a qué hora se le puede hablar al general?
> —No se le puede hablar a ninguna; amaneció crudo —respondió Pancracio—. ¿Qué quiere?

As illustrated in the above two excerpts, speech is followed by several spaces and a closing dash when it is interrupted by interpolated text in the same paragraph. Another dash and a period or comma close the interpolated material and mark the resumption of speech by the same character. Pauses in speech are marked by suspension points consisting of three closely spaced periods. Dialogue within dialogue is usually marked by guillemets, as in the following:

—¿Quién es este curro? —preguntó Anastasio.

—Yo estoy de centinela, oí ruido entre las yerbas y grité: «¿Quién vive?» «Carranzo», me respondió éste vale... «¿Carranzo? No conozco yo a ese gallo...» Y toma tu Carranzo: le metí un plomazo en una pata...

Capitalization Spanish does not capitalize nouns or adjectives denoting affiliation with a place (hence, for example, *norteamericano,* "North American"; *un norteamericano,* "a native of the U.S. or Canada"), membership in a religious group (*católico,* "Catholic") or political party (*falangista,* "Falangist"; *comunista,* "Communist"), or adjectives deriving from proper names (*sanmartiniano,* "of General San Martín"). Days of the week and months are also not capitalized (*Hoy es jueves, tres de mayo,* "Today is Thursday, the third of May"). In titles of books, usually only the first word is capitalized (*El amor en los tiempos de cólera*), while in titles of periodicals major words are usually capitalized (*El País, Revista Española de Lingüística*). Major words are usually capitalized in names of organizations (*Organización de Estados Americanos, Universidad Nacional Autónoma de México*).

Word Division The regular rule in Spanish is that words must be divided after one or more vowels, and not between vowels: *se-ño-ri-ta, fue-go, tie-ne.* This rule applies even when each of two vowels in succession constitutes a distinct syllable, so that *creer* and *leer,* for example, cannot be broken, and *reata* can only be broken *rea-ta.* A single letter may not end a line, so that *agua* and *animal* cannot be broken as *a-gua* and *a-nimal.* The digraphs *ch, ll,* and *rr,* which represent single sounds, are treated as if they were single letters (*bo-rra-cho, tie-rra, aque-lla*). Groups of two consonants are normally separated (*tiem-po, al-gu-na, for-mar-se*), except for the consonants *p, b, f, t, d, k, g* preceding *l* or *r* (hence, *pa-la-bra, se-cre-to, ma-dre, aza-frán, pe-li-gro, pa-tria, no-ta-ble, ci-clo, re-fle-xión, re-gla*). Groups of three consonants within a word not ending in the above pairs will ordinarily have an *s* in the middle, and will be divided after the *s: cons-ti-tui-do, trans-pa-ren-te, obs-tá-cu-lo.*

Exceptions to these rules may be found with prefixed and compound words. In such cases the break is normally made between the major components of the word, i.e., the prefix and the base or the major elements of the compound: *des-apa-re-ce, in-útil, cen-tro-ame-ri-ca-no.* The first- and second-person plural pronouns are customarily broken *nos-otros* and *vos-otros.*

Diacritics and Special Characters The acute accent may appear on all five vowel letters (á Á, é É, í Í, ó Ó, ú Ú) and the diaeresis is used over *u* (ü Ü). The tilde over *n* (ñ Ñ) is the only special consonantal character.

French

Punctuation The outward-pointing double angle brackets called *guillemets* serve in French as quotation marks:

Roman d'aventure, conte philosophique, cette œuvre d'une rare vérité est l'un des « classiques » de notre temps.

...il y avait de plus, contre les quatre colonnes de la mairie, quatre manières de gaules, portant chacune un petit étendard de toile verdâtre, enrichi d'inscriptions en lettres d'or. On lisait sur l'un : « Au Commerce » ; sur l'autre : « A l'Agriculture » ; sur le troisième : « A l'Industrie » et, sur le quatrième : « Aux Beaux-Arts ».

All punctuation not belonging to the quoted matter is placed outside the guillemets. Traditionally the guillemets are separated by a space from the quoted material. Note that the second passage above illustrates the customary French typographical practice of separating semicolons and colons from the preceding word by a space, though this style is not regularly adhered to in newspapers or magazines and is usually not copied when extracted French text is printed in English.

In dialogue, as in Spanish, speech by different characters is usually marked by indention and a dash, but there is no closing dash separating the speech from interpolated text, and no dash marking the end of the interpolation and the resumption of speech:

Charles se donna jusqu'au coin de la haie, et enfin, quand on l'eut dépassée :
—Maître Rouault, murmura-t-il, je voudrais bien dire quelque chose.
Ils s'arrêtèrent. Charles se taisait.
—Mais contez-moi votre histoire! Est-ce que je ne sais pas tout! dit le père Rouault, en riant doucement.
—Père Rouault..., père Rouault, balbutia Charles.

As in Spanish, unspaced suspension points are used to mark pauses in speech. In some publishers' styles, a series of interchanges between different characters will be opened and closed by a single set of guillemets. Guillemets are also used to mark quotations within dialogue. When quotes occur within quotes and both quotes end at the same place, a single guillemet serves to close both of them:

—Il a dit : « C'est moi le meilleur nageur de « nous trois ». Et il ne s'est pas vanté.

Capitalization In French, adjectives denoting ethnicity, affiliation with a place, or geographical race are usually lowercase (*japonais, parisien, la race noire*), and corresponding nouns denoting language are also lowercase (*le japonais,* "Japanese" = "the Japanese language"). The corresponding nouns denoting people, however, are capitalized (*les Japonais,* "the Japanese"; *un Parisien,* "a Parisian"); nouns denoting race may fluctuate (*les noirs* or *les Noirs,* "the Blacks"). As in Spanish, days of the week (*mardi*) and months (*janvier*) are not capitalized. Nouns or adjectives denoting religious or political affiliation (*bouddhiste, catholique, gaulliste, communiste*) are also not capitalized, though *Juif* ("Jew") used as a noun is generally an exception, and usage fluctuates with nouns designating members of Christian religious orders (*les Jésuites* or *les jésuites*). Adjectives derived from proper names are usually not capitalized (*pascalien,* "of Pascal"). The generic noun in names of streets, boulevards, squares, and so forth is traditionally not capitalized (*avenue Louis Roche, boulevard St. Ger-*

main, place de l'Opéra), unless the place is used metonymically (as *le Quai d'Orsay* designating the French ministry of foreign affairs). Likewise, the generic noun is lowercase in certain geographical names (*le mont Blanc, la mer Rouge, le golfe Persique*). In names of buildings the generic word may or may not be capitalized (*Musée du Louvre* or *musée du Louvre*).

In names of organizations, only the first noun is usually capitalized (*l'Union européenne, Centre nationale de la recherche scientifique*), though sometimes other important nouns in the name will also be capitalized (*Organisation des Nations unies, Rassemblement pour la République*). Note that initialisms formed from these names (*C.N.R.S., R.P.R.*) use all capitals. In hyphenated organizational or geographical names, on the other hand, both words are capitalized (*les États-Unis, les Pays-Bas, le Comédie-Française*).

With titles of books and periodicals, the most common practice is to capitalize only the first word and any other words that would be capitalized in normal prose (*Le vocabulaire des institutions indo-européennes, A la recherche du temps perdu*). A variant style is to capitalize both an initial article and the first following noun, or a following noun and adjective if the adjective intervenes between the noun and article (*La Planète des singes; Le Petit Prince*).

Word Division   Rules for breaking words at the end of a line in French are similar to those for Spanish; that is, words are normally divided after a vowel and never divided between vowels: *di-vi-sé, cha-peau, théâ-tre*. Internal and final *e* is counted as a syllable even when the *e* is mute (i.e., not normally pronounced): *ap-pe-ler, ef-fi-ca-ce-ment, qua-tre*. A group of two consonants between vowels is split between the consonants (*par-tie, con-nais-sait, es-pèce*); exceptions are combinations in which the second consonant is *r* or *l* and the first consonant is one other than *r* or *l* (*sa-ble, pro-blè-me, é-troi-te*). The digraphs *ch, th, ph*, and *gn* are treated as if they were single letters and are not broken: *a-che-ter, ca-thé-dra-le, gra-phie, mon-ta-gne*. Combinations of more than two consonants are normally broken after the second consonant, unless the rules regarding *r/l* combinations and digraphs apply: *cons-truc-tion, obs-cu-ri-té, mar-cher*. A break is not allowed after an apostrophe (*au-jour-d'hui*, not *au-jourd' / hui*).

Words derived from productive prefixes may be broken between the prefix and the base word even when the above rules are violated: *in-sta-ble, re-struc-tu-rer*. This applies particularly to the prefixes *dé-* and *pré-*, which are nearly always separated from the base word: *dé-sta-li-ni-sa-tion, pré-sco-lai-re*. The rules may also be abrogated in the case of compound words made up of Greco-Latin elements, with the break being made between major components of the word (*stra-to-sphère* rather than *stra-tos-phère*).

In careful typesetting, a single letter will not be left at the end of a line, and a new line will not begin with a single consonant plus mute *e*, but especially in journalism these rules are not always observed, and breaks such as *mê-me* and *a-mé-ni-té* may be found.

Diacritics and Special Characters   Both the acute and grave accents may appear over *e* (é É, è È), but the grave accent alone over *a* and *u* (à À, ù Ù) The circumflex accent can occur over any vowel letter (â Â, ê Ê, î Î, ô Ô, û Û).

The diaeresis may be used over *e, i,* and *u* (ë Ë, ï Ï, ü Ü). The combination of *o* and *e* is usually written as a ligature (œ Œ), though setting it as *oe* is not unacceptable if necessary. The sole consonantal diacritic is *c* with a cedilla written below it (ç Ç). In some printers' styles, a string of words set entirely in capitals may dispense with all over-the-letter diacritics, leaving only the cedilla.

Italian

Punctuation   The use of an apostrophe in Italian to mark deletion of a vowel is common. When the following word begins with a vowel, there is no space after the apostrophe: *una buon'amica, quell'albero, non c'è pane.* When the following word begins with a consonant, there is a full space: *ne' tuoi panni, un po' di tiempo, a mo' d'esempio.*

Italian employs both English-style quotation marks (Italian *virgolette alte*) and guillemets (*virgolette basse*), with much variation in usage. Some publications, such as the popular magazine *Espresso,* use English-style marks to highlight technical terms or idiosyncratic words and guillemets to enclose directly quoted speech. Treatment of dialogue in fiction varies from publisher to publisher; probably the most common practice is to introduce successive speeches with indention and a dash, with interpolated material in the same speech opening and closing with a dash. As in Spanish and French, guillemets are used for a quotation inside another quotation.

Capitalization   In respect to differences from English, capitalization practices in Italian are similar to French and Spanish. Adjectival derivatives of place-names and adjectives denoting ethnicity are not capitalized (*il popolo italiano, formaggio svizzero*), and a corresponding noun denoting a language is lowercase (*studiare l'italiano*). There is much fluctuation in the treatment of corresponding nouns denoting people. Capitalization is usually more common in reference to a nation (e.g., *gli Italiani*) and lowercasing in reference to individuals (e.g., *c'erano due italiani,* "there were two Italians"); *i Romani* would most likely refer to the ancient Romans and *i romani* to the inhabitants of the modern city.

Titles of books and periodicals usually begin with a capital letter and are otherwise capitalized as normal prose (*La coscienza di Zeno, I dialetti delle regioni d'Italia, Studi di grammatica generativa*). However, in short titles, especially very familiar ones, all important words may be capitalized, and both the uncapitalized and capitalized versions may be considered correct (*La divina commedia/La Divina Commedia, Orlando furioso/Orlando Furioso, I promessi sposi/I Promessi Sposi, Corriere della sera/Corriere della Sera*).

Forms of the polite pronouns *Lei* and *Loro* and the corresponding possessive pronoun *Suo* are ordinarily capitalized.

Word Division   More than in other Romance languages, Italian attempts to divide words after a vowel and before a consonant or consonants whenever possible. The letter groups *ch, gh, gli, gn, qu,* and *sc* (when before *e* or *i*), which represent single consonant sounds, are not divisible. The traditional rule is that any consonant group with which it is possible to begin a word will be carried over to the next line when it occurs internally in a word; hence clusters consisting of any consonant (other than *l* or *r*) followed by *l* or *r* will not be divided, nor will clusters beginning with *s*. The following examples illustrate these principles: *a-mo-re, fi-lo-so-fo, a-qua-rio, la-ghi, bi-scia, fi-glia-stro, ca-pri-no, de-sti-no, ri-spo-sta, e-sclu-sio-ne.* Breaks are made between double consonants and other consonant groups: *fat-to, poz-zo, ac-qua, cor-sa, al-to, ap-pren-do, bac-te-rio, im-por-tan-za.* Diphthongal and triphthongal combinations of vowels, which usually contain *i* or *u*, are not divisible unless a vowel or vowel group forms a distinct syllable; hence *maestro* and *eroe* are divisible as *ma-e-stro* and *e-ro-e*, but *aiuola* can only be broken as *a-iuo-la* and words such as *miei, più,* or *tuo* cannot be broken. Words should not be broken after an apostrophe; thus, for example, *dell'amico* can only be divided *del-l'a-mi-co.*

Diacritics and Special Characters Italian as printed in the 1980s and '90s may have a grave accent over all five vowel letters (à À, è È, ì Ì, ò Ò, ù Ù) and an acute accent over *e* (é É). Acute accents were formerly used over other vowel letters and a circumflex accent over *i* (as in *studî*, the plural of *studio*), but these practices are now considered old-fashioned. There are no consonantal diacritics or special characters in Italian.

Portuguese

Punctuation In Portugal, guillemets are usually employed as quotation marks, while English-style inward-facing commas are the norm in Brazil. Note that Portuguese does not follow the Spanish practice of beginning questions and exclamations with punctuation.

Capitalization Portuguese capitalization rules are essentially identical to Spanish. There is some variation in the treatment of ethnic names and noun derivatives of geographic names, which may sometimes be capitalized (*os brasileiros* or *os Brasileiros, os índios* or *os Índios*). In Brazil, major words in the titles of both books and periodicals tend to be capitalized.

Word Division Syllable division in Portuguese follows basically the same rules as Spanish. The digraphs *ch, lh,* and *nh* are indivisible, though the clusters *ss* and *rr* are divisible (*der-ro-tar, pês-se-go*). Note that the vowel combinations *ai, au, ei, eu, iu, oi, ou, ui, ãe, ão,* and *õe* represent diphthongs and cannot be divided.

Diacritics and Special Characters Portuguese employs a variety of diacritics over vowel letters. The acute accent may appear over any vowel (á Á, é É, í Í, ó Ó, ú Ú) and the circumflex accent over *a, e,* and *o* (â Â, ê Ê, ô Ô). In current usage the grave accent appears only over *a* (à, À). A tilde may appear over *a* and *o* (ã Ã, õ Õ). As in Spanish, the diaeresis may appear over *u* (ü Ü) and as in French, a cedilla may appear under *c* (ç Ç).

Latin

Punctuation Classical texts as published today use the same punctuation as modern European languages. Quotation marks, if used, vary with the country of publication.

Capitalization Texts in Classical Latin follow the same basic rules of capitalization as modern European languages; that is, proper names and the first word of a sentence are capitalized. In texts published in English-speaking countries, and often in texts published elsewhere, proper adjectives are capitalized (*scriptores Romani, lingua Latina*). Names of the months and the words *Kalendae, Idus,* and *Nonae* in dates are capitalized (e.g., *Ianuarius; Idus Martiae; ante diem octavum Kalendas Iulias,* conventionally abbreviated *a.d. VIII. Kal. Iul.*).

A general convention in citing the titles of ancient, medieval, or modern works is to capitalize only the first word of a title and any other words that would normally be capitalized (*De rerum natura, Ab urbe condita, De bello Gallico.*) Works written in English with Latin titles, however, usually follow English conventions and all major words are capitalized (*Principia Mathematica, Religio Medici*).

Word Division The traditional doctrine is that a word has as many syllables as it has vowels and diphthongs. In practice, this means that a word is divided after a vowel or diphthong and before a single consonant, with the exception of *x,* which is usually not carried to the next line (*de-ae, a-ci-e, fi-li-us, fe-ro-ci-ta-te, dix-it, sax-um*). The letters *u* and *i,* when used in classical texts instead of *v* and *j* as consonants, are treated like any other consonants (*e-ie-ci, uo-ca-ri*). The groups *qu, gu, ch, ph,* and *th* are treated as single consonants (*lo-qua-cem, lin-gua, ar-chi-tec-tus*). Double consonants are separated (*mit-to, in-ter-ro-gas-set*). Groups of two or more consonants are divided after the last consonant, except for clusters of a consonant (other than *r* or *l*) and *r* or *l* (*pa-trem, cas-tra, ex-ter-nus, abs-tu-le-runt, ex-em-pla, om-nis, in-te-gra-re*).

Compounds and words formed with prefixes are usually divided along the boundaries of the components, even if the above rules are violated: *ab-est, ob-la-tus, di-sto, du-plex.*

Diacritics and Special Characters Latin as normally printed has no diacritics or special characters, though texts for learners and work of a linguistic nature may show a macron or breve over a single vowel (ā Ā, ē Ē, ī Ī, ō Ō, ū Ū, ă Ă, ĕ Ĕ, ĭ Ĭ, ŏ Ŏ, ŭ Ŭ).

Polish

Punctuation Polish, like German, traditionally uses split-level quotation marks („"). Both inward- and outward-pointing guillemets (» «, « ») may also be used. Dialogue in fiction is rendered in the general European manner, that is, by indenting speeches by separate characters and beginning each speech with a dash.

Capitalization Like other European languages, Polish does not capitalize days of the week or months. Nouns denoting nationality or ethnicity and nominal derivatives of countries or regions are normally capitalized (*Polak, Amerykanin, Kaszuba, Ślązak*), though names for inhabitants of cities or towns are not capitalized (*warszawiak, londyńczyk*). All corresponding adjectives denoting nationality, ethnicity, etc., begin with a lowercase letter (*język polski, ser szwajcarski*). In titles of periodicals all important words are capitalized (*Gazeta Wyborcza, Prace Filologiczne*), while titles of literary works have only an initial capital (*Ogniem i mieczem, Historia literatury polskiej*). All major words are capitalized in names of organizations and institutions (*Narody Zjednoczone*, "United Nations"; *Towarzystwo Miłośników Języka Polskiego*, "Society of Lovers of the Polish Language"; *Wydział Historii Uniwersytetu Jagiellońskiego*, "Department of History of the Jagellonian University"); in this respect, Polish follows English more than do most other European languages.

Word Division Polish divides after a vowel and before a single consonant (*nie-na-ru-sze-nie*) and splits groups of two identical consonants (*pan-na*). Note that the various combinations of consonant + i + vowel constitute a single syllable and cannot be divided (*cia-sto, mie-li, nio-sła*). The digraphs *ch, cz, dz, dź, dż, rz,* and *sz* are indivisible (*du-chem, to-czyć, no-dze, jeż-dżę, mo-rze, du-sza*), unless the *d* of *dz* and *dż* forms part of a prefix. As with Russian, rules regarding division of internal consonant clusters—of which Polish has a great abundance— are flexible: the word *iskra*, for example, can be broken *is-kra, isk-ra,* and even *i-skra*, though not *iskr-a*, since a single vowel letter should not be carried over to the next line. When the structure of a word is clear, division along the boundaries of its components is preferred, though not absolutely obligatory; hence *pol-ski* is the preferred division, though *po-lski* and *pols-ki* are tolerated. Words formed with prefixes, however, should keep the prefix intact (hence, *przed-stawić, nad-u-żyć, ob-o-rać, roz-strzyg-nąć*). (The principal prefixes ending in a consonant are *bez-, ob-, nad-, naj-, od-, pod-, przed-, przeciw-, roz-,* and *wez-/wes-;* those ending in a vowel are *do-, na-, o-, po-, prze-, przy-, u-, wy-,* and *za-*.) Compounds are also divided along the boundaries of their major components (*kraj-obraz, noc-leg, staro-słowiański*).

Diacritics and Special Characters Polish employs an acute accent over several consonants (ć Ć, ń Ń, ś Ś, ź Ź) as well as over the vowel *o* (ó Ó). A single dot (not a háček) may also be written over z (ż Ż); this character is completely distinct from the accented z. The letter *l* has an ordinary form and a form written with a slanting slash through it (ł Ł). There are two additional vowel diacritics, a hook (Polish *ogonek*, literally, "little tail") under the letters *a* and *e* (ą Ą, ę Ę). This hook curves to the right, unlike a cedilla, which should under no circumstances replace it.

Czech

Punctuation Czech uses double and single split-level quotation marks („ " , '), and occasionally inward-pointing guillemets (» «). Czech fiction employs either the double quotation marks or the general European system of indention and dashes.

Capitalization Months and days of the week are not capitalized. Czech capitalizes nouns denoting ethnicity and nominal derivatives denoting inhabitants of countries, regions, or cities (*Čech, Američan, Afričan, Pražan*), though corresponding adjectives denoting nationality, ethnicity, etc., begin with a small letter (*americká univerziteta, český román, ementálský sýr*). Most names of languages are nouns ending in the suffix *-ina;* these are invariably lowercase (*čeština, angličtina*), as are the adverbial forms meaning "in (a given language)" (e.g., *česky, anglicky*). Titles of both books and periodicals capitalize only the initial letter and proper nouns (*Slovanské starožitnosti, Nenesitelná lehkost bytí; Naše řeč, Časopis lékařů českých*). Names of organizations and institutions also capitalize only the initial word (*Spojené národy,* "United Nations"; *Česká republika,* "Czech Republic"; *Janáčkova akademie múzických umění,* "Janaček Academy of Musical Arts").

Word Division As with most other languages, Czech divides words after a vowel and before a single consonant (*prá-ce, dou-fat, dě-ku-je-me*); note that *l* and *r* in Czech can count as vowels (hence, *vl-ně-ný, vr-bo-vý,* and even *vtr-hl* are possible). To a greater degree than is the case with Polish or Russian, the guidelines for breaking consonant groups (as set out, for example, in *Pravidla českého pravopisu* ["Rules of Czech Orthography"] published in 1993 by the Czech Academy of Sciences) make division according to word structure obligatory. These rules extend not only to prefixes (e.g., *do-mlu-vit, na-jde, na-zdar, nej-lé-pe, ne-jsem, ne-lze, pře-tlak, roz-hra-ní, sou-struh, nad-u-ží-vat*), but also to inflections and suffixes (e.g., *vrať-me, pad-nuv-še, tisk-li, dět-ství, měst-ský, zvlášt-ní, ka-men-ný*). Where the structure of a word is not recognizable from the standpoint of a contemporary native speaker, on the other hand, considerable latitude is allowed (e.g., *bá-sně* or *bás-ně, do-ktor* or *dok-tor, se-stra, ses-tra,* or *sest-ra* are all considered acceptable). Some of the more common prefixes are *bez-, do-, na-/ná, nad-, ne-/ně, nej-, ob-, od-, po-, pod-, pro-, pře-, před-, při-, roz-, sou-, u-/ú-, vy-,* and *za-*. However, nothing but familiarity with the language would allow one to distinguish *nej-lé-pe,* where *nej-* is the prefix, from *ne-jsem,* where *ne-* is the prefix. As in other Slavic languages, compounds are divided along the boundaries of their major components (*tmavo-vlasý, samo-uk, boje-schoupnost, kolem-jdoucí*).

Diacritics and Special Characters Czech employs a profusion of diacritics over letters, which lend the language a very distinctive typographic appearance. The háček (Czech, "little hook") is used over *c, n, r, s,* and *z* (č Č, ň Ň, ř Ř, š Š, ž Ž). In addition, *d* and *t* may be followed by an apostrophe, which should be set closer to the letter than an actual apostrophe would be (ď, ť); when capitalized, the apostrophe is replaced by a háček (Ď, Ť). An acute accent may be found over all vowel letters as well as *y,* which represents a vowel (á Á, é É, í Í, ó Ó, ú Ú, ý Ý). Finally, a háček may occur over *e* (ě Ě) and a small circle over *u* (ů Ů).

Classical Greek

Normally only words or phrases in Classical or Ancient Greek are transliterated in works intended for a nonscholarly audience. Anything more than a phrase should probably be set in Greek type, particularly if the intended reader is expected to have some understanding of the original, whether or not it is translated. Quotation marks are not used around anything set in Greek. Untransliterated Greek passages must include accent and breathing marks; for the norms of their placement, a Greek grammar or textbook should be consulted. Classical Greek punctuation uses a raised dot (˙) in place of both an English colon and semicolon, and a semicolon (;) in place of an English question mark.

Transliteration The following system is the customary one for transliterating Greek:

Greek alphabet	Name of letter	Transliteration
A α	alpha	a
B β	beta	b
Γ γ	gamma	g
Δ δ	delta	d
E ε	epsilon	e
Z ζ	zeta	z
H η	eta	ē
Θ θ	theta	th
I ι	iota	i
K κ	kappa	k
Λ λ	lambda	l
M μ	mu	m
N ν	nu	n
Ξ ξ	xi	x
O ο	omicron	o
Π π	pi	p
P ρ	rho	r (rh *initially*)
Σ σ (*but* ς *when last letter in a word*)	sigma	s
T τ	tau	t
Y υ	upsilon	y (*but* u *after* a, e, i); *sometimes* u *in all positions*
Φ φ	phi	ph
X χ	chi	kh
Ψ ψ	psi	ps
Ω ω	omega	ō

In Greek all words that begin with a vowel have an apostrophe-like diacritic written over them to indicate whether or not they begin with an *h* sound. This diacritic, called a "smooth breathing" when it faces outward (') and a "rough breathing" when it faces inward ('), is not duplicated in transliteration. A rough breathing, however, is represented by adding an initial *h* to the word in transliteration (e.g., ἁμαρτία = hamartia). Initial ρ (r) in Greek is always written with a rough breathing over it and is conventionally transliterated *rh*. A double ρ (r) inside a word is usually transliterated *rrh* (e.g., ἐπίρρημα = epirrhēma).

Greek has three diphthongs in which the first vowel is long (α, η, ω). The second element of these diphthongs is invariably iota and is conventionally written under the letter ("iota subscript"). In transliteration, the iota is written next to the vowel (e.g., βουλῇ = boulēi, δήμῳ = dēmōi).

The three accent marks employed by Greek are acute (´), grave (`), and circumflex (ˆ), at least one of which occurs over a vowel letter in most Greek words. The accents are not customarily transliterated.

The velar nasal sound [η] (the *ng* in *sing*) only occurred in Greek before κ, γ, χ, and ξ. It was spelled with γ (called "gamma-nasal"), though this is usually transliterated as *n* in English. Hence ἄγκυρα is transliterated *ankyra*, ἄγγελος as *angelos*, and σφίγξ as *sphinx*.

The letter upsilon (υ) is usually transliterated *y* when it is not the second element of a diphthong, though a more recent practice is to transliterate it *u*. (The borrowed English words *hubris* and *kudos* have this transliteration.) The choice of transliteration should be left up to the author.

Word Division   Rules for dividing Greek words are simple at least in theory. A single consonant between two vowels is carried over to the next line (*a-gō, so-phi-zō*). Any consonant group that can begin a word is carried over to the next line. Since Greek permits a fairly wide range of initial consonant clusters, this rule is not all that helpful to those lacking a knowledge of the language, and it is perhaps easier to define the set of clusters that cannot begin a word. Words cannot begin with (in Greek terms) a mute and its corresponding aspirate, so that πφ, τθ, or κχ must be broken (hence, *Sap-phō, tit-thē, sik-khos*). Combinations of a liquid (λ, ρ) or a nasal (μ, ν) (including γ when it functions as "gamma-nasal") must also be broken (*an-thos, el-pis, er-gma, en-khos* [spelled ἔγχος]), though the group μν, which can begin a word, is not breakable (*me-mnē-mai*). Double consonants are also broken (*tha-las-sa*). Prefixes should be divided from the conjoined word: *eis-phe-rō, an-a-gō, syn-e-khō*. Common prefixes that end in a consonant include *an-, ap-, eis-, ex-, hyp-, hyph-, kat-,* and *kath-*.

Russian

Transliteration   Russian is written in the Cyrillic alphabet, which was in large part adapted from a form of the Greek alphabet used in the early Middle Ages. Several Slavic languages of the Balkan Peninsula, a number of languages spoken in the area of the former Soviet Union, and Mongolian in the Republic of Mongolia are also written in Cyrillic.

The most common ways of transliterating Russian Cyrillic letters are shown below. As can be seen, the majority of letters are transliterated identically in all systems.

Russian alphabet	U.S Board on Geographic Names	Library of Congress system	Slavists' system
А а	a	a	a
Б б	b	b	b
В в	v	v	v
Г г	g	g	g
Д д	d	d	d
Е е	e (ye *initially, after vowels, & after* ъ, ь)	e	e
Ё ё	ë (yë *initially, after vowels, & after* ъ, ь)	ë	ë

Russian alphabet		U.S Board on Geographic Names	Library of Congress system	Slavists' system
Ж	ж	zh	zh	ž
З	з	z	z	z
И	и	i	i	i
Й	й	y (see also below)	ĭ	j
К	к	k	k	k
Л	л	l	l	l
М	м	m	m	m
Н	н	n	n	n
О	о	o	o	o
П	п	p	p	p
Р	р	r	r	r
С	с	s	s	s
Т	т	t	t	t
У	у	u	u	u
Ф	ф	f	f	f
Х	х	kh	kh	x
Ц	ц	ts	t͡s	c
Ч	ч	ch	ch	č
Ш	ш	sh	sh	š
Щ	щ	shch	shch	šč
Ъ	ъ	”	″	″
Ы	ы	y	y	y
Ь	ь	’	′	′
Э	э	e	ė	ė
Ю	ю	yu	i͡u	ju
Я	я	ya	i͡a	ja

The U.S. Board on Geographic Names system is the method most commonly used for rendering place-names and personal names, and is the method preferred by some publishers for bibliographic citations. A variant of this system, which might be called the "general system," omits " and ', so that the Cyrillic letters ъ and ь (called in Russian твердый знак, "hard sign," and мягкий знак, "soft sign") are not represented at all. The "general system" also deals with masculine singular adjective endings differently (see below).

The Library of Congress system is a more faithful rendering of Russian Cyrillic, though as given above, with the ligature marks and diacritics, it is little used outside of library cataloging systems. A completely acceptable compromise is to use the Library of Congress system without the ligature marks over t͡s, i͡u, and i͡a (representing Cyrillic ц, ю, and я) and without the diacritics over ĭ and ė (representing Cyrillic й and э), but retaining ″ and ′ for Cyrillic ъ and ь. This is probably the most commonly used system in, for example, bibliographical citations in books on Russian history intended for anything but the most narrowly specialist audience. (The use of prime marks rather than apostrophes for ъ and ь is preferred, but not absolutely obligatory.)

The Slavists' system borrows c, č, š, and ž from Czech, Croatian, and other Slavic languages written in Roman script; it comes closer than any other system to rendering each Cyrillic letter with one Roman letter. This system is de rigueur in scholarly publications treating Russian literature or linguistics, both for words in text and for bibliography, but it is not often seen in publications aimed at a more general audience.

The Russian letter ё is rarely written with the diacritic outside of dictionaries and textbooks for foreigners, though it differs completely in pronunciation from e, representing [o] instead of [e] in a stressed syllable. It is not usually transliterated as *ë* unless the Russian text in question uses it. Occasionally in the "general system" it will be transliterated *yo* or *o*, especially in names (e.g. *Alyosha*, representing Russian Алёша, conventionally written Алеша). There is no sign of its presence, however, in transliterations such as *Gorbachev* or *Khrushchev* (Russian Горбачёв, Хрущёв, conventionally written Горбачев, Хрущев), which if more phonetically transliterated would be *Gorbachov* and *Khrushchov*.

The endings of masculine singular adjectives (and nouns declined as adjectives, which include many surnames) pose a special problem, because the "general system" typically simplifies the exact Cyrillic transliteration. All four possibilities are shown in the chart below.

Cyrillic	*"General system"*	*U.S.B.G.N.* system	*L.C.* system	*Slavists'* system
-ый	-y	-yy	-yĭ (simplified -yi)	-yj
-ий	-y (*or* -i)	-iy	-iĭ (simplified -ii)	-ij

Hence a name such as Russian Горький, the city now and in the pre-Soviet period known as Нижний Новгород (Nizhnii Novgorod), can be transliterated *Gorky, Gorki, Gor'kiy, Gor'kiĭ, Gor'kii,* or *Gor'kij.*

Punctuation A dash, which may or may not be preceded or followed by a space, is used in a fairly wide number of syntactic situations in Russian. Russian lacks a copular verb in the present tense (i.e., an equivalent of the verb *to be*), and a dash is sometimes used in copular sentences to separate subject and predicate:

> Moya sestra — uchitel'nitsa, a brat — zootekhnik.
>
> Pis'mo Chaadayevu — unikal'nyye «memuary» poeta o tselom periode s iyulya 1834 po oktyabr' 1836 goda.

Guillemets (Russian *kavychki*) serve as quotation marks in Russian. Dialogue in fiction is punctuated much as in other European languages, without quotation marks and with utterances by different speakers indented and beginning with a dash:

> Vse, krome Panteleya, seli vokrug kotla i prinyalis' rabotat' lozhkami.
>
> —Vy! Dayte parnishke lozhku! — strogo zametil Panteley. —Chay, nebos' tozhe est' khochet!
>
> — Nasha eda muzhitskaya!.. — vzdokhnul Kiryukha.

Dialogue within dialogue is placed inside guillemets.

Capitalization Capitalization practices in Russian are not significantly different from those in Western European languages. The first word of a sentence and proper names are capitalized, while the months and days of the week are not. Nouns and adjectives denoting ethnic groups or derived from place-names are not capitalized (*angliyskiy,* "English" (adj.); *anglichanin,* "Englishman"; *moskovskiy,* "of Moscow"; *moskvich,* "inhabitant of Moscow"). In the titles of books and periodicals capitalization extends only to the first word and any other words that would normally be capitalized.

Capitalization patterns for governmental bodies and nongovernmental institutions are idiosyncratic. In the names of major governmental bodies on a national level and major international bodies, all important words may be capitalized (*Verkhovnyy Sovet Rossiyskoy Federatsii,* "Supreme Soviet of the Russian Federation"; *Organizatsiya Ob"edinennykh Natsiy,* "United Nations"; *Sovet Bezopasnosti,* "Security Council"). In the names of bodies deemed to be of lesser importance (especially foreign ones), and in the names of academic and educational institutions, only the first word and proper nouns are capitalized (*Federatsiya nezavisimykh profsoyuzov Rossii,* "Federation of Independent Trade Unions of Russia"; *Verkhovnyy sud SShA,* "U.S. Supreme Court"; *Akademiya nauk Rossii,* "Russian Academy of Science"; *Moskovskiy gosudarstvennyy universitet,* "Moscow State University").

Word Division   Rules for word division at the end of a line are not significantly different in Russian from those in other European languages. A single consonant following a vowel is carried over to the next line, and clusters of two identical consonants are broken in the middle (*lyu-bov', dya-den'-ka, re-bya-ta, mas-sa, kon-nyy*). The letters ъ ("), ь (') and й (y) must not be carried over to the next line. Words containing prefixes should be broken between prefix and stem (*pri-slat', ot-stranyat',* not *pris-lat', ots-tranyat'*), and compounds should be broken between major components (*part-org, spets-stav-ka*). (The most common syllabic prefixes are (in Cyrillic order) *bez-, voz-, vy-, do-, za-, iz-, na-, ne-, o-/ob-, ot-, pere-, po-, pod-, pre-, pri-, pro-, raz-/ras-, so-,* and *u-*.) Naturally, digraphs in transliteration that represent single letters in Cyrillic—including the double digraph *shch* (representing щ)—should not be broken.

Clusters of three or four consonants inside Russian words are quite common. The Russian texts on orthography and punctuation of the last four decades that set out rules for carrying over words tend to be very flexible in regard to ways of breaking such clusters; thus, the word *rodstvo* (родство), for example, can be divided *rod-stvo, rods-tvo,* or *rodst-vo.* The rules promulgated in the U.S. Government Printing Office *Style Manual* (1984), which are recommended by some style manuals, are much more restrictive. They treat clusters of *b, p, g, k, f, v* plus *l* or *r* as unbreakable, as well as *dv, dr, tv, tr, zhd, ml,* and clusters containing *sk* and *st,* including *sk* and *st* themselves. It is not clear that there is any particular virtue in following these rules, and they leave unresolved the question of how to divide words such as *volkhvy* or *skol'zkiy.* For short textual extracts or titles in a bibliography, there is no reason not to be as flexible as the Russians.

Arabic and Hebrew

Transliteration   The transliteration of Arabic and Hebrew are complex subjects that will not be discussed in detail here. This complexity arises in part from the diversity of transcription systems, especially for Arabic. More significant, though, is the fact that, as normally written, neither language indicates all vowels, though it is conventional to transliterate with vowels. (Similar problems arise with other languages written in Arabic script, such as Persian and Urdu.) Hence, it can be quite difficult to accurately transliterate a passage in either language simply with the aid of a dictionary and a minimal knowledge of the writing systems.

In transliterating Arabic, it is conventional to join the definite article *al* to a following noun (e.g, *al-Islam*). Phonetic assimilations of the *l* of *al* to a following consonant are usually not indicated.

Capitalization Neither Arabic nor Hebrew have distinctions between upper- and lowercase, so capitalization is purely a consequence of transliteration. Proper nouns are capitalized when transliterated more or less as in English. The usual practice in citing the titles of books, journals, or articles or the names of organizations is to capitalize only the first word and any proper noun. Book and journal titles are italicized, and titles of articles are placed within quotation marks.

Word Division Divisions should be made in any way that is reasonably close to general European practice, i.e., single consonants after a vowel should be carried to the next line, double consonant groups should be broken, and consonant clusters should be broken in a phonetically plausible-looking manner.

Chinese and Japanese

Romanization—Chinese Chinese is written in a system of logographic characters, in which each character represents both a single syllable and a single word. Chinese characters have their own internal structure, which has no necessary relation to the sound of the syllable. Romanizations of Chinese are based not on the structure of the character but on the sounds of the spoken syllable that correspond to the character. Though the characters are to a large degree superdialectal (that is, they can in theory be given a phonetic value in any Chinese dialect), Romanizations normally give characters the phonetic value they have in Modern Standard Chinese (derived from the "Mandarin" or Northern dialect as spoken in Beijing). Different systems of Romanization exist for other dialects, such as Cantonese.

The two best-known Romanizations rendering the pronunciation of Modern Standard Chinese are the Wade-Giles system, traditionally used in English-speaking countries, and Pinyin, used in the People's Republic of China. Since the introduction of Pinyin into press-agency releases by the People's Republic several decades ago, the use of Pinyin has spread, and Chinese words are now normally written in Pinyin in English-language publications of all varieties, whether journalistic or scholarly. Pinyin has become the norm for both common nouns and proper nouns, including personal names and place-names. The only generally acknowledged exceptions are a handful of historical names, such as Sun Yat-sen and Chiang Kai-shek. (These forms are renderings of their names in southern dialects, and the equivalents in Modern Standard Chinese—*Sun Yixian* and *Jiang Jieshi*, respectively, in Pinyin—are phonetically quite different.)

Place-names present a special problem. A number of traditional English-language names for Chinese cities and provinces—sometimes called the "Postal Atlas" names—have a *k* or *ts* where the Modern Chinese form of the name is spelled with a *q* or *j* in Pinyin. Well-known examples are *Peking* (Modern Standard Chinese: *Beijing* in Pinyin, *Pei-ching* in Wade-Giles), *Tientsin* (*Tianjin* in Pinyin, *T'ien-ching* or *T'ien-chin* in Wade-Giles), *Tsingtao* (*Qingdao* in Pinyin, *Ch'ing-tao* in Wade-Giles). A few other traditional English names (*Canton, Port Arthur*) have no relation at all to the Chinese names (respectively, *Guangzhou* and *Lüshun*). The use of the Modern Chinese name in works of a historical nature can sound anachronistic, and decisions about which form to use should in most cases be left up to the author. The only essential is to maintain consistency.

Tables giving the correspondences between Wade-Giles and Pinyin for all syllables of Modern Standard Chinese can be found in a number of reference works, such as the Chinese-English dictionary published by the Beijing Foreign Languages Institute in 1979 (reprinted in a number of versions by western publishers). Such tables have also appeared in books about China directed toward a general audience, such as Jonathan Spence's *The Search for Modern China* (1990).

Pinyin uses four diacritics (macron, acute accent, haček, and grave accent) to mark the four tones of Modern Standard Chinese. (Superscript numbers serve the same function in the Wade-Giles system.) These tone markings are normally only shown in works of a linguistic character, where they are essential. The apostrophe, which in Wade-Giles distinguishes aspirated from unaspirated consonants, is only used in Pinyin to separate syllables in a compound that could be read as a single syllable (hence the compound place-name *Xi'an* is written with an apostrophe to distinguish it from the single syllable *xian*).

Capitalization—Chinese Capital letters are purely an artifact of Romanization, since the Chinese character system has nothing analogous to lower- or uppercase letters. Personal names and place-names are capitalized, though syllables following a hyphen in a name are normally not capitalized. Treatment of book and periodical titles varies. The usual practice is to capitalize all words of works in classical Chinese literature; for example, *Yi Jing* (known in English as *The Book of Changes*), *Hong Lou Meng* (known in English as *The Dream of the Red Chamber*). Titles of modern works cited in a bibliography, however, usually have only the first word capitalized; likewise, the title of an article would be placed in quotes and have only the first word capitalized. In names of organizations, institutions, movements, etc., usually all words are capitalized, especially if the name is not italicized.

Word Division—Chinese A sensible policy is to divide along the boundaries of Chinese syllables. In Modern Standard Chinese, in which a syllable can only end in a vowel letter, *n, r,* or *ng*, this means that *n* and *r* should not be carried to the next line when they end a syllable, and that *ng* should not be divided.

Romanization—Japanese Japanese is customarily written in a mixture of Chinese characters and characters from two native Japanese syllabaries (in which each written character represents a vowel, a consonant-vowel combination, or the consonant *n*). Depending on factors such as whether or not they occur in a compound, the Chinese characters may be given either a Sino-Japanese reading (representing an old borrowing of the phonetic word from Chinese along with the corresponding character) or a Japanese reading (in which the meaning of the Chinese character is represented by a native Japanese word). An additional complexity is that some Chinese characters have more than one Sino-Japanese reading, owing to the fact that Chinese words were borrowed at different times and from different dialects; the particular reading used in a given compound must simply be learned.

The customary Romanization in use in English is the Hepburn system. It is basically this system which is used in the widely available series of bilingual dictionaries of the Japanese publisher Kenkyusha. (The other major system, the *kunreishiki* or "cabinet ordinance system," is used in Japan and in linguistic publications in the English-speaking world.) In exact Romanizations of Japanese names, titles, or isolated words or phrases, vowel length is shown by a macron, though the common forms of names such as *Tokyo, Kyoto,* or *Togo* conventionally omit the macrons. (Some of Kenkyusha's dictionaries, however, indicate long vowels by doubling the vowel letter.)

Capitalization—Japanese As with Chinese, there is nothing in the Japanese writing system analogous to upper- and lowercase, and capitalization is merely a by-product of Romanization. Romanized titles of literary works usually capitalize only the first word and proper nouns (e.g., *Genji monogatari,* "The Tale of Genji"; *Takahama Kyoshi zenhaiku shū,* "The Collected Haiku Poems of Kyoshi Takahama"). Book and article titles in Japanese are normally treated in bibliographies in the same way as Chinese titles. Institutional and organizational names usually capitalize all words, though names of this sort are so often simply translated that they seldom appear outside of scholarly works.

Word Division—Japanese End-of-line breaks in Japanese pose few problems because Japanese syllables normally end in either a vowel letter or a single *n,* and there are virtually no syllable-initial consonant clusters.

9 Tables and Illustrations

Tables and Graphs   172
Art   193

By means of tables and illustrations, information can frequently be presented more clearly, concisely, or vividly than textual explanation alone can achieve.

Issues of design relating to art are taken up in Chapter 13, "Design and Typography," and issues of printing in Chapter 14, "Typesetting, Printing, and Binding."

Tables and Graphs

Whenever a significant amount of data, especially numerical data, needs to be presented systematically, the author should consider creating a table or graph. However, tables and graphs should never duplicate data already presented in the text itself, and they are generally unnecessary for small amounts of data that can easily be provided in prose. Being somewhat expensive to typeset, tables should be employed only when they can significantly clarify the presentation of data.

Since there often is not enough room for an entire table on the manuscript page where it would be expected to appear, tables in a manuscript are traditionally provided on pages separate from the rest of the manuscript, one table to a page; only the briefest tables are generally integrated with the manuscript text. These table pages are not numbered sequentially with the rest of the manuscript; instead, each should be marked with the number of the manuscript page where it is first referred to—for example, "msp. 29"—and often the author's last name as well.

The author should mark, in the manuscript page margin, the point where any unnumbered table should go (e.g., "Insert College Degrees table here"), or leave a wide space in the manuscript for a note ("[College Degrees table]"). If the tables are numbered and a reference appears in the text (e.g., "This discipline continues to grow, as shown in Table 3.19"), the copy editor will usually call out such references. In addition, the editor or designer will normally give the typesetter a blanket instruction, in the design specs or elsewhere, that each table should be inserted as close as possible to the first text reference.

Today both manuscript and tables will normally be prepared on computer, and standard computer programs permit tables to be inserted anywhere. In normal screen view, tables are unaffected by page breaks. To ensure that manuscript tables print out with as few breaks as possible, the author can insert page breaks immediately above and below each table.

Because of the complex formatting required for typesetting, even computer-generated tables will almost always be entirely rekeyed by the typesetter. Nevertheless, tables in manuscript should look much as they are intended to look in print, except that they should normally be double-spaced. Only runover lines in column heads and items should be single-spaced. If the author specifies a table with horizontal rules, these should be drawn in pencil.

Standard word-processing programs usually offer a variety of automatic table formats, many with shaded backgrounds. Though shading or color may look attractive on-screen, only the simplest black-and-white designs should be submitted to a publisher, especially if camera-ready tables have been requested. Shading requires halftone screening and rarely improves the clarity of printed tables.

Tables should always exhibit several essential qualities:

1. *Simplicity* Strive for concision. A series of short tables may be more useful than one long and complex table.

2. *Consistency* If the table consists of words rather than figures, all the entries in a column should be grammatically parallel. Aim for consistency in terminology, abbreviations, and format within all related tables.

3. *Compactness* Omit any redundant material. Consider combining two tables whenever one column appears identically in both.

4. *Clarity* Choose the column headings and stub items judiciously. Figures are easier to compare when arranged vertically than horizontally. Make figures easy to interpret; for example, consider adding an extra column of percentages next to a column of figures if the percentages would make the raw numbers more meaningful, or vice versa.

Readability is another consideration, but one often left primarily to the editor or designer. The design should make the columns as even as possible and allow adequate space between them for clarity but avoid leaving excessive space. In long or wide tables, a horizontal line space or rule after every fifth entry (or even every other entry) can help guide the reader's eye.

The best way for an author to absorb the principles of table creation is to study published tables from a variety of good sources.

Tables for magazine or journal articles must often conform to the publication's specific styling requirements. The author should scan back issues for examples of the preferred style. Tables published in books usually need only be styled consistently with the other tables in the same book.

Table Elements

Table number In works that contain only a few tables, they may be unnumbered and may be cited by phrases such as "the table above" and "in the following table." But in texts with a significant number of tables, they are almost always identified by number. The accompanying text should always refer specifically to each table in turn—by means of a reference such as "The results of a recent survey, shown in Table 9.3," "Table 9.3 shows the results of a recent survey,"or simply "See Table 9.3"—and the text reference should precede the table.

Tables should normally be numbered separately from illustrations (including graphs), since they are traditionally handled separately at all stages of production.

Tables may be numbered consecutively throughout an entire book, or as a separate series within each chapter. In the chapter-by-chapter system, Table 2.1 (or Table 2-1) would be the first table of Chapter 2, Table 3.14 (or Table 3-14) would be the fourteenth table of Chapter 3, and so on. In journals, tables are numbered article by article, each beginning with Table 1. In books, chapter-by-chapter enumeration is often desirable for the editor, who would otherwise have to renumber every subsequent table in the book if a single table were removed or added.

The table number is usually set above the table, either flush left or centered, with the title directly below it. Alternatively, it may be set on the same line as the title, usually separated from the title by a period, a dash, or an em space. When set on a separate line, it is often set all-capitalized (e.g., "TABLE 3.4" or "TABLE 3-4"); when run in with the title, its style often matches that of the title.

Title The title of a table, like all caption titles, should be concise. The title should be a noun or a noun phrase (e.g., "Social Interation in Mobile Home Parks"). Any extra information can be provided in a brief parenthetical tag or subtitle, the column heads, a table footnote, or the text. Articles (*a, an, the*) are usually omitted, as are unnecessary phrases like "Summary of," and no period follows the title.

Table titles are usually capitalized *headline-style;* that is, all words except for internal articles, coordinating conjunctions, prepositions, and the *to* of infinitives are capitalized. Occasionally only the first word and proper nouns are capitalized, in what is known as *sentence-style* capitalization. Capitals-and-small-capitals style (e.g., "INCIDENCE OF DENGUE IN SELECTED CONGO TOWNS") is also acceptable, though less widely used. All three styles are preferred to an all-capitalized title.

Titles of tables of numerical data often end with a brief parenthetical explanation of some aspect of the data that follows. The phrase "(in thousands)," or simply "(000)," allows the author to eliminate the extra zeros in a table consisting of round numbers. Thus, 450,000 would become 450; 3,500 would become 3.5; and so on. Other such phrases include "(percent)," or "(%)"— meaning that all the figures represent percentages—and "(for the year ended Dec. 31, 1997)." The note "(1990 = 1)" or "(1990 = 100%)" would be used for annual economic data expressed as a proportion or percentage of the figures for 1990. "(N = 532)" would indicate the number of individuals in a surveyed group, which might be discussed only in percentage terms in the table itself. If the title is short, such information may be included in the title itself—for example, "World Sales in Thousands of Dollars" or "U.S. Fiber Consumption (millions of pounds) and Prices (dollars per pound)."

The title may be followed by a *headnote* explaining some aspect of the table, such as how the data were obtained or limitations in the data. More often, such explanations appear in a note below the table.

Stub The leftmost column of a table is called the *stub.* Tables are usually defined as consisting of both rows and columns; thus, a stub is a component of any proper table. (This distinguishes tables from parallel lists with headings.) Stub items can obviously be regarded as headings in just the way that column heads are. To reflect this, the stub sometimes will be italicized; more rarely, it will be set boldface. However, the stub has traditionally tended not to be distinguished typographically from the column entries at all.

A heading over the stub is not always necessary; for example, the heading "Year" may usually be omitted over a stub consisting of a list of years. When provided, such headings are usually set flush left even if the other column heads are centered.

The stub items, like items in any list, should be logically and grammatically parallel. They are normally capitalized sentence-style. They are not numbered. (In the rare instances when the items are referred to by number in the text, an Arabic number in parentheses precedes each item.)

Occasionally brief notations such as "(in dollars)" or "(at end of year)" may follow a stub item instead of being set as footnotes.

Stub items sometimes require headings within the stub itself. These headings may be set off by indenting all the items below them; they may additionally or alternatively be set in italics, boldface, or all-capitals. If the headings are boldface, the items will usually be roman. Extra line spacing may be added above and below each set of items under a head. Rarely, two levels of heads may be required within the stub. Extra indention, with or without added line spacing and a third type style, is usually required to distinguish the second-level heads.

When such headings are used, no data usually appears in each heading's own row. However, a row of totals may sometimes appear in the heading row, while the data that sum to those totals appear in the item rows below. See the following two alternative versions.

	Amount ($000)	Percent of sales
Standard cost of goods sold		
Prime costs	860,000	40
Factory overhead	740,000	35
Total standard cost	1,600,000	75
or		
Standard cost of goods sold	**1,600,000**	**75**
Prime costs	860,000	40
Factory overhead	740,000	35

When stub items run over to a second line, the runover line standardly aligns horizontally with the corresponding entries to its right. However, if at least one of the corresponding items has a runover, the first lines of the stub item and each item to its right should align.

When an unavoidably long stub item runs over to a second line, the runover line is usually indented one em space (about two character spaces). If any of the stub lines are headings governing indented stub items below them, any runovers—whether of headings or of the items below them—should be indented one em more than the indented items.

When a stub includes at least one level of heading, the heading may often be turned into a *cut-in heading* (also called a *crosshead* or *table spanner*). Cut-in headings govern the entire width of the table (and are usually centered on the table's width) but are inserted, or *cut in,* under the column heads; thus, the table title and the column heads are not repeated. See Table 9.1 for an illustration of the parts of a table described in this and the following sections.

Column headings   *Column headings* are words or concise phrases (usually noun phrases) that categorize the data below them. The column head should not be much wider than the widest items in the column beneath it; narrowing the head may result in one or more runover lines. There should be at least an em space between the widest parts of adjacent headings.

Table 9.1   The Parts of a Table

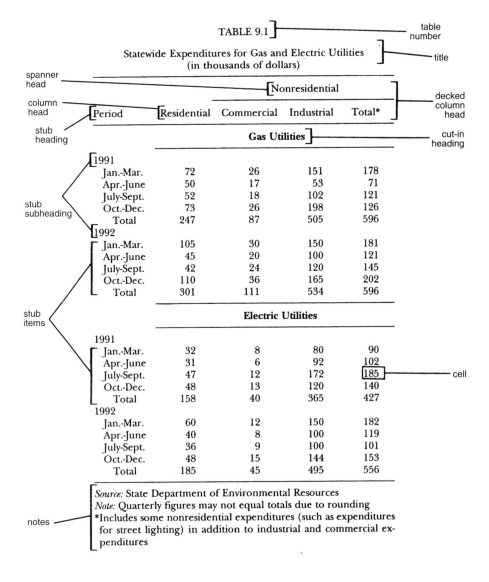

TABLE 9.1 — table number

Statewide Expenditures for Gas and Electric Utilities
(in thousands of dollars) — title

Period	Residential	Nonresidential		
		Commercial	Industrial	Total*
Gas Utilities				
1991				
Jan.-Mar.	72	26	151	178
Apr.-June	50	17	53	71
July-Sept.	52	18	102	121
Oct.-Dec.	73	26	198	126
Total	247	87	505	596
1992				
Jan.-Mar.	105	30	150	181
Apr.-June	45	20	100	121
July-Sept.	42	24	120	145
Oct.-Dec.	110	36	165	202
Total	301	111	534	596
Electric Utilities				
1991				
Jan.-Mar.	32	8	80	90
Apr.-June	31	6	92	102
July-Sept.	47	12	172	185
Oct.-Dec.	48	13	120	140
Total	158	40	365	427
1992				
Jan.-Mar.	60	12	150	182
Apr.-June	40	8	100	119
July-Sept.	36	9	100	101
Oct.-Dec.	48	15	144	153
Total	185	45	495	556

Labels for the figure: spanner head, column head, stub heading, stub subheading, stub items, notes; and decked column head, cut-in heading, cell.

Source: State Department of Environmental Resources
Note: Quarterly figures may not equal totals due to rounding
*Includes some nonresidential expenditures (such as expenditures for street lighting) in addition to industrial and commercial expenditures

Column heads are frequently set with headline-style capitalization, though sentence-style capitalization and all-capitals are also used. Roman, boldface, and italic type are all commonly used for column heads. Any abbreviations, figures, or symbols used in column heads should observe the same style used in the body of the table. A period never follows a column head.

Column heads may be positioned horizontally in various ways. They may be set flush left over the column, flush right over the column, or centered over the column. Only long words should be divided.

Since neither the stub column head nor the rightmost column head should ever run into the margin, the design must be altered if centering either head would force it to do so. Thus, the stub column head is frequently set flush left on the table itself (the stub items may also be set flush left, even if the following columns are all set flush right), and the right-hand column head is frequently set flush right.

Since most columns of numbers are right-aligned, their heads are also often right-aligned above them. Headings over word columns, and the columns themselves, may be left-aligned (since this is typical of standard prose). Tables with gridlines tend to look best when the headings are centered horizontally (and vertically) within the cells or grid boxes.

The visual effect is the paramount consideration. Thus, the editor should ideally consider the actual manuscript tables, test the effect of various alternative designs on them, and choose one design that will best serve most of the book's tables, and convey any recommendations to the designer. If the design must be slightly altered for a few tables, it is unlikely that the reader will notice, but the goal should be a consistent appearance for the entire book.

When column heads are of different lengths, they may align at either top or bottom; such alignment should be consistent from table to table.

Column heads should normally be set horizontally—that is, like all the rest of the text—but may be set vertically if necessary to save space. A combination of horizontal and vertical column heads in one table is acceptable, but the stub column head is never set vertically. Vertical column heads are generally set flush left on the column.

Like a table title, a column head may be followed by a brief phrase that explains something about the data below. (See "Title" above.) A phrase may apply to more than one column head by being spread across both columns:

1990   1995
(thousands of dollars)

In such cases, however, the phrase may really belong in the table title.

A *spanner head* governs two or more column heads below it. It may or may not be set in larger type than the column heads or in a different type style; it is normally followed by a rule below that spans the width of the affected columns. The combination of a spanner head and the column heads below it is often called a *decked head*, since it consists of two decks or tiers. (These may also be termed *stacked heads*.)

two-column spanner head:	Temperature	
	Maximum	Minimum

four-column spanner head:	Dissolved oxygen (ppm)			
	Mean	Range	Mean saturation (%)	Saturation range (%)

A decked head may occasionally consist of three tiers of headings; however, such headings may become hard to read and can often be avoided.

Columns The table's data appear as items in its columns; the combined data are often called the table *body* or *field*.

Words in columns are capitalized sentence-style or not at all. If the column head or the table title specifies such things as units of measurement—e.g., "(ppm)" or "($US)"—these are not repeated in the columns.

A column head may occasionally have no meaningful application to a particular stub item, in which case the point where the stub row intersects with the column—called a *cell*—either is left blank or shows the abbreviation "NA" or "n.a.," meaning "not applicable." A centered em dash, or three or more ellipsis points, conventionally means "data not available." (It is sometimes important to distinguish between "not applicable" and "not available," though not all tables do, and ellipsis points or "NA" are often used for both. The author may wish to explain such symbols in a general footnote.) When a quantity is zero, a zero appears in the cell.

Some tables increase their data-holding capacity by adding extra information to items in a column instead of adding another column. This is commonly done when adding raw numbers to a list of percentages that reflect them or when showing two units of measurement.

Alignment Table columns must be precisely aligned horizontally and vertically. A stub item must always align horizontally with the row it governs. As mentioned earlier, the last runover line of a stub item, rather than the first line, normally aligns with the corresponding data to its right. However, if the column entries themselves have runovers, the first lines of both the stub item and the column item should align (see Table 9.3).

Vertical alignment is equally important. Items are seldom centered within a column. Words are nearly always set flush left on the column. A column of whole numbers usually aligns flush right; a column that includes some mixed fractions (e.g., "4 3/4") aligns on the rightmost whole digit; and a column of decimal numbers aligns on the decimal points.

Commas in numbers will naturally affect their alignment. Normally commas mark off each group of three digits to the left of the decimal point in all tabular numbers.

In columns that contain dollar amounts, decimal points and zeros are omitted when the columns contain only whole-dollar amounts. However, if at least one of the amounts contains a cents figure, the decimal points and zeros must be added throughout.

In a column consisting only of dollar amounts, the dollar sign is usually placed (1) next to the first item, (2) next to the total amount if there is one, and (3) next to the first item following any break in the column such as a subheading, a subtotal, or a horizontal rule. If some of the items are not dollar amounts—for instance, if some amounts are measured in foreign currency—the dollar sign must be repeated as needed. In a stub, dollar signs should be repeated with all dollar amounts.

Dollar signs should normally align down the column; thus, the dollar sign beside the top number may be followed by one or more spaces. Exceptions occur (1) when not every item in the column is a dollar amount, or (2) when the column contains inclusive figures that consist of two dollar amounts, in which case the internal connecting symbols align instead.

$7–9	$10 to $50
$102–123	$50 to $150
$24–30	$150 to $200
$1,014–1,178	

The conventional rules for listing decimal numbers are listed below.

Decimal places should not be carried farther than necessary; rounded-off numbers usually provide enough data for valid comparisons. When some numbers in a column are carried one or two places to the right of the decimal point, however, the others should normally add one or two zeros as necessary to align them at the right.

3.85
18.00
12.50
7.00

In columns consisting of decimal fractions both greater than and less than a whole number, a zero is usually added to the unit column on the left of each decimal fraction that is less than a whole number. If all the items are decimal fractions less than a whole number, the zero is optional; however, a zero is traditionally added to the very first number in the column if it is less than a whole number.

5.43	0.4
0.20	.6
0.60	.6782
8.81	.3

A lone zero is usually aligned in the unit column without a decimal point; in some tables, the zero is centered in the column or the zero amount appears as "0.0."

67.2	67.2	67.2
54.3	54.3	54.3
0	0	0.0
56.0	56.0	56.0

Columns consisting entirely of decimal fractions align on the decimal points.

Columns with combinations of figures and words may align on the right or the left or may be centered.

When parentheses enclose some of the items in a column (indicating a negative amount in economic data), the figures usually align on the right, with the closing parenthesis falling just outside the column.

Plus or minus signs that appear at the left of a set of figures do not affect the vertical alignment. The symbols themselves may be aligned, but more often they are set close to the figures. A plus or minus sign that follows a figure falls outside the right-alignment.

A column consisting only of Roman numerals aligns at the left.

Aligning a column of dates may require that extra space be inserted. The dates in some tables may look better centered.

Sept	27	1898
Oct	3	1899
Nov	13	1899–1900
		1901–2

If the stub consists of a column of dates, the month alone may be set well to the left for the sake of clarity.

Oct	10
	20
	31
Nov	10
	20
	30

Totals The word "Total" usually appears at the foot of the stub, and the total figures themselves in one or more columns to the right. The word may be omitted if the figures are obviously totals. "Total" is typically indented farther than any other stub item; grand totals are usually indented farther than subtotals.

Total numbers should be highlighted in some way. They may be set bold; more often, they are set off with a line space above and below. Sometimes there is a short horizontal rule above the total (representing the addition line under the last number in an addition column), and sometimes also—primarily in accounting tables—a double underscore below; these are set the full width of the total figure, including the currency sign.

In a column consisting of percentages that add up to 100 percent, the total is optional. If the numbers do not add up to 100 percent, an exact total percentage should be given, along with a general footnote such as "Percentages do not equal 100 because of rounding."

As mentioned, totals and subtotals will sometimes appear opposite a stub heading and above the items they sum. In such cases, the heading usually is set flush left and often in boldface type.

Columns of words Some tables consist of words rather than figures. Since such *word tables* are often intended to be read like text, they tend to use abbreviations sparingly, though articles are often omitted.

Word tables look best when they are simple, with brief entries and no rules. Runover lines are often indented, as in Table 9.2, unless rules or line spaces serve to separate one item from another. If the columns include long

Table 9.2 Beaufort Scale

Beaufort Number	Name	Wind Speed		Description
		mph	kph	
0	calm	<1	<1	calm; smoke rises vertically
1	light air	1–3	1–5	direction of wind shows by smoke but not by wind vanes
2	light breeze	4–7	6–11	wind felt on face; leaves rustle; wind vane moves
3	gentle breeze	8–12	12–19	leaves and small twigs in constant motion; wind extends light flag
4	moderate breeze	13–18	20–28	wind raises dust and loose paper; small branches move

items with runover lines, these usually align at the left. If the items are brief—say a word or two, with few or no runover lines—the columns may look best centered.

Rules Rules are sometimes used in tables to guide the reader's eye and to separate densely packed columns or rows of figures. Rules can usually be replaced by horizontal and vertical spacing, as they generally are today. An author submitting a table for publication should omit most rules, since the decision whether to use rules is best left to the editor or designer.

Tables conventionally use only three full-width horizontal rules: one below the title, one below the column heads, and one below the table but often above any footnotes. Any or all of these may be omitted. Rules below spanner heads are set exactly the width of the columns governed by the head. Cut-in heads may have full-width rules above and below them. Additional external rules may separate the entire table from the text above and below.

Most table rules are either hairline or half-point rules, but heavier rules may be used to set off larger divisions. A very complex table might use double rules below the caption and at the end of the table, and heavy single rules below column heads, decked heads, and cut-in heads.

Vertical rules are sometimes used to separate columns, especially in crowded statistical tables. But where enough space is provided between columns, vertical rules are usually not necessary. Vertical rules are often used to separate the halves of doubled tables (see page 185). When vertical rules are needed, the columns—but not necessarily each column item—should be centered between the rules. Cut-in heads should have space above and below them that interrupts any vertical rules.

Other table elements *Leaders* are periods set in a row to guide the eye from one column (usually the stub) to the next. They are spaced like ellipsis points, and each point aligns vertically with those above and below it. Since they look somewhat old-fashioned and tend to clutter a table, they are rarely used today. Instead, the space between columns is usually shrunk to make the horizontal alignment more evident, which may require breaking or shortening a few of the stub entries. Alternatively, a line space or rule after every fifth entry, or even light background shading of alternate entries or alternate groups of five entries, can aid the eye in a similar way (see Table 9.3).

Table 9.3 Nations of the World

Country	Area			Population (latest est.)	
	square miles	square kilometers	rank	total (midyear 1995)	rank
Botswana	224,607	581,730	47	1,549,000	145
Brazil	3,300,171	8,547,404	5	155,822,000	5
Brunei	2,226	5,765	167	281,000	173
Bulgaria	42,855	110,994	103	8,406,000	82
Burkina Faso	105,946	274,400	73	10,324,000	71
Burundi	10,740	27,816	145	5,936,000	95
Cambodia	70,238	181,916	89	9,608,000	76
Cameroon	183,569	475,442	53	13,233,000	60
Canada	3,849,674	9,970,610	2	29,463,000	32
Cape Verde	1,557	4,033	169	392,000	169
Central African Republic	240,324	622,436	43	3,141,000	128
Chad	495,755	1,284,000	22	6,361,000	93
Chile	292,135	756,626	38	14,210,000	59
China	3,696,100	9,572,900	3	1,206,600,000	1

Braces may occasionally be used to enclose adjacent items in a column to indicate a subcategory.

	% of total value	% of labor force
Agriculture	10.3	71.4
Mining	58.2⎫	
Manufacturing	2.5	
Construction	1.9	
Finance	0.9 ⎬	10.0
Trade	6.1	
Public utilities	0.3	
Transportation and communications	2.3⎭	
Public administration, defense⎫		
Services ⎬	17.5⎬	18.6
Other ⎭		
TOTAL	100.0	100.0

Footnotes Tables are frequently footnoted. Table footnotes may include notes lacking reference symbols that identify the table's source, explain the meaning of abbreviations, or describe the limitations of the data, and notes indicated by a number or other reference mark that explain specific items in a column.

Footnotes are positioned just below the table and often set in smaller type. Footnotes begin flush left; runover lines are either set flush left or indented to align below the first word of the footnote (rather than the reference number or symbol).

The author often has a choice of whether to include certain data in the table itself or in footnotes. Sometimes a column or row with very few different values can be removed from the table and the information moved to a couple of footnotes. If a table has too many notes, on the other hand, the author may move footnote information to column heads or add a new column of data.

The three common types of footnotes are source notes, other general notes, and specific notes, and they should be listed in that order.

Source notes The first note below the table is often a *source note.* Source notes are required when the table is reprinted from another source or when the table's data were derived from another source. (The author must generally obtain written permission to use such copyrighted material; see "Copyright and Permissions" beginning on page 319.)

The form of the source note should match the bibliographic style used elsewhere in the work (see section beginning on page 210). When borrowed data has been used in a new table, the note is commonly introduced by the word *"Source:"* (or *"Sources:"*) or *"Note:"* or by phrases such as "Data from . . ." or "Adapted with permission from. . . ." When an entire table or part of a table is being reprinted, the page on which the original table was published should be included.

Source notes are sometimes set as headnotes just below the table title; this more prominent position may be specifically requested by a copyright holder.

Other general notes General notes contain information pertaining to the table as a whole, such as the quality of the data, how the data were obtained, and the meaning of any nonstandard abbreviations or symbols used throughout the table. A general note is normally unnumbered and often introduced instead by the word "Note" below the table; if a table has more than one general note, the notes should be run together in a paragraph headed "Notes." A single important note may be designated a headnote and placed below the title.

Specific notes Specific footnotes are introduced by reference marks—superscript numbers, letters, or symbols—that correspond to the reference marks that follow specific items in the table. Each note may begin on a separate line, or the notes may run together like general notes, each separated from the next by a space of about two ems.

If numbers are used for note references in the text, tables should use either superscript lowercase letters or the older footnote symbols for their own footnotes. (In mathematical tables, superscript numbers or letters both might be mistaken for exponents and so should be avoided in any case.) The traditional footnote symbols are used in the order *, †, ‡, §, ‖, ¶, #. When there are fewer than five footnotes, the asterisk and dagger may be used in the order *, **, †, ††.

Each table should have its own set of notes. Each set of specific footnotes begins with a [1], [a], or *. It is best to sequence the footnote symbols in reading order: row by row, from left to right. Any reference mark may be used more than once within a table; in fact, it is common for a single footnote to explain more than one item in a table.

Reference marks are positioned directly after the pertinent figure or word with no intervening space. Footnote symbols hang in the space between columns and do not affect alignment.

An item may carry reference marks to two or more separate footnotes (e.g., "405[a,c]" or "405[1,3]").

Instead of superscript figures or letters, a few publications prefer to use parenthesized footnote reference marks—lowercase letters, numbers, or even capital letters—set on the baseline. If such nontraditional reference marks are used, they should be clearly identified as footnote symbols.

Table Length and Width

A table should ideally fit onto a single page. An editor who discovers that a table is too large to do so should look for ways to reduce it. If none of the standard methods works, the table may have to be set broadside, across a page spread, or on successive pages.

Reducing table size The author should be encouraged at the outset to bear in mind the realities of page size when designing any original tables. Often a table that is too wide may simply be broken by the author into two separate tables, and a long table may be reconceived into a shorter one.

When a table looks as though it will be too wide or long when typeset, its width or length should be systematically checked. This has traditionally required making a careful count of its lines (for length) and characters per line (for width). However, tables created on computer and submitted on diskette permit author and editor to experiment with electronically reformatting a large table in a variety of ways.

If the table is too wide, consider the following ways of narrowing it:

1. If any stub items or column heads are too long, try to devise a shorter phrasing that will still be clear and accurate.
2. Replace words in the stub or column heads with standard abbreviations. Any abbreviations that will not be readily understood may be explained in a footnote. (Ideally, any word abbreviated in one table should be abbreviated in all of them.)
3. Run any long stub items or column heads onto a second line; divide individual words if necessary.
4. If any long entries within a column are contributing to the table's excessive width, consider whether an element common to all the entries in the column could be incorporated into the column head instead.
5. If one or several items in a column includes some special element, consider replacing it with a footnote reference and using the footnote to explain it.

6. Consider splitting the table in two. If the column categories are not closely related to each other, this may actually result in a clearer presentation of the data.

While wide tables can often be narrowed, long tables are frequently hard to shorten, especially if the number of stub items is fixed (listing all the nations of the world, for example). However, it may turn out that all the stub items need not actually appear in the same table, and that a shorter table may actually make the data more accessible.

If necessary, a table may be reversed, the stub items becoming the column heads and vice versa. Obviously, this will be useful only where the table's shape will change significantly as a result, and is not desirable if it makes the column heads inconsistent with those of other similar tables.

As a final option, a large table may simply be photographically reduced, so that it appears with smaller type than the rest of the tables. The table number and title should, if possible, be kept at their full size.

Broadside tables Large tables that are broader than they are long may often be set broadside, with the stub at the bottom of the page. Such tables should be set on a left-hand page if possible. If the table is shorter than the page is wide, it is centered on the page. The running head and folio are usually omitted on broadside pages.

When broadside tables begin on a verso (left-hand) page and continue onto a recto (right-hand) page, there is no need to repeat the column heads or a heading within the stub, but if the table runs over to the next verso page these heads should be repeated. A two-page broadside table should always begin on a verso page. (See "Continued tables" below.)

Doubled tables Some tables are so long and narrow that they may be divided into two (or more) sections which are run side by side below the title. Column heads are repeated over each section and must align horizontally. If the table divides under a heading in the stub, the heading must be repeated. A vertical rule may separate the table sections. (See Table 9.4.)

Table 9.4 Easter Dates

Year	Ash Wednesday	Easter	Year	Ash Wednesday	Easter
1997	Feb. 12	Mar. 30	2005	Feb. 9	Mar. 27
1998	Feb. 25	Apr. 12	2006	Mar. 1	Apr. 16
1999	Feb. 17	Apr. 4	2007	Feb. 21	Apr. 8
2000	Mar. 8	Apr. 23	2008	Feb. 6	Mar. 23
2001	Feb. 28	Apr. 15	2009	Feb. 25	Apr. 12
2002	Feb. 13	Mar. 31	2010	Feb. 17	Apr. 4
2003	Mar. 5	Apr. 20	2011	Mar. 9	Apr. 24
2004	Feb. 25	Apr. 11	2012	Feb. 22	Apr. 8

A table that is very wide but not long may, as a last resort, be divided in two and its second half set below its first half. The stub items must naturally be repeated in the second half. (See Table 9.5.)

Table 9.5 Doubled Table

Price and Earnings Indexes (1985=100)

	1987	1988	1989	1990
Consumer price index	105.7	109.9	115.2	121.4
Hourly earnings index	103.9	106.7	110.0	113.6
	1991	1992	1993	1994
Consumer price index	126.6	130.4	134.2	137.0
Hourly earnings index	117.3	120.1	123.0	125.9

Spread-width tables Spread-width tables are very wide tables spread across two facing pages. The number and title may be set on the left-hand page; if they are instead centered over the table, breaking between the two pages, no words should be divided at the break. At the point where the table divides, the two parts should be flush against the inside margins. If a spanner head or cut-in head will govern columns on both pages, it should be repeated on the new page, followed by "(continued)" or "(cont.)." If necessary to aid the reader, the stub items may be repeated in the far right-hand column of the facing page.

Footnote symbols used in spread-width tables are sequenced from left to right horizontally across the spread, row by row. The number of footnote lines on each page should be approximately equal; however, if all the references occur on the right-hand page, all the notes should appear there.

Continued tables *Continued tables* are tables that require at least one page turn to be read.

Continued tables present no particular problems to the author working on a computer. If a long table is not created on computer, the author should type "Table continued" at the bottom of the first page, and the table number followed by "(cont.)" at the top of any succeeding pages. Column heads should be repeated on each new page. If the table breaks under a heading within the stub, the heading should be repeated, followed by "(cont.)."

On the typeset pages, unnumbered general notes and numbered footnotes that refer to column heads should be set at the foot of the first page of the table; they are not repeated on the succeeding pages. Other numbered footnotes should generally appear on the page where the reference occurs; a numbered note that refers to items on more than one page may be repeated on each page where the reference appears. In very long tables, all the numbered footnotes may be placed at the end of the table.

Copyediting and Proofreading Tables

The copy editor is always responsible for checking the accuracy and presentation of tables, which will often require even more concentrated attention than the rest of the text. (See Chapter 12, "Production Editing, Copyediting, and Proofreading.")

If the tables will not be numbered in the published work, each should be given a temporary production number by the copy editor. This, along with the author's last name and the number of the manuscript page where the table is first referred to, should be written at the top of each table page.

The first reference to each table should be marked in the margin of the manuscript if the author has not already done so.

All tables must be evaluated in their textual context. If any table essentially duplicates the text, the author should be queried as to whether either the table or the redundant text should be deleted. If information in the table and text conflicts, the author must be asked which should prevail. References to the tables within the text must be checked for appropriateness and accuracy.

The copy editor should ask a series of questions about every table.

Is the title brief, clear, appropriate, and accurate?

Does each column head and stub item make sense?

Are the columns and rows properly aligned?

Are any italics and boldface used consistently? Is capitalization consistent? Does the styling conform with the design specs?

Are all figures consistently styled as to number of decimal places, commas, currency symbols, etc.?

Are all totals correct?

Are the abbreviations necessary, consistent, and understandable?

Do the footnotes correspond with their reference marks? Are they in proper sequence and consistently styled?

After the initial editing pass through the manuscript, the copy editor should subsequently review all the tables as a group, so as to catch any stylistic and factual inconsistencies from table to table.

Wherever rules and gridlines are shown, the in-house editor should be asked whether these are to be retained. If the copy editor has been given the design specifications, it may be possible to mark any necessary rule deletions or additions.

The copy editor should watch for any particularly wide or long tables. Though it usually is not the copy editor's responsibility to cut down such tables, they should be flagged to draw the author's and in-house editor's attention to them. When a table will have to be set broadside or spread-width, the editor or copy editor should instruct the typesetter to "Set table broadside" or "Set table across facing pages." A table that will have to be continued to a second page should be marked "Begin table on left-hand page."

Since continued tables will rarely break at the same point on the printed page as in the manuscript, the design specs should specify how they are to be handled. If the specs fail to do so, the editor (not usually the copy editor) should write special specs stating where the table number or title and column heads should be repeated, and where "continued" lines should appear and how they should be styled.

Proofreading typeset tables requires special attention to alignment, spacing, and typography. If the tables are not incorporated with the text in the first proofs, any editorial notations written on the manuscript that concern the positioning of the table may have to be carried to the margins of the proofs (e.g., "Insert Table 3.19 about here," or simply "Table 3.19"). In page proofs, the proofreader must check for any references like "the table below" to see if they correspond to the actual placement of the table. Any spread-width tables must be checked to ensure that they align across the two pages. (This alignment will have to be checked once again at the blues stage.)

Graphs and Maps

Graphs, in the broad sense of the word—that is, diagrams that display data graphically, for the sake of vividness or concision—straddle the boundary between tables and art. Graphs that are not submitted as camera-ready art by the publisher can usually be set by the typesetter. Depending on their design, graphs may be line art or continuous-tone art, black-and-white or colored. (See "Art" beginning on page 193.)

Pie charts One of the simplest graph styles is the *pie chart,* which marks sections of a circle to show the proportional parts of a whole, in percentages or numbers (see Figure 9.1). The size of each section is determined by converting these numbers to the appropriate number of degrees within a 360° circle. The best pie charts are often those with fewest sections: more than six or seven may make a chart too complex. Pie charts have traditionally been arranged clockwise from 12 o'clock, with the largest section first and the smallest section last, but this arrangement is entirely optional today. Each section usually has a distinctive pattern or shading or color, all of which are identified in a legend next to the chart. Alternatively, all the section labels may appear outside the circle next to their appropriate sections, in which case shading or patterns are unnecessary. Labels placed inside the sections themselves are often less successful, since the narrowness of the smallest sections often forces those labels to be severely abbreviated or simply moved outside the circle.

Pie charts are now almost always created on computer, since even an ordinary office program can transform raw numerical data into a correctly proportioned pie chart.

Figure 9.1   Pie Chart

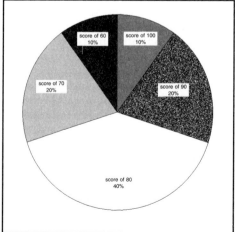

Bar and column graphs *Bar graphs*, like the one illustrated in Figure 9.2, can supply a great deal of information in a compact space by using bars of various lengths. Like pie charts, bar graphs make proportional comparisons visually compelling, but the bar form allows the display of more information than pie charts. First, a large number of bars may be used. In addition, each bar may be subdivided into sections so that different kinds of data (such as data for three different years) can be shown within a single bar. Alternatively, such data may be presented in groups of multiple bars, each bar representing a unit to be compared with the others in the group. Regardless of the bar graph's design, the various types of data may be distinguished by the color, pattern, or shading of each bar or bar section.

Figure 9.2 Bar or Column Graph

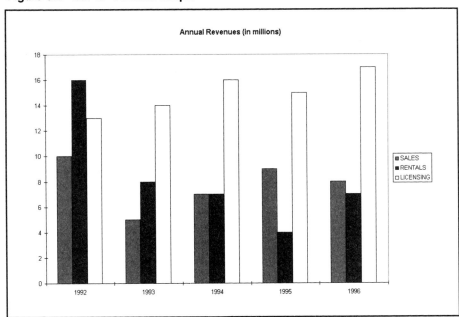

The bars may be either horizontal or vertical. Vertical bar graphs are often called *column graphs.* On a column graph, the categories of variables are listed across the bottom, the units of measure along the vertical axis. On a horizontal graph, the categories are listed at the left (see Figure 9.3), the units of measurement at the bottom. The length of the labels (on either axis) may dictate which type of bar graph to use. Lengthy category labels can usually be accommodated more easily on a horizontal graph, lengthy measurement labels more easily on a vertical graph. However, it is generally best to stick with a single graph orientation throughout a given work.

The bars may extend below the horizontal axis (on a column graph) or to the left of the vertical axis (on a horizontal graph) to indicate losses or other

Figure 9.3 Horizontal Bar Graph

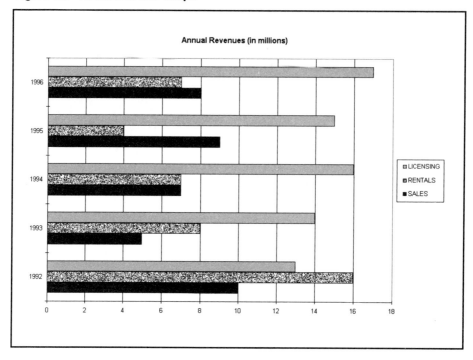

negative numbers. Obviously, the value or measurement axis must also be extended below or to the left on such graphs.

Like pie charts, bar graphs are generally created on computers today. The user selects a desired type of graph, selects a pattern or color to symbolize each kind of data, and enters on a standard table the data to be illustrated, and the computer automatically generates the proportioned image and legend. One standard design option allows for a variety of "three-dimensional" bar-graph designs; however, this purely decorative option—in no sense does such a design add a new "dimension" to the data—may impair rather than enhance the clarity of the data's presentation.

Line graphs Line graphs depict a continuous process, such as a change over a period of time, by means of one or more lines plotted on a grid. Like bar graphs, line graphs have traditionally been plotted on graph paper. (Light-blue gridlines on printed graph paper will disappear when photographed; black or brown lines will not.) Today, like other graphs, they are more often created on computer.

Each axis of a line graph should be labeled clearly. The vertical axis normally represents measurements and the horizontal axis represents time units. The vertical axis is usually about two thirds the length of the horizontal axis. The graph should be roughed out before the final form is chosen; if the intervals along the vertical axis are too large in relation to those on the horizontal axis, for example, the graph line will be misleading. (For some purposes it may be desirable to exaggerate one or the other element.)

The numbers along the vertical axis should begin with the lowest number relevant to the graph. This will frequently be zero, but often not.

If a vertical axis will have a large unused space—say, the area from 500 to 3,000 kilograms on a scale that goes up to 4,000 kilograms—a break may be inserted in the axis. This is usually shown by two parallel slash marks through the axis or parallel jagged lines that extend across the entire graph, with white space in between. If the only activity in a graph occurs in the high numbers (e.g., weekly activity in a stock market that remains in the 6,000–7,000 range), the vertical axis may simply begin with a high number, and the reader will assume correctly that there is nothing to be shown in the omitted lower range.

To compare two or more trends or processes, line graphs may display more than one line (see Figure 9.4). For the sake of clarity, the graph should show no more than five or six lines, and the marking of the vertical axis should permit the lines to be spaced widely enough to be legible, especially if the figure is being reduced for reproduction. Each line should be clearly identified with a label or key. If there are only two or three lines, one may be dotted and another dashed to distinguish them from a continuous line; when more lines

Figure 9.4 Line Graph

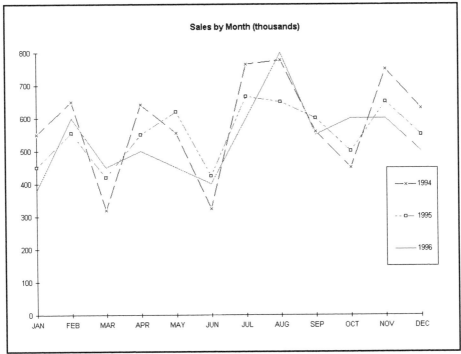

are shown, it is preferable to mark each with a symbol (or color, if the graph will be in color) that readily identifies it. Each symbol (e.g., a tiny square or diamond) may appear on the line itself at each point where it intersects a gridline.

The labels along each axis must be large enough to be legible. All labels, and especially number labels, should be set horizontally where possible.

Any graph consisting of points plotted on a double-axis grid may be called a *scattergraph* or *scatter diagram*. Line graphs are thus simply a type of scattergraph in which the points are connected by lines. Occasionally the lines will be omitted and the points shown by themselves. In any point graph that shows two or more processes, each point must be distinctively identified as representing its own category, since there is no line to make clear its connection with the others in its sequence. This is usually done by replacing each simple point in a line with the same distinctive symbol (square, diamond, triangle, circle, etc.), giving each set a distinctive color (if available), or both.

Flowcharts Charts that essentially consist of labeled boxes connected by lines may show hierarchies, sequences of steps in a process, or relationships between the parts of a whole. Flowcharts and organization charts are common examples, as are charts that diagram the various elements of a working system. Such charts are often created on desktop computers, since the art functions of standard computer programs permit the user to assemble text boxes and straight connecting lines with little effort. Unless they are prepared carefully, however, such charts may look better when produced by a professional typesetter.

Maps Maps vary greatly in the kind and amount of detail they contain. *Political maps* focus on political entities such as countries, states and provinces, and cities and towns. *Road maps* primarily display information needed by travelers— not only roads, cities, and towns, but landmarks and points of interest, including their size and importance, distances between marked points, highway exit numbers, and so on. *Topographical maps* emphasize the landscape, especially the land elevation. They usually show roads as well, but much less conspicuously. *Specialized maps* may illustrate any of a great variety of distributions—crop production, electoral returns, consumer buying patterns, crime rates, and so on. *Locator maps* usually show the location of a country, state, or area within a larger context. They generally show no interior detail; in fact, the area in question is often shown in solid black. A small locator map often accompanies and complements a larger map of the country or state.

A map will often combine two or more of these functions. The greater the variety of information to be conveyed, the greater variety of visual means will be needed. Sophisticated maps generally require the use of color, which may be used to indicate topographic and specialized detail. For simpler maps, color and even shading are generally unnecessary. Line-art maps (possibly employing various hatching patterns) are adequate to show political features, basic topography, roads, and distributions of many kinds.

The map's legend, which should ideally be set within the border as an integral part of the map itself, should provide a key to its graphic features, and compass direction and scale must also normally be specified.

Art

Art, in publishing terms, is simply any graphic material that is not typeset. Art may thus include all kinds of illustrations—technical photos, maps, charts and graphs, diagrams, and so on—that might not be considered particularly artistic. The distinction between art and text is lessening as art comes to be incorporated into electronic layout files at earlier and earlier stages of production as a result of the importing of scanned art and the computer generation of new art.

Art reproduction is a dauntingly technical subject, about which neither author nor editor is generally obliged to have a sophisticated knowledge. This section will attempt to provide a useful introduction to its basic processes and terminology; see also Chapter 13, "Design and Typography," for further discussions dealing with graphic materials. See the Bibliography for further reading.

Line Art

Line art is any image that can be reproduced using only pure black and white; it usually includes lines and areas of black on a white background. It is the simplest and least expensive type of art to reproduce. Standard types of line art include pen-and-ink drawings and unshaded diagrams, graphs, clip art, and maps. Even a page of standard text (e.g., a facsimile of a book page or a business letter) may be treated as a piece of line art. Line art can easily be scanned on an inexpensive scanner and incorporated into a digital page layout.

The graphic artist preparing line drawings generally uses black india ink on glossy, heavy, white drawing paper to achieve the best contrast. High-contrast art reproduces well and provides sharp detail. (Photocopies tend to reproduce less well, though clean, high-quality photocopies will often give good results.) A mock shading effect can be achieved in line art by using patterns of lines or dots. Such patterns can be purchased ready-made on pressure-sensitive paper, cut into shape, and stuck down on the areas where simulated shading is desired. (See Figure 9.5.)

Basic line-art diagrams are now often created on computer even by fairly unskilled users. In computer-generated art, areas can be filled in with patterns of lines and dots automatically; even the art functions in standard word-processing programs can provide a variety of these "fill" patterns.

Continuous-Tone Art and Halftones

Black-and-white art that contains shades of gray is referred to as *continuous-tone art* (as is color art, a special category of continuous-tone art that will be treated separately) or *grayscale art.* Black-and-white photographs, black-and-white reproductions of paintings, many drawings, and diagrams and maps that contain shaded sections are examples of continuous-tone art.

Before it can be printed, such art must be transformed into a mass of dots of pure black and white. In the traditional method, the art is photographed through a glass screen on which is printed a tight grid of lines. This grid breaks up the image into hundreds of tiny dots, each of which is read by the camera

Figure 9.5 Line Art

as pure black or white. The resulting image, called a *halftone*, is then rephotographed for printing with the text. Very fine screens are used for high-quality printing on coated paper, the coarser screens for newspaper-quality printing. (The choice of screen fineness is based on the type of paper the art will be printed on and its ink-absorption qualities.) The eye is usually fooled into perceiving halftones as continuous-tone art, though in coarser newspaper images the reader can easily make out the individual dots of the halftone screen. (See Figure 9.6)

Newer methods are now displacing this traditional technology. Screens printed on film sheets, called *contact screens*, can be placed directly on the art itself instead of photographing it through a glass screen. The dots themselves

Figure 9.6 Halftone Images at 80 and 133 lpi

can be of graded density, which produces a more subtle reproduction of grays. More commonly today, the halftone dots are electronically generated by means of special computer programs that convert an original image into tiny square *pixels* (picture elements) that can be used to produce dots in output; the result may closely approach the subtlety of the original continuous-tone art.

Today most art is prepared for printing by using a *flatbed* or *drum scanner* to convert it into a computer file that can be saved and manipulated using special graphics software. The scanning software separates the art into pixels. The scanned art can then be placed in the page layout with the copy by the type-setter or graphic designer. After corrections have been made, the entire file is sent to an *imagesetter*, which outputs the file as film negatives or positives or as paper that can be used as camera-ready mechanicals to be shot, stripped, and plated by the printer. Many printers are bypassing the film stage altogether by etching or exposing the information from the computer file directly onto a plate, in the so-called *direct-to-plate process*. (See also Chapter 14, "Typesetting, Printing, and Binding.")

The *resolution* (clarity of detail) of the final film output is determined by the printing requirements. For high-quality printing on coated paper, the editor or art director will typically ask for a film resolution of about 133–175 *lines per inch*, or *lpi* (a line being a row of the dots that make up the halftone). For the uncoated paper used for newspapers and most books, the desirable output is usually 80–120 lpi; since uncoated paper absorbs more ink, the lower density of dots reduces the possibility of the ink collecting in between the dots and creating undesirably dense areas.

The resolution of the film can also be stated in *dots per inch*, or *dpi*. A typical high-resolution output by an imagesetter would be 1200–2500 dpi; home and office laser printers, by contrast, may print at the relatively low resolution of 300–600 dpi.

The editor or art director should indicate the scanning resolution required for the art based on the intended file output size and type and the printing process. In general, the higher the resolution, the sharper the image quality and the larger the digital file. High-resolution files can sometimes be prohibitively large for some uses. For instance, if an image was scanned for use on a computer monitor—as in a Web page—it should have a low scanning resolution (perhaps no more than 72 dpi), since many monitors cannot support higher resolutions and a larger file will be slow to display. For printing, however, a high-resolution scan is necessary to achieve the greatest detail possible for the intended quality of paper, colors of ink, and printing process. A rule of thumb is to scan an image at 2½ times the intended output lpi. For instance, a halftone that will be printed in a book using uncoated but good-quality paper may be output at 120 lpi, but the original grayscale photograph would be scanned at about 300 *ppi (pixels per inch)*.

High-contrast reproduction can be produced by artificially enhancing the contrast between light and dark in an image by means of a computer algorithm that directs the black dots to disappear altogether in areas where there are few of them, producing a pure white, and the white areas to disappear in areas where the black dots are heavily predominant, producing a pure black. High-contrast reproduction enhances the dramatic qualities of a piece of art.

For another high-contrast effect that may be less expensive and clearer to reproduce, continuous-tone art can be produced as line art. In this process, any area that would have more than 50 percent black shading (or some other chosen percentage) automatically prints as pure black, while any area that would be less than 50 percent black (or some other complementary percentage) automatically prints as pure white. (The original art simply needs to be marked "Reproduce as line art.")

Any photograph submitted for publication should be a glossy, unretouched black-and-white continuous-tone print with sharp detail and high contrast. It should not be cropped or mounted by the author; instead, the author may use a photocopy of the picture (which may double as an overlay) to indicate any desired cropping.

Transparencies such as slides can be an equally high-quality medium for the creation of halftones.

If the author's "original" of a piece of art was taken out of a book, magazine, newspaper, or brochure, it will have to be *rescreened*, since it was already screened for its original publication. This is certainly not ideal; however, rescreening can today be quite successful, especially if a *fineline* process is used, and the reader may not notice any deficiency in the image's quality. On the other hand, a careless rescreening, especially of a coarse newspaper halftone, can look unacceptably poor.

Halftones and color art are sometimes segregated to a *gallery* or *insert*—a section printed on inserted signatures (usually eight or sixteen pages) of glossy stock, or sometimes unglossy *matte* stock. The glossy coating enhances graphic detail, and the whiteness of the stock permits maximum contrast. However, halftones are often quite acceptable when printed on standard book stock throughout the book, especially if the book is printed on bright-finish paper.

The editor should be alert to the quality of the halftone proofs returned by the printer or service bureau. For black and grayscale pages, there are three common proofing systems. A *digital proof,* usually an early proof from the typesetter or designer, may be nothing more than a laser printout. After the book has been completed, the pages can be output through an imagesetter to a coated paper (a low-resolution proof at this stage will be less expensive and will be adequate to confirm the positioning, sizing, and cropping of the images). After film has been output and stripped together, a *blueprint,* made from the high-resolution film, can be useful for checking text and images. (Dylux is one common brand name for blueprints.) For pages that contain halftones, a contact *photoprint* of the film will give the editor the closest approximation of the final printed art. (Velox is a common trademark name for photoprints.)

If, after a comparison of the proof with the original (which should have been returned with the proof), it appears that a significant amount of the image's detail, contrast, or sharpness has been lost, the art should be returned to the printer with specific requests for improvement.

The halftone process is also used when background shading is to be applied to some area of the page that would otherwise be white, such as a box or sidebar. (This use of the process does not properly come under the topic of art, since it is created by the typesetter or printer.) The darkness or lightness of the shading is referred to in terms of *screens.* A 90 (80, 70) percent screen will produce a dark-gray background, a 10 (20, 30) percent screen a light-gray background. A screened background naturally reduces the contrast with any type printed on it; any screen of 50 percent or higher will make black type printed over it hard to read. When the background screen (whether of black or some other color) is darker than about 50 percent, *dropout type*—that is, type that prints white as a result of "dropping out" all color—becomes easier to read than standard black type.

Color Art

Color is becoming more and more common in publications of all kinds. Attractive though it is, however, color is generally a luxury, since except for a few kinds of material—particularly fine art and complex maps—it is not needed for conveying essential information. However, whenever a publisher sees a book as "competing" with another publisher's book of the same genre—particularly a textbook—color can quickly come to seem a necessity.

Most color printing employs the *four-color process,* and thus is called *four-color* or *process printing.* The colors involved in standard four-color printing are always the same: cyan (blue), yellow, magenta (red), and black. To most eyes, combinations of these four colors seem to provide all the colors of the rainbow, and all but the most lavish books and magazines are printed entirely in four colors.

Four-color printing requires several expensive steps. In particular, the original art must be *separated* into the four individual colors, and it must usually be printed on a four-color press—a press with four printing cylinders, each of which applies a different color to the page passing through. The manufacturing cost of a book printed in four colors throughout may be several times those of a one-color book of the same length.

Rather than print books entirely in four colors, publishers often use color inserts or galleries (usually 8- or 16-page signatures) of higher-quality paper. It may also be possible to print certain proportions of a book in color—two out of three pages, for example—and the manufacturing manager should be consulted if such a possibility seems desirable.

Color art is usually submitted in a form corresponding to the way it was created, and the form of submission is often specified in the artist's contract. Color art created on computer is submitted on disk, or may even be transmitted electronically from artist to publisher.

Commissioned paintings and drawings may arrive in their original form, or the artist may have already had them scanned onto a computer. Color photographs will generally be submitted as slides or larger transparencies.

Color separation Like grayscale images, scanned color photographs and art must go through the halftoning process before they can be printed. During the separation process, when film is produced, halftone screens are created for each of the three primary printer's colors (cyan, magenta, yellow, or CMY) plus black (K). When printed with the colored inks, the overlapping dots merge to create a wide range of color.

There are different technologies today for separating original color art into its constituent colors. For years the standard method was to photograph the art with a large stationary camera that employed three different colored filters in succession. Because of the principle of additive color, photographing through a red filter produces the cyan negative, photographing through a green filter produces the magenta negative, and photographing through a blue filter produces the yellow negative. The negatives themselves are not actually colored; they simply display clear and opaque areas that permit the printing of the proper constituent colors if they are properly labeled and employed. The black negative is often essential for providing contrast, sharpness of outline, and saturation of color. Printing inks are never ideally pure, and thus reproduction must generally be adjusted in subtle ways to obtain the best results.

Today the device most commonly used for separation is the *drum scanner.* The art is attached to a small whirling cylinder, and three beams of light (red, green, and blue, or RGB) that have been passed through colored filters are tracked across the art. The data they pick up is fed directly into a computer, which produces separations by calculations based on the data obtained from the three beams. Preset controls permit the operator to manipulate the color as needed. Original art submitted on flexible paper or light cardboard can be wrapped around a cylinder; art on stiffer material will need to be photographed first, a separate step that will cost extra and may change the original color. The *flatbed scanner,* with its flat surface, can accommodate inflexible art with comparable results.

Editors may be sent color proofs for approval, along with the originals for comparison (even when review will involve the art department as well, as it almost always will). Reviewing color art calls for a sharp eye for color levels and fineness of detail. Color proofs are also sometimes marred by *moiré* patterns, which occur when the dot patterns of the various printing screens line up irregularly to produce a visibly imperfect texture. Problems in *registration,* which result when the four negatives are not precisely aligned with one another and produce ghostly double images, are less frequent today, since manual alignment of negatives is becoming rare.

There are several common proofing systems for viewing color art. Since color proofs made from the final film can be very expensive, an early digital proof of the art in place with copy and captions is advisable. From digital proofs, the editor and art director will be able to approve the size and placement of art in relation to the text but not the quality of the color (see "Proofs" on page 206). Since most digital color proofs are continuous tone, the halftone screening process is not visible in them.

After the pages with art have been output to film, proofs can be provided by means of any of several different color proofing systems, most of which use a process of laminating colored filmlike material or layers of colored toners. (Common brand names include Matchprints, Fujis, Waterproofs, and Chromalins.)

Two-color printing and color matching systems Midway between black-and-white and full-color is two-color printing. In two-color printing, one of the colors is almost always black because that is the color in which the text is generally printed. The second color is added to enliven the text page; in a given book it might be visible, for example, as a screened background color in sidebars, in a thick colored rule under running heads, as the color of all A-heads, and as a "fill" color in line art. A second color is rarely necessary, but can be attractive enough to warrant the added expense of printing on a two-color press, which is still significantly cheaper than four-color printing.

When only a single color is to be added to black, this *spot color* may be chosen from a standard manufacturer's catalog of colored inks, any of which can print directly from a single printing cylinder, thus requiring only a two-color press. The most widely used *color matching system*—so called because they permit the precise matching of a preferred color with a color represented in the system—is the Pantone Matching System, more familiarly known as PMS. Another is the TruMatch system. Such spot color is also sometimes used in four-color printing when the editor or art director adds a fifth color—often for use as a background or sidebar color. This spot color will be easier to control on press if it is separate from the four-color process plates.

Color screens—areas of color diluted with a proportion of white—are commonly called for in the specifications for two-color books. Like halftone screens, color screens are requested in terms of percentages: the specs may call for 20 percent background screens for all sidebars, for example, or 25 percent color "fills" for two-color art.

Duotone art is halftone art in which a single spot color has been added to the black. This produces a characteristic effect somewhat like printing a picture on colored paper stock. When the background screen is light, the effect can be quite subtle. A light brown screen can produce the "sepia" effect of an old photograph, for example, and a light blue screen can produce a metallic effect. Designers find duotones useful in moderation; however, since any such screen will result in lessened contrast, duotones should not be overused, and should rarely if ever involve screens darker than 50 percent.

Illustration Elements

Much of what was said about table numbers, captions, and credit lines applies to illustrations as well.

Illustration numbers Like tables, illustrations are often identified by number within a book or article. Numbering is optional when illustrations are few or when they are only casually related to the text; it is rare in encyclopedic books, in popular books, and in books for young people, but is common in textbooks and technical books.

Even when the illustrations in the published work will not be numbered, each must be assigned a temporary number for use throughout the production process.

Art is usually identified by the word "Figure" (or "Fig.") followed by an Arabic numeral. The figure number appears in the caption and in any text references to the illustration.

Like tables, figures may be numbered either consecutively throughout the book or chapter by chapter. Chapter-by-chapter numbering is standard in highly illustrated technical works and textbooks.

All illustrations are usually numbered together, no distinction being made between photographs and other kinds of artwork. An exception is sometimes made for maps, which may be numbered separately ("Map 1," "Map 2," etc.).

Captions Most illustrations call for captions. Though captions tend to be limited in what they can include (often for the sake of consistency), they need not be dull. An imaginatively worded caption can enhance its illustration considerably, and authors should be encouraged to provide interesting captions wherever possible.

An illustration caption almost always includes a title or headline, which is often preceded by an identification number. The number and title normally appear on the same line, separated by a period or dash or simply a space. Caption titles generally consist of a brief phrase (e.g., "Goya, *Saturn Devouring His Children,* oil on canvas," or "View of the market place (1788), situated in the older area of Higher Buxton")—which may often be followed by a sentence of interesting description. Further text following the title is often set in less obtrusive type—roman type following a bold title, for example. This may consist of complete sentences, or it may be a legend explaining the symbols or labels used in the illustration, as in the following example.

> **Fig. 2.24** A Cell and Its Organelles. *A,* nucleolus; *B,* nucleus; *C,* cytoplasm; *D,* mitochondrion; *E,* Golgi apparatus.

The design specs should specify type style, capitalization (headline-style vs. sentence-style), and positioning. (See Chapter 13 and the section beginning on page 343.)

Though captions may take any number of forms, captions for given types of material within a given book or article should be consistent in structure as well as style. If one caption begins with a bold title, they all should; if one provides the date and medium for a depicted work of art, so should the rest.

When sections of a figure or people in a photograph are being identified, the identifications should proceed from left to right, row by row, and generally from top to bottom (or clockwise, if appropriate). An introductory phrase usually describes the picture. The individuals are then introduced, beginning with a phrase such as "Top row," "From left," or "Left to right." Rows are usually described as "top" or "back," "center," and "bottom" or "front." If there are many names, each row's listing may begin a new line. The major actor in the scene is often identified first (e.g., "Ambassador Charles Bragdon signs the 1976 agreement . . ."); others are identified by their actions or their location in the picture (e.g., "Delegates Mary Ellen Stewart, left, Gilles Berton, center, and David Ponzi, right, look on").

The parts of a figure should generally be located similarly ("left," upper right," etc.). When this is inadequate to locate the parts of a complex figure, identifying symbols—usually letters or numbers—may be used to refer to corresponding symbols in the illustration. Such letters are usually lowercased and italicized.

> **Figure 4.6** Old World sucker-footed bat *(Myzopoda aurita),* photo by Harry Hoogstraal. *(a)* ventral view of skull; *(b)* palate; *(c)* head and thumb disk; *(d)* lateral view of skull. Photos from Proc. Zool. Soc. London.

A symbol or abbreviation that appears in more than one figure should normally be explained in each figure's caption. If a common symbol key is prepared for a set of similar figures, each caption should refer to it (e.g., "For explanation of abbreviations, see key to Figure 1").

Credit and permission lines Any illustration reproduced from another source calls for a statement acknowledging the source and, if the source is copyrighted, stating that permission to use or adapt the illustration has been granted. (See "Copyright and Permissions" on page 319.) Figures drawn by the author do not require credit lines; however, a line reading simply "Illustration by the author" can ensure that credit will not be given to another source. Similarly, it is unnecessary to credit figures drawn for hire, but as a courtesy the artist may be credited with a simple acknowledgment (e.g., "Map by Mary Kennedy"). Though there is no legal obligation to credit illustrations from the public domain, such acknowledgment not only represents a courtesy but is frequently helpful to the curious reader.

Illustrations are often provided free of charge by companies and institutions. Credit lines for such figures are often stipulated by the institution, but normally take a form such as "Photographs by Frank Smith, courtesy of the Stambolian Museum" or "Photograph courtesy RHS International, Inc."

All credit lines in a given work should be typographically similar. A brief credit line conventionally appears in small type (often italics) immediately below or alongside the illustration. Simple credit lines may include only the name of the artist or photographer, often preceded by "courtesy [of]" if no permission fee was charged; credit may instead be given to a donor institution (whose name may be preceded by the copyright symbol © if appropriate) or to a picture agency. When full bibliographic information is included in a bibliography, only a short form of the reference is necessary. Credit and permission lines can become undesirably prominent if set in the same type size and style as the caption; thus, run-in credit lines should be set in a contrasting style (e.g., roman if the caption is bold, italic if the caption is roman), a smaller type size, or within parentheses. (Acknowledgments may also appear as footnotes.)

> Antietam today. *Photo by Frank Smith.*
>
> **Loggerhead shrike.** Photo courtesy of A. Cruickshank/VIREO.
>
> **Figure 16** Rutherford B. Hayes at 25 (Reprinted, with permission, from Alan A. Jones, *Hayes of Ohio,* p. 44. © 1990 by Midatlantic Publishers.)
>
> Fig. 3.6 The Romanov family tree, 1918. *Adapted from Black and Turner, 1976, p. 132.*

Labels A label is any word, letter, or symbol in an illustration that identifies a particular part of the figure. The words inside the boxes of an organizational chart are labels, as are the words and numbers that denote the coordinates of a graph.

For the sake of consistency, labels in a given publication should look more or less alike. Thus, a flowchart with italic or sans-serif or all-cap labels should not normally be followed by one with bold or serif or lowercase labels. (For this reason, label style is stipulated in the design specs whenever the typesetter will be setting labels for art.)

Lowercase letters, with their greater variety of form, are easier to read than capital letters, though all-capitalized labels may be used to distinguish a different category or level of labels. If the illustration will be reduced for publication, the labels must naturally be large enough to be read easily at the smaller size.

Labels have traditionally been added in several different ways, some of which have largely fallen out of use. They may be drawn by a graphic artist, stenciled, or typed separately (preferably on reproduction-quality paper) and pasted onto the artwork. *Transfer letters* are letters (other elements such as circles and rules are also available) printed on the back of a clear plastic sheet that can be transferred to another surface when it is rubbed firmly with a flat tool; however, it is hard to align them well enough to create entire words that will look acceptable. *Stick-on letters* suffer from the same problem. On computer-generated art today, labels are simply keyboarded as part of the text file. A typesetter will set labels separately or will position typeset labels on scanned-in artwork.

Obtaining Art

The author's contract will generally spell out whether responsibility for a book's art rests with the author or the publisher. Regardless of who is required to furnish the art, the likely sources for the art will be similar. An author may commission a local artist or photographer to illustrate the book; the publisher may do the same. The author or publisher may instead approach a stock-photo archive, or perhaps several different archives, to provide the art. (Stock photos are usually cheaper than commissioned photos, but not always.) Archives now are available on the World Wide Web, and some even offer art that can be downloaded to a local computer. The annual *Literary Market Place* provides listings of photographers, artists, art services, and stock-photo agencies that do extensive book work; each listing details their experience and specialties.

Museums and larger historical societies are good sources for reproductions and photos from their collections. Government agencies (including the Library of Congress) can be especially useful sources of maps and pictures; their Web sites may be good places to start a search. Manufacturers often provide pictures of their own technology, often requiring only a credit line in return. National professional and amateur organizations, unions, broadcasting networks, film companies, foreign consulates or travel offices, the United Nations—the possible sources are almost endless. Such art requests are usually handled through a public-relations or corporate-communications department. Technical illustrations (now very often created on computer) are also available through art services.

Books often profit from using the work of a single artist or photographer exclusively, which will help ensure a coherent graphic conception throughout. The author or editor who finds it desirable to commission new art and to work with the artist or photographer should first examine his or her portfolio (which may be available on a Web site) to see if the style matches what is needed.

Price will often be a consideration. A bible of the field for artists and designers—which also provides an excellent overview of art technology and artistic practice in general—is the regularly updated *Graphic Artists Guild Handbook: Pricing & Ethical Guidelines.* (See also Bibliography.)

Photographs are subject to several common failings, particularly including inferior composition and inadequate light-dark contrast. Photos may have lifeless or unconvincing models, or may simply show irremediably dull situations which the provided captions fail to bring to life. Often a photograph's failings can be overcome by judicious cropping or by reproduction that enhances contrast. A publisher's art department will often be able to salvage quite unpromising illustrations. But sometimes the editor will decide that a photo simply cannot be saved and will encourage the author to drop it from the book.

Copyright, ownership, and *model releases* (which convey the permission of a person depicted in a photo to publish the photo) often become critical when new photos and art are commissioned. Freelance artists may be well-versed in contractual matters, and editors should be just as knowledgeable. The author and editor will have to decide whether exclusive rights to the work are needed, which will often be the case especially if a book is expected to be republished in electronic or other form. If exclusive rights are needed, a *work-for-hire contract* conveying all rights in the art to the publisher may be sought by the publisher; however, artists often are reluctant to part with all rights in their work by signing work-for-hire contracts. Exclusive rights naturally will not be available for any pictures from a stock agency.

Clip art, in its original sense, is art to be clipped from books of illustrations (usually special collections, or *clip books*, intended specifically for this purpose) for use in a design project. Today clip art is more commonly incorporated into an electronic document by means of a scanner or taken directly from an electronic clip-art archive. Though clip art is traditionally line art, it commonly appears today as continuous-tone or even color art. Since clip art is not created for the specific project in which it may be used, it provides a cheap but often not thoroughly satisfactory solution to illustration problems, and many readers today will readily spot it for what it is. Electronic clip art can, however, be readily manipulated using standard graphics software, thereby creating a customized look for a given project. And where clip art is primarily intended to serve a modest design purpose (in the form of borders or small recurrent ornaments, for example) rather than to fulfill any more serious illustrative function, it may be very useful for a wide variety of projects.

Handling Illustrations Editorially

If a published work is to include art, the author is normally asked to submit either rough drafts or camera-ready artwork with the manuscript. The contract should specify whether the publisher requires the submission of finished artwork or will provide the services of an artist to produce polished versions from the sketches—and, if the latter, at whose expense.

Illustrations should be submitted on separate sheets, generally one for each figure. Each sheet should be marked with the illustration's number—either the number that will identify it in the text or a temporary production number for art that will not be numbered in the text—and some identification of the project, such as the author's last name. Either the first reference to each illustration should be marked in the manuscript margin or space in the text following the first reference should be left for insertion notes such as "[Figure 4.1]." If the proper orientation of the picture might be ambiguous, the top should be indicated on the back or on a tissue overlay by the word "TOP" at the top or simply an arrow pointing to the top.

Any notations on the back of an illustration, especially a photograph, should be done lightly with a soft pencil—never a ballpoint pen—so that they will not show up in relief on the other side. Using a label that has been filled out before being stuck onto the back of the art is even safer, though label glue can have detrimental effects on a photo over time. The best method is often to keep each photo in a clear plastic labeled sleeve. Photos and original art should never be folded or stapled. Paper clips should be used, if at all, only with extra thicknesses of paper slipped under them to protect the art from being dented. All finished artwork should be kept (by both author and editor) in large envelopes backed with stiff cardboard. Ideally, each piece should be kept between two pieces of light cardboard and should have its own tissue overlay—a piece of tissue taped across the back of the art at the top and folded down to cover the whole front. Overlays must always be used with any media that are prone to smudging, such as charcoal and pastels. A tissue overlay can serve other purposes than protection; the figure number and other identification can be written on it (but never while the art is underneath the tissue), flaws or other aspects of the image can be indicated by circles and comments on the overlay, or the portion of the picture that will be reproduced can be outlined on it.

Illustration captions, which will be typeset, have traditionally been submitted together on a separate sheet or sheets. (If the illustrations will be unnumbered in the text, each caption must have a temporary identification number—circled, to prevent its being set—to match that of the illustration's temporary number.) Today, however, most typesetters find it easier to handle captions that are integrated with the rest of the text.

As mentioned earlier, the in-house editor and copy editor will almost always be responsible for several other tasks regarding illustrations, which may be divided up differently depending on the editor and the project. (If the author was properly instructed at the outset, preferably by means of an "Author's Guide" from the publisher, several of these will already have been done and the editors' own tasks made simpler.) These will include at least the following duties:

1. Make a list of all art received from the author that is not part of the electronic file. (If the author has provided such a list, check off each piece on it.) Note any missing art referred to in the text.

2. Make sure each piece is properly identified.

3. Consider whether each illustration is of adequate quality and fulfills its intended role in the text; ask the author if any pieces of doubtful value can be deleted or replaced (or if even more art may be necessary).

4. Prepare a type list of any labels (words, numbers, math symbols, etc.) that will have to be typeset; next to each set of labels, specify its typeface and size (e.g., "8-pt Bask.") or, if the labels have been "spec'd" by the designer, typemark them as appropriate. Edit the labels as necessary for consistency and clarity.

5. For the purpose of a castoff, estimate how much space each illustration will take and the total space that all the illustrations will require. Be sure all captions and credit lines have been provided.

6. Call out in the margin the first text reference to each illustration if the author has not done so. Check for consistency between any description in the text and the figure's number, caption, and labels.

7. Edit the captions and credit lines, noting any style decisions on a style sheet, and mark them up according to the design specs (if provided).

8. Check the permissions file to see that permission has been obtained for all illustrations that may be copyrighted, and that the information needed for each credit line has also been obtained, bearing in mind that any photograph showing an identifiable person who is still living may require a written release.

Illustrations must be in camera-ready form before being shot or scanned. If any appear to be of dubious quality, they should be reviewed by a designer or production specialist before being sent out for pre-press handling.

Photographs should be in the form of glossy prints or transparencies. (As mentioned, photographs printed on glossy stock in books or magazines have already been screened once and do not qualify.) Photocopies may be suitable for line art (never for continuous-tone art); however, they are often of inadequate quality even for line art and should be reviewed by an expert eye before being scanned. Computer-generated graphics should be submitted either in electronic form or as printed out on a laser printer on repro-quality paper. Drawings done in light pencil or wash should be checked by a designer or production expert to determine whether they will photograph and reproduce adequately without requiring special techniques.

Artwork was traditionally often mounted on *boards*—large pieces of cardboard—for protection and easier handling. Today, any art to be scanned on a drum scanner (without being photographed beforehand) must be flexible and therefore should simply be laid between pieces of cardboard. Flatbed scanners can, however, usually accommodate rigid art.

Photocopies should always be kept when illustrations are sent out to be photographed or scanned.

Cropping and sizing Most photographs benefit from *cropping*—the cutting away of portions of the picture, usually unwanted background, in order to give it a new or sharper focus and to permit enlargement of significant objects in the picture. To crop a photograph, the editor or designer must first identify the "picture within the picture," which is best done by placing two L-shaped pieces of cardboard over the picture and moving them to frame any desired shape and size of rectangle. When the best image has been determined, *crop marks*—usually two short lines indicating each edge of the new image—are drawn in the margin. Crop marks can be drawn (lightly) on a tissue overlay. A glossy print may often be marked with a grease pencil (whose marks can be wiped off glossy surfaces), and a nonglossy print with a soft erasable pencil.

Most art submitted for publication will appear at a different size in the published work. Art is usually reduced—or *shot down*—to the size at which it will be published, since such reduction minimizes any flaws in the art and allows the artist to work on a more comfortable scale. Since too great a reduction can cause loss of detail and legibility, however, the editor or designer should always test the effect of a proposed reduction by making photocopies.

Sometimes art must be enlarged instead, especially when transparencies such as slides are being used. Though good transparencies usually take enlargement well, the risk of enlargement is that the texture will become coarse and any flaws will be magnified.

Reduction percentages can easily be calculated by means of a proportional scale or wheel (such as designers often use) or a calculator, or by doing the simple math. Divide the desired width by the original width and change any resulting decimal figure into a percentage (e.g., .76 = 76%, 1.22 = 122%). A brief instruction such as "Shoot at 75%" (or just "75%") should be written on the back, in the margin, or on an overlay. Art that is not to be reduced or enlarged should be marked "S/S" for "same size."

Proofs The printer or photographer returns to the publisher a set of illustration proofs. Each must be checked to see that the illustration has been cropped and sized properly, that it has not been *flopped* (printed backward, as a result of flopping the negative over), and that no new flaws have been introduced. If corrections are needed, the art is returned.

At the first- or galley-proof stage, any notations in the manuscript margins about the position of illustrations must be carried forward to the proof margins. It is also a good idea to recheck the text references, in case any revisions to the text have rendered them inconsistent with a figure or its caption. If any changes have been made to an illustration, the editor must reread the caption and any text references to make sure they are still accurate.

At the second-proof stage, the meticulous editor will once again check each illustration and caption against its text references to be sure the art's content and positioning are consistent with the references. If any holes have been left for illustrations that have still not been incorporated into the proofs, the holes should be measured to be sure they will accommodate the sized art, caption, and framing white space called for in the design specs. On a proof of an entire page that includes text with art in place, the art will often appear in low-resolution form. The standard term for art intended only to fill the space where a higher-quality print will eventually appear is *FPO* ("for position only") *art*. However, the editor or art director will additionally want to see high-quality, high-resolution proofs of all art (photoprints or color proofs made from the film) at some point before receiving the printer's proofs (bluelines), so that the quality of the scan or repro can be adequately confirmed in time to correct it.

10   Notes and Bibliographies

Footnotes and Endnotes   210
Parenthetical References   217
Other Systems   220
Bibliographies   223
Special Types of References   231

A writer who borrows a quotation, idea, or piece of information from another work is traditionally required to acknowledge the borrowing in some way, and in serious nonfiction writing such acknowledgment is normally done by means of reference notes, usually in tandem with a bibliography. Thorough documentation of this kind is the distinguishing mark of scholarly writing. Scholarly documentation accomplishes several things: (1) it gives proper credit for work done by others and makes plagiarism more difficult, (2) it directs the reader to sources that may be of interest, (3) it may take the place of a lengthy explanation, (4) it can strengthen an argument by marshaling respectable published support, (5) it indicates the extent and quality of the writer's research, and (6) it can guide the interested reader to other relevant works that may not actually have been cited.

Most published nonfiction omits bibliographic references altogether. Most readers are somewhat put off by references, and omission of references tends to be conducive to a more relaxed tone. Articles in popular magazines, for example, never employ reference notes, relying instead on casual mentions of any sources within the running text itself (e.g., "As Hawking observed in his *Brief History of Time,* . . . ," "At a symposium in New York in March 1948, Margaret Mead criticized Kinsey's report, complaining that . . .").

Not all notes are simple bibliographic citations. So-called *substantive* or *content notes* may be used for discussions of subjects ancillary to the main topic being discussed. Such discussions, which might otherwise simply appear within parentheses, are usually moved out of the main text whenever they are long enough or digressive enough to represent an undesirable interruption of the main line of discussion.

Source documentation is widely dreaded, especially by younger writers, who may regard the practice as almost impossibly arcane, difficult, and time-consuming. However, much of the difficulty is often simply the result of disorganized research. The demands of documentation become much easier if the researcher has been systematic and meticulous about jotting down a complete and accurate bibliographic record of each work studied at the time it is first looked at (as well as being painstakingly accurate in copying the passages themselves). Once the complete record is in hand, formatting—and, if necessary, reformatting—the data usually becomes a relatively simple task.

Nevertheless, there indeed exists a bewildering variety of conceivable types of citations, and the unlucky researcher will from time to time encounter unusual and exacting citation problems. If an analogous citation cannot be found in the endnote lists in a scholarly journal, the best advice is often simply to provide the reader with all genuinely relevant information in a concise form broadly consistent with the style of the other citations. The accuracy and adequacy of the information are always more important than achieving some "perfectly" consistent form, especially when there may well be no other comparable entry with which the problematic entry truly need be absolutely consistent.

Since no style manual can describe in detail more than a fraction of the bibliographic styles now in use, the writer submitting an article to a particular journal should always follow any instructions to authors in the journal's front or back matter and study carefully the references in its articles, the latter being unquestionably the most efficient way of learning its particular (and possibly unique) style. If a manuscript prepared on computer will be submitted to more than one journal, the original can be changed easily from one journal's style to another's, each different form being preserved as a separate electronic file. Within a given discipline, such changes will usually be minor. Book publishers, unlike journals, generally permit a reasonable range of different documentation styles, though they can be expected to require (or impose) internal consistency just as rigorously as do journals.

Several style manuals have established themselves as the standard guides to bibliographic form and other style issues in the various disciplines. In the humanities particularly, but also importantly in the social and natural sciences, the *Chicago Manual of Style* has long held a privileged position, especially in book publishing, and its treatment of bibliographic citation is the most comprehensive of all. In the life sciences and physical sciences, *Scientific Style and Format: The CBE Manual for Authors, Editors, and Publishers* is the most widely followed authority. In the social sciences, the *Publication Manual of the American Psychological Association* (APA) is commonly relied on. College and university departments usually prescribe certain manuals for use by undergraduates and generally by graduate students as well: those most often assigned are perhaps Kate Turabian's *Manual for Writers of Term Papers, Theses, and Dissertations* and (especially in the humanities) the *MLA Handbook for Writers of Research Papers*. In the business office, the *Gregg Reference Manual* has been standard for many years. See the Bibliography for publication data on these and other authorities for individual professional fields.

Ordinary word-processing programs now make the job of inserting references far simpler than it was in the precomputer era. Their important functions include automatic renumbering of notes whenever new notes are added or existing ones are deleted, automatic reformatting of pages to accommodate footnotes, and automatic changing of footnotes to endnotes (or vice versa) throughout. These functions take only a few minutes to master and can save the user immense amounts of time.

Special software programs today provide automatic formatting of the elements of bibliographic citations in any of a large number of styles used in the humanities, social sciences, and natural sciences. Using an on-screen template, the user types each element into its appropriate box, and the program automatically creates the format in the chosen bibliographic style. For many students and scholars, this capacity can be of modest assistance. However, the main task will still lie in what precedes the formatting of the elements—that is, the careful gathering of all the essential documentation data and the judicious deployment of the source material within the new text.

References usually take one of three forms: footnotes, endnotes, or parenthetical references. Footnotes, set at the bottom of the page, can be more convenient than notes at the end of an article, chapter, or book for the serious reader, who is thereby spared the need of constantly flipping back and forth. Computer programs have largely freed typists and typesetters from the arduous task of calculating text-block lengths to accommodate footnotes of varying lengths, thus largely neutralizing an older argument against footnotes. However, footnotes are often disliked by more casual readers accustomed to a relaxed style of presentation. They may also be felt to make pages less attractive, and a heavily footnoted work may have ungainly pages that consist as much of footnotes as of normal text. Partly for these reasons, endnotes have become increasingly common in recent decades, and are now sometimes even employed with no actual reference numbers in the text (see "White-Copy System" beginning on page 221).

Scholarly works in the natural sciences and to a somewhat lesser extent in the social sciences and humanities employ parenthetical references, highly condensed bibliographic references set within parentheses right in the running text. Parenthetical references have been found to be extremely efficient in scientific writing, where professionals expect to encounter them frequently. Since the scientific articles cited tend to be short and highly focused on a single research finding, bald citations devoid of page references or any accompanying discussion are usually felt to be adequate. In the social sciences and especially the humanities, parenthetical references—which do not allow for even brief "content" discussions—must generally be at least supplemented by footnotes or (more commonly) endnotes.

In the humanities, footnotes and endnotes have traditionally been preferred throughout, but in recent years there has been a trend in the humanities toward using parenthetical references where appropriate. The name of the cited text's author is often worked smoothly into the text itself, so such references tend to shrink to mere parenthesized page references that hardly disturb the flow of the text. This extreme concision is nevertheless often inappropriate to the types of references a humanities scholar is likely to cite and the kinds of points the scholar is likely to make, and it is thus usually necessary to combine the two modes of citation. In writing intended for a more general public, parenthetical references are almost never seen, since they inevitably break up a text in a way that most people reading primarily for pleasure dislike.

The choice of reference type is actually rarely left to the writer. For term papers and theses, professors often require a specific reference style that is standard in their field; scholarly journals almost always impose a house policy for all their articles; a publisher of books for a professional audience may apply a general policy on documentation to all its books; a large corporation may specify a single mode of documentation for its reports; law firms generally follow the standard style of the legal profession; and so on.

Rules for documentation in serious writing were developed to ensure thoroughness and internal formal consistency. But as this variety of treatment reminds us, documentation data may be deployed in a variety of ways without losing any of its content or scholarly value.

This chapter seeks to provide an introduction to every significant issue of documentation and to provide consensus versions—versions that can be translated readily into the special style of any given journal or authority—of citation style in the humanities and sciences. Since most aspects of documentation style are more easily comprehended through examples than through discussion, a number of details will be found in the examples themselves but not otherwise referred to.

For discussions of permission to use copyrighted material, see "Copyright and Permissions" beginning on page 319.

Note: Wherever alternative ways of styling particular elements are mentioned in this chapter, such alternatives should not be randomly mixed. Instead, one or the other style alternative should be adopted and maintained throughout a given work.

Footnotes and Endnotes

Footnotes and endnotes use sequential superscript numbers to key bibliographic information about sources (author, title, place of publication, publisher, date, and page number) or ancillary discussions to specific text passages. Notes that appear at the bottom of the page are called *footnotes;* otherwise identical notes that appear at the end of an article, chapter, or book are called *endnotes.*

The superscript numbers are generally placed immediately after the material to be documented, whether it is an actual quotation or a paraphrase of language used in the source, or sometimes after the name of the source's author. The number is normally placed at the end of a paragraph, sentence, or clause, or at some other natural break in the sentence; it follows all punctuation marks except the dash.

> As one observer noted, "There was, moreover, a degree of logic in the new LDP-SDPJ axis, in that the inner cores of both parties felt threatened by the recent electoral reform legislation";[7] this opinion seems to have been shared by various other commentators.[8]

The numbering is consecutive throughout a paper or article. In a book, it almost always starts over with each new chapter.

The note itself, usually set in type one or two points smaller than the text type, begins with the corresponding number. The number may either be set as a superscript or set on the line and followed by a period; the latter is now more common in typeset material.

> [4] I. L. Allen, *The City in Slang* (Oxford, 1993), 156.
>
> *or*
>
> 4. I. L. Allen, *The City in Slang* (Oxford, 1993), 156.

Both footnotes and endnotes normally provide full bibliographic information for a source the first time it is cited. In subsequent references to the source, the information is abridged (see "Subsequent References to Books and Articles" beginning on page 215).

Whenever data that would normally appear in a note—particularly the author's name or the source's title—appears in the text itself, adequately identified as the source of the quotation or information, it may be omitted from the note.

When endnotes are employed in a book, the task of locating a particular endnote should be made as easy as possible for the reader by providing running heads on each page of endnotes that individually specify which pages of the main text are covered by that page of endnotes—for example, "Notes to pp. 305–316," "Notes to pp. 317–330," etc. In addition, the endnotes for each book chapter or section should be preceded by a bold heading ("Chapter 1," "Chapter 2," etc.).

Superscript letters (used in alphabetical order, and always lowercase) or superscript marks are occasionally substituted for reference numbers when footnotes are employed. Both are commonly employed for table footnotes to indicate that they are not part of the larger chapter reference sequence. In tables of technical data, use of letters will avoid the risk that numerical superscripts will be mistaken for mathematical exponents, and use of marks will avoid the smaller risk that letters could similarly be taken for exponents. The traditional marks are listed below in the order normally used.

* (asterisk)
† (dagger)
‡ (double dagger)
§ (section mark)
‖ (parallels)
¶ (paragraph mark)
# (number or pound sign)

This sequence usually begins anew with each page. If more than seven notes are needed in a sequence, numbers or letters should be used instead. When less than five are needed, the asterisk and dagger may be used in the order *, **, †, ††.

The following paragraphs describe the various elements of initial references.

Books

The basic elements of book citations are (1) the author's name, (2) the book's title, (3) the place of publication, publisher, and date of publication, and (4) the page or pages where the information appears.

Author's name The author's name is written in normal order, and followed by a comma. The names of two or more authors are listed in the sequence shown on the book's title page. If there are more than three authors, the first author's name is followed by *et al.* (for *et alii* or *et aliae,* "and others"), set in roman type. If a publication is issued by a group or organization and no individual is mentioned on the title page, the name of the group or organization (sometimes called the *corporate author*) may be used instead. If the corporate author is the same as the publisher, or if for any reason no name appears on the title page, the name may be omitted and the book title may begin the note.

4. Elizabeth Bishop, *One Art,* ed. Robert Giroux (New York: Farrar, Straus & Giroux, 1994), 102.

15. Bert Hölldobler and Edward O. Wilson, *The Ants* (Cambridge, Mass.: Belknap–Harvard Univ. Press, 1990), 119.

8. Charles T. Brusaw, Gerald J. Alred, and Walter E. Oliu, *The Business Writer's Handbook,* 5th rev. ed. (New York: St. Martin's, 1997), 182–84.

22. Randolph Quirk et al., *A Comprehensive Grammar of the English Language* (London: Longman, 1985), 135.

12. New York Times Staff, *The White House Transcripts* (New York: Bantam, 1974), 78–79.

6. *Information Please Almanac: 1998* (Boston: Houghton Mifflin, 1997), 324.

Title of the work The title is italicized in keyboarded and typeset manuscripts (underlined in typed or handwritten material). Each word of the title and subtitle is capitalized except for internal articles, coordinating conjunctions, and prepositions. A colon separates the title from any subtitle even if no colon is used on the title page. In hyphenated compounds, the second (third, etc.) element is generally capitalized as if there were no hyphen. Prepositions of four or more letters are often capitalized.

44. Alan Lloyd, *The Wickedest Age: The Life and Times of George III* (London: David & Charles, 1971), 48.

20. *The Post-Physician Era: Medicine in the Twenty-First Century* (New York: Wiley, 1976), 14.

3. Arthur Miller, *A View from [From] the Bridge* (1955; New York: Viking, 1987), 11.

Editor, compiler, or translator If no author is mentioned on the title page, the name of the editor, compiler, or translator is placed first in the note, followed by the abbreviation *ed.* (or *eds.*), *comp.* (*comps.*), or *trans.* In works listing the original author and title, the name of an editor, compiler, or translator is preceded by the abbreviation *ed., comp.,* or *trans.* or some combination of them.

7. Arthur S. Banks, Alan J. Day, and Thomas C. Muller, eds., *Political Handbook of the World: 1997* (Binghamton, N.Y.: CSA Publications, 1997), 293–95.

14. Simone de Beauvoir, *The Second Sex,* trans. and ed. H. M. Parshley (1953; New York: Knopf, 1993), 446.

Part of the book If a reference is to one part of a book (such as an article, short story, or poem in a collection), the part's title is enclosed in quotation marks. Titles of chapters of a work by a single author are usually ignored.

4. Grace Paley, "Dreamer in a Dead Language," *Later the Same Day* (New York: Farrar, Straus & Giroux, 1985), 9–36.

10. Ernst Mayr, "Processes of Speciation in Animals," *Mechanisms of Speciation,* ed. Claudio Barigozzi (New York: Alan R. Liss, 1982), 1–3.

Name of a series If a book belongs to a series, the series name should be included. If the book is a numbered volume in the series, the volume number is also included. The series name is capitalized headline-style but not italicized.

> 4. George W. Stocking, Jr., ed., *Functionalism Historicized: Essays on British Social Anthropology,* History of Anthropology Series, vol. 2 (Madison: Univ. of Wisconsin, 1984), 173–74.

Edition   If a work is other than the first edition, the number or the nature of the edition is shown.

> 11. Albert C. Baugh and Thomas Cable, *A History of the English Language,* 4th ed. (Englewood Cliffs, N.J.: Prentice Hall, 1992), 14.
> 29. *A Handbook for Scholars,* rev. ed. (New York: Oxford, 1992), 129.

Volume number   If a work has more than one volume, the total number of volumes follows the title and edition, and the number of the volume cited precedes the page number, with an unspaced colon between them.

> 3. Ronald M. Nowak, *Walker's Mammals of the World,* 5th ed., 2 vols. (Baltimore: Johns Hopkins Univ., 1991), 2:661.

Publication data   The city of publication, the short name of the publisher, and the year of publication, in that order, follow next, enclosed in parentheses. A colon follows the city name, and a comma follows the publisher's name. If the city is a small one, the abbreviated state name (or country name) should be included; state names should all take either their older traditional form or the official post-office form. If the city or publisher is not known, use *n.p.* (for *no place* or *no publisher*); if the year is not given, use *n.d.* (for *no date*); if the pages are unnumbered, use *n. pag. (no pagination).*

Publishers' names are now commonly abbreviated, in both notes and bibliographies, to the most concise form that will still remain unambiguous for the reader. Thus, University of Oklahoma Press may be cited as "Univ. of Oklahoma," "U of Oklahoma P,"or even simply "Oklahoma"; W. W. Norton & Co. becomes simply "Norton"; and so on. The writer should adopt a basic level and style of abbreviation for publishers' names and observe it throughout.

> 13. Vitalij V. Shevoroshkin and T. L. Markery, *Typology, Relationship and Time* (Ann Arbor, Mich.: Karoma [Publishers, Inc.], 1986), 15.
> 28. Dan Sperber, *On Anthropological Knowledge: Three Essays* (New York: Cambridge [University Press], 1985), 20.

Reprint   A reprint of an older work should include the original year of publication (if known) followed by a semicolon, the word "reprint," and the reprint data.

> 36. Douglas C. McMurtrie, *The Book: The Story of Printing and Bookmaking,* 3d ed. (1943; reprint, New York: Dorset, 1990), 235.

Page number   The number of the page or pages on which the cited material can be found is preceded by a comma and followed by a period; the abbreviation *p.* or *pp.* is now usually omitted. For inclusive numbers, either the elided style (see paragraphs 11–12 on page 97) or the unelided style should be used consistently.

> 33. Roland Barthes, *Writing Degree Zero,* trans. Annette Lavers and Colin Smith (New York: Farrar, Straus & Giroux, 1977), 106–8 [or 106–108].

Articles

The following paragraphs describe specific elements of first references to articles in periodicals. Their basic elements are (1) the author's name, (2) the article's title, (3) the periodical's name and issue, and (4) the page or pages referred to. As with book references, any of this data included in the text itself can be omitted from the note.

Author's name The author's name is treated like that of a book author. Writers of book reviews or letters to the editor are treated like authors.

> 10. Renato Rosaldo, "Doing Oral History," *Social Analysis* 4 (1980): 89–90.
>
> 7. Gordon A. Craig, review of *The Wages of Guilt: Memories of War in Germany and Japan*, by Ian Buruma, *New York Review of Books*, 14 July 1994: 43–45.

Article title The article's title is capitalized headline-style, enclosed in quotation marks, and not italicized.

> 5. Richard Preston, "A Reporter at Large: Crisis in the Hot Zone," *New Yorker*, 26 Oct. 1992: 58.

Periodical name The periodical's name is italicized and capitalized like the title of a book. If the word *The* begins the name, it is generally omitted.

> 31. Richard Harris, "Chicago's Other Suburbs," *[The] Geographical Review* 84, 4 (Oct. 1994): 396.

Periodical volume, number, and date If a periodical identifies its issues by both volume and number, both may be specified (in Arabic rather than Roman numerals); a comma separates the two elements, but no punctuation precedes the volume number. However, a periodical whose pages are numbered consecutively through an annual volume actually needs only the volume number. The volume number is followed by the year, in parentheses; if the season, month, or precise date appears on the journal, it may optionally be included as well. Popular weekly and monthly magazines, including those that bear a volume-and-number designation, are normally referred to only by date. The name of the month is usually abbreviated *(Jan., Feb., Mar., Apr., May, June, July, Aug., Sept., Oct., Nov., Dec.)*, and a precise date, as for a weekly or a newspaper, should be inverted (e.g., "29 Feb. 1996"). When no volume number is used, the date is preceded by a comma and followed by a colon.

> 6. John Heil, "Seeing Is Believing," *American Philosophical Quarterly* 19 (1982): 229.
>
> 15. John Lukacs, "The End of the Twentieth Century," *Harper's*, Jan. 1993: 40.
>
> 10. Sam Dillon, "Trial of a Drug Czar Tests Mexico's New Democracy," *New York Times*, 22 Aug. 1997: A4.
>
> 8. Harold S. Powers, "Tonal Types and Modal Categories in Renaissance Polyphony," *Journal of the American Musicological Society* 34 (1981) [*or* 34, 3 (Fall 1981)] 428–70.

Page number The number of the page or pages on which the cited material can be found is always included. The page number is separated from the issue date by a colon and a space, and the abbreviation *p.* or *pp.* is omitted. As in book citations, inclusive numbers should employ either the elided or the un-elided style throughout.

Unpublished materials

When an unpublished work is cited, the title (if any) follows the author (if known) and is enclosed in quotation marks and capitalized like a book or article title. If the work is untitled, a descriptive title, not enclosed in quotation marks, should be used instead. The date (if known), any identification or cataloging number, and the name and location of the institution where it can be found, should follow. If the pages are numbered, a page reference should be included. A thesis or dissertation citation should include the granting institution and the year.

> 14. "Pedigree of the Lister family of Ovenden and Shibden Hall," SH:3/LF/27, Calderdale Archives Dept., Halifax, West Riding, Yorkshire.
>
> 7. Clive Johnson, letter to Elizabeth O'Hara, 9 Nov. 1916, Johnson Collection, item 5298, California State Historical Society, San Marino, Calif.
>
> 1. "Noster cetus psallat letus," MS 778, Fonds Latin, Bibliothèque Nationale, Paris.
>
> 30. Linda R. Spence-Blanco, "Structure and Mode in the Lassus Motets," Ph.D. dissertation, Indiana Univ., 1995, 132–35.

Subsequent References to Books and Articles

Later references to a previously cited source employ a shortened form of the data in the first note. This may include the author's last name, a shortened form of the title, and a page reference; it never includes a periodical name, the publisher's name or location, or the publication year. As with initial references, if the author's name or the title appears in the running text introducing the quoted material, they need not be repeated in the note.

> 9. Bishop, 68.
> 22. Hölldobler and Wilson, 19–20.
> 31. Quirk et al., 450.

If more than one work by a given author has been cited, the author's name should be followed by the name of the book, usually shortened, unless the title has just been mentioned in the text.

> 9. Bishop, *One Art,* 68.

A shortened reference to an article in a periodical should include the author's last name, the title of the article (often shortened), and the page number.

> 14. Lukacs, "End," 41.

Though the shortened style is almost universally employed in footnotes and endnotes today, a few writers still use the traditional Latin abbreviation *ibid.* where appropriate. *Ibid.* (for *ibidem,* "in the same place") is used only when referring to the work cited in the immediately preceding note. It may be used several times in succession. When used without a page number, it indicates the same page of the same source as in the note immediately preceding.

> 10. Simone de Beauvoir, *The Second Sex,* trans. and ed. H. M. Parshley (1953; reprint, Knopf, 1987), 600.
> 11. Ibid., 609.
> 12. Ibid.

The Latin abbreviations *op. cit.* (for *opere citato,* "in the work cited") and *loc. cit.* (for *loco citato,* "in the place cited") are very rarely used today but are often encountered in older works. *Op. cit.* refers to the source cited earlier (with other notes intervening) but not to the identical page or pages.

> 19. Sheldon and Eleanor Glueck, *Unraveling Juvenile Delinquency* (New York: Commonwealth Fund, 1950), 23.
> 20. Don C. Gibbons, *Delinquent Behavior* (Englewood Cliffs, N.J.: Prentice-Hall, 1972), 341.
> 21. Glueck, op. cit., 30–34.

Loc. cit. refers strictly to the same page or pages of the same source cited earlier, with references to other sources intervening.

> 13. W. T. Sanders, *Cultural Ecology of the Teotihuacan Valley* (State College, Penn.: Pennsylvania State Univ., 1965), 312–13.
> 14. Sabloff and Andrews, op. cit., 160.
> 15. Sanders, loc. cit.

Substantive Notes

Substantive or *content notes*—notes providing additional information, commentary, or cross-references—are provided when the author desires to supply a piece of nonessential information, usually not primarily bibliographic, without interrupting the main flow of the text. Such notes are keyed to the text in the same sequence as bibliographic notes, as in the following list.

> 1. Lyon Richardson, *A History of Early American Magazines* (New York: Thomas Nelson, 1931), 8.
> 2. Total average circulation per issue of magazines reporting to the Bureau of Circulation rose from 96.8 million in 1939 to 147.8 million in 1945.
> 3. For a particularly compelling account of this episode, see James P. Wood, *Magazines in the United States* (New York: Ronald Press, 1949), 92–108.
> 4. Richardson, 42.
> 5. For more details, see Appendix.

Texts that use parenthetical references (see below) for all purely bibliographic notes frequently simultaneously use footnotes or endnotes for substantive notes. Any note that refers to a book or article that is not the source of material used in the text (as in note 3 above) also becomes a footnote or endnote.

An unnumbered *source note* is frequently placed at the beginning of each part of a collection of works by different authors to provide information about the individual author or to state where the selection was originally published, and may also acknowledge those who assisted the author or provide other miscellaneous information. Source notes are normally not keyed to the text with a reference number or mark. (The logical place to put the mark would be on the title or the author's name, where most editors and designers are reluctant to use such symbols.) Such notes are conventionally placed at the bottom of the first page of the article or chapter, regardless of which style of documentation is being used in the text itself.

> Dr. Muller holds the Rothbart Chair in Sociology at the University of Wisconsin, Madison. The research for this article was partly funded by a grant from the Ganz Foundation.
>
> Reprinted, with permission, from the *Kansas Quarterly* 10 (1978), pp. 42–50.

Parenthetical References

Parenthetical references are highly abbreviated bibliographic citations enclosed in parentheses within the running text itself, which direct the reader to bibliography entries containing the full bibliographic data.

Parenthetical references have the advantage of providing essential information within the text without seriously impeding the reader. Such references originated in the natural sciences. Scientific research articles tend to be brief, sharply focused on a single survey or experiment, and readily summarizable; such articles obviously lend themselves well to bare parenthetical references. Parenthetical references are common in the social sciences as well. They are also often encouraged in the humanities, and even show up occasionally in writing for a broader general audience. However, they are not popular among readers reading for pleasure. Such stripped-down references are also often inadequate in the humanities, where nuances of meaning rather than hard experimental findings are often at issue. And substantive notes can rarely be handled by parenthetical references at all, and must take the form of footnotes or endnotes even if the bulk of a work's references are being treated parenthetically.

A parenthetical reference, like a superscript note reference, is placed either immediately after the quotation or piece of information whose source it refers to or after the author's name. It falls outside of quotation marks but inside commas, periods, semicolons, colons, and dashes. The following example (from Frank B. Gill's *Ornithology*) exemplifies the style used in the sciences:

> R. Haven Wiley (1974) suggests that this is the primary reason that open-country grouse display in leks whereas forest grouse tend to display solitarily. Birds-of-paradise that display in leks are species that inhabit forest borders and second-growth forest, where predation risk tends to be higher than in primary forest (Beehler and Pruett-Jones 1983). Conspicuous display on traditional sites, however, may attract predators and thereby counter any possible advantages. The Tiny Hawk of Central America, for example, seems to specialize on lekking hummingbirds as prey (F.G. Stiles 1978).

Note how the parenthetical shrinks to the year alone when an author's name appears in the text, and how initials are provided to distinguish F.G. Stiles from another Stiles in the bibliography. The corresponding bibliography entries read as follows:

Beehler, B.M., and S.G. Pruett-Jones. 1983. Display dispersion and diet of birds of paradise: A comparison of nine species. Behav. Ecol. Sociobiol. 13: 229–238.

Stiles, F.G. 1978. Possible specialization for hummingbird-hunting in the Tiny Hawk. Auk 95: 550–553.

Wiley, R.H. 1974. Evolution of social organization and life history patterns among grouse (Aves: Tetraonidae). Q. Rev. Biol. 49: 201–227.

Author-Date References

A parenthetical reference to a work normally consists simply of the author's last name followed by the year of the work's publication. This style, known as the *author-date* (or *name-year*) *system*, is the parenthetical style used universally in the natural sciences and widely in the social sciences. The alternative *author-page system* (see page 219) is seen in the field of literature and less often in other fields within the humanities. It should be noted that the two styles are often combined; especially in the social sciences, both year and page are very frequently included in the same parenthesis.

Unlike most texts employing footnotes and endnotes, those employing parenthetical references absolutely require a bibliography, since the author's last name followed by a year obviously does not adequately identify a source except for readers very familiar with the literature of their field. The bibliography will generally be alphabetically ordered by the authors' last names, so as to permit the reader to easily locate the source referred to. And in such bibliographies the author's name is usually followed immediately by the year of the work's publication, thereby matching the information given in the parenthetical reference and ensuring maximum ease of lookup.

Often a bibliography will contain works by more than one person with the same last name, or more than one work by a single author from the same year, with the result that a simplest form of author-date reference will be ambiguous. In cases of confusable last names, initials should be added to the last name in the reference (as in the "F.G. Stiles" reference above). Where a single author has published two cited works in the same year, a letter should follow each date: "(Wells 1992a)," "(Wells 1992b)," etc. Any such letters must also be attached to the date in the bibliographic entry.

If a work has two or more authors, the reference must reflect the style and order of the authors' names employed by the bibliography. A reference to a work by two authors will take the style "(Krieger and McCann 1997)"; a work with three authors might read "(Krieger, McCann, and Forster 1988)"; a work with four or more authors, "(Krieger et al. 1990)." A corporate-author name may be abbreviated—e.g. "(Amer. Chem. Soc. 1994)"—as long as abbreviating will not make the bibliographic listing hard to find. A work lacking an official author should be referred to by its title (shortened) if that is how the bibliographic entry will begin: for example, "(*Chicago Manual [of Style]* 1993)."

Two or more works by the same author can be shown within one parenthesis: "(Corelli 1988, 1990)." Citations to separate works by different authors can also be combined: "(Nilsson 1979; Flagstad and Melchior 1982)."

If a longer work is cited, it may be necessary to include a page reference, since page references are rarely permitted in the accompanying bibliography. A page number should be separated from the year by a comma or a colon and may be preceded by *p.* or *pp.:* "(Huizinga 1922, 424)," "(Huizinga 1922: 424)," or "(Huizinga 1922, p.424)." If a multivolume work is cited, the volume number can be included as well, separated from the page reference by a colon: "(Radcliffe and Laing 1985, 2:466)." A reference to an entry in a dictionary or encyclopedia should begin with the name of the actual entry if this will be the headword of its bibliography entry: "('Zoroastrianism and Parsiism,' *Ency. Britannica*)." References to classic literary works that have been published in various editions often cite stanzas, lines, verses, chapters, books, or parts rather than page numbers.

For unpublished or nonprint sources that will not be listed in a bibliography, such as telephone interviews or letters to the author, the reference must include all the data a bibliography entry would have included: the name of the source, the type of communication, the location if applicable, and the date: "(Clarissa Sackville, personal interview, Tunbridge Wells, Conn., 10 Sept. 1996)."

As with other types of references, whenever the running text immediately preceding the parenthetical reference provides any information that would normally appear in the reference, the parenthetical may omit that data.

Author-Page References

Since articles in the humanities tend to be longer and more discursively wide-ranging than scientific articles, and also less likely to be quickly superseded by articles of more recent date, a reference style that includes page references has traditionally been thought more desirable than a style that omits them in favor of a date. Thus, the type of parenthetical reference most used in certain humanities fields provides the author's last name and a page reference but omits the year of publication. This style, prescribed by the influential *MLA Handbook for Writers of Research Papers,* is used very widely in college and graduate-school term papers and theses and in journals in the field of English. It is less common in the other humanities and infrequent in the social sciences. However, as mentioned, the addition of a page reference to an author-date citation, effectively melding the two systems, is now fairly common especially in the social sciences. Such author-date-page references are endorsed by the widely followed *Publication Manual of the American Psychological Association* (APA).

When more than one work by a given author is cited, references to those works must include a shortened version of their titles (which thus take the place of the date in sciences style). Such shortened titles almost always include (and may consist solely of) a noun. Thus, citations to Jan Tschichold's *The New Typography* and *The Form of the Book* might read "(Tschichold, *Typography* 45)" and "(Tschichold, *Form* 117–18)." Note that the APA manual would call instead for the style "(Tschichold, 1991, pp. 117–18)"—but only where a page reference seemed to be needed.

Otherwise, author-page references observe the same rules as author-date references. For example, they can accommodate multiple author names and diverse citations within a single parenthetical just as author-date references do.

Like other parentheticals, they are normally placed immediately after the documented quotation or piece of information or after the author's name, outside any quotation marks but inside (i.e., to the left of) commas, periods, semicolons, colons, or dashes.

More often than in scientific writing, writers in the humanities try to mention the name of cited authors in the running text, a practice that reflects the generally more personal nature of humanities writing. This generally results in parentheticals that consist solely of a page number; such short references hardly interrupt the flow of the text, and most readers so inclined can readily learn to ignore brief numerical interpolations.

> In his *Autobiography* Yeats recalls telling Wilde, half in compliment, "I envy those men who become mythological while still living," and receiving the reply, "I think a man should invent his own myth" (87–88).

Other Systems

Number (Citation-Sequence) System

A newer style of citation, primarily employed in scientific journals (including *Science* and *Nature*), is the one sometimes known as the *citation-sequence system*, a method combining features of the endnote and parenthetical-reference styles.

In the citation-sequence system, each reference source is given a number corresponding to the order of its first appearance in the article. Less commonly, the numbering may reflect instead the alphabetical order of the authors' names. (When numbering according to alphabetical order, the author will be able to assign the final numbers only at the very end of the writing process.) The broader term *number system* covers both the citation-sequence and the alphabetical numbering methods. Regardless of which ordering is used, once a source has been cited, every subsequent citation employs the same number. The numbers are either set like footnote references or set full-size and enclosed in parentheses or brackets. The sources are listed at the end in numerical order (which may reflect either alphabetical or citation sequence).

The example below (from the *New England Journal of Medicine*) illustrates how the method works.

> No antimicrobial drug given alone is adequate therapy for H. pylori. For example, bismuth or amoxicillin given alone eradicates H. pylori rapidly in just over 20 percent of patients.[48–50] H. pylori rapidly becomes resistant to metronidazole alone, resulting in very poor rates of eradication.[62] Treatment with clarithromycin alone may be more effective; in one study an eradication rate of 44 percent was achieved with a high dose (2 g daily) given for 14 days.[55]

The corresponding entries in the nonalphabetical reference list are as follows (note that these follow a style employing minimal punctuation and italicization):

> 48. Chiba N, Rao BV, Rademaker JW, Hunt RH. Meta-analysis of the efficacy of antibiotic therapy in eradicating Helicobacter pylori. Am J Gastroenterol 1992;87:1716–27.

49. Tytgat GNJ. Treatments that impact favourably upon the eradication of Helicobacter pylori and ulcer recurrence. Aliment Pharmacol Ther 1994; 8:359–68.

50. Penston JG. Helicobacter pylori eradication—understandable caution but no excuse for inertia. Aliment Pharmacol Ther 1994;8:369–89.

55. Peterson WL, Graham DY, Marshall B, et al. Clarithromycin as monotherapy for eradication of Helicobacter pylori: a randomized, double-blind trial. Am J Gastroenterol 1993;88:1860–4.

62. Rautelin H, Seppala K, Renkonen OV, Vainio U, Kosunen TU. Role of metronidazole resistance in therapy of Helicobacter pylori infections. Antimicrob Agents Chemother 1992;326:163–6.

(Since alphabetical order is irrelevant in the citation-sequence system, the authors' names actually need not be inverted as they are here. In addition, all dates follow the journals' names here, since there are no parenthetical references that would require the dates to be moved forward.)

Note the advantages of this system. The page remains uncluttered by parenthetical references and footnotes. Several citations can be combined inconspicuously in a single parenthesis or superscript (separated by commas). Ideally, the writer will feel encouraged to provide the authors' names in the running text wherever the reader will find them useful and to omit them wherever they seem unnecessary. The system allows for maximum concision, producing reference lists of minimal length.

It also has some disadvantages. Like any endnotes, notes in the citation-sequence system require the curious reader to turn to the end of the article whenever the author or title is not named in the running text. Like parenthetical references, citation-sequence notes are intended only for purely bibliographic notes, and any substantive notes must generally be handled as separate footnotes or endnotes, since such discussions will generally relate to only one particular reference to a given source rather than to all the references to that source.

An exhaustive discussion of this and related systems is provided in Mary-Claire van Leunen's *A Handbook for Scholars* (see Bibliography).

White-Copy System

When a serious book is seeking to reach both a scholarly audience and an audience of laypeople, the author or editor will often choose a documentation style that actually omits all references from the main text while retaining complete documentation at the end of the volume. This so-called *white-copy system* thereby allows the layperson to read an entire work without being constantly reminded of its documentation. At the same time, it permits the scholarly reader to seek out the documentation at will; though he or she is not alerted to the existence of individual references, the assumption is that any serious reader will sense which text passages require documentation, and in any case will not be looking for documentation except where it is of particular interest.

The system is fairly simple to employ, only slightly more laborious than normal endnotes. Consider the following example (from Kip S. Thorne's *Black Holes and Time Warps*):

> . . . As Robert Serber recalls, "Hartland pooh-poohed a lot of things that were standard for Oppie's students, like appreciating Bach and Mozart and going to string quartets and liking fine food and liberal politics."
>
> The Caltech nuclear physicists were a more rowdy bunch than Oppenheimer's entourage; on Oppenheimer's annual spring trek to Pasadena, Hartland fit right in. Says Caltech's William Fowler, "Oppie was extremely cultured; knew literature, art, music, Sanskrit. But Hartland—he was like the rest of us bums. He loved the Kellogg Lab parties, where Tommy Lauritsen played the piano and Charlie Lauritsen [leader of the lab] played the fiddle and we sang college songs and drinking songs. Of all of Oppie's students, Hartland was the most independent."
>
> Hartland was also different mentally. "Hartland had more talent for difficult mathematics than the rest of us," recalls Serber. "He was very good at improving the cruder calculations that the rest of us did." It was this talent that made him a natural for the implosion calculation.
>
> Before embarking on the full, complicated calculation, Oppenheimer insisted (as always) on making a first, quick survey of the problem. . . .

The corresponding endnotes read:

> 212 ["Hartland pooh-poohed . . . liberal politics."] Interview—Serber.
>
> 212 ["Oppie was extremely cultured; . . . most independent.] Interview—Fowler.
>
> 212 ["Hartland had more talent . . . rest of us did."] Interview—Serber.
>
> 212 [Before embarking . . . quick survey of the problem.] Here I am speculating; I do not know for sure that he carried out such a quick survey, but based on my understanding of Oppenheimer and the contents of the paper he wrote when the research was finished (Oppenheimer and Snyder, 1939), I strongly suspect that he did.

As this example illustrates, the references can be keyed just as precisely as if superscripts appeared on the text page itself. (The accompanying reference list is divided into a section of taped interviews and a standard bibliography.) Notice that the list includes both substantive and bibliographic endnotes. If specific page references had been necessary, they could have been dealt with by an entry such as the following:

> 213 ["I miss terribly . . . in their absence."] Rabi et al. (p. 257).

The corresponding entries in the bibliography read as follows:

> Fowler, William A. Taped interview. 6 August 1985, Pasadena, California.
> Oppenheimer, J.R., and Snyder, H. (1939). "On Continued Gravitational Contraction," *Physical Review* **56**, 455.
> Rabi, I.I., Serber, R., Weisskopf, V.F., Pais, A., and Seaborg, G.T. (1969). *Oppenheimer*. Scribners, New York.
> Serber, Robert. Taped interview. 5 August 1985, New York City.

White-copy endnotes may include either full initial references or (as here) a condensed style similar to that of parenthetical references, pointing the curious reader to a bibliography for the rest of the data.

Like standard endnotes, white-copy endnotes usually benefit from running heads that indicate which text pages are covered by each page of endnotes.

The white-copy system seems unlikely to be adopted by scholarly journals or for books exclusively aimed at a scholarly readership. But it is increasingly favored by authors and editors of fairly weighty books that are seen to have the potential to attract a large audience if presented to readers in a palatable form.

Bibliographies

Works in which sources are documented generally end with an alphabetized list of the work's references, which also often includes works not specifically referred to. Such a bibliography, often helpful in footnoted works, is essential in works with parenthetical references, since these brief references only point the reader toward the complete data in a bibliography.

Works with footnotes or endnotes traditionally provide full bibliographic data in initial references, so a bibliography will generally be somewhat redundant in such works; however, even in footnoted works a bibliography will enable the serious reader to scan the writer's sources rapidly, identify useful sources for further reading, and survey the significant publications in a general field at a glance. Annotated bibliographies, with their helpful descriptions, serve additionally to guide the reader to recommended sources. Thus, footnoted (or endnoted) books generally include bibliographies. Footnoted articles, on the other hand, frequently forgo bibliographies altogether, since it is usually so easy for the reader to scan the notes themselves.

Broadly speaking, there are two different styles for bibliography entries: one for the the humanities and general writing, and one for the natural and social sciences.

Bibliography entries in the humanities essentially repeat the data contained in the initial footnote to each source, simply inverting the author's name and altering some of the punctuation. Entries in science bibliographies include all the data that humanities entries include but with various differences in style and format.

In sciences style the year of publication immediately follows the author's name; this places the same data included in the parenthetical references right at the beginning of each entry, and thus permits the reader to quickly identify the source cited in a given parenthetical reference. The other differences between the two styles are these: In the sciences, (1) initials (not separated by spaces) are generally used instead of the author's first and middle names, (2) all words in book and article titles are lowercased except the first word, the first word of any subtitle, and proper nouns and adjectives, and (3) article titles are not enclosed in quotation marks. Increasingly in scientific publications, (4) the author's first and middle initials are closed up without any punctuation, and (5) book and journal titles are not italicized.

In each set of examples below, the first group illustrates humanities style and the second illustrates sciences style. These examples, like the examples of in-text references described earlier, by no means exhaust the possible variations on these two basic systems; variant styles are recommended by various professional organizations and academic disciplines. An examination of the references in a professional or scholarly journal will reveal the minor ways in which its preferred style differs from the examples here. (The discussions preceding these examples inevitably repeat some of the information provided earlier in the "Footnotes and Endnotes" section.)

For guidence on alphabetizing entries, see Chapter 11, "Indexes."

Books

A bibliography entry for a book should include all the following elements that are relevant. (Note that most of the humanities entries in the sample bibliography entries beginning below match those shown under "Footnotes and Endnotes" beginning on page 212.)

Author's name The author's name comes first. Names of coauthors are listed in the same order as on the title page. The name of the first author is inverted so that the surname comes first and serves as the basis for alphabetization. The names of additional authors are generally not inverted (though scientific style varies in this respect). In humanities style, names are shown as they appear on the title page. In sciences style, the first and middle names are always abbreviated. In humanities style, if there are more than three authors, only the first author's name is generally shown, followed by *et al.* (set in roman type); in sciences style, either the first three names are listed and followed by *et al.* or as many as six names are listed. A period follows the final name.

In sciences style, the year of publication (with a period after it) normally follows the author's name.

Humanities Bishop, Elizabeth, *One Art*. Ed. Robert Giroux. New York: Farrar, Straus & Giroux, 1994.

Hölldobler, Bert, and Edward O. Wilson. *The Ants*. Cambridge, Mass.: Belknap–Harvard Univ. Press, 1990.

Brusaw, Charles T., Gerald J. Alred, and Walter E. Oliu. *The Business Writer's Handbook*. 5th rev. ed. New York: St. Martin's, 1997.

Quirk, Randolph, et al. *A Comprehensive Grammar of the English Language*. London: Longman, 1985.

New York Times Staff. *The White House Transcripts*. New York: Bantam, 1974.

Information Please Almanac: 1998. Boston: Houghton Mifflin, 1997.

Sciences Chandrasekhar, S. 1983. *The mathematical theory of black holes*. New York: Oxford.

Mayr, E., and P.D. Ashlock. 1991. *Principles of systematic zoology*. 2d ed. New York: McGraw-Hill.

Morris, M.S., K.S. Thorne, and U. Yurtsever. 1988. Wormholes in spacetime and their use for interstellar travel. *Amer. J. of Physics* 56, 395.

Lorentz, H.A., A. Einstein, H. Minkowksi, et al. 1923. *The principle of relativity*. Reprint: New York: Dover, 1952.

Work in America Institute. 1980. *The future of older workers in America*. New York: Work in America Institute.

McGraw-Hill yearbook of science and technology: 1997. New York: McGraw-Hill.

Title   In the humanities, the title of a book or journal is generally italicized. In the sciences, such a title is usually italicized but often not. In the humanities, headline-style capitalization (all words capitalized except for internal articles and prepositions) is standard; in the natural and social sciences, both headline-style and sentence-style capitalization (only the first word and proper nouns and adjectives capitalized) are used. (The titles of sample book references in the sciences in this chapter are set italic and use sentence-style capitalization.) Titles in the humanities include any subtitles, whereas subtitles are often omitted in science bibliographies.

> *Humanities*   Maxmen, Jerrold S. *The Post-Physician Era: Medicine in the Twenty-First Century.* New York: Wiley, 1976.
>
> *Sciences*   Hartshorne, C. 1973. *Born to sing[: An interpretation and world survey of bird song].* Bloomington: Indiana Univ. Press.

Editor, compiler, or translator   In entries for books that have an author, the name of an editor, compiler, or translator—preceded or followed by the abbreviation *ed., comp.,* or *trans.* or some combination of these—follows the title. If no author is listed, the name of the editor, compiler, or translator is placed first, followed by a comma and *ed., comp.,* or *trans.*

> *Humanities*   Beauvoir, Simone de. *The Second Sex.* Trans. and ed. H. M. Parshley. 1953; New York, Knopf, 1993.
>
> Banks, Arthur S., et al., eds. *Political Handbook of the World: 1996–97.* Binghamton, N.Y.: CSA Publications, 1997.
>
> *Sciences*   Robinson, I., A. Schild, and E.L. Schucking, eds. 1965. *Quasi-stellar sources and gravitational collapse.* Chicago: Univ. of Chicago Press.

Part of the book   When a bibliography entry cites only one part of a book, such as an essay in a collection or an article from a symposium, the name of that part is given first as a title in roman type. In humanities style, it is enclosed in quotation marks; in sciences style, it is not. The book title follows. Titles of chapters of nonfiction works by a single author are omitted.

> *Humanities*   Culler, Jonathan. "Derrida." *Structuralism and Since: From Levi-Strauss to Derrida,* ed. John Sturrock. New York. Oxford Univ. Press, 1981: 154-80.
>
> *Sciences*   Mayr, E. 1982. Processes of speciation in animals. *Mechanisms of speciation,* ed. C. Barigozzi. New York: Alan R. Liss.

Name of a series   If the book is part of a series, the series name (unitalicized) should be included, as well as the volume number if any.

> *Humanities*   Stocking, George W., Jr. *Functionalism Historicized: Essays on British Social Anthropology.* History of Anthropology Series, vol. 2. Madison: Univ. of Wisconsin Press, 1984.

    Sciences   Genoway, H.H. 1973. *Systematics and evolutionary relationships of spiny pocket mice, genus Liomys.* Special Publications of the Museum 5. Lubbock: Texas Tech Univ. Press.

Edition   If a book is other than the first edition, the number or other description of the edition ("2d ed.," "1992 ed.," "Rev. ed.," etc.) follows the title.

    Humanities   Baugh, Albert C., and Thomas Cable. *A History of the English Language.* 4th ed. Englewood Cliffs, N.J.: Prentice Hall, 1992.

                    van Leunen, Mary-Claire. *A Handbook for Scholars.* Rev. ed. New York: Oxford Univ. Press, 1992.

    Sciences   Gill, F.B. 1995. *Ornithology.* 2nd ed. New York: W. H. Freeman.

Volume number or number of volumes   In an entry that cites a multivolume work, the total number of volumes (e.g., "9 vols.") comes next. There is usually no need to cite the volumes actually used, since this will appear in a note or parenthetical reference. If only one volume was consulted, that volume alone is listed as an entry so that the text references can omit volume numbers.

    Humanities   Boyd, Brian. *Vladimir Nabokov.* 2 vols. Princeton, N.J.: Princeton Univ. Press, 1990–91.

    Sciences   Nowak, R.M. 1991. *Walker's mammals of the world.* 5th ed. 2 vols. Baltimore: Johns Hopkins Univ. Press.

Publication data   The city of publication (with the state abbreviation if necessary) and the name of the publisher follow; in humanities style, the year of publication follows the publisher.

    A colon follows the city name. In humanities style, a comma follows the publisher's name, and a period follows the date. In the sciences, a period follows the publisher's name, the date having already appeared after the author's name. If the place or publisher is unknown, use *n.p;* if the date is unknown, use *n.d.* However, any part of the publication data that is known but not printed on the title page may be added in brackets.

    If the title page lists more than one city, only the first appears in the bibliography. If a special imprint name appears above the publisher's name, it may be joined to the publisher's name with an en dash (e.g., "Golden Press–Western Publishing"). Short forms of publishers' names (e.g., "Wiley" for "John Wiley & Sons, Inc.," "Dover" for "Dover Publications, Inc.") are now fairly standard in bibliographies just as in notes; the abbreviated style, if used, should be used consistently. The word *and* and the ampersand (&) are equally acceptable within publishers' names; one or the other should be used consistently for all publishers.

    For a multivolume work published over a period of several years, inclusive numbers are given for those years. For works about to be published, "in press" is substituted for the date.

    Humanities   Shevoroshki, Vitalij V., and T. L. Markery. *Typology, Relationship and Time.* Ann Arbor, Mich.: Karoma [Publishers, Inc.], 1986.

                    Sperber, Dan. *On Anthropological Knowledge: Three Essays.* New York: Cambridge [Univ. Press], 1985.

    Sciences   Kuhn, T. 1962. *The structure of scientific revolutions.* Chicago: [Univ. of] Chicago [Press].

Reprint   A citation of a reprint should specify the original publication year (if known).

    Humanities   McMurtrie, Douglas C. *The Book: The Story of Printing and Bookmaking.* 3d ed. 1943. Reprint, New York: Dorset, 1990.

    Sciences   Lorentz, H.A., A. Einstein, H. Minkowski, et al. 1922. *The principle of relativity.* Reprint, New York: Dover, 1952.

Page references   Page numbers are normally added to book entries in a bibliography only when the entry cites a discrete portion, such as an article or story in a collection, in which case inclusive page numbers for the complete piece are shown. If that portion is in a volume of a multivolume work, both volume and page number are given.

    Humanities   Fernandez, James W. "The Argument of Images and the Experience of Returning to the Whole." *The Anthropology of Experience,* ed. Victor W. Turner and Edward M. Bruner, 159–87. Urbana: Univ. of Illinois Press, 1986.

    Sciences   Hunter, L., et al. 1991. Shorebird and wetland conservation in the western hemisphere. *Conserving migratory birds,* ed. T. Salathé. Cambridge, Eng.: International Council for Bird Preservation.

Articles

Citations to journals, like citations to books, follow a style parallel to that used in footnotes.

Author's name   The author's name follows the same style as for book entries. Writers of signed reviews or of letters to the editor are treated like authors.

    Humanities   Rosaldo, Renato. "Doing Oral History." *Social Analysis* 4 (1980): 89–90.

        Craig, Gordon A. Review of *The Wages of Guilt: Memories of War in Germany and Japan,* by Ian Buruma. *New York Review of Books,* 14 July 1994: 43–45.

    Sciences   Ho, P.T.C., and A.J. Murgo. 1995. Letter to the editor. *N. Eng. J. of Med.* 333:1008.

Article title   In humanities style, the title and subtitle are enclosed in quotation marks and capitalized headline-style. In sciences style, article titles omit the quotation marks and use sentence-style capitalization; any subtitle is generally omitted. (A few journals in the natural sciences omit the article title altogether.)

    Humanities   Preston, Richard. "A Reporter at Large: Crisis in the Hot Zone." *New Yorker,* 26 Oct. 1992: 58–81.

    Sciences   Penrose, R. 1995. Gravitational collapse and space-time singularities." *Phys. Rev. L.* 14:57.

Periodical name The periodical's name is italicized in the humanities and usually but not always in the sciences. Unlike book titles, periodical titles are capitalized headline-style in bibliographies in the sciences as well as the humanities. Any *The* at the beginning of a title is dropped. In the sciences, journal titles are generally abbreviated; each discipline has a standard set of abbreviations for its journals. (The citations in a scholarly or professional journal are the best source for such abbreviations in a given field.) Outside of the sciences, journal titles are generally not abbreviated. Titles that begin with the words *Transactions, Proceedings,* and *Annals* are traditionally inverted (thus, *Proceedings of the American Philosophical Society* becomes *American Philosophical Society Proceedings*). Names of newspapers are treated as they appear on the masthead, except that any initial *The* is omitted. A place-name is added in brackets if it is needed to identify the paper, and a particular edition ("Evening edition," "New England edition") may have to be identified.

> *Humanities* Harris, Richard. "Chicago's Other Suburbs." *[The] Geographical Review* 84, 4 (Oct. 1994): 396.
>
> Perlez, Jane. "Winning Literary Acclaim, A Voice of Central Europe." *[The] New York Times,* New England Final ed., 9 Sept. 1997: B1–2.
>
> *Sciences* Goodwin, G.G., and A.M. Greenhall. 1961. A review of the bats of Trinidad and Tobago. *Bull. Amer. Mus. Nat. Hist. [Bulletin of the American Museum of Natural History]* 122:187–302.

Periodical volume, number, and date Periodicals whose issues are primarily identified by volume and number should be identified in that way in a bibliography. Those whose issues are instead identified primarily by date must be identified by date instead. Numbers are not commonly used unless the issue is paginated independently of the volume as a whole and the number is needed to identify the issue. If the volume number corresponds to a particular year, the year in parentheses follows the volume number. In the sciences, the year is omitted here, having already appeared next to the author's name.

Some periodicals use a seasonal designation in addition to a volume and number designation; the pages are often numbered independently of the volume as a whole. Popular monthly and weekly magazines are referred to by date, as are newspapers. Precise dates are given in day–month–year order. Names of months with more than four letters are usually abbreviated.

Some scientific journals print the volume number in boldface to distinguish it from adjacent page or issue numbers.

> *Humanities* Heil, John. "Seeing Is Believing." *American Philosophical Quarterly* 19 (1982): 224–48.
>
> Lukacs, John. "The End of the Twentieth Century." *Harper's,* Jan. 1993: 39–58.
>
> Dillon, Sam. "Trial of a Drug Czar Tests Mexico's New Democracy." *New York Times,* 22 Aug. 1997: A4–5.
>
> Powers, Harold S. "Tonal Types and Modal Categories in Renaissance Polyphony." *Journal of the American Musicological Society* [or *JAMS*] 34, 3 (Fall 1981) [*or . . .* 34 (1981)]: 428–70.

Sciences   Glanz, W.E. 1984. Food and habitat use by two sympatric *Sciurus* species in central Panama. *J. Mammal.* 65:342–46.

Conway, Morris S., and H.B. Whittington. 1979. The animals of the Burgess Shale. *Scientific American* 240 (Jan.):122–33.

Page numbers   Inclusive pages for *the whole article* are normally provided at the end of the entry, preceded by a colon and followed by a period. For newspaper entries, it may be necessary to add a section letter as well (e.g., "B6"). When an article is continued on later pages after a break, those pages should be cited as well (e.g., "38–41, 159–60"); alternatively, a plus sign following the opening page number ("38+") may take the place of all subsequent numbers.

Humanities   Friedrich, Otto. "United No More." *Time*, 4 May 1987: 28–37.

Sciences   Lemon, R.E., and C. Chatfield. 1971. Organization of song in cardinals. *Anim. Behav.* 19:1–17.

Unpublished Materials

Unpublished materials often itemized in source listings include not only theses and dissertations but also a bewildering variety of other documents, particularly those that may have come to be housed in archives—letters, receipts, reports, balance sheets, music manuscripts, legal briefs, evidentiary materials, memoranda, handwritten notes, speeches, book manuscripts, and so on. (Often the author will provide a separate list of archival documents.) It would hardly be possible to dictate a comprehensive set of guidelines for citing such documents. However, the writer who is careful to note down every identifiable cataloging or identification criterion on first being shown the materials and to reproduce these in a fairly consistent format in the bibliography is unlikely to be criticized.

The author's name should be treated just as for a book or article. Any formal title should appear just as it does on the work, enclosed in quotation marks and capitalized like the title of a book or article. If the work has no official title, a descriptive title, not enclosed in quotation marks, should be used instead.

If the work is dated, the date must be included. If the date is known but does not appear on the document, it should be enclosed in brackets.

The final essential information is the cataloguing or identification number—or whatever information is necessary to identify and locate the document in its collection—along with the name of the collection, its parent institution (if any), and the city.

Humanities   "Pedigree of the Lister family of Ovenden and Shibden Hall." SH:3/LF/27. Calderdale Archives Dept., Halifax, West Riding, Yorkshire.

Johnson, Clive. Letter to Elizabeth O'Hara. 9 Nov. 1916. Item 5298, Johnson Collection, California State Historical Society, San Marino.

"Noster cetus psallat letus." MS 778, Fonds Latin, Bibliothèque Nationale, Paris.

Spence-Blanco, Linda R. "Structure and Mode in the Lassus Motets." Ph.D. dissertation. Indiana Univ., 1995.

Sciences   Maxwell, J.C. Letter to J.O. Hartwell, 9 June 1850. Bonneville
                 Archive, King's College Library, Cambridge Univ., Cam-
                 bridge, England.

Bibliography Order and Format

For ease of scanning, bibliographies are traditionally set with flush-and-hang
indention—that is, with the initial line of each entry set flush left and the subsequent lines indented. All the entries are normally listed together alphabetically, whether the first word is an author's surname or the title of a book.
(Initial articles in titles are ignored in determining alphabetical order.) Special
types of entries—recordings, artworks, films, personal interviews, archival documents, etc.—may be segregated in separate lists. Bibliographies are occasionally
divided into categories by subject matter; however, such divisions are usually
desirable only for bibliographies that represent recommended-reading lists in a
variety of discrete subject areas (as in this book's bibliography).

After the first listing of an entry by an author (or the coauthors) of more
than one listed work, the name (or names) is replaced in succeeding adjacent
entries by a long (three-em) underline or dash (usually typed as six hyphens).
It is followed by a period, or by a comma and an abbreviation such as *ed.,* just
as a name would be. The underline or dash substitutes for the author's or
coauthors' full name or names. However, it may be used only when all the
names are exactly the same in the adjacent entries; otherwise, all the names
must be written out.

A work by a single author precedes a work by that author and another; and
works *written* by an author usually precede works *edited* by the same person.

In the humanities, the various works by a single author or group of coauthors are ordered alphabetically by title. In the sciences, they are ordered by
date; if an author has published more than one article during a year, each can
be distinguished by a letter (often italicized) appended to the year (1995a,
1995b, etc.), which must also appear in any text references.

Depending on its scope, a list of sources may be headed "Bibliography,"
"List of References," "Literature Cited," "Works Cited," or "References Cited."
(The term *bibliography* has been used broadly in this chapter to cover all these
possibilities.) A list headed "Bibliography" traditionally lists all the works a
writer has found relevant in writing the text. A "List of References" includes
only works specifically mentioned in the text or from which particular quotations or pieces of information were taken. Writings in the sciences often use
the heading "Literature Cited"; however, only "literature"—published works—
actually cited can be included on such a list, and bibliographic information for
unpublished works must be provided within the text itself. (Works in press may
be considered literature.) The heading "References Cited" allows the inclusion
of unpublished works. "Works Cited" allows the inclusion of the references described below under "Special Types of References."

In an *annotated bibliography,* entries are followed by a sentence or paragraph
of description, in order to lead the reader to the most useful works for further
study. A bibliography may be selectively annotated, or every single entry may
include an annotation. The descriptive part may either be run in with the entry
or be set off by spacing, indention, italics, or smaller type.

Trow, George W. S. *Within the Context of No Context.* 1981; New York: Atlantic Monthly, 1997.
A short, strange, elegant meditation on television and post–World War II American culture. After almost two decades, its aphoristic insights seem more uncannily prescient and disturbing than ever.

The elements and options of bibliography design can best be understood by studying the bibliographies in a variety of publications.

Special Types of References

Cited sources frequently include items that do not fit neatly into any of the categories described above. Several of these types of references (recordings, films, artworks, literary classics, etc.) appear almost exclusively in humanities writing, almost always identified concisely in the text itself. Thus, most of the illustrative examples below illustrate a single style of bibliography entry, from which the corresponding note or parenthetical reference can easily be generated.

Nonprint Sources

Nonprint entries will often be listed separately from standard bibliographic items. Many bibliographies omit nonprint entries altogether; however, if the decision is made to include them, it should be done systematically.

Personal communications The name of a person who supplied information in a personal communication is listed first, styled like an author's name. A descriptive word or phrase—"personal communication," "telephone interview," etc.—follows, unitalicized and without quotation marks. The place (if applicable) and date of the communication are also given.

Sandage, Allen. Personal interview. Baltimore, 13 Sept. 1985.

Such sources are rarely included in a list of references; more often, the information is worked into the running text or provided exclusively as a footnote or endnote; in scientific publications it is usually given in the form of a parenthetical reference with no corresponding bibliography entry.

. . . seemed a rather feeble construct (A. Sandage, pers. interview, 13 Sept. 1985).

Speeches Speeches and lectures are identified by (1) speaker's name, (2) speech title, in quotation marks (or a descriptive name if the speech has no formal title), (3) name of the meeting, sponsoring organization, or occasion, (4) place, and (5) date.

Halcott-Sanders, Peter. "Armenia 1915—Rwanda 1994." LeSueur Memorial Address. Lafayette Hall, New Orleans. 2 November 1994.

Television or radio program Broadcast programs are occasionally cited in reference lists. The title of the program is usually listed first, in italics. If it is an episode of a series, the episode title is enclosed in quotation marks and the name of the series follows in roman type. If the text reference is to a particular performer, director, or other person, that person's name may be listed first and thus determine the basis for alphabetization. The names of the performers, composer, director, or other participants may follow the title. The network, the local station and city, and the date of the broadcast complete the citation.

> Burns, Ken. *Baseball.* 8 episodes. PBS. WGBY-TV, Springfield, Mass. 28 Sept.–16 Nov. 1994.

Sound recordings   How recordings are listed in a discography frequently depends on the writer's focus. The participants in a recording may be numerous and various enough that it may sometimes be necessary to create entries for which no readily available model exists. A work devoted to performers will generally alphabetize a list of recordings by performers' names. (In orchestral recordings, this will usually be the conductor's name rather than the ensemble's.) Alternatively, a listing might alphabetize by composers' or songwriters' names. If a discography is entirely devoted to a single performer or composer, that person's name should naturally be omitted from all the entries. Common foreign terms (*Quatuor, Coro, Dirigent,* etc.) may be silently translated (as they have been in the first example below). The recording's title, the recording company's name, the year, and the catalog number follow, and other information may be added as needed.

> Abbado, Claudio, cond. Gustav Mahler, *Symphony No. 3.* Vienna Philharmonic Orch. and Chorus; Jessye Norman, soprano. 2-CD set. Deutsche Grammophon, 1982. 2741010.
>
> Cruz, Celia, with David Byrne. "Loco de Amor." On David Byrne, *Rei Momo.* Cassette tape. Luaka Bop/Sire Records, 1989. 925990-4.

Films and videotapes   Films, film scripts, and videotapes are usually listed by either title or director. However, as with sound recordings, if such participants as writers, performers, or composers are the focus of the text, their names may be listed first, or such participants may be listed subsequently in a consistent order. (As with recordings, a filmography devoted to a single person will omit that person's name from all entries.) The title (italicized) is usually followed by whatever other names may be needed to identify the work. A descriptive term such as "Filmstrip," "Slide program," or "Videocassette" should be added if appropriate, followed by the production company and the year. A catalog number and any other relevant information may be added as appropriate.

> Tourneur, Jacques, dir. *Out of the Past.* With Robert Mitchum, Jane Greer, and Kirk Douglas. Screenplay: Geoffrey Homes (pseud. of Daniel Mainwaring), James M. Cain, and Frank Fenton (both uncredited). Cinematography: Nicholas Musuraca. RKO. 1947.

Artworks and crafts   Artworks are occasionally cited in reference lists. References to artworks generally begin with the artist's name, which is followed by the title (italicized), the year it was created, and the name and city of the museum or collection. The work's medium (or media) and sometimes its dimensions and a catalog number may be included as well. If the artist is unknown, the abbreviation "Anon." may begin the entry; for crafts, "Anon." may more often be omitted throughout. A descriptive title for an untitled work is not italicized.

> Repin, Ilya Yefimovich. *Zaporozhian Cossacks*. Oil on canvas. 1891. State Russian Museum, St. Petersburg.
>
> High chest. 1725–35. Boston, Mass. Pine, maple, tulip poplar. 69½ x 40¼ x 22½. Winterthur Museum, Wilmington, Del. 52.255.

Microforms Normally published material that has been microfilmed for storage is cited as if the actual works had been handled, with no mention of the microform process. Only materials that exist only or primarily on microfilm or microfiche—including archival materials, reports, privately printed works, and works published originally as microfiche sets—need to have that fact acknowledged. If they are available from a commercial service, it should be named. If the microphotography was done by the archive or library that is storing it, the latter's name and location must be given.

> Wiener Stadt- und Landesarchiv [Vienna State and Provincial Archives]. *Todten Protokoll* [List of Deceased Persons] (24 Oct. 1771). Microfilm.
>
> Russian Academy of Sciences Library, St. Petersburg (BAN). *Catalogue of Foreign Language Books and Periodicals to 1930.* 992 microfiche. London: Chadwyck-Healey.

Government and Legal Publications

If a publication by a government agency has a named author, that name may appear first. However, most government publications are officially authored by an agency rather than an individual. The name of the government (e.g., "U. S.," "Montana," "Chicago") usually comes first, then the names of the department (if applicable) and agency. The title (italicized) should be followed by any series or publication number used by the agency. Most U.S. government publications are published by the Government Printing Office, which is usually abbreviated *GPO;* however, references to congressional documents, and often other references to U.S. government sources, omit the GPO publication data altogether. Standardized abbreviations are often used in these references, but names may instead be spelled out, especially in works intended for a general audience.

> U.S. Bureau of the Census. *Geographical Mobility, March 1994 to March 1995.* Current Population Reports, Series P-20, no. 37 (1996).
>
> *United States Government Manual 1996/97.* Washington, D.C.: GPO, 1996.
>
> U.S. Office of Technology Assessment. *Informing the Nation: Federal Information Dissemination in an Electronic Age.* OTA-CIT-396 (1988).
>
> Texas Dept. of Information Resources. *Video Conferencing Standards.* SRRPUB 5-1 (1995).

Congressional documents and bills Citations of Congressional documents normally list the following elements: (1) "U.S. House of Representatives" or "U.S. Senate" and the name of the committee or subcommittee, if applicable, (2) the document's title, (3) the document's number or other description,

(4) the date, and (5) the page reference. The number and session of Congress are often included as well. The *Congressional Record* is identified only by date and page number.

> U.S. House Special Committee on Aging. *The Early Retirement Myth: Why Men Retire before Age 62.* Publ. 97-298 (1981).
> *Cong. Rec.* 2 Aug. 1996: S9466–69.

In citations of congressional bills, *H.R.* is the conventional abbreviation for "House of Representatives" and *S.* for "Senate." In citations of congressional reports, *H.* is used instead of *H.R.* For both bills and reports, the number and session of Congress follow the document title.

> H.R. 898 (Balanced Budget Act), 105th Congress, 1st Session.

Laws, regulations, and constitutions References to laws, regulations, and constitutions should be documented in the notes and bibliography whenever complete data is not provided in the text.

The legal profession itself almost invariably follows the citation forms stipulated in *The Bluebook: A Uniform System of Citation* (see Bibliography), and almost anyone writing or editing legal books must be thoroughly familiar with the *Bluebook*'s recommendations. However, its highly condensed forms, which are optimally efficient for professionals, are opaque to most laypeople. Thus, any author writing about a legal subject for a wider audience who intends to use *Bluebook* style should consider providing a guide to interpreting the citations in the prefatory matter or as a headnote to the endnotes or bibliography. Otherwise, any abbreviations should be limited to those readily understood by the public.

In general, federal laws are published in the United States Code (U.S.C.), and each state publishes its laws in its own series. In most series, the volume number precedes the name of the set. Wherever possible, the act's name (if it has one) should be included.

> Americans with Disabilities Act, 42 U.S.C. §1201 et seq. (1990).
> Minn. Stat. § 289.23.

Federal regulations codified in the *Code of Federal Regulations* or the *Federal Register* are identified by volume number, section or page number, and date.

> 32 C.F.R. § 199 (1994).
> 43 Fed. Reg. 54221 (1978).

Roman numerals are traditionally used for constitutional articles and amendments.

> Indiana Constitution, Art. III, sec. 2, cl. 4.

Court cases Titles of court cases are italicized within the text (e.g., *Surner* v. *Kellogg, In re Watson*) but not in bibliographies. The *v.* (for *versus*) is usually set roman.

A citation to a court case provides not only (1) the name of the case, but also (2) the number, title, and page of the volume in the multivolume set where it is recorded, and (3) the date. The name of the court that decided the case is usually included with the date if it is not mentioned in the running text. As in standard citations, the volume number precedes the abbreviated name of the multivolume series and the first page of the decision or regulation follows the name. (Inclusive page numbers are not used in legal references.)

> Turner Broadcasting System, Inc. v. Federal Communications Commission, 512 U.S. 622 (1997).
> Barker v. Shalala, 40 F.3d 789 (6th Cir. 1994).
> Palsgraf v. Long Island Railroad Co., 248 N.Y. 339 (1928).

Classic Literary Works

Since older classic literary works are usually available in different editions with different paginations, documentation of classic novels, stories, plays, and poems frequently includes the divisions of the work (chapter, book, part, act, scene, line) in addition to the page numbers of the edition being cited. (In long poems and verse plays with numbered lines, only the lines are cited.)

> This exchange closely resembles one in *Mansfield Park* (410; vol. 3, chap. 9).

Numerals alone are used in footnotes and endnotes and especially in parenthetical references whenever they can be easily understood without accompanying abbreviations or words such as *chap. (chapter), v. (verse), act, sc. (scene),* or *l.(line),* particularly in extended discussions of a given work. (Bear in mind that the abbreviations for *line* and *lines, l.* and *ll.* are easily mistaken for the numbers 1 and 11.) Frequently two numerals are used together, the first indicating a large division of the work and the second a smaller division, separated by a period or sometimes a comma: thus, "book 4, line 122" becomes "4.122." For the act and scene of a play, capital and lowercase Roman numerals may be used ("III.ii"), but Arabic numbers are now more common ("3.2").

> The redoubtable Mrs. Marwood has just pronounced that "For my part, my Youth may wear and waste, but it shall never rust in my Possession" (2.1).

Divisions of literary works are hardly ever cited specifically in bibliographies.

The Bible

The Bible is listed in bibliographies only when a particular edition is specified in the text; such editions follow standard bibliographic form. Whether or not an edition is specified, a standard text reference (whether provided as a note or a parenthetical) includes the name of the biblical book, set roman and often abbreviated, followed by Arabic numerals representing chapter and verse, separated by a colon (or, less often, a period). Such information commonly appears in parentheticals even in nonscholarly writing. If a book has two parts, an Arabic numeral precedes the book's name. Page numbers are never used in such citations.

> (Gen. 1:1)
> (Job 38:4-41)
> (2 Chron. 16:1-2)

Electronic Sources

Computer software References to computer software are normally treated just like book references except that the medium is added after the title. The city name is frequently dropped, and additional information, such as the operating system the software is designed for, may be added if appropriate.

> *Import/Export USA.* CD-ROM. Detroit: Gale Research, 1997. Windows.
>
> *Eighteenth-Century Fiction.* CD-ROM. London: Chadwyck-Healey.

On-line sources Since many on-line sources are highly subject to change or deletion, any on-line text likely to be cited—including personal e-mail messages—should always be either downloaded onto a disk or printed out and stored on paper (with a notation of the date accessed) as a permanent record.

There is no universally accepted standard for citing on-line sources, but since most such sources can now be accessed by using a Web browser, it is generally adequate to indicate the document's URL (uniform resource locator)—for materials available on Web, Gopher, FTP, or Telnet servers—somewhere in the citation, usually following the date on which the electronic document was published, posted, or last revised (if known). Thus a typical citation of an on-line source would show the author's name, the title of the document, the title of the complete work (such as the name of a periodical) in italics, the date, and the full URL. A URL is composed of the protocol used (*http, gopher, ftp,* or *telnet*), the server's identification, the directory path, and the file's name.

> Agmon, Eytan. "Beethoven's Op. 81a and the Psychology of Loss." *Music Theory Online* 2, 4 (1996). http://boethius.music.ucsb.edu/mto/issues/mto.96.2.4/mto.2.4.agmon.html
>
> Miller, James. "I Dream of Genie." *Avatar.* Feb. 1997. http://www.avatarmag.com/departments/fx/default.htm
>
> Davies, Al. 1997. Mitral Valvular Prolapse Syndrome. *Medical Reporter* 2, 11 (Feb.). http://www.dash.com/netro/nwx/tmr/tmr0297/valvular 0297.html
>
> CERT. "The CERT Coordination Center FAQ." (Aug. 1997). ftp://info.cert.org/pub/cert_faq (3 October 1997).
>
> Dalhousie, Duncan. "Scottish Clans On-Line." (19 May 1996). gopher://dept.english.upenn.edu:70/11/Scotts/Clan.txt (3 Oct. 1997).

In many cases it is necessary or desirable to include the date of access as well. The widely followed MLA guidelines for styling electronic citations place the date of access in parentheses at the end of the citation. Note that the date of access will often be the only date shown, since many on-line documents do not include dates.

> Walker, John. "Resources for Learning French." http://www.fourmilab.ch/francais/lfrench.html (12 Aug. 1997).

When a document is accessible only through a proprietary on-line service, the name of that service should be included in the citation:

> McGrath, Peter. "U.S. Open History." *Newsweek Interactive.* 15 Sept. 1997. America Online.

Periodicals published on paper that happen to be accessed on-line may be cited just like normal periodicals, with no acknowledgment of their on-line status, if it is clear that the text has not been altered for the on-line version.

References to mailing lists or newsgroup postings should begin with the author's name, include the subject line (or a made-up descriptive subject line), and provide the name and electronic address of the mailing-list server or newsgroup and the date posted. A personal e-mail message can be called "Personal communication" with no mention of its electronic medium.

Marchand, Jim. "L'humour de Berceo." (1 Oct. 1997). Medieval Texts Discussion List. Medtext-1@postoffice.cso.uiuc.edu

Massey, Neil. "Year 2000 and Sendmail 8.86." (1 Oct. 1997). comp.mail.sendmail

Many mailing-list discussions are archived after messages are posted. Archives are usually maintained on the mailing list's server and may also be available through a Web page. An archived message is cited in its original form unless the message was accessed through a Web server rather than the list server or newsgroup.

McCarty, Willard. "The Fate of Universities." 13 June 1997. Humanist Discussion Group. http://www.iath.virginia.edu/lists_archive/Humanist/v11/0097.html

11 Indexes

Index Types and Formats   239
The Elements of an Index Entry   240
Preparing the Index   246
Special Problems   259
Producing the Final Copy   266
Index Design and Typesetting   268

An index is a list of key words and phrases that makes information accessible by pointing to all the specific places in a book or long report where pertinent information appears. Not all such publications include indexes. For instance, indexes are usually omitted from corporate annual reports, books arranged alphabetically (such as dictionaries and directories), and publications short enough to allow readers to find all the necessary information from the table of contents. However, most nonfiction books include an index of one sort or another. This chapter describes the various types of indexes in use today, the elements of those indexes, and how to go about writing, editing, and designing indexes.

Professional indexers are responsible for most book indexes published today, and they have set a high standard. This chapter provides the information essential for an author or beginner hoping to produce a professional-quality index. Any prospective indexer should study several good published indexes against the texts they cover, which may be the best way to acquire the kind of editorial judgment necessary to produce an index of professional quality. Anyone intending to become a professional indexer should also read at least one of the books devoted to the subject (see Bibliography).

Responsibility for a book index is commonly left to the author, who may choose either to create it him- or herself or to pay a professional indexer to do so (perhaps through the publisher, who will generally have a list of freelance professionals). However, the publisher will frequently absorb the cost of producing an index. The book contract should specify such responsibility.

The ideal index would be one created by an author who has thoroughly mastered indexing technique, can set aside the uninterrupted block of time necessary to produce the index rapidly (indexing usually begins with arrival of the first page proofs and ends soon after arrival of the final pages, which may be a very short interval), and has a strong sense of how his or her reading audience will intuitively search for information. Though such ideal conditions rarely exist, authors nevertheless often create excellent indexes.

Most indexing projects can be delegated to freelance professionals with full confidence that they will do the book justice. However, technical and scientific books may present a challenge to a nonspecialist indexer, and an author who cannot find a specialist might consider hiring a colleague in the field instead.

Contracts with professional indexers are generally very simple. Professional indexers usually charge a set fee per book page or per index entry, which may go up or down for exceptional cases. Aside from the fee, the basic stipulations will be the approximate length—often given in terms of the approximate total number of lines or headings (entries, subentries, and sub-subentries)—and the deadline date. If multiple indexes will be required, that must be specified. Contracts today also commonly specify that the index be submitted both on diskette and as paper manuscript.

If the contract does not state otherwise, the indexer can assume that a single index is desired and that it should include subentries. The indexer should ask the editor to send an index style sheet with the page proofs; the style sheet should spell out any desired specifications not contained in the contract, which may include the format (indented or paragraph-style), alphabetization method, number of entry levels, style of referencing illustrations, use of boldface or italic locators, and so on, all of which are discussed on the following pages.

Index Types and Formats

Simple Indexes

The most basic type of index is composed entirely of main entries, with no subentries. The main entry typically consists of a heading followed by its page references. This type of index, sometimes called a *simple index,* is suitable for short, uncomplicated texts that will be indexed by amateurs. However, most publications calling for an index require one with subentries.

Single vs. Multiple Indexes

A single index that combines all kinds of entries is appropriate for most publications. However, some books are best served by multiple indexes. Some biographical and historical works, for instance, contain a separate index of personal names or titles of works, and some books about law contain a separate index of legal citations, or *table of cases.* Other types of works may lend themselves to other types of indexes—medical terms, first lines of poems, place-names, and so on.

Multiple indexes are not common, however (partly because users tend to find it more convenient to use a single index), and they should be considered only when (1) the index is lengthy to begin with, (2) a large percentage of the total index would consist of the special entries under consideration, and (3) it would be a real service to the reader to provide more than one index.

A compromise solution is to combine all entries in a single index but set each type of entry in a different type style: for example, caps and small caps for one class of entry, italics for another, and roman for another.

Indented and Paragraph-Style Formats

If an index contains subentries, the indexer must decide which of two formats to use: the *indented* (also called *entry-a-line*) format or the *paragraph* (also called *run-in* or *run-on*) format.

In an indented index, each new main entry, subentry, and sub-subentry begins on a new line. In a paragraph index, all subentries are run in to form a single paragraph headed by the main entry. Examples of each format are shown below. (For a discussion of how to punctuate them, see pages 251–253.)

indented format: Questionnaires by mail, 205–210
        accuracy, 207–209
        anonymity of, 313
        costs, 232–234
        sampling, 210–218
          collecting data from, 212–216
          selecting the sample, 211
        speed, 234–236

paragraph format: Questionnaires by mail, 205–210;
        accuracy, 207–209; anonymity
        of, 313; costs, 232–234; samp-
        ling, 210–218, collecting data
        from, 212–216, selecting the
        sample, 211; speed, 234–236

Indented indexes are far more common, especially in complex works such as reference books. One advantage of the indented format is that it is very easy for the reader to scan. Another is that it facilitates the use of sub-subentries.

The paragraph format, however, is favored by some publishers because it uses less space. Moreover, if entries have only a few subentries and no sub-subentries, it is not hard to locate a desired topic. Paragraph indexes are frequently found in histories and biographies, especially those in which the order of certain subentries is chronological instead of alphabetical.

The Elements of an Index Entry

The principal elements of an index entry are the main heading, subheadings, locators, and cross-references.

Main Headings

A main heading is almost always a noun, gerund, or noun phrase, the first word of which is the keyword—that is, the word the reader is likely to think of when consulting the index. The natural order of a phrase may have to be changed in order to get the keyword into initial position. A comma is used to mark any inversion of natural order.

natural order: Personalized exercise program
        Indented index
        Disadvantages of photocopying
        History of the Society of Jesus

index order: Exercise program, personalized
        Index, indented
        Photocopying, disadvantages of
        Society of Jesus, history of

Adjectives, adverbs, conjunctions, interjections, prepositions, pronouns, and verbs cannot normally function by themselves as main headings, although several of these may be used as subheadings. (If such a word is being discussed *as* a word—e.g., if the word *per* or *hopefully* is discussed in a book on English usage—it may be listed *in italics* as a main index entry.) In a heading, modifiers generally follow the keyword. Sometimes, however, the keyword will be an adjective that is the first word of a familiar compound and far more likely than the following noun to be the word that a reader will naturally be looking for. Such adjective-plus-noun compounds are usually not inverted for indexing.

Civil rights	Hazardous waste
Electoral college	Nuclear power
Genetic code	Basic training

Similar noun-plus-noun compounds are usually not inverted either.

Computer graphics	Reference works
Health care	Tax law

In cases where the decision whether to invert the natural order of a compound could go either way, two separate entries may be made, one in natural order and one in inverted order. The full entry should appear at the form that seems more likely to be consulted, with a cross-reference to it at the other entry. If the entry lacks subentries, it is usually a kindness to the reader to create a double entry by simply repeating the page references rather than providing the cross-reference.

natural order: Decimal fractions, 30, 85, 112–113

inverted order: Fractions, decimal. *See* Decimal fractions
    or
  Fractions, decimal, 30, 85, 112–113

Subheadings

Subheadings are used to make information easier to find, keeping main headings from being followed by long, discouraging lists of undifferentiated page numbers.

without subheadings: Minutes, 202, 205, 355, 388,
    410, 419, 571, 573–579, 600

with subheadings: Minutes, 571, 573–579, 600
    capitalization in, 202, 205
    certification of, 576
    corporate, 410, 419
    paper quality, 388
    resolutions, 576
    shorthand notes and, 355
    typing of, 576–579

If the text warrants it, the indexer may break the entry down into three levels—main entry, subentry, and sub-subentry. Fourth-level entries (sub-sub-subentries) should be avoided. In fact, even sub-subentries are omitted from most indexes, and indexers can generally avoid them by slightly modifying the subentries.

Subheadings, like main headings, are indexed alphabetically by the first important word, but in subheadings this keyword does not necessarily come first. Inversion is generally less necessary, and consequently less common, in subentries than in main entries. Thus, a subheading may begin with a preposition or conjunction that helps show the subentry's precise relationship to the main heading, but is disregarded when alphabetizing. (For more on alphabetizing subheadings, see page 258.)

> Numerals, 215–218, 281
> in addresses, 198
> at beginning of sentence, 215
> in dates, 215, 394
> enumerations, 215
> ordinals, 217, 218
> punctuation with, 221, 223–224,
> 229
> and symbols, 218

There must always be a logical relationship between heading and subheadings. If there is a grammatical relationship as well, the heading can be combined with each subheading to make a meaningful phrase. Many indexers try to phrase subheadings so that any prepositions or conjunctions follow the keyword rather than precede it, thus making the alphabetical order more apparent.

> Minutes, 45, 88–96
> certification of, 95
> corporate, 89
> format of, 91–92
> shorthand notes and, 90

A purely logical relationship will often suffice; for example, the simple subheading "resolutions" under this "Minutes" heading would undoubtedly be sufficient even without a preposition or conjunction. However, such omissions often risk making the entry hard to understand.

Subheadings may occasionally be listed in chronological rather than alphabetical sequence; this is most common in histories and biographies, where an arrangement of topics by date is often appropriate.

> Presidential campaigns, 54, 186–199;
> of 1948, 187; of 1952, 188; of
> 1956, 188; of 1960, 189–191;
> of 1964, 192; of 1968, 193–194
>
> France, 13, 47–48; before World
> War I, 33, 48; during World
> War I, 58–60, 89–90; at Paris
> Peace Conference, 76, 78–84;
> in interwar period, 86–87, 172–175,
> 184–86; fall of in 1940, 187–188;
> during World War II, 190–194

Page References and Other Locators

Locators—that is, page references as well as alternative locators such as subsection and paragraph references (e.g., "8.22.3b")—are listed in numerical sequence from lowest to highest, separated by commas. In a multivolume work, a volume number may precede the locator; for example, "2:172" would mean page 172 in volume 2.

Inclusive page numbers   Inclusive page numbers tell the reader exactly how far the discussion of a topic extends. For example, the sequence "212–216, 219–220, 222" tells the reader that a lengthy discussion of the topic on pages 212–216 is followed by briefer mentions. If the interruptions in this discussion had been very brief, the indexer would have simply written "212–222." When a discussion of a topic is continuous from, say, page 24 to page 25, the indexer would enter "24–25"; if there are two separate, discontinuous references to the topic on these pages, the indexer would instead enter "24, 25." (Inclusive page numbers are joined by a typed hyphen, which will be typeset as an en dash.)

There are two standard ways to style inclusive numbers. The clearest method is to provide all numbers in full; for example, "232–234," "504–506." The alternative is to elide (or shorten) them; for example, "232–34," "504–6." Indexes most commonly use elided numbers, since they save space. (For details on styling elided numbers, see paragraph 12 on page 97.)

Throughout this chapter, the nonelided style is used.

Older indexes sometimes employ two less-specific indicators of extended discussions. *Passim* (Latin for "here and there") has traditionally signified irregular mentions of a subject following its main discussion. For example, "Corrosion, 55–77 *passim*" could refer to what we would now usually specify more precisely by (for example) "Corrosion, 55–61, 62, 64, 67–68, 75, 77."

The abbreviation *ff.* (for *folios*, meaning leaves or pages of a book) following a page number—as in "Trade, international, 530 *ff.*"—indicates a continuing, but interrupted or less important, discussion. Today such an entry would instead provide inclusive page numbers and (optimally) a list of subheadings, some of whose locators might not fall within the inclusive page numbers of the main entry.

> Trade, international, 530–540
>   Chamber of Commerce, 537, 549
>   Commerce Department, 533–535
>   Export–Import Bank, 537–538
>   financing exports, 537–539, 582

Locators for nontext references   Nontext materials such as tables, diagrams, photographs, and maps are sometimes identified as such in the index, especially if they appear on a different page from the pertinent text. One way to identify illustrations is to print any numbers that locate such material in italic or, less commonly, boldface type. A note at the beginning of the index can explain the procedure.

> Agincourt, Battle of, 100, *101*   Bactrian camel, 115–116, **117**
> Aircraft, 208, *209*   Badger, 70, **72–75**
> Alexander I, 171, *171*, 173

Another common method is to precede or follow the locator number by an identifying term such as *illus.* (or *ill.*), *map,* or *table,* printed in italics or enclosed in parentheses. These special locators are usually listed in sequence with the other locators.

> Brazil, 204–209, *map* 210, 335, 376
> Data files, foreign, 53–56, 59 (illus.), 110

Less commonly, they follow the page references.

> Medical history, 183–185, 294–295, *ill.* 186

Locators for footnotes and endnotes   Footnotes and endnotes that merely document a bibliographic source are not indexed. But notes that provide supplementary discussions may be indexed. In a note reference the abbreviation *n* (for *note*) is added to the page number. (If the note is on the same page with similar information that is being indexed anyway, the note reference is unnecessary.)

> Genoa, 43, 74n, 86–87

A reference to one of several numbered footnotes at the bottom of a single page may or may not include the footnote number; the indexer should establish a consistent policy on this point. However, any reference to an endnote (a note listed with the rest of the notes at the end of an article, chapter, or book) should include the note number. Whenever a note is identified by number, one of the following forms is used:

> 22n.3   *or*   22n3
> 22nn. 2, 4   *or*   22n2, 22n4

Some indexers like to make such references clearer by enclosing them in parentheses.

> 22 (n3)
> 22 (nn. 2,4)

Cross-References

Cross-references direct index users to subjects they might otherwise miss when looking for a keyword other than the one the indexer has chosen for the principal reference. The choice of what and how to cross-reference requires careful thought, since there must be enough cross-references to guide the users but not so many as to overload the index and insult their intelligence.

There are two kinds of cross-references, *see* references and *see also* references.

See references   The more common is the *see* reference, which tells the reader that all information on the heading's topic is covered by another heading. (For the use of *see* references to subentries, see page 255.)

> Journal titles. *See* Periodical titles

See references can guide the reader:

1. from an abbreviation or a popular or older term to an official or current term

   FDA. *See* Food and Drug Administration, U.S.
   Burma. *See* Myanmar

2. from a person's pseudonym to his or her real name, or vice versa

   Parley, Peter. *See* Goodrich, Samuel G.
   Tokyo Rose. *See* D'Aquino, Iva Toguri
   Blair, Eric Arthur. *See* Orwell, George
   Mortenson, Norma Jean. *See* Monroe, Marilyn

3. from a woman's married name to her birth or professional name, or vice versa

   Cronyn, Mrs. Hume. *See* Tandy, Jessica
   Murry, Kathleen. *See* Mansfield, Katherine
   Newbold, Edith. *See* Wharton, Edith

4. from the defendant's name to the plaintiff's name in a legal citation

   Smith, Colby Corp. v. See *Colby Corp. v. Smith*

5. from one form of a corporate name to another

   Mark D. Bancroft and Sons, Inc. *See* Bancroft, Mark D., and Sons, Inc.

6. from any other kind of listing possibly expected by a reader to the principal entry

   Quotations, long. *See* Block quotations
   Tape, magnetic. *See* Magnetic tape
   Virgule. *See* Slash

Double entry A double entry is sometimes preferable to a *see* reference, especially when the heading has no subheadings and few locators. The two "Journal titles" entries below take about the same amount of space, but the second will save time for the reader who happens to look it up.

| *cross-reference:* | Journal titles. *See* Periodical titles
Periodical titles, 56–57 |
| *double entry:* | Journal titles, 56–57
Periodical titles, 56–57 |

If the "Periodical titles" entry contained subheadings or a long list of locators, the cross-reference would be preferable.

See also references The second type of cross-reference is the *see also* reference, which usually comes at the end of an entry and directs the reader to additional information on a closely related subject. (For the use of *see also* references with subentries, see pages 255–257.)

Evaluation, 154–156, 303, 305. *See also* Rating systems

> Professionals, career, 245–251. *See*
>   *also* Managers; Middle management

The indexer should obviously avoid circular cross-reference entries that do not lead to additional information.

> Pine trees. *See* Trees
> Trees, 396. *See also* Pine trees

For the styling of entries and cross-references, see pages 255–257.

Preparing the Index

Marking the Page Proofs

The indexer works from page proofs, the stage of production at which final page numbers are assigned to the pages. It is inefficient to work from unpaged first (or galley) proofs, because so much time must later be spent looking for the same material on the page proofs and copying the page numbers. In addition, there is always the chance that the galleys will be heavily edited, requiring time-consuming revision of the index. Working from galleys is efficient only when a work is to be indexed according to locators other than page numbers.

It is a good idea to scan through the whole work at the outset to gain some sense of its scope, purpose, and terminology before beginning to read and mark the page proofs systematically.

What to mark on page proofs As you read, always keep the index user in mind by asking yourself, Is this information likely to be looked up? If so, under what word? If more than one possible keyword occurs to you, note them in the margin. Look for significant nouns. Proper nouns are the most obvious, but resist the temptation to index those that appear in very casual references or in lists of examples. All terms that are defined or glossed within the text itself (and generally italicized as well), should be indexed.

Certain parts of a book are not indexed; these include prefaces, glossaries, bibliographies, chapter summaries, review questions, and any footnotes that merely provide source references. However, some material ancillary to the main text should be indexed if indexing may prove useful to the reader, including introductions, important bibliographical references within the body of the text, tables and charts (but not separate items within them), appendixes, footnotes and endnotes that contain discursive text, and illustrations and maps.

How to mark proofs Underline or circle key words and phrases as you read. You may want to write additional words that summarize the information in the margins, or to add synonyms and related phrases for the terms you have underlined (for use as possible cross-references). If multiple indexes are required, separate colors can be used to flag each type of entry—for example, blue for authors' names and red for subject entries.

A dash or colon after an entry (either as underlined in the text or added

in the margin) can indicate that it will be a main heading; a dash or colon before the word can indicate a potential subheading. If you underline a proposed
subheading in the text, write the probable heading in the margin. (Whether a
given term will be a heading or a subheading may not become obvious until
the final editing.) Indicate inversions with a slash or a transposition sign at the
point of inversion. (Experienced indexers often develop individual shortcuts
and may not need to mark each heading or subheading in detail.)

A page proof marked for indexing is shown in Figure 11.1. Proposed index entries are underlined, and inverted text is shown by a slash before the
keyword (such as "court action, types of"). Cross-references are indicated by a
circled "XR" in the margin, and the main term is circled in the text. An alternative possible heading "Legal procedures" is enclosed in brackets, to be considered when the final entries for the index are compiled.

Phrasing of Headings

As mentioned earlier, the indexer should stick as closely as possible to the author's phrasing, and should carefully follow the author's spelling and use of
capitals, italics, quotation marks, and accents.

Choose whether to make a particular keyword either singular or plural; the
plural form is usually suitable for both singular and plural references.

Be concise. In subheadings, avoid unnecessary prepositions like *concerning*
and *regarding*, and retain only those words that are needed to clarify the meaning
or the relation of main heading to subheading. In the example below, some of
the relationships are purely logical, so no connecting words are needed, while
other relationships are specified by conjunctions or prepositions.

> Paragraphs
>   conjunctions and
>   in correspondence
>   development and strategy
>   indention
>   omission of
>   of quoted material

If two different topics require identical headings because they are
homonyms, make separate entries and identify each heading with a modifier or
other explanatory word or short phrase. (For details about alphabetizing such
entries, see page 258.)

> Creeper (bird), 224
> Creeper (plant), 361–362
>
> References, employment, 145–147
> References, in manuscript, 222–226

Compiling the Index Entries

Although index entries may be prepared chapter by chapter as you finish
marking the page proofs, it is usually best not to begin preparing them until
most of the proofs have been read and marked. Closely examining a large por-

Figure 11.1 Page Proof Marked for Indexing

---

22   AMERICAN LAW AND THE JUDICIAL SYSTEM

The office of the *public/defender* is now active in many states. Public defenders provide legal counsel for people of limited means in both trial and appellate courts.

Court Procedures   [Legal procedures]

Legal procedures vary from state to state and from court to court. This lack of uniformity has led legislatures and bar associations to try to reduce the number of disparities among various jurisdictions by standardizing court procedures, legal terminology, and legal documents. Standardizing legal procedures : is of great value to the courts and the legal profession in the efficient administration of justice and the handling of cases in court.

In an effort to simplify common law pleading, Congress in 1938 adopted a set of rules known as the *Federal Rules of Civil Procedure.* These rules set out each step in a civil proceeding, including the method of preparing required documents in all federal courts. Since then, the majority of the states have adopted similar rules. Consequently, the rules of procedure in the state courts are to a certain extent now uniform.

Types of Court Action

The courts have responsibility in three general areas—criminal, civil, and equity law. In most jurisdictions, the same courts try cases in all three areas. In a few jurisdictions, special courts known as chancery courts hear equity cases, and some states have separate courts for civil and criminal cases. Under the Federal Rules of Civil Procedure, there is no longer a distinction between law and equity in the preparation of pleadings in civil law cases.

Criminal actions An individual or a group breaking a law designed to protect society from harm is considered to have committed a crime. Because the public has suffered as a result of the crime, the people of the state or of the United States bring the action; they are represented in court by a public official who may be known as a *district attorney,* a *public prosecutor,* or a *United States attorney.* The jurisdiction of each court determines the types of crimes that are to be prosecuted there. Courts of limited jurisdiction generally hear lesser crimes, or misdemeanors, while courts of general jurisdiction try the more serious crimes, or felonies.

Civil actions A civil case may arise when the actions of an individual or a group cause harm to another, who then goes to court seeking compensation for that harm. The injured party, called the *plaintiff* or *complainant,* asks the court to grant damages in the form of a payment of money. In some jurisdictions, if either party in the case requests it, a jury may hear the trial. If neither party requests a jury, the judge renders judgment after hearing both sides. In civil actions the party who brings the action must present a *preponderance of evidence* or the action will fail.

Equity actions In most jurisdictions equity actions are encompassed within civil actions, although a few states provide separate courts of equity. In equity

tion of the work will provide a perspective that may help you determine the best headings throughout.

After the entries have been marked on the page proofs, the information is transferred to the index file, either by keyboarding them into a word-processing file—by far the more common method today—or by writing or typing them on index cards in the traditional manner. Regardless of the system used, the basic steps are similar. (Experienced indexers may combine some of these steps into one procedure.)

1. Transfer information from page proofs. Make a separate entry for each reference, consisting of only one heading or subheading and one locator. Type the keyword first, followed by any modifiers. Do not enter subheadings under a heading at this point, even if you are certain they will appear that way in the final index. It will be simple to group individual subheadings together later on, but frustrating to try to separate entries already compiled under one heading.

2. Add one locator to each entry. Note where a particular reference ends; check the next page to see if the discussion continues. Make a separate entry for each reference to a particular heading. For example, two separate entries would be necessary to record references to "E-mail systems" on pages 25 and 28 of a work. If you list more than one locator for a heading, and later find that the heading must be subdivided or consolidated with a similar heading, collating the locators in numerical order will become considerably more difficult.

3. Include explanatory comments. Explanatory comments should further identify the topic or key a prospective subheading back to its prospective heading. Type these comments in all caps or boldface, enclose them in brackets, or otherwise mark them so that they are not copied onto the final index manuscript. Their function is only to aid your subsequent sorting job. After typing each entry, double-check the information, especially the spelling of proper nouns and scientific or technical terms and the accuracy of locator numbers.

4. Make cross-reference entries. Make a separate entry for each cross-reference.

5. Edit the entries. It is at this point that final decisions are made about phrasing and the relative significance of headings. Editing should ideally be done only after the markings from the complete page proofs have been transferred to the file, because only then does the indexer have a full understanding of the work. However, because of time pressure, indexers usually edit the entries for each chapter as it is received. Begin with the first chapter of page proofs and reread each entry to make sure the information is accurate. As you read, ask yourself:

Is the material significant enough to index?

Do the headings and subheadings make sense? Are they headings the reader is likely to look up?

Are all the cross-references necessary? Are additional ones needed?

Are all the cross-references still valid, or should they be revised in view of your subsequent editing of the entries?

Does the wording of the cross-references precisely match that of the entry headings referred to?

The final step is to add proper capitalization and punctuation, as described in the "Styling of Entries" section below.

6. Sort the entries. Group together entries that have the same heading, putting the locators in numerical order. Group all identical subheadings together under their main headings; delete any redundant headings or subheadings. Place cross-references in proper order within the entry. The Sort function on your computer can order entries as they are keyboarded; however, subentries often must be ordered manually. (For sorting methods with dedicated indexing software, see the section beginning on page 267.) Eliminate any unintended duplication. If you see several closely related subheadings with only one or two locators each, consider consolidating them. Conversely, any subheading with a large number of locators might be broken down into sub-subheadings, and a main entry with a large number of subheadings may often be broken down into two separate entries.

Examples of unedited and edited index entries that have been compiled from a marked-up page proof are shown in Figures 11.2, 11.3, and 11.4.

Figure 11.2 Unedited Index Entries (computer list)

Public defender, 22
Defender, public. *See* Public defender
Court procedures, 22-28
Legal procedures   [Court procedures]
Legal procedures: standardization, 22
Federal Rules of Civil Procedure, 22
Procedure, rules of, 22
Court action, types of, 22-23
Chancery courts, 22
Civil Procedure, Federal Rules of, 22
Criminal actions, 22
District attorney, 22
Public prosecutor, 22   [xr District attorney]
United States attorney, 22   [xr District attorney]
Courts of limited jurisdiction, 22
Courts of general jurisdiction, 22
Civil actions, 22
Plaintiff, 22, 24
Complainant, 22.   [xr Plaintiff]
Preponderance of evidence, 22
Evidence, preponderance of. *See* Preponderance of evidence
Equity actions, 22-23
Courts of equity, 22-23

Figure 11.3 Sorted and Edited Index Entries

Chancery courts, 22
Civil actions, 22
Civil Procedure, Federal Rules of, 22
Complainant. *See* Plaintiff
Court actions
   civil, 22
   criminal, 22
   equity, 22–23
Court procedures, 22–28
Courts
   of equity, 22–23
   of general jurisdiction, 22
   of limited jurisdiction, 22
Criminal actions, 22
Defender, public. *See* Public defender
District attorney, 22, 26
Equity actions, 22–23
Evidence, preponderance of. *See* Preponderance of evidence
Federal Rules of Civil Procedure, 22
Legal procedures
   standardization, 22
   See also Court procedures
Plaintiff, 22, 24
Preponderance of evidence, 22, 28
Procedure
   rules of, 22
Public defender, 22
Public prosecutor. *See* District attorney
United States attorney, 22, 25. *See also* District attorney

Styling of Entries

To ensure consistency, indexers observe strict style rules for the punctuation, capitalization, and indention of entries. The following paragraphs present general rules that apply to most kinds of entries. The styling of cross-references is discussed on pages 255–257, and styling of some problematic kinds of entries is discussed in the section beginning on page 259.

Punctuation Commas are used (1) to separate a keyword from its modifier(s) in an inverted entry phrase, (2) to separate each heading and subheading from its locators, and (3) to separate locators.

Periods are used only to separate an entry from a cross-reference that follows it; they are never used to mark the end of an entry (other than an abbreviation). Some indexers prefer to use a comma to set off cross-references.

Figure 11.4 Selected Entries on Index Cards

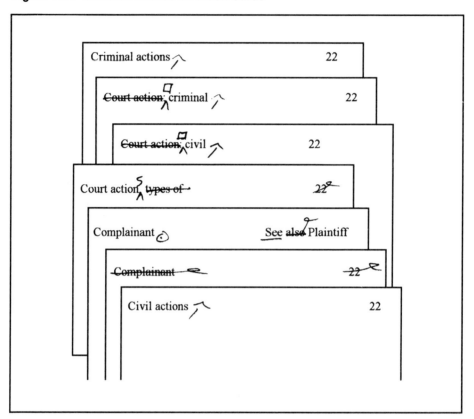

Semicolons are used to separate the parts of a multiple cross-reference. In paragraph indexes, semicolons separate the subentries.

Indented index An indented index requires less punctuation than a paragraph index, since indention itself serves to separate the parts of an entry. A main heading that is followed by subheadings may or may not have its own locators, depending on whether the indexer finds references that are best regarded as belonging to the broad topic. If a main heading lacks its own locators, it is normally unpunctuated.

```
Bankruptcy law
    forms, 356, 358
    judges, 11
    referees and receivers, 19

Bankruptcy law, 10, 23–26, 355–358
    forms, 356, 358
    judges, 11
    referees and receivers, 19
```

Less commonly, a colon follows a heading or subheading without locators of its own.

> Exposures:
>   filters and, 33–35
>   how determined, 36–38
>   time:
>   interiors, 44–45, 58
>   with microscope, 100–102
>   for stars, 122

Occasionally an indented index will run in the first subentry on the same line with the main heading, separating them with a colon.

> Waves: longitudinal, 99
>   seismic, 94–96
>   sound, 96
>   surface, 90

Paragraph index In a paragraph index, semicolons are used to separate subentries. If a main heading has its own locators, they are followed by a semicolon; if it has no locators, a colon separates it from the first subheading.

> Mineral deposits, 20–28, 199; coal,
>   55–57; formation of, 17, 23–26;
>   petroleum, 126–130

> Mineral deposits: coal, 55–57; for-
>   mation of, 17, 23–26; petroleum,
>   126–130

If the subentries are divided into sub-subentries, commas are used to separate the latter from one another and from their subentry. (For more on sub-subentries, see pages 241–242.)

> Questionnaires by mail, 205–210;
>   accuracy, 207–209; anonymity
>   of, 313; costs, 232–234; samp-
>   ling, 210–218, collecting data
>   from, 212–216, selecting the
>   sample, 211; speed, 234–236

Capitalization Most indexers capitalize the initial letters of main entries and lowercase those of subentries. Some prefer to lowercase all entries (except proper nouns and adjectives).

Certain main entries should always be lowercased, even in an index that capitalizes its main entries. For example, the particles in proper names that are indexed by a lowercase particle (e.g., "de Klerk, Frederik Willem") are usually not capitalized. (For more on styling personal names, see pages 259–263.) Any abbreviation normally printed in lowercase letters keeps its form as a main entry (e.g., "f-stop" or "pH measurement"). For such names and abbreviations, always follow the author's capitalization.

Italic and boldface type   Sometimes headings or locators are italicized or boldfaced to distinguish them from the surrounding text. Italics are used for such items as titles of books, foreign terms, and names of law cases (following the style used in the text itself), as well as for *see* and *see also* in cross-references. Sometimes italics denote locators for illustrations or other nontext references, as discussed on pages 243–244.

> Afterlife, 218, 290, 355–356, 358
> *Against Catilene* (Cicero), 218
> Agdistis, 288–289
> *Ager* (land), 148
>
> Douglass, Frederick, 115, 274, 294–295
> *Dowdell v. United States*, 449
> Draft riots, 214, 249
> *Dred Scott* case, 184–185, 295–296, 370

Boldface type may be used to indicate a major topic or the locators for the principal discussion of a topic. Sometimes boldface is reserved instead for the volume number in a locator. In scientific indexes, boldface type is often used for illustration locators or definitions of terms. Punctuation following a boldface reference should not be boldface. Any special uses of italic or boldface type should be explained in a note at the beginning of the index.

> Football, 283, **403–404**
> Ford, Henry, 65, **409–410**, 741
> Ford Foundation, 262, 835
>
> Legume, **7:**247–248
> Lehigh River, **1:**280
>
> Abdomen, 11, **167–169**, 345, 403
> Accessory heart, **249**
> Air sac, 83, **379**, 390–392

Indention   For ease of scanning, all indexes are set with hanging indention; that is, the first line of each main entry begins flush left, while all subsequent lines of the entry are indented to some degree.

The usual unit of indention in typeset indexes is one em. Thus, in an indented index the main entry begins flush left, subentries are indented one em, and sub-subentries are indented two ems, as in the first example below. Runover lines for all entries—main entries as well as subentries and sub-subentries—are indented the same amount from the left margin, usually one em more than the largest subheading indention.

> *indented format:*   Telephone communications, 10–12,
> > 34–35, 61, 255–260
> > local calls, 255
> > long-distance calls, 256–260,
> > > 267–269
> > > bill-to-third-party calls,
> > > 257
> > > collect calls, 257
> > > credit-card calls, 258–259
> > PBX systems, 34–35, 48

In paragraph indexes, the main entry begins flush left and all runover lines are indented the same amount.

> *paragraph format:*   Telephone communications, 10–12,
> 34–35, 61, 255–260; bill-to-third-
> party calls, 257; collect calls, 257;
> credit-card calls, 258–259; local
> calls, 255; long-distance calls,
> 256–260, 267–269; PBX systems,
> 34–35, 48

Cross-Reference Style

Cross-references should match exactly the phrasing, capitalization, and punctuation of the heading or subheading they refer to. Only in rare cases when the heading is exceptionally long should it be shortened in a cross-reference.

Multiple *see also* references are listed in alphabetical order and separated by semicolons.

> *See also* Library; Reference works; Research

Cross-references do not end with periods, even though they read like sentences.

See and *see also* are italicized in most indexes. When the heading referred to (e.g., a book title or a Latin species name) is already italicized, *see* and *see also* are frequently set roman to distinguish them from the italicized headings.

The initial *s* in *see* and *see also* is usually capitalized. However, when a cross-reference is enclosed in parentheses (as in many paragraph indexes) or preceded by punctuation other than a period, the *s* is lowercased.

To direct the reader to other headings that are too numerous to list, the indexer may employ general cross-references, normally in italics.

> Herbs, wild, 560–567. *See*
> *also specific herbs*
>
> Government, state, 134, 136–137.
> *See also* Governors; *names of*
> *individual states*

Cross-reference to a subentry   A cross-reference directing the reader to a subentry generally begins with the words *see under* or *see also under* followed by the main heading.

> Syrinx. *See under* Sound production
>
> Syrinx, 51. *See also under* Sound production

An alternative method is to specify both the main entry and the specific subentry, separated by a colon.

> Syrinx. *See* Sound production: in syrinx
>
> Syrinx, 51. *See also* Sound production: in syrinx

A double entry may always be substituted for a *see* reference, particularly if it will not require any more space.

> Syrinx, 51, 56–57

Cross-reference styles for indented and paragraph indexes *See* references are always run in with their headings or subheadings. However, the position and punctuation of *see also* references depend on whether the reference is attached to a main entry or a subentry, and whether the index format is indented or paragraph-style.

In most indented indexes, *see also* references are run in with their entries.

> Taxes, 233–252. *See also* Tax
> collection systems
> federal estate tax, 233–237
> life estate, tax consequences
> of. *See* Life estate
> state inheritance tax, 240–
> 246, 251

Alternatively, the *see also* reference can be set as a separate subheading, always the last one in any list. A *see also* reference from a main heading is set as a subheading; a *see also* reference from a subheading is set as a sub-subheading. Both are frequently enclosed in parentheses.

> Trustees, 54–56, 75–80
> college, 433, 467
> as guardians, 77–80
> (*See also under* Banks)
>
> Columns, 261–275
> breaking, 266–267
> length of, 273–274
> parallel, 283
> (*See also* Tables)
> width of, 265, 267–269

In paragraph-style indexes, a *see* reference always immediately follows the heading it applies to (as shown on page 244), and a *see also* reference that applies to a subheading immediately follows that subentry. *See also* references that pertain to the main heading may either follow it immediately or, more commonly, appear at the end of the complete entry.

> Tundra (*see also* Alpine ecosystem;
> Arctic ecosystem): biotic community, 225–227; soils, 221–222; and
> taiga, 220
>
> Tundra: biotic community, 225–227;
> soils, 221–222; and taiga, 220. *See*
> *also* Alpine ecosystem; Arctic ecosystem

In both paragraph and indented indexes, cross-references that apply to a subheading always follow the subentry immediately. In a paragraph index they are enclosed in parentheses.

> Territory: boundaries, 22–25; breeding and nonbreeding, 25–29;
> functions of, 20–21; maintenance

of, 26–27 (*see also* Chickadee,
territorial behavior of). *See also*
Aggression; Breeding

Note that *see* and *see also* within parentheses in a paragraph index are low-ercased when they are not preceded by a period.

Alphabetizing

Several rules of alphabetization apply to all methods of indexing.

Word-by-word vs. letter-by-letter There are two basic ways to alphabetize. The *word-by-word system* alphabetizes entries by the first word of a phrase. If two headings have identical first words, the second word is considered, then the third, and so on up to the first comma, colon, or period. The word-by-word system is the one familiar to file clerks, who are taught that "nothing comes be-fore something": that is, that a group of letters followed by a space (i.e., "nothing") is filed before any identical group of letters followed immediately by additional letters, a hyphen, or an apostrophe.

Capital gains	High Top Fire Tower
Capital stock	Highlands Audubon Society
Capital-intensive industries	High's Station
Capitalism	Highways, maintenance of

In the *letter-by-letter system*, or "dictionary style" (so called because it is com-monly used in dictionaries), every letter is considered in sequence up to the first comma, period, or colon; word spaces are ignored.

Civil Aeronautics Board	National Insurance Act of 1911
Civilian Conservation Corps	Nationalization of industries
Civil War	National Labor Relations Board

The letter-by-letter system makes alphabetizing a little easier for the in-dexer, while the word-by-word system can be easier for the reader because it groups identical single words together. But the differences are minor, and ei-ther system can at times produce awkward-looking series.

word-by-word	*letter-by-letter*
Bank Holding Company Act	Bankers in government
Bank of America	Bankers Trust
Bankers in government	Bank Holding Company Act
Bankers Trust	Bank of America
East African Common Market	East African Common Market
East India Company	"Eastern banking establishment"
"Eastern banking establishment"	Eastern Europe
Eastern Europe	East India Company

Both alphabetical systems are in wide use; the word-by-word system is slightly more common.

General rules for alphabetizing Quotation marks, apostrophes, and accent marks are ignored in alphabetizing. Hyphens (*Pan-African, bill-to-third-party calls,* etc.) are also disregarded, and the linked elements are considered as a single unit, regardless of whether the word-by-word or letter-by-letter system is being used.

Bentley, Thomas	Queen Anne's lace
"Bentley's Miscellany"	Queen bee
Bento Gonçalves (Braz.)	Queen-of-the-night
Benton, Thomas Hart	Queen's crown

Words followed by a comma or colon are alphabetized before any identical words followed by additional words with no intervening punctuation.

> *Capital: A Critique of Political Economy*
> Capital, convertibles as source of
> Capital, cost of
> Capital budgeting
> Capital expenditures

In alphabetizing subheadings, any introductory article, conjunction, or preposition is usually ignored.

> Abbreviations, 400–410
>   of academic degrees, 338, 405
>   with apostrophe, 346, 403
>   at beginning of sentence, 401
>   capitalization of, 404
>   in dates, 405–406

However, some indexers prefer to alphabetize by the subheading's first word, regardless of its relative importance.

> Abbreviations, 400–410
>   at beginning of sentence, 401
>   capitalization of, 404
>   in dates, 405–406
>   of academic degrees, 338, 405
>   with apostrophe, 346, 403

Identical headings that are distinguished by parenthetical explanations are alphabetized according to the words in parentheses; the order may be alphabetical or chronological:

> References (employment)
> References (manuscript)
>
> Grey, Sir George (1799–1882)
> Grey, Sir George (1812–1898)

Words that are spelled alike but that have different meanings have traditionally been sorted according to the following order: (1) name of a person, (2) name of a place, (3) common noun, (4) title of a work.

> Lévis, Québec
> Levi's (jeans)

civil disobedience
Civil Disobedience (Thoreau)

However, this rule is no longer widely followed, and parenthetical identifiers following the entry proper will usually provide a basis for alphabetization.

Special Problems

Some kinds of entries tend frequently to pose particular kinds of indexing problems. Those discussed in this section are (1) personal names, (2) place-names, (3) titles of works, (4) abbreviations, (5) numerals, and (6) legal citations.

Personal Names

Most personal names are easily indexed: the surname comes first, followed by a comma and the given name or names. But some foreign names, especially those beginning with articles or other prefixes, and names with titles attached require the indexer to understand and follow certain conventions.

Pseudonyms A person's name may have to be indexed in more than one place. For instance, authors who write under a pseudonym usually are indexed under their real names, though the reverse may also occur. The same may apply to entries for married women and their birth or professional names. (For details on cross-references, see the section beginning on page 244.)

> Bell, Currer. *See* Brontë, Charlotte
> Godwin, Mary Wollstonecraft. *See* Shelley, Mary Wollstonecraft
>
> Twain, Mark. *See* Clemens, Samuel Langhorne
> *or*
> Clemens, Samuel Langhorne. *See* Twain, Mark

A person's name indexed by the more commonly known form may also include the original name in parentheses.

> Titian (Tiziano Vecellio), 34, 186
> Vecellio, Tiziano. *See* Titian

Supplemental identification Any information that might be needed to help the reader identify a person listed in the index—such as a title, brief modifier, or dates—should be added in parentheses.

> Charles II (King of Great Britain)
> Charles III (King of France)
> Charles III (King of Spain)
>
> Baker, Josephine (entertainer)
> Baker, Sara Josephine (physician)

Compound names Compound surnames, with or without hyphens, are indexed according to the individual's preference or, if that is unknown, the most familiar usage. The desired form may be found in the text. If the author consistently refers to the person by a given short form of the surname, that form should be retained in the index. It is always a good idea to include a cross-reference from the alternative form of the name or make a double entry.

cross-reference:	Williams, Ralph Vaughan. *See* Vaughan Williams, Ralph
	Vaughan Williams, Ralph, 43, 95–98
double entry:	Bulwer-Lytton, Edward, 65, 121
	Lytton, Edward Bulwer-, 65, 121

Saints Christian saints are indexed by their given names. Modern-day saints are indexed under their family name; it may be necessary to add parenthetical identification.

Luke, Saint
Mary Magdalene, Saint
Cabrini, Saint Frances Xavier (Mother Cabrini)

Names with abbreviations or roman numerals Personal-name designations such as *Jr., II, III,* and *IV* follow the given name, separated by a comma.

Kennedy, John F., Jr.
Markey, Richard, III

Courtesy titles Courtesy titles—*Mr., Mrs., Miss, Ms., M., Mme, Mlle,* etc.—are deleted from indexed names unless (1) a married woman is indexed under her husband's name—for example, "Beach, Mrs. H. H. A. (Amy Marcy)"—or (2) the courtesy title is in the title of a work—for example, *Mr. Smith Goes to Washington.*

Academic and professional titles Academic and professional titles that precede a name (such as *Professor* or *Doctor*) and degrees that follow a name (such as *Ph.D.* or *M.D.*) are usually deleted from indexed personal names.

Honorific, clerical, and military titles Honorific titles such as *Dame, Lady, Lord,* and *Sir* that precede personal names are retained in an index but ignored in alphabetizing. The same is true for clerical and military titles that precede a personal name.

Grey, Sir George
Grey, Lady Jane

Smith, Rev. James S.
Smith, Msgr. James T.
Smith, Gen. James W.

Nobility and popes Royalty, nobility, and popes are normally listed under the names by which they are most familiarly known. Cross-references and double entries are commonly used to index such names.

Charles, Prince of Wales
Charles XII, King of Sweden
Clement VIII, Pope (1592–1605)

Edward VIII. *See* Windsor, Duke of
Windsor, Duke of, 234, 336

Names with particles Personal names that begin with particles (articles, prepositions, or other prefixes) can be difficult to alphabetize. A general rule is that English and American names derived from other languages are indexed with the prefix first, uninverted. Likewise, any name that is most familiar in this country in the form that includes the prefix is generally indexed in that form.

Dos Passos, John
La Guardia, Fiorello H.
Van Allen, James A.

Della Robbia, Luca
Du Barry, Madame Jeanne
Von Braun, Wernher *or* Braun, Wernher von

Other, less familiar foreign names should be alphabetized according to the customs of the country and its language. Some of these customs are explained under "Foreign Names" below.

Names of institutions and businesses Personal names that appear in names of institutions and businesses are not inverted. However, cross-references or double entries may sometimes be necessary.

H&R Block
Norton Simon Museum
Oral Roberts University

Daniel O'Connell and Sons, 54
O'Connell (Daniel) and Sons, 54

Foreign names When in doubt about the form of any foreign name—its spelling, its capitalization, or whether to invert the particle or other element—the indexer should follow the author's treatment of the name in the text; for further guidance, consult a standard reference source such as *Merriam-Webster's Biographical Dictionary*. Cross-references and double entries should be provided as needed.

In French and Belgian surnames, the preposition *de* is usually ignored in alphabetization, while the article *la* usually is not.

Lesseps, Ferdinand de
La Salle, Antoine de
La Tour, Georges de

Italian surnames retain forms of the preposition *de* in indexes, and so do Dutch names. However, the *de* in Spanish surnames and the prepositions *von* and *van* in Dutch and German names are standardly inverted.

De Sica, Vittorio
De Vries, Hugo
Soto, Hernando de
Bismarck, Otto von

Spanish surnames, when compound in form, are usually indexed under the first element of the compound.

> García Gutiérrez, Antonio
> Pérez Galdós, Benito
> Santos-Dumont, Alberto

However, many Spanish surnames are single rather than compound, and some Spanish-speakers use two given names and only one surname. Sometimes *y* joins the two parts of the compound surname. In the names of married women, the birth name frequently precedes *de* and the husband's name.

> Jiménez, Juan Ramón   Gutiérrez de Rivera, María Jesús
> Zorrilla y Moral, José   Rojas de Pérez, Ana

The first syllable of a Chinese name is usually the family name, under which the name should be indexed; thus it is not necessary to invert traditional Chinese names. However, many Chinese now invert their names in accordance with Western practice, and these names should be inverted in an index. Any two-syllable name (often hyphenated) is generally a conflation of the two one-syllable given names, which will identify the remaining one-syllable name as the surname (as in "Mao Zedong").

The traditional order of Japanese names places the family name first; thus, no inversion is required when indexing historical Japanese names. Modern Japanese names may usually be treated like Western names—that is, the last name should be the one alphabetized; however, some Japanese still prefer the traditional order.

A cross-reference should be made from any other form that might have become familiar in the West.

> Diem, Ngo Dinh. *See* Ngo Dinh Diem
> Teng Hsiao-Ping. *See* Deng Xiaoping

Again, the author's own treatment of foreign names should be your principal guide.

Alphabetizing personal names   The following principles govern the standard alphabetization of personal names.

Names with contractions (such as O'Neill or D'Angelo) are alphabetized as if they were solid words.

Names that begin with *Mc, Mac,* or *M'* may be alphabetized in either of two ways. The more common method is to list the names as if all were spelled *Mac,* though each name retains its actual spelling. The alternative method is to alphabetize them strictly according to their actual spelling.

> *indexed as if spelled* Mac: *indexed letter by letter:*
> McAdam, John   MacArthur, Douglas
> MacArthur, Douglas   *Macbeth*
> McAuley, James   Machiavelli, Niccolò
> *Macbeth*   McAdam, John
> McCarthy, Mary   McAuley, James
> Machiavelli, Niccolò   McCarthy, Mary

Personal names that begin with *Saint, St., Sainte,* or *Ste.* are always alphabetized as if they were spelled in full, though they may keep their abbreviated form if that is the form used within the text. These compound names are also alphabetized as if they were a single word.

Sagan, Carl
St. Clair, Arthur
Sainte-Claire Deville, Henri-Étienne
St. Johns, Adela Rogers
Saint-Léon, Arthur
Salk, Jonas

Initials in an inverted personal name precede spelled-out names beginning with those initials.

Smith, J. C.
Smith, J. M.
Smith, J. Morris
Smith, James E.

Place-Names

Place-names are indexed by the form that appears in the text. Any alternative forms that are common or that are mentioned by the author should be cross-referenced.

Denali. *See* Mt. McKinley
Livorno. *See* Leghorn

Many place-names need to be further identified geographically.

Springfield, Mo.
Washington (state)
Washita River (Okla.)

Choosing the keyword is not always easy. Generally, the keyword is the specific element of the name rather than a generic word like *Lake* or *Mount.*

Louise, Lake   Lookout Mountain
Good Hope, Cape of   Salton Sea
Rushmore, Mount   Michigan, University of

A few place-names beginning with a generic word are traditionally not inverted. However, the indexer should consider adding cross-references or double entries for such uninverted entries.

Cape Cod
Rio Grande
Lake of the Woods

Foreign-language place-names (both U.S. and foreign) that begin with articles are usually alphabetized according to the article.

Des Plaines   Al Kugrah
El Paso   El Fasher

La Jolla   La Paz
Los Angeles   Le Mans

Names of cities and towns are never inverted in an index. Thus, towns named for geographical or manmade features whose first element is a generic word always keep their natural order when indexed.

Lake Charles, La.
Mount Vernon, N.Y.
Fort Collins, Colo.

Titles of Works

The titles of books, periodicals, poems, plays, stories, articles, and works of art follow the same style in an index as in the text itself. Any internal punctuation is disregarded for alphabetizing purposes. If a title begins with an article (*A, An,* or *The*), the title is usually inverted. Some indexers prefer to keep the article in original position, but in all cases the article is ignored in alphabetizing.

Golden Bough, The *or* *The Golden Bough*
"Rose for Emily, A" *or* "A Rose for Emily"

Initial prepositions, no matter how small, stay in place and determine alphabetical order.

Imagists
In the Shadow of the Glen
Irish Literary Theatre

Titles that appear as subheadings keep their initial articles in normal position. Like main headings, however, they are always alphabetized according to the first word that follows the article.

Hardy, Thomas
   Far from the Madding Crowd
   A Pair of Blue Eyes
   The Return of the Native

In an index of first lines of poetry, initial articles not only are kept in natural order but also determine the alphabetical order.

The well was dry beside the door
The west was getting out of gold
There sandy seems the golden sky
There's a place called Faraway Meadow

Foreign titles of works, like English titles, are alphabetized by the first main word following any initial article. But if the reader might not recognize the article for what it is, the indexer should also list the title with the article first as a cross-reference.

Esprit des Lois, L' (Montesquieu)
L'Esprit des Lois. See Esprit des
   Lois, L'

Adding information that pinpoints the title's identity will sometimes help the reader.

> *Life* magazine
> *No More Parades* (Ford)
> *Times* (London)

Any work of art may be indexed as a main entry, with the artist's name in parentheses. Alternatively, the work's name may be listed as a subheading under the artist's name. If only a few works are indexed under the artist's name, they should be alphabetized with the other subheadings; if many works are listed, they may be grouped together at the end of the artist entry as subentries under the subheading "works."

Titles that appear only in footnotes, endnotes, or parenthetical references that merely identify the source of information are never indexed.

Abbreviations

Most indexes make minimal use of abbreviations, because spelled-out words are usually expected by the reader. (Since abbreviations are very common in scientific and technical works, however, they appear frequently in the indexes to such works.) But if an abbreviation is very common and the author uses it in the text, the indexer should enter it. A less familiar abbreviation should be indexed by its spelled-out form, with a cross-reference at the abbreviation.

> GNP, 55, 76, 123–125
> Gross national product. *See* GNP
>
> New York Stock Exchange (NYSE), 87, 134
> NYSE. *See* New York Stock Exchange

Familiar abbreviations whose spelled-out forms are very lengthy (such as "AFL-CIO") are acceptable without a cross-reference to the spelled-out form. Short forms of state and province names used only to identify places within that state or province (e.g., "Jamaica, N.Y.") naturally do not require cross-references.

Abbreviations are alphabetized letter by letter.

> Cassette tape
> CAT
> Catalog
> CD-ROM
> Cell

Numerals

When numerals are used as index headings, they are often alphabetized as if they were spelled out; alternatively, they may be grouped at the head of each alphabetical section and listed in numerical sequence.

> *Two's Company,* 91, 167
> *2001: A Space Odyssey,* 192, 241
> *Two Tickets to Broadway,* 140
> *Typhoon,* 271

2,4-D, 186
Daffodil, 237
DDT, 67–69
Deciduous forest, 132–139

A series of headings intentionally listed in numerical sequence ignores the alphabetical order.

Gross domestic product
   1993, 243
   1994, 247
   1995, 251
   1996, 258

Numbers used as prefixes with chemical terms are ignored in alphabetizing.

hydrogen, 118–120, 243
6-hydroxydopamine, 182
hydroxylase, 291

Legal Citations

Citations to law cases should generally be indexed under the names of both adversaries, through either cross-reference or double entry. When the federal government is a party to the action, "United States" usually is not abbreviated. Law case names are italicized.

Marston v. United States, 25, 36–38
United States, Marston v. See *Marston
   v. United States*

Case citations beginning with phrases such as *Ex parte, Ex rel.,* and *In re* should be inverted so that the personal name of the party is the keyword.

Jones, Clyde M., Estate of, 133
Smith, In re, 48

Producing the Final Copy

The index manuscript should use single-column format, in order to facilitate any subsequent markup. It should be double-spaced throughout. If typesetting codes or tags are being added before each main heading and subheading, all entries can be typed flush left; if not, runover lines and subheadings should be indented.

If it has been decided how to mark entries that are continued from one page to another, use that form where needed at the top of a new page, even though these will mostly disappear from the typeset version (see page 270).

Most published indexes leave extra space before the beginning of each alphabetical section, and the manuscript should do so as well. In some indexes each section is headed with the appropriate letter (A, B, C, etc.) as well.

For a multiple index, a separate heading (such as "Index of Pharmaceutical Terms") should be typed above each index.

The index manuscript should be proofread carefully against the edited entry list or index cards.

A copy of the index should be kept, along with the page proofs and the original unedited index file or notecards, until the index is printed in its final form.

Computer Sorting

The most practical computer aid to the indexer is the Sort function, which will automatically put a list of words or phrases of any length into alphabetical order. The Sort function can save the indexer an enormous amount of time; however, it has certain limitations.

The Sort function cannot sort subheadings under individual main headings if they are formatted like a normal indented index (i.e., indented on the column by means of the tab key or the space bar). However, it can easily alphabetize subentries if each one is preceded by its main entry. For example, the set of entries

Artichokes: Hearts of Artichokes à la Isman Bavaldy, 11
Asparagus: Madame Loubet's Asparagus Tips, 82
Artichokes: Stuffed Artichokes Stravinsky, 241
Artichokes: Artichokes à la Barigoule, 275
Beets: Purée of Beetroot, 276

can automatically be sorted into

Artichokes: Artichokes à la Barigoule, 275
Artichokes: Hearts of Artichokes à la Isman Bavaldy, 11
Artichokes: Stuffed Artichokes Stravinsky, 241
Asparagus: Madame Loubet's Asparagus Tips, 82
Beets: Purée of Beetroot, 276

which can in turn be edited fairly easily into

Artichokes
    Artichokes à la Barigoule, 275
    Hearts of Artichokes à la Isman Bavaldy, 11
    Stuffed Artichokes Stravinsky, 241
Asparagus
    Madame Loubet's Asparagus Tips, 82
Beets
    Purée of Beetroot, 276

Bear in mind, however, that any prepositions or conjunctions with which subheadings begin will determine their automatic alphabetizing.

A given program may only be able to alphabetize according to either the word-by-word or the letter-by-letter principle. Thus, if alphabetization according to the alternative principle is required for some reason, a good deal of editorial work may be necessary to finish the job.

Computer Indexing Programs

Basic computer office programs include indexing capabilities that go beyond simple sorting. However, these are not intended for text to be sent to a typesetter, but rather only for documents that will be entirely produced on the computer.

Such indexing programs are fairly simple to use, though producing the index still requires a good deal of work. The indexer (who in such cases is usually also the editor) scrolls through the document on-screen, highlighting or flagging each appearance of a term that should appear in the index. For every such appearance, the indexer must call up a dialog box, where the term can be edited into the precise form it will take as an index entry. If the term will be a subentry, the main entry under which it will appear can be entered at the same time. Cross-references can also be entered. The index automatically generates a locator for each appearance; thus, when the indexer reaches the end of the document, the entire formatted index with all page references will itself be complete. If some late-stage text editing turns out to be needed, the program will automatically change any page references for topics that have moved as a result, and will remove any page references that apply to text that has been removed. (It will not automatically *add* references, however.)

Such programs can be useful for lengthy business reports, as well as for theses and dissertations. But since all the locators in such an index will be valid only for the computer-generated pages, most of the locators would have to be changed if the document were sent out to be typeset. For this reason, such programs will not be of much help to anyone indexing material whose final form will be typeset pages.

Standard computer programs provide a second method of indexing computer-generated documents as well. This involves creating a so-called concordance file, consisting of the list of terms you want to appear in the index keyed to the various forms those terms might actually take in the document. This saves the editor from having to mark every appearance of every indexable term throughout. However, the concordance method, being somewhat more "automatic," will generally produce a less sensitive index, and it cannot generate subentries.

Indexing programs for professional indexers are also available. These dedicated, or stand-alone software programs offer a variety of features, including choice of format (indented or paragraph) and alphabetization method (letter-by-letter or word-by-word), cross-reference verification, spell checking, and automatic punctuation. They may also be programmed to ignore specific words when alphabetizing entries, such as prepositions and conjunctions used in subheadings. They thus enable the indexer to view the index in alphabetized, formatted form as he or she inputs the entries from page proofs or index cards. (For a list of indexing software, contact the American Society of Indexers.)

Index Design and Typesetting

Design and Markup

Though index designs are never complicated, they must generally be carefully calculated to ensure that the index fills a specified number of pages. The principal design variables include the type size, the number of columns, whether right margins will be justified, whether end-of-line word breaks will be allowed, and what indentions will be used.

Basic page design Indexes are usually set in two columns per page and in type about two points smaller than the main text. However, before committing to this design, the editor should know how heavily the book was indexed and how many pages have been allotted for the index. A book index must generally be fit into the number of pages left in a signature (which is generally 16 pages, but sometimes 8, 24, or 32 pages), or the end of a signature plus another complete signature. Its length must thus usually be balanced with that of the book's front matter, which is generally designed at the same time as the index, after the rest of the page proofs have been approved (see discussion on pages 314–315). Assuming the desired length of the index is between two and five percent of the total pages in the book, the design just described will probably work well if the indexer took between six and ten references per page, which tends to be the average. If there are fewer references per page, the index will be on the short end of this range; if there are a dozen or more references per page, the index may exceed it.

Some indexes are set three columns to the page, and a large-format book may have a four-column index. Multiple-column indexes, which permit the use of very small type, represent an efficient use of space, especially for indented indexes with their many short lines.

Five-point type is unacceptably small for an index. Eleven-point type is awkwardly large, and the index should never be set in type larger than the text.

Nevertheless, index length can be greatly altered by design. An index that would fill 30 pages of 10/12 type might fit into 13 pages of 6/7 type. If simultaneously converted from indented style to paragraph style, the same index might shrink to 10 pages. If, on the other hand, the editor discovers that the index can't be made to fill up most of the remaining pages of a signature at a reasonable type size, added leading (up to about 14-point) can be used to bulk it out. The same index that filled 30 pages when set in 10/12 type might fill 35 pages in 10/14 type.

Casting off the index Casting off an index manuscript—that is, estimating its eventual typeset length—is usually somewhat simpler than casting off a book manuscript, since the design elements do not vary from beginning to end. However, it may also be more critical, since at this late production stage the index will have to fit the specific number of pages left in a partly filled signature (or one or more complete signatures plus the remaining blank pages of the preceding signature).

Assuming the index was received on diskette, the editor may simply choose to format the index on a computer—setting the text block to match that of the book, setting the index in two (or more) columns, choosing a desired type size and leading, and setting the approximate indention for subentries and turn lines—and then note the computer's indication of how many pages the chosen design will produce. (Since the computer's type will vary somewhat from the typesetter's, even in typefaces with the same name, the editor must allow for some minor deviance in the page allotment.)

If the index is received only as manuscript, the editor may type a small portion of the index into the computer, format it as described above, note how many pages it requires, and then simply calculate the proportion of the whole index that the excerpt represents.

In a more traditional method, the editor counts the number of lines on a page of index manuscript and multiplies by the number of index manuscript pages to get the total number of manuscript lines. Then the editor calculates the depth of the book's text block in terms of points, divides the desired leading into it, multiplies by the number of columns, and finally divides the total number of entries by the resulting figure to get the approximate number of pages that the index will require using the intended design.

Right-hand margins and word breaks Most indexes are set ragged right rather than right-justified. Because of the narrow column widths, a justified right margin will frequently result in both crowded and widely spaced lines of type, and the end-of-line word breaks that are so frequent in narrow justified columns can make the index hard to read.

In ragged-right style, words rarely need to break between lines. Because of the narrow column, however, long words will sometimes result in unsightly short lines above them if no end-of-line breaks are permitted. The editor may choose to instruct the typesetter to hyphenate whenever a line would otherwise be shorter than a specified length.

Indention As discussed earlier, indented indexes have traditionally employed one-em indention for subentries, two-em for sub-subentries, and three-em for all runover lines (two-em if there are no sub-subentries). If the editor discovers that the index is in danger of running long, these indentions can be reduced; 4-, 8-, and 12-point indentions will generally be adequate to ensure a minimum acceptable clarity, and can reduce an index's length by five percent or more.

Continued entries When an entry breaks at the end of a right-hand page and continues after the page turn, the main-entry heading is usually repeated at the top of the new column, followed by the word *continued* (or *cont.*) in italics or parentheses or both. In an indented index, the heading and notation appear by themselves on the first line of the new column; in a paragraph index, they precede and are run in with the new subentry. Some editors also like to use a *continued* notation for an entry carried from the bottom of a left-hand page to the top of the opposite page.

Instructions for the typesetter On the first page of the marked-up index manuscript, the editor identifies the book by author and title and tells the typesetter the page of the book where the index will begin (e.g., "Index begins on book page 586"). On the same page, or on a separate sheet, the editor provides complete specifications for the index's design, such as the following:

> *Index Specifications*
> Running heads: Set word "Index" on both left and right pages.
> Title: Set word "INDEX" in 24-pt Baskerville caps, fl left, 8 pts below 1-pt rule x 28 pi fl top on text block. Sink 5 pi b/b to first head letter.

Head letters: At head of each alpha section, set capital head letters (A, B, C, etc.) in 9-pt Bask., fl left on col; allow 2 pi b/b from last entry above, 12 pts b/b to first entry below.

Entries: 9/9 Bask. x 13½ pi. Set double col; right col aligns left on 14½-pi indent. Set main entries fl left on col; subentries indent 1 em. Both main-entry and subentry turns indent 2 ems from fl left. Set cols ragged right; to prevent short lines, break words whenever more than approx 24 pts space would otherwise be left at end of line. If entry breaks over page turn, repeat main-entry head fl left followed on same line by word "(*cont.*)." Set all hyphens between inclusive nos. as en dashes.

Proofreading

While reading the typeset page proofs, the proofreader should be particularly attentive to transitions from column to column, especially where the *continued* notation is used. Any alphabetical division that begins near the bottom of a column should have at least two lines of entry text below it; otherwise, the new section should begin at the top of the next column. A single line followed by a line of space at the end of an alphabetical section should never appear at the top of a column, nor should a line consisting solely of one or two locators. The proofreader can fix such breaks by asking for space to be added to or deleted from an existing space, by marking the columns on a pair of facing pages to run a line (or even two lines) shorter or longer than on other pages, or by identifying entries or subentries that could be either squeezed onto one line less or expanded to run over onto an extra line.

12   Production Editing, Copyediting, and Proofreading

Overview 272
The Manuscript   274
Copyediting the Manuscript   275
Proofs and Proofreading   301
Parts of a Book   313
Copyright and Permissions   319

Editorial production may be handled by a large staff of specialists or by a single person. A large book publisher may employ a staff of acquisitions editors, developmental editors, general editors, production editors, copy editors, designers, and proofreaders. A small company may require only one editor to handle all production tasks. In this chapter, the tasks are somewhat arbitrarily allocated to an *in-house editor*, with overall responsibility for getting the author's manuscript into print; a *designer*, who designs the book's interior; a *copy editor*, who does the principal editing of the manuscript for style, consistency, and correctness; and a *proofreader*, who checks typeset proofs against manuscript copy.

Production editing comprises most of the tasks involved in turning a new manuscript into a bound book—tasks that are often the responsibility of editors with titles other than Production Editor. It includes many functions dealt with at greater length in other chapters, particularly Chapters 9, 13, and 14.

Overview

The process of producing a bound book from a book manuscript usually encompasses at least the steps listed below.

1. The author submits a manuscript, generally in both electronic and printed form, which will often already have gone through one or more revisions or rewritings as a result of reviews by an agent, a high-level editor, or several academic experts, depending on the nature of the manuscript.

2. The manuscript (also called *typescript* or *copy*) is given to a copy editor for copyediting.

3. The copyedited manuscript is sent to the author for review.

4. A designer (sometimes the in-house editor) designs the book's interior, producing a set of *design specifications,* or *specs* (see Chapter 13, "Design and Typography").

5. The typesetter, or *compositor,* sets *sample pages* that show how the proposed design will look in print; these are reviewed in-house, and the specs are altered if necessary.

6. The typemarked (or electronically coded) manuscript, which now incorporates all editorial changes, is sent to a typesetter, who sets it according to the design specs.

7. The typesetter returns *first* or *galley proofs.*

8. The editor sends a set of proofs to the author for review, and another (or sometimes the same set when it is returned) to a proofreader. The author's own corrections are carried to the proofreader's *master proof,* which is then returned to the typesetter, accompanied by any illustrations, in camera-ready form (see Chapter 9, "Tables and Illustrations").

9. The typesetter makes the corrections by resetting parts of the copy, which is then combined with any art—sometimes initially in the form of a *dummy* of the book made from photocopies or on a computer—to produce *second* or *page proofs.*

10. The editor or proofreader checks the proof corrections (and may ask for several revised proofs) and returns them to the typesetter.

11. The typesetter, after incorporating any further corrections, sends high-quality prints *(repro proofs)* or film negatives or an electronic version of the final pages to the printer.

12. The printer uses film to create a complete set of film proofs *(book blues),* which are sent to the editor for review.

13. The editor carefully reviews the book blues and returns them to the printer with all necessary corrections marked.

14. The printer makes the corrections, creates the printing plates, and starts the print run. At the very beginning of the run, the printer sends an early set of actual book signatures—called *folded and gathered sheets (F&G's)*—to the editor for review.

15. The printed signatures go to the binder to produce bound books.

Some of these steps may become complex, especially when there is a large amount of artwork or when the manuscript is divided into sections that go through each stage at a different time. Scheduling is extremely important. Since typesetters and especially printers try to schedule their jobs to take advantage of every working minute, an editor's missed deadline may mean that work may be put off for weeks while the typesetter or printer completes other previously scheduled jobs. Thus, the handling of manuscript and proof must be carefully scheduled so that deadlines can be met without sacrificing editing and proofing quality. Editors generally keep a wall chart listing each of their various projects and each editorial steps involved in turning manuscript into bound books. Each cell will often show a target date, next to which will be filled in the date each stage is actually completed. A complicated book being handled section-by-section may even require a separate chart on which each chapter or section occupies its own row or column.

The Manuscript

Author's Manuscript Checklist

The author's manuscript must be submitted in a form that will make the editing as efficient as possible. Most authors now prepare their manuscripts on computers and submit them on diskette with accompanying hard-copy printouts. The author is usually asked to submit at least two printed copies of the manuscript. The manuscript should be typed or keyboarded on good-quality paper, using one side of the page only. All the pages should be the same size; any tearsheets (pages taken from a previous edition or another published source) or other larger or smaller pieces should be taped or reproduced onto $8\frac{1}{2}'' \times 11''$ paper. To allow for editing, all copy must be double-spaced, including tables, footnotes, and bibliographies, and margins at least one inch wide must be left on all sides. Right margins should not be justified. The printout should be clear and easy to read; some publishers will not accept dot-matrix printing.

Ideally the manuscript should be typed with the "Show ¶" function activated, so that all spacing shows up in the form of dots on-screen. A single space should follow periods and other end punctuation, and the manuscript should be checked thoroughly for inadvertently added spaces elsewhere as well.

The manuscript should be complete, including its title page, dedication, table of contents, list of illustrations (tables, maps), foreword, preface, acknowledgments, tables and illustrations (with captions), glossary, bibliography, and appendixes as appropriate—everything that the author intends to appear in the printed book except the copyright page and index. (See "Parts of a Book" beginning on page 313.)

The author may be asked to add generic coding of text elements (paragraphs, headings, etc.), following a code list provided by the editor. More often, coding will be entered by the publisher or typesetter. (See Chapter 13, "Design and Typography.")

Some publishers prefer to deal only with hard copy in the actual editing stages. In such cases, the author submits only the paper manuscript, which must be identical to the retained diskette. The copyedited manuscript will be returned to the author, who then enters all the suggested emendations that are found acceptable and returns the hard copy along with the diskette. (This may provide an added incentive for accuracy and consistent styling by the author when originally submitting the manuscript.) Where extensive changes have been requested, the editor may ask that new paper manuscript reflecting the changes be returned.

The author should particularly ensure that all the following tasks have been done:

1. Number the text pages throughout in the upper right-hand corner. For any pages added subsequently, add sequential letters to the previ-

ous page number (e.g., 18A, 18B). Number the front matter with lowercase roman numerals (i, ii, iii, iv, etc.). Use separate numbering sequences for tables or illustrations ("Table 1," "Table 2," etc.; "Figure 1," "Figure 2," etc.); if there are many, include the chapter number ("Table 2.1," "Table 2.2," etc.).

2. Include adequate bibliographic information for each source of quoted material.

3. Obtain permission for any copyrighted material quoted in the text or used in preparing tables or graphs and for photos and artwork, and include a file of completed permission forms obtained from each copyright holder. The publisher should have supplied blank permission forms and instructions. (See "Copyright and Permissions" beginning on page 319.)

4. Type all footnotes or endnotes on a sheet separate from the text, regardless of their intended eventual placement on the printed page. Check the sequence of note numbers in the text and the notes themselves. For the bibliography, follow a standard bibliographic style. (See Chapter 10, "Notes and Bibliographies.")

5. Review all cross-references for necessity and accuracy. Table and figure numbers (in separate sequences) must match their text references. Cross-references to pages should read "see page 000" or "see page ▮▮▮ " at this stage; add the actual manuscript page number (circled) in the margin for later use. Cross-references to headings rather than page numbers can reduce the potential for error and the cost of inserting page numbers in the page proofs. (For more on cross-references, see the section on page 294.)

6. Place each table or graph on a separate page. Highlight their suggested placement within the text by a text reference (e.g., "As Figure 5.5 shows, . . ." or "The following table . . . "). If there is no text reference, include a circled note in the margin (e.g., "Insert Fig. 5.5 here") or on a separate line at the appropriate point in the text. Include a concise caption for each figure. Type a list of all tables or illustrations; such a list may be typeset to follow a table of contents in the printed book, or may instead be used only by the editor as a checklist (suggest which in a note on the copy). (See Chapter 9, "Tables and Illustrations.")

7. Submit all art in a separate folder along with a list of the art in the order in which it will appear. Enclose the art in heavy cardboard for protection. (See "Tables and Illustrations.")

8. Send the manuscript well wrapped by an express courier service or by registered mail (always retaining a backup copy).

Copyediting the Manuscript

In book publishing, editorial work is generally divided into at least two tasks. An upper-level editor—frequently the same editor who has acquired the manuscript for the publishing house—reads the manuscript critically, focusing on such large issues as conception, organization, and tone. This higher-level editing is often known as *manuscript editing* or *line editing,* names which distinguish it from what is known as *copyediting.* This may follow similar work already done by an agent who proposed the book to the editor. (Increasingly, in-house editors are allowing agents to take over much of this responsibility.) If the manuscript is a textbook or a serious nonfiction work, it may also be sent to outside reviewers who are expert in the subject. The editor may send the manuscript back to the author more than once for revision.

Occasionally the principal editor will act as the copy editor as well. In fact, some regard the distinction between manuscript editing and copy editing as artificial, especially in cases where the in-house editor may give the manuscript only cursory attention and the copy editor finds it necessary to do extensive recasting and reorganizing. Nevertheless, for the sake of clarity we will treat the two jobs as if they were strictly segregated, and this chapter will devote itself largely to the job of the copy editor and the more easily distinguishable proofreader.

Copyediting is often the most important stage in preparing a manuscript for publication, especially at a time when in-house editors are feeling increasing pressure to acquire large numbers of books and have less and less time for properly vetting them. The copy editor will sometimes be more of a specialist in the subject matter than the in-house editor. It is therefore often left to a first-rate copy editor to turn an awkward, eccentric, incoherent manuscript into a cogent and creditable text. However, the copy editor is normally expected to consult with the in-house editor before attempting any editing that goes beyond the limits of standard copyediting.

Of the many things copyediting attempts to do, the most fundamental is to impose a thorough consistency and formal correctness on a manuscript. Systematic thoroughness is the greatest copyediting virtue. Errors and inconsistencies that elude the copy editor and are discovered only at the proofreading stage are expensive to correct.

A copy editor must naturally have mastered the standard rules of English style. But he or she should also be an avid reader of good prose, since wide and thoughtful reading is what most reliably produces the kind of taste and critical discrimination that form the solidest foundation for an editor's judgment.

Some manuscripts are still copyedited in-house. However, most are sent out to freelance copy editors, who, thanks to overnight courier service, may live 2,000 miles away from the publisher's offices. Most copy editors charge by the hour and submit a final bill at the end of a project; a few editorial projects are contracted on a flat-fee basis. The hourly rate will often assume an average editing speed of approximately six to seven pages an hour.

The copy editor should be supplied (usually by the in-house editor) with colored pens or pencils and special copyediting tags or flags. The latter are pieces of colored paper, about 2″ × 4″ in size, with a gummed edge that, when moistened, can be stuck firmly to the side of a manuscript page. (Pressure-sensitive tags, such as Post-its, are more prone to fall off and should not normally be used for serious copyediting—though they can be very useful for notes to oneself in the course of a project.) Notes and queries to the author or in-house editor are written on the side of the tag with the adhesive edge (often continuing to the other side), which is then stuck to the back edge of the page next to the text it discusses and folded over the front of the page. Depending on who is being addressed, "Au" (for "Author") or "Ed" (for "Editor") is then written on the side that shows when the tag is folded over; the manuscript page number should also be written at one corner of the tag. Alternatively, different-colored tags may be used for author and editor queries, or author queries may all be stuck on one side of the page and editor queries on the other. (Very brief queries may usually be written in the margins of the manuscript, though some editors discourage marginal queries.) (See Figure 12.1 for a copyediting tag.)

These tags remain in place until the in-house editor determines they should be removed. He or she will remove any tags addressed to "Ed" as soon as the issue addressed has been dealt with. The author should be instructed to address any queries directed to "Au"—either by making alterations to the manuscript or by writing brief answers on the tag itself—but not to remove the tags, since the in-house editor must make the final determination of how adequately each issue raised has been dealt with. All such tags should be removed by the editor before the manuscript goes to the typesetter, however. If a tag contains text to be inserted, it may be photocopied onto an 8½" × 11" sheet, along with instructions for insertion.

Figure 12.1 Copyediting Tag (both sides)

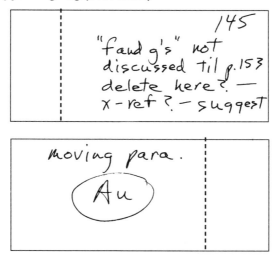

It goes without saying that the copy editor should make every effort to write clearly. If pencil is used, the pencils must be kept sharp; a dull pencil can make small handwriting very hard to read, and an in-house editor should never have to trace over such editing to make it clear enough for the typesetter.

Tact is of paramount importance for the copy editor. Authors vary greatly in their sensitivity to having their work edited, but many are quick to take offense at what they may consider high-handed editing. (Since there is usually no personal contact between copy editor and author, there may be no conversational opportunity to soften the effect of one's blunt editorial comments.) A style of querying that might strike most people as merely brusque may be genuinely insulting to an author, and the "correcting" of an author's idiosyncratic but nonetheless acceptable usages may give as much offense as correcting a person's grammar at a cocktail party. The result may be angry exchanges between the author and in-house editor, making the latter disinclined to hire the copy editor for the next project.

A few specific suggestions: Avoid using any language that might sound superior or self-righteous. Never use exclamation points in your messages to the author. Never simply write a question mark (or two or three) without explaining what it is you don't understand. Write frequent brief notes to accompany your emendations, generally worded as questions—such as "Au: OK?" or "Is this a bit clearer?" or "Maybe too informal?"—even where they may not be strictly necessary. And remain sensitive to the many legitimate style differences that continue to exist even among educated writers.

In conjunction with tact, a copy editor must cultivate a certain humility. He or she must always remember that the book is basically the author's, and that an attitude that regards a manuscript as a canvas on which to exercise one's own creative power is always inappropriate. The copy editor will rightly be faulted for permitting misspellings, inconsistencies, and flagrant errors to slip by, but it is the author who will receive near-exclusive credit or blame for the book as a whole.

An in-house editor may specify that a manuscript requires light editing, moderate editing, or heavy editing. Light editing may be quite cursory (and the copy editor's billable hours will be expected to reflect this), whereas authorization for heavy editing conveys broad latitude to shape the manuscript's prose. Moderate editing is naturally the norm, and this is the level that the present chapter basically addresses.

Basic Tasks

The copy editor is almost always obliged to do the following:

1. *Style the manuscript.* Most changes that a copy editor makes are "mechanical" or stylistic changes—in punctuation, capitalization, abbreviations, numbers, etc.—intended to conform the style of the text to a standard uniform style. Consistency is a major goal. Inconsistencies can easily appear even in the best writing, and removing those that might prove misleading or distracting is often the copy editor's principal job. A style sheet is an essential aid; see "The Style Sheet" beginning on page 281.

2. *Rewrite where necessary.* Rewriting the author's prose where its intention is unclear or its style awkward is a copyediting responsibility that must be handled judiciously, since it is all too easy to change the author's meaning inadvertently. The copy editor must always be careful not to appear to be substituting his or her own style for the author's. A query to the author may be preferable to attempting to rewrite passages that the copy editor may not completely understand.

3. *Rearrange content as needed.* Words, sentences, paragraphs, or whole sections may have to be transposed and sequences renumbered. Passages of text may have to be relegated to a note or an appendix, and vice versa. It is often best to alert the in-house editor if it appears that many such changes will be necessary.

4. *Verify data, as appropriate.* Freelance copy editors are generally responsible for verifying spelling of names and proper nouns, dates, foreignisms, and similar information. Query any odd-looking quotations, bibliographic references, dates, and names that cannot be verified. For a book in a specialist field, it is usually advisable to have on hand (perhaps from a library) several reputable and current reference books in the field, with which to check such information.

5. *Check headings.* Headings should be vetted for consistency and parallelism, organizational logic, and relevance to the text that follows them. Typing up the headings of each chapter in outline form is the best way of checking its organization. Check that the table of contents precisely reflects all the titles and headings.

6. *Verify all cross-references.* Check the author's cross-references and add new ones if necessary. (See "Cross-References" on page 294.)

7. *Check all sequences.* All numerical lists, all numbered footnotes or endnotes, all alphabetically arranged lists (such as bibliographies and glossaries), and all table or figure numbers must be in order.

8. *Regularize bibliographic style.* In general, the author's bibliographic style should be accommodated as far as possible; imposing consistency should be the copy editor's chief aim.

9. *Delete extra spacing.* On word-processed manuscripts, check that extra spaces have not been added inadvertently between words, and mark any such spacing for deletion. (If the manuscript is submitted to the typesetter on diskette, it is likely that such extra spacing will show up in the typeset proofs.)

10. *Review all tables.* Tables may need to be revised for accuracy, clarity, and consistency. (See Chapter 9, "Tables and Illustrations.")

11. *Review the artwork.* If the content of any illustrations or charts seems unclear or inadequately related to the text, bring the problem to the author's attention. Be sure all captions are styled and worded consistently. (See Chapter 9.)

12. *Check for possible instances of copyright violation, plagiarism, libel, or other potential legal problems.* Query the author as to whether permission has been obtained to reproduce any materials potentially protected by copyright. Tactfully query the author or alert the editor about passages written in a different—and usually superior—style that you suspect have been plagiarized. Point out any potentially libelous statements; these may include negative claims of dubious veracity about named individuals in nonfiction and even recognizable depictions of public figures in fiction.

13. *Keep a list of items that may require permission.* These may include quotations, illustrations, tables, and even data reedited from a given source. Include page references on the list. Alternatively, each item may be flagged. As a general rule, material more than 75 years old is in the public domain. (See "Copyright and Permissions" beginning on page 319.)

14. *Remove sexual and other bias.* Rewrite the copy to remove potentially offensive bias if you have permission to do so from the in-house editor.

15. *Renumber the pages if necessary.* Page numbers should appear on all copy except tables and illustrations, which usually are numbered sequentially by themselves.

16. *Typemark the manuscript.* If instructed to do so, add all the marks and notations that the typesetter will need to set the text in accordance with the design specifications. (Typemarking requires that the in-house editor provide a list of text elements and their abbreviations; see "Typemarking" on pages 296–297.)

Because of this variety of duties, the copy editor always goes through a manuscript more than once. A quick first read, perhaps without even a pen or pencil in hand, will acquaint the editor intimately with the text's organization, tone, vocabulary, and general problems. A slow and painstaking second pass will be the main occasion for fixing most errors of spelling, punctuation, grammar, parallelism, order, and general consistency. For very simple texts, this much may be adequate. But in a text with various elements, it is often best to make a separate pass through the manuscript for each of them. In a text with tables, for example, making a separate pass looking only at the tables will ensure maximum focus on their format, content, consistency, and sequence. Separate passes for captions, footnotes, A- and B-heads, and so on—each of which will naturally go very quickly compared to the initial reading and markup—will be similarly useful.

Marking Up the Manuscript

Copy editors communicate with typesetters by using a set of standard conventions, symbols, and codes. Most of these are described and illustrated in the following section.

Manuscript page numbers must be complete and in sequence. They should appear at the upper right corner, where they can be readily scanned by anyone who handles the manuscript. Any pages inserted later should be identified with a letter following the number of the preceding page; pages 4A and 4B would thus fall between pages 4 and 5. The additional instruction on the bottom of page 4 "p. 4A follows" will alert the typesetter. For added clarity, the notation "follows p. 4" may be written at the top of page 4A. If the manuscript fills up with numerous lettered pages, however, the entire manuscript should be renumbered. If pages are deleted, change the number on the preceding page to include the missing pages. Thus, for example, if pages 15 and 16 were deleted, page 14 would be renumbered "14–16," which would will tell the typesetter to expect page 17 to follow; the message "follows p. 14" can be added on page 17 as well.

Editorial revisions should be made as close as possible to normal reading order. In those frequent cases where they must be written several inches away, a line should be drawn connecting the inserted material to the insertion point.

Special instructions to the typesetter are often necessary but should be kept as brief as possible. These should be written in the margin rather than on flags. All such instructions should be circled to distinguish them from actual revisions. They may begin with the abbreviation "Comp" (for "Compositor") to make it clear who is being addressed (e.g., "Comp: Disregard horizontal lines").

Most longer text insertions are bracketed rather than fully circled. However, circled insertions that are clearly linked to their insertion points will not be confused with instructions.

The right margin may be reserved for editorial notations, and the left margin for typemarking. A heavily revised manuscript, however, will usually require editorial notations in both margins as well as between the lines.

Beginners understandably prefer using pencil rather than pen, though a fine-point pen is easier for the typesetter to read and will not smudge. If more than one person will be marking the copy, each should use a single identifying color. The copy editor's own mistakes should be whited out or erased rather than crossed out. Mistakes made by the author, in contrast, should never be erased but only crossed out; the author's original should always be visible behind the deletion marks.

The Style Sheet

Copy editors almost always work with a style sheet. There are two basic kinds. One is a list of preferred stylings which the in-house editor may give to the copy editor along with the manuscript reflecting the publisher's "house style." (These may even be full-fledged style manuals.) The other kind of style sheet, the subject of this section, is created by the copy editor while reading the manuscript. On it the copy editor notes his or her final style decision for each individual entry, whether it is based on the author's own preference, the editor's preference, or the publisher's style sheet. Though its principal use is often as a memory aid for the copy editor who creates it, it can also be useful for the in-house editor and the proofreader.

Many publishers provide their own printed blank style-sheet forms. In the absence of a standard form, a simple style sheet can be created easily by drawing a wide grid (perhaps six boxes per page) on two or three sheets of paper. Each of the first several boxes should be headed with three or four sequential letters of the alphabet; the remaining boxes may be given such headings as "Numbers," "Abbreviations," "Tables," "Captions," "Punctuation," "Notes," "Bibliography," "Cross-References," and "Miscellaneous." (See Figure 12.2.)

While working through the manuscript, the copy editor enters on the style sheet the preferred style for each word (phrase, abbreviation, etc.) about which there may be any doubt. It is not necessary to list words that appear in the general dictionary the editor will be following, except in cases where the author (or the specialized profession for which the book is being written) clearly has a strong preference for a different spelling or style than the one listed first in the dictionary. It is often helpful to include the number of the page where the word first appears; if the copy editor changes his or her mind late in the project, this will make it easier to comb the manuscript and change the word throughout.

When fiction is being edited, the style sheet is the best place to keep track of the spelling of characters' names and the identities of those bearing the names, since authors have often been known to change such names or characters inadvertently as a long novel progresses.

The entries should be brief. For example, if a hyphen will be used in the adjective *health-care*, the editor should write simply "health-care (adj)" in the H box. This will serve as a reminder throughout the editing project that the hyphen should always be included in the adjectival form, whereas the noun *health care* will probably remain unhyphenated (and perhaps need not be listed on the style sheet at all).

Some further examples will help illustrate the use of the style sheet. The entry "résumé" would show that the word should always include the accent marks. The entry "President (U.S. only)" will show that in all references to the office of the U.S. president the word should be capitalized. The entry "west-northwest (text)—WNW (tables)" would illustrate the two styles to be followed for *all* compass directions. "Concours d'elegance (rom)" would show that the term is to be set in roman type rather than italics, and without its French accents. "W. E. B. Du Bois" shows that there will be a space between "Du" and "Bois" and that "Du" will be capitalized.

Under "Abbreviations," an entry might read "CIA," as a reminder that the periods should be removed wherever the form "C.I.A." appears and that full capital letters rather than small caps will be used. The entry "e.g., i.e." shows that these abbreviations will always be italicized.

Under "Captions," the entry "Brahms: Symphony No. 3, IV" could indicate that the standard caption form for all multimovement compositions would include the composer's last name, a colon, a standard simple styling of the composition's name, a comma, and the movement number written as a Roman numeral.

Under "Numbers," the entry "1980s" will indicate that all similar decade names will omit an apostrophe before the *s*, and the entry "5,200" announces that four-digit numbers use the optional comma. The simple entry "ten, 11" will indicate that all numbers up through ten are to be spelled out, while all higher numbers will be expressed in digits. The entry "one-half, one-fourth, three-fourths (in running text); all fractions with units smaller than tenths in running text set solidus" says that hyphens are to be used in the spelled-out form of fractions, and that fractions with large numerators or denominators will be set in digits as split or solidus fractions (e.g., "16/5") rather than as vertical or built-up fractions ("$\frac{3}{4}$"). Other entries can clarify the choice between such alternative forms as "2d" and "2nd," "1988–90" and "1988–1990," and "two million dollars" and "$2 million."

Under "Punctuation," the entry "series comma" will indicate that a comma is always to be used before *and* or *or* at the end of a series. "Set punc. following bold text rom in running text" would convey that boldface type should not normally extend to the punctuation that follows bolded words and phrases.

In the "Notes" and "Bibliography" sections, several sample footnotes or endnotes and their corresponding bibliography entries can illustrate the chosen style for a variety of types of bibliographic references.

Under "Cross-References," any standard form or forms for cross-references can be listed.

An experienced copy editor will need to make only a modest number of entries on a style sheet—perhaps no more than twenty for an undemanding book— since reliance on a standard dictionary and style manual will decide all but a small number of spelling and styling questions. However, a technical manuscript or a complex novel may well require many more.

When the style sheet is finished—after the copy editor's last reading of the manuscript—it is submitted with the manuscript, and may subsequently be copied and used by the author, the in-house editor, the typesetter, or the proofreader.

A style-sheet page is shown in Figure 12.2.

Copyediting Marks

The standard copyediting marks are illustrated in the example of a copyedited passage in Figure 12.3. The marks themselves are, for the most part, the same as proofreaders' marks; both are listed in Table 12.1.

Insertions and substitutions The symbol commonly used to indicate an insertion is a caret placed at the point of insertion; the addition is written over the caret and above the line. If a character is added in midword, only a caret is needed below the insert. If a character is added to the beginning or end of a word, a close-up sign may be added for clarity. Any large insertion should be enclosed in a brace extending from the caret. A long insertion that will not fit easily between the lines may be written in the margin, with a line drawn from the brace to the caret. Any additions within the margin must be written horizontally; the typesetter should not have to tilt the page in order to read any passage. Any insertion too long to fit in the margin should be typed on a separate sheet—never on a slip of paper stapled or stuck to the edge of the manuscript page. For a long insertion on page 24, a caret would be drawn at the insertion point, the instruction "Insert 24A" would be written and circled in the margin, and the new text would be typed on a sheet numbered 24A. Be sure it is obvious to the typesetter whether the insert should be run in with the preceding or following text or set as a separate paragraph. Several brief inserts can be typed on one sheet if they are all to be inserted on the same manuscript page and if each is clearly identified ("Insert A," "Insert B," etc.).

When words are substituted for the author's own, the original word or phrase is crossed out and the replacement text is written above the deleted passage, without a caret.

Deletions Material can be deleted by simply drawing a heavy line through the unwanted copy, being careful to begin and end the cross-out line precisely so that no characters or punctuation marks are missed, no extra characters are mistakenly deleted, and nothing is left ambiguous.

The delete sign, a line with a loop at the end, may be used to delete a single character, a word, or a whole line of copy. To cut a large section such as a

Figure 12.2 Style Sheet

MNOP	QRST	UVWXYZ
mid-1990s 23	St. Paul 34	Web 161
Midwestern 41	résumé 61	unequaled 189
ms. 49	re-create 86	
President 58 (U.S. only)	Quality Circle 117	
managed care (n., adj.) 64		
P/E ratio 128		

Abbrev.	Numbers	Punc.
WNW (table) 33	1990s	series ⌐
kph 41	5,200	Jones's
CPA 59	ten, 11	
Sr., Jr. 103	2d	
e.g., i.e.	1988-90	

paragraph, draw a box around it with the delete loop extending from one side, and draw a large X through the copy.

A single character may be crossed out with a simple slash whenever the deletion loop might interfere with an accompanying close-up sign.

To delete an underscore, attach a delete mark to its end; to delete only part of an underscore, divide it with a vertical line or lines and place delete marks only on the appropriate sections. If the copy is crowded, write "ital" or "rom" in the margin, circle the pertinent sections of the underscored material, and connect those sections and the margin notation with a line if necessary.

When the copy is heavily marked up, add close-up signs, run-in signs, or arrows to guide the typesetter from one part of the copy to another, and rewrite isolated single words and punctuation marks in their new positions so that they do not get lost. Most punctuation marks should normally appear immediately after the word they follow; however, a comma, semicolon, period, or other mark, written prominently, may be added at the beginning of an insertion or continuation if it cannot be written clearly next to the preceding text.

Close-up A close-up sign indicates a deletion of space. The close-up sign often consists of two arcs, but a single arc is usually adequate, especially if the copy is already heavily marked. It is frequently used to turn two or more separate words into a single word, or, with a deletion mark, to turn a hyphenated word into a closed-up word. Where a word breaks at the end of a line, deleting the hyphen and drawing close-up marks (which simply end in the margin) tells the typesetter that the hyphen is not properly part of the word. This generally only needs to be done where there is a realistic possibility of a mistake; however, some editors will ask that every end-of-line hyphen be marked for either retention or deletion.

When deleting several words—and especially wherever the next word being retained might possibly otherwise be overlooked by the typesetter—a large close-up mark can guide the typesetter from the beginning of a deletion to its end.

Capitals, small capitals, and lowercase letters Three underscores drawn below lowercase letters indicate a change to capital letters. A single lowercase letter can be capitalized by simply drawing the capital letter boldly over it so as to cover it. Any handwritten capitals that might be mistaken for lowercase can be reinforced with triple underscoring.

Small capitals are indicated by drawing a double underscore below capital or lowercase letters. A combination of three and two underscores indicates a combination of capitals and small capitals.

The lowercase symbol, a slash mark through a letter, is used to change a capital letter to lowercase. To change a word or phrase typed all in capitals to lowercase, slash the first letter to be lowercased and extend the top of the slash as a horizontal line across the top of the rest of the word or phrase. (Some copy editors simply slash the first letter for lowercasing and omit the horizontal continuation.)

In addition to the marks in the text, abbreviations such as "cap" (for "capitals"), "lc" ("lowercase"), "sm caps" ("small capitals"), and "caps/sc" ("capitals and small capitals") may be written in the margins if necessary for clarity.

Spaces The space symbol (#) instructs the typesetter to insert a word space, the amount of spacing between adjacent words on a line. To separate two words that were inadvertently closed up, draw a slash between them; the space symbol may be added to the upper end of the slash. Sometimes a *thin space,* smaller than a word space, may be needed—for example, on either side of operational signs in mathematics; this is usually indicated by a slash drawn where the space is desired and the note "thin #" circled in the margin. Occasionally a *hair space* ("hair #"), smaller than a regular thin space, is needed between two characters that might cause confusion when closed up entirely, such as a single quotation mark set next to a double quotation mark.

Italic, boldface, and roman type Italic type is indicated by a single underscore. (Italic capital letters thus require four separate underscores, with the note "ital caps.") For lengthy italic copy, simply write and circle "ital" in the margin and circle or bracket the passage. To change an italic word or phrase to roman, underscore or circle the italicized text and write and circle "rom" above it or in the margin. To mark a change from a large block of italic type, write "rom" in the margin as a precaution.

When marking already typeset copy, such as a tear sheet (a page torn from a printed book—often the previous edition of the book being edited—that will be reset), there is no need to underscore words that are already italicized.

Boldface is frequently used for headings and captions; design specifications usually dictate what text elements will be set bold, and the copy editor need not reiterate the specs by marking them up. To boldface a word or passage within the running text, draw a wavy underscore below it. If it is more than a line long, it may instead be clearly bracketed and the abbreviation "bf" written in the margin. To change boldface to roman, circle the affected words and write "lf" (for "lightface") in the margin. As always when writing *l*'s, make a distinct cursive loop.

Boldface italic type is indicated by a straight underscore with a wavy underscore below it (and if necessary the note "bold ital" in the margin).

Punctuation Punctuation marks can be added or changed to different marks as described below (in alphabetical order).

Apostrophe An apostrophe can be added by means of an inverted caret above the line at the insertion point.

Brackets Square brackets can usually be drawn in place. Parentheses can be converted to brackets by simply tracing the brackets heavily over the parentheses so as to obscure them.

Colon If a colon needs clarification or if it has been created from a period by drawing in the second point, a small circle or oval may be drawn around it. A semicolon can be changed to a colon by drawing two heavy dots over the semicolon so that the tail of its comma is obscured.

Comma A comma that is not clear—one inserted or retained next to a deletion, for example—should be highlighted by a caret drawn over it. Any added comma may be clarified by putting a caret above it.

Dashes The em dash, usually typed as two hyphens, is marked for the typesetter with a numeral 1 over the hyphens (or hyphen, if the author has typed just one) and a capital M below them. To call for dashes longer than one em, write a larger number over the hyphen—for example, 3 for a three-em dash. In print, the em dash is usually closed up tight to the text on both sides; close-up marks should be added if there is space between the hyphens and the surrounding text in the manuscript. (Newspaper style, and the house style for some book publishers, calls for spaces between the dash and the surrounding text.)

The en dash is usually represented in manuscript copy by a single hyphen. To change a hyphen to an en dash, write a 1 above the hyphen and a capital N below it. In an index, or in other types of copy that contain many en dashes, only the first one or two en dashes need be indicated, followed by a circled "etc."

Ellipsis points To add ellipsis points, simply draw three (or four) circled dots. Ellipsis points generally have spaces between them (except in newspaper text, where they are generally set without spaces). If they are closed up in the manuscript, the editor should simply make a series of vertical lines between them. Ellipsis points in mathematical copy are often raised off the baseline; to typemark these, place a caret above and an inverted caret below each point, or write "ctr points" in the margin.

Exclamation point An added exclamation point should be written clearly so that it is not mistaken for other symbols (*l*, *1*, /, etc.) that it may resemble.

Hyphen Any hyphen inserted by the copy editor, and any hyphen that is part of an inserted word, should be doubled so that it looks like an equal sign. To ensure that the typesetter retains the hyphen in a hyphenated word or compound that breaks on its hyphen at the end of a line, such end-of-line hyphens should be doubled. As mentioned earlier, any end-of-line hyphen in the manuscript that denotes a syllabic break but might mistakenly be retained by the typesetter (and might represent a hyphen mistakenly keyboarded by the author) should be marked for deletion with a slash through it and a close-up mark (which simply extends out into the margin). End-of-line hyphenation that is not potentially ambiguous usually need not be marked for retention or omission, though some editors prefer it be done in every case.

Parentheses Added parentheses should be drawn carefully, since handwritten parentheses can easily look like various other symbols. They should be slightly oversize. One or two tiny horizontal lines drawn through each handwritten parenthesis will help the typesetter recognize them.

Period A point enclosed in a small circle denotes a period; it should be used whenever needed for clarity. To change a comma to a period, simply circle the typed comma. To change a colon or semicolon to a period, draw a circle around its lower half so that the circle goes through the upper point.

Question mark Since question marks are used so frequently as shorthand for queries of various kinds, an added question mark can be clarified by the circled note "set ?"

Quotation marks An inverted caret under inserted quotation marks can help identify them when they might be misread. Potentially confusing combinations of single and double quotation marks can be clarified by putting separate inverted carets under the single and double quotes.

Semicolon A semicolon that might not be conspicuous should be highlighted by placing a caret over it. A comma can be changed to a semicolon by adding a point over it and a caret over the point. To change a semicolon to a comma, draw a caret over the comma so that it covers the point of the semicolon. To change a colon to a semicolon, draw a tail on the lower point and then a caret above the new semicolon.

Slash Since a handwritten slash can look confusingly like the number 1 or the letter *l*, it should be accompanied by the circled note "set slash."

Transposition The transposition sign—a line curving over one element and under another—is used to indicate transposition of characters, words, phrases, or sentences. Often the marginal note "tr" is added. To switch two words on either side of a word that will remain in place, the line should curve over the first word, under the second, and over the third.

When the material to be transposed is typed on more than one line, the editor usually circles one of the elements and shows its new position with a line leading from it to a caret or arrow at the insertion point. More complicated transpositions may have to be rewritten.

All transpositions must be marked with care and double-checked especially for punctuation of the reordered text. To delete punctuation when transposing, draw the curved line *through* the punctuation mark.

Run-in text The run-in sign—a sinuous line that leads from copy on one line to copy on another—is used to run them onto the same line. When a messy deletion of intervening material has been made, a run-in line can guide the typesetter to where the retained copy resumes.

Stet The instruction "stet," Latin for "let it stand," is used to restore words mistakenly crossed out. Draw a series of heavy dots below the deleted material (erasing the cross-out line, if necessary, to make the text legible) and write "stet" in the margin.

Spell out or abbreviate To indicate that a number is to be written out or an abbreviation is to be spelled in full, the editor simply circles the number or abbreviation, and may also write "sp" above it or in the margin. This should be done only when the intended change is unambiguous. For example, the circled fraction "1/2" could be set as either "one half" or "one-half," a circled "100" could be set as either "one hundred" or "a hundred," and the circled abbreviation "pt." could conceivably be spelled out as "point," "pint," "part," or something else. Thus, it is often better to cross out the abbreviation and spell out its replacement.

Conversely, a spelled-out number may be circled to indicate that it should be set as digits—but again only where the intended form is absolutely clear.

When a spelled-out word is to be abbreviated, however, the abbreviation should be written explicitly rather than left to the typesetter.

Align Proper text alignment is usually more of a concern for proofreaders than for copy editors, but alignment of tables and other columns or lists may occasionally need to be clarified at the manuscript stage. To show vertical alignment, draw a pair of parallel vertical lines against the left or right side of the lines of copy that should be aligned left or right. To show horizontal alignment, draw two parallel horizontal lines under the type that must align. An additional instruction is usually written in the margin—for example, "Align stubhead left w/stub items" or "Align all figure cols right."

Diacritics and other special symbols Copy editors should know the names of special symbols, including the Greek alphabet, diacritics, and basic mathematical symbols, since any symbol that might be uncommon or confusing should be described or named in the margin the first time it appears. (See Chapter 6, "Mathematics and Science," and Chapter 8, "Foreign Languages.") If the author has written > in a table, for example, it may be necessary to clarify the symbol by writing and circling "greater than" in the margin. Similarly, any odd spellings or stylings that are intentional but that the typesetter might misread or be tempted to "correct" should also be noted, either by placing stet points below the text or by writing "follow copy" in the margin. When there might be confusion between a zero and a capital O, or between the numeral 1 and the letter l, write in the margin "zero," "cap oh," "one," or "ell."

Diacritical marks should be added to foreign words if the author has omitted them. In the margin next to the line, either write and circle the name of the diacritic or rewrite the word, making the diacritics prominent. (A properly typed diacritic, or one that the author has drawn in clearly, usually does not require any further marking.) The most common diacritics (most of which are available in word-processing programs as special characters) are the following:

é	acute accent	ö	diaeresis
è	grave accent	ç	cedilla
â	circumflex	ō	macron
ñ	tilde	ŭ	breve
ă	haček		

Subscript and superscript In handwritten or unclear copy, place a caret over any subscript (as in chemical symbols) and an inverted caret below any superscript (such as footnote numbers).

Indention and paragraphs Manuscript copy must sometimes be marked to tell the typesetter whether lines should be set flush left or right, centered, or indented, as well as the specific amount of indention.

In most publications the first lines of paragraphs are indented, except for those immediately following headings. Instructions on paragraph indention should be included in the design specifications.

When paragraph divisions are clear, there is no need to mark them further. However, when the starting point of a paragraph is obscure or when the editor wants to begin a new paragraph in midline, a paragraph symbol (¶) should be drawn next to its first word. A line-break symbol may be inserted instead or additionally. In running text, it will be understood that the line-break symbol by itself denotes a new paragraph; in other contexts, the symbol may be ambiguous without clarification of its meaning.

To remove a paragraph's indention—for instance, for the first paragraph that follows a heading—draw the move-left symbol (which resembles an opening bracket) flush left on the text block. The move-right symbol (which resembles a closing bracket) is rarely used except to mark math copy or to reposition a credit line. Either symbol may be clarified by a note in the margin telling the typesetter to set the text flush left ("fl l"), flush right ("fl rt"), or flush with some particular part of the copy.

When marking a specific amount of indention for an item not covered by the design specs, *em quads* are often used. These tiny squares are placed just to the side of the line to be indented. The simple em quad indicates one em of space. A number written within the quad indicates a multiple of an em space (thus, a 3 in the quad tells the typesetter to set a three-em space); alternatively, the editor may draw in multiple empty quads, one for each space requested.

An *en quad*, drawn as a quad with a slash through it, is occasionally still used, mainly in numbered lists to indicate the amount of space between the period following each numeral and the text of the item. Such measurements will normally be stipulated in the design specs and usually need not be indicated on the manuscript.

An em quad or en quad can be extended vertically down the page by a vertical line descending from it. Em and en quads are usually drawn only at the beginning of an indented section to familiarize the typesetter with the desired format; the circled instruction "etc." will indicate that the spacing should continue in the same way.

Headings

In addition to running text, such text elements as headings, lists, cross-references, extracts, and bibliographic notes usually require special attention.

Almost any long piece of nonfiction can benefit from the inclusion of headings, since headings help the reader mentally organize the material and find specific passages. Thus, authors should be encouraged by their editors to employ headings in most manuscripts, and copy editors should feel free to suggest them where appropriate.

Headings should by themselves form an outline of the manuscript. To check the organization of a text, the copy editor will find it very helpful to copy out all the headings for each chapter in a vertical list resembling an outline. Any heading inconsistencies that are revealed by doing so—gaps, lack of parallelism, and so on—should be corrected or pointed out to the author.

Headings are usually nouns or concise noun phrases. (Newspaper headings, which usually describe events, will often use a complete sentence as a heading.) The copy editor should confirm that each heading accurately and concisely summarizes the text that follows. The text immediately following a heading should never depend on any words in the heading for an antecedent.

Table 12.1 Copyediting and Proofreading Marks

Text change	Copyediting example	Proofreading example (with marginal mark)
align or straighten	Venus: Roman goddess of love Mars: Roman god of war	Venus: Roman goddess of love Mars: Roman god of war (align)
apostrophe	cats dish	cats dish
boldface type	Warning: Not for internal use	Warning: Not for internal use (bf)
brackets	*The Message Is the Medium* [sic]	*The Message Is the Medium* (sic) [/]
capital letters	crossed the missouri River	crossed the missouri River (cap)
center	]My Thirteenth Year [	]My Thirteenth Year[(ctr)
close up	went for ward slowley	went for ward slowley
colon	as follows; rice, beans,	as follows rice, beans, (:)
comma	peas corn carrots celery	peas corn, carrots celery
deletion	attended this the conccert	attended this the conccert
diacritics	the entrée was entrecôte	the entre was entrecte é/ô
ellipsis	"Warm, winning, heart- breaking"./././	"Warm, winning, heart- breaking"
em dash en dash	That year--that is, the 1996-97 season	That year--that is, the 1996-97 season

Table 12.1 *(continued)*

Text change	*Copyediting example*	*Proofreading example*
em space **en space**	▭ C. Designations 2.▨Primary sources	▭ C. Designations ▭ 2. ˬPrimary sources ▨
hyphen **retain hyphen**	a well-known scene- stealer	a well known scene- = stealer
insertion	three pieces ˬblueberᵣy pie (ᵒᶠ above, r above)	three pieces ˬblueberˬy pie ᵒᶠ / r
italic type	"It was w̲u̲n̲d̲e̲r̲b̲a̲r̲!"	"It was w̲u̲n̲d̲e̲r̲b̲a̲r̲!" (ital)
line break (or paragraph)	end of line. New line. To reʒd- it the manuscript	end of line. New line. To reʒd- (#) (bb) it the manuscript
lowercase	The President was called at 3 A̸.M̸.	The President was called at 3 A̸.M̸. (lc)
move left **move right**	⌐ It was a dark and stormy night. --Shakespeare ⌐	⌐ It was a dark and stormy night. ⌐ --Shakespeare ⌐ ⌐
move up **move down**	Fungible ⌐Assets⌐ ⌊Unique⌋ Assets	Fungible ⌐Assets⌐ ⌐⌐ ⌊Unique⌋ Assets ⌊⌋
paragraph	paragraph ends. Paragraph starts	paragraph ends. Paragraph starts (#) ˬ
parentheses	arrived Tuesday ﴾June 3﴿	arrived Tuesday ˬJune 3, ˬ ﴾ / ﴿
period	That was enough⊙ Unbelievable⊙ It paused⊙ Nothing has changed⊙	That was enough⊙ Unbelievable⊙ ⊙/⊙ It paused⊙ Nothing has changed⊙ ⊙/⊙
question mark	So he really wants it.?	So he really wants it/ (set ?)
quotation marks	liked the song ˅Laura˅	liked the song ˅Laura˅ ˅˅/˅˅

Table 12.1 *(continued)*

Text change	Copyediting example	Proofreading example
roman type	He (noticed) the mistake. (rom)	He (noticed) the mistake. (rom)
run in (no paragraph)	end of line.) New line to be run in	end of line.) New line to be run in (run in)
semicolon	Akron, Ohio; Ogden, Utah;	Akron, Ohio, Ogden, Utah, ;/;
slash	the team's owner/manager (slash)	the team's owner,manager (set slash)
small caps	from 423 B.C. to A.D. 310	from 423 B.C. to A.D. 310 (sc)/(sc)
space	words that are runtogether./.	words that are runtogether ... #/#/#
spell out **abbreviate**	bought ③ apples on (Mon.) (thirteen) in the (United States)	bought ③ apples on (Mon.) (sp)/(sp) thirteen in the United States 13/○/○
stet (let stand)	waved the white flag	waved the white flag (stet)
subscript **superscript**	CO2 C14	CO2 2 C14 14
substitution	Gogh the Van Dyke exhibit	the Van Dyke exhibit Gogh
transpose	beginning,/end\ middle moves after and before	beginning,/end\ middle (tr)/∧ moves after and before (tr)/(tr)
wrong font		(Type Design) (wf)

All the headings at a given level should generally be grammatically parallel or otherwise consistent in form and style. (Heading design is discussed in Chapter 13, "Design and Typography.")

Lists

Lack of grammatical parallelism is perhaps the most common problem in lists, and copy editors will frequently have to recast list entries to achieve a necessary consistency.

Run-in lists—lists that occur as part of normal-looking sentences—may sometimes need to be clarified by the addition of parenthesized numbers, especially when the items are long or complex.

Displayed lists—that is, lists set off in vertical format—may be numbered, bulleted, or unnumbered and unbulleted. Numbered lists are usually desirable when the order or number of items is mentioned in the text or otherwise significant.

To change an author's run-in series to a vertical list, insert line-break symbols (deleting any commas or semicolons between the items by drawing the symbol through them), add initial capital letters if necessary, and change any numerals in parentheses to numerals with periods. To change an author's displayed list to run-in form, use run-in lines to connect the items, add punctuation after each item, change any capitalization as needed, and delete or restyle the numbering.

Cross-References

Cross-references will often have to be inserted for the sake of the reader's convenience where the author has not provided any, and those provided by the author may have to be rephrased for accuracy and stylistic consistency. Examples of cross-reference style (illustrating, for example, whether "chapter" is capitalized and whether "page" is abbreviated) should be included on the copy editor's style sheet.

Wherever the author refers to another page of the manuscript, the copy editor changes the number to 000 (or one or more small black squares) so that the manuscript page number will not be typeset. The 000 alerts the proofreader, editor, author, and typesetter to the fact that, later on when page proofs arrive, the appropriate cross-reference page numbers will have to be added. The copy editor writes the manuscript page number of the original reference in the margin to facilitate finding the new position of the original cross-reference at the later proof stages. The proofreader is responsible for carrying over all these notations to the margins of the proofs.

Cross-references that refer to chapters or sections rather than specific pages will avoid the necessity and expense of adding page references at the proof stage. However, the reader will usually be grateful for a precise page number.

Extracts

Extracts are quoted excerpts from other sources that are set off from the running text, usually by spacing, left (and often right) indention, smaller type size, or (usually) a combination of all three.

Excerpted text that runs to four lines or longer is generally set off as an extract, whereas shorter quotations are generally run in. Where longer quotations have been run in by the author, therefore, the copy editor may have to mark them to be set off. (More rarely, the editor may have to mark brief excerpts set off by the author to be run in instead.) This is done by simply inserting line-break symbols at the beginning and end of the extract, bracketing the passage with a vertical line in the margin, and adding the circled note "extract" (or, if the copy editor is typemarking the manuscript, the typemarking symbol for extracts instead). Any quotation marks enclosing the excerpt should be deleted, since setting text off makes such quotation marks redundant. The copy editor usually need not instruct the typesetter further about how to set extract text, since the design specs will cover extracts.

Notes and Bibliographies

For the formatting of notes and reference lists, the copy editor should be familiar with the various stylings discussed in Chapter 10. The author and in-house editor often agree on a particular format at the outset of a publishing project.

For ease of typesetting, many publishers prefer notes to be set as endnotes rather than footnotes. If the author has provided footnotes but the in-house editor desires endnotes instead, the copy editor must write in the margin next to the first footnote "Set all footnotes together at end of chapter [article, book]," and at the end of the chapter (or article or book) provide the new head "Notes" and write "Insert footnotes 1–00 here." If the author has typed endnotes when footnotes are desired instead, the copy editor should instruct the typesetter to "Set all endnotes as footnotes throughout."

A distinction is sometimes made between simple bibliographic notes, which are equally acceptable as footnotes or endnotes, and substantive or content notes, which are usually placed at the bottom of a page. In such cases, the substantive notes may employ a different set of reference symbols (*, †, etc.). The editor's job is made easier, in either case, if the author has been instructed to type all notes on pages separate from the text.

The copy editor should always be alert to the possibility that material in a given note might better be included in the body of the text, or vice versa, and should query the author wherever it seems desirable.

The copy editor should check the position of all reference symbols, moving them to more appropriate locations where necessary. Reference symbols in mathematical copy, in particular, may be mistaken for exponents or other symbols.

Reference symbols in the text usually appear as superscripts. Call the typesetter's attention to them by means of circled notations in the margin such as "fn 7," which will also be helpful to the copy editor making a late pass through the manuscript to recheck the notes alone. This late pass should include (1) checking numerical sequence, (2) confirming that the reference numbers correspond to the proper notes, (3) seeing that the publishing data in each note is complete, standard, and consistently styled (including consistency in any shortened forms), and (4) making sure all the references are signaled in the margin by hand so that the typesetter will spot them easily.

In editing bibliographies, the copy editor must be sure to (1) check alphabetical order, (2) compare each text reference with its bibliography entry to see that they correspond in every detail, (3) verify that the entries consistently follow a standard bibliographic style, and (4) query the author about any works that seem to have been overlooked.

Art and Tables

Any first reference to a piece of *art*—the term broadly used for any material not set by the typesetter—must be signaled, or *called out,* in a circled note in the manuscript margin, which should include the art's number (or, if it is unnumbered, a brief title).

The copy editor should be alert to the role the art is intended to play in the text. If an illustration does not seem to adequately illustrate its intended point, the author should be queried.

Any description of the art in the text must be completely accurate.

Any art apparently borrowed from another published source should be flagged with a query as to whether permission has been obtained. If the copy editor has the permission file, it should be systematically checked against the art file.

Hand-drawn diagrams may have labels that will have to be typeset. All such labels should be styled consistently (and otherwise edited if necessary) by the copy editor.

Any photographs or art that will become camera copy (as opposed to photocopies) must naturally be treated with great care. If a photograph must be numbered for identification, write the number on the back lightly in pencil. Keep all camera-copy art between protective cardboard, in a drawer if possible, and never set other materials on top of it.

All tables should be edited together for the sake of consistency. (It is thus helpful if the author has segregated them into a separate file.) The wording and styling of headings and stub entries should be regularized from table to table where the author has failed to do so, as should any terms and phrases that recur in the tables. Mark for alignment any table entries that have not been properly aligned horizontally or vertically. Query any tables that seem poorly conceived or structured. Text references to tables, like references to art, must be called out in the margin.

For further discussion, see Chapter 9, "Tables and Illustrations."

Mathematical Copy

Style and markup rules for mathematical copy are described in Chapter 6, "Mathematics and Science."

Typemarking

Typemarking is the marking of a manuscript with circled codes that identify its various type elements—headings of different levels, lists of different types, set-off material, chapter titles, and the like. By directing the typesetters to the appropriate item in the design specifications, these codes ensure that each element will be set according to the designer's wishes. It is often the copy editor who will be asked to typemark the manuscript, using a list of typemarking codes provided by the in-house editor. (Alternatively, typemarking may be done in-house, either before or after the copyediting phase.) This may be a standard list provided for every project, and the copy editor may have to select from its elements only those that actually are used in the manuscript being edited. There is generally no need for a copy editor to see the actual design specs, since basic typemarking has much more to do with analysis of the text than with actual design. The typemarking will usually be done in a color different from those used for editing. Some publishers, in fact, ask that each element be marked in its own color (as stipulated on an instruction sheet), the colors thereby becoming the primary signal for the element.

Though typemarking is largely mechanical and can go very fast, some pitfalls often lurk in a manuscript. If the copy editor has turned a run-in list into a set-off list, it must be given its appropriate mark; if the author has typed some of the headings incorrectly (if some typed as A-heads should instead be B-heads, for example), the copy editor must typemark them correctly; and so on.

The editor may request a memo from the copy editor that lists all the elements actually used, along with the page where each first appears, and possibly also the pages where any unusual examples of the element show up.

For more on typemarking, see Chapter 13, "Design and Typography."

Copyedited Pages

Figure 12.3 shows two pages of copyedited text, illustrating the use of many of the marks described above.

Trafficking the Copyedited Manuscript

The copyedited manuscript will normally be returned to the editor, who will read all queries addressed to "Ed," and may also check the overall quality of the job and add further queries or marks (usually in different-colored pen). The editor then sends it on to the author, perhaps with a standard printed sheet of instructions on interpreting copyediting marks, responding to queries (with the injunction not to remove any flags or erase any marks), and generally dealing with the edited manuscript. The author will usually be encouraged to return the manuscript within a few weeks, as the schedule requires.

When the manuscript returns, the editor will frequently have to reconcile the responses to the queries and clean up the manuscript for the typesetter. The flags are removed at this point (and may be saved in an envelope for possible later reference); the information on some of them may have to be transferred to the text. Where the author has decided to reject the copyeditor's or editor's suggestions, the editor will generally acquiesce. However, when these decisions seem to be the result of misunderstanding or when they may create problems of consistency, a call to the author may be necessary.

When the final issues have been resolved, the manuscript and diskette are sent to the typesetter, along with the specs (revised if necessary). Generally all changes will have been entered on the diskette by the publisher. Sometimes this task will be left to the typesetter, and sometimes, as mentioned earlier, the

Figure 12.3 Copyedited Text

John Wallis, a mathematician and Member of the Royal Society, published in 1658 a grammar, written in Latin, for the use of foreigners who wanted to learn English. Wallis, according to George H. MacKnight, abandoned much of the method of Latin grammar. Wallis's grammar is perhaps best remembered for being the source of the much discussed distinction between "shall" and "will." Wallis's grammar is also the one referred to by Samuel Johnson in the front matter of his 1755 dictionary. John Dryden deserves mention too. He defended the English of his time as an improvement over the English of Shakespeare and Johnson. He is the first person who worried about the preposition at the end of a sentence we know prepositions of. He eliminated many such from his own writings when revising his works for a collected edition. He seems to have decided the practice was wrong because it could not happen in Latin.

C. C. Fries tells us that 17th-century grammars in general were designed for either foreigners or for school use, in order to lead to the study of latin. In the 18th century, however, grammars were written predominately for English speakers, and although they were written for the purpose of instructing, they seem to find more fun in correcting. A change in the underlying philosophy of grammar had occurred, and in perhaps the first eighteenth-century grammar, A Key to the Art of Letters, published in 1700 it is made explicit by a schoolmaster named A. Lane. He thought it a mistake to view grammar simply as a means to learn a foreign language and asserted that "the true End and Use of Grammar is to teach how to speak and write well and learnedly in a language Already known, according to the unalterable Rules of right Reason." Gone was Ben Jonson's appeal to custom.

The 18th-Century Grammar

There was evidently a considerable amount of general interest in things grammatical among men of letters, for Addison, Swift and Steele all treated

Figure 12.3 *(continued)*

grammar in one way or another in The Tatler and *The* Spectator in 1710, 1711, and 1712. In 1712, Swift published yet another proposal for an English academy (it came within a whisker of succeeding); John Oldmixon attacked Swift's proposal in the same year. Public interest must have helped create a market for the grammar books that began appearing with some frequency about this same time. And if controversy fuels sales, grammarians knew it; they were perfectly willing to emphasize their own advantages by denigrating their predecessors, sometimes in abusive terms.

We need mention here only a few of these productions. Pride of place must go to Bishop Robert Lowth's *A Short Introduction to English Grammar* (1762). Lowth's book is both brief and logical. Lowth was influenced by the theories of James Harris's *Hermes* (1751), a curious disquisition about universal grammar. Lowth apparently derived his notions about the perfectability of English grammar from Harris, and he did not doubt that he could reduce the language to a system of uniform rules. Run in: His favorite mode of illustration is what was known as false syntax, examples of linguistic wrongdoing from the King James Bible, Shakespeare, Sidney, Donne, Milton, Swift, Addison, Pope—the most respected names in English literature. He was so sure of himself that he could permit himself a little joke; discussing the construction where a preposition comes at the end of a clause or sentence, he says, "This is an idiom, which our language is strongly inclined to."

Lowth's grammar was not written for children. Lowth's approach was strictly prescriptive; he meant to improve and correct, not describe. He judged correctness by his own rules—mostly derived from Latin grammar—which frequently went against established usage. But he did what he intended to so well that grammarians subsequently fairly fell over themselves in haste to get out versions of Lowth suitable for school use, and most subsequent grammars—including Noah Webster's first—were to some extent based upon Lowth's.

author will be asked to enter the changes. Camera-ready art is not usually included at this stage; however, if the editor expects to receive page-style first proofs, properly sized photocopies of the art may be sent, or the size of each art hole may be specified in the margin next to its text reference.

Electronic Editing

As mentioned, most manuscripts are created electronically and submitted on computer diskette in addition to paper. However, most book editing continues to be done on paper. The marks on a copyedited manuscript are generally keyed into the electronic file after they have been approved by the author and editor. This is generally done in-house; alternatively, the diskette and paper manuscript may be sent straight to the typesetter and the corrections may be keyed in there.

The typemarking on the manuscript may also be keyed into the manuscript, in the form of generic coding. (See Chapter 13, "Design and Typography," and Chapter 14, "Typesetting, Printing, and Binding.")

The submission of manuscripts on diskette has led to experimentation with on-screen editing. Word-processing programs now include editing functions that go beyond the kind of editing most users employ for their own writing.

With these functions, deleted text need not simply disappear, but rather is struck through with a deletion line. Any substituted text appears next to it underscored and in color. (Other display options are also available.) The subsequent reader (author or editor), using a distinctive color of type, can accept or reject the change and make further alterations. Other colors can serve to identify the marks of other participants.

Alternatively, a cleanly edited file can be electronically compared with a copy of the original file, using a special file-comparison function that causes the differences between them to appear in highlighted form.

Queries and comments can be written to the author and editor in much the way footnotes are added electronically. The user presses a combination of keys, a numbered tag appears at the designated point in the text, a window for the query simultaneously pops up, and the user types the query in it. The author can answer the appropriate queries (in a separate color and with a different identifying tag), and the in-house editor can weigh the issues and make a final decision.

In this way, the manuscript's editorial "history" is preserved as it passes from hand to hand. At the end of the process, a copy of the file showing all the emendations and queries it has accumulated may even be preserved for the record while the clean final file is sent to the typesetter.

Certain marks that would appear on a manually edited manuscript will not appear on a version that has been edited with the help of an editing program. For example, electronic text moved from one place to another will show up struck through at one point and added at its new location but with no line linking the two.

Computers with special equipment can adapt this system to a "pen-editing" system. Such systems allow users to employ an electronic "pen" with which to write on the screen itself—crossing out passages, writing in substitute text above them, writing comments in the margins, and so on. The computer soon learns to "read" the handwriting of a new user and convert it quickly to the computer's own cursiv. script. Once an emendation is accepted by a subsequent reader, the crossed-out text disappears, and the cursive script is converted into standard type and replaces the previous text.

The editing functions on word-processing programs were designed for work on small documents, particularly office documents that might need to go to various people for comments and additions. On larger projects they perform less well. Since very little text is ever visible on-screen, book editors grow frustrated at lacking the browsing freedom that is so helpful for achieving a sense of perspective within a lengthy manuscript. Most professional editors find on-screen editing—including "pen-editing," which was conceived with an eye to larger editorial projects—to be alienating and counterintuitive, and are far more comfortable working on paper. It remains to be seen whether on-screen editing will become the preferred editing mode of the future.

Proofs and Proofreading

The proofreader performs an indispensable role in the later stages of the publishing process, somewhat narrower than that of the copy editor but by no means lacking in scope for discrimination and judgment.

Book publishers generally make use of freelance proofreaders, though they will usually also have in-house proofreaders on the staff for smaller jobs. Magazines and especially newspapers more often keep all their proofreading in-house. (Typesetters almost always employ their own proofreaders, so most proofs that arrive at publishers' offices have already been proofread. However, publishers rarely rely solely on a typesetter's proofreading.)

Like copy editors, proofreaders normally work for an agreed-upon hourly fee. Since proofreading is a more "mechanical" task than copyediting, it usually goes faster, and proofreaders are often expected to work at a rate of approximately ten pages per hour—a rate that will vary considerably depending on the size of the pages and the type, as well as the technical difficulty of the material.

The proofreader's main job is to compare manuscript copy with proof—reading small sections of copy against the corresponding sections of proof, character by character—and to mark the proofs so that they follow the copy and the design specifications (a copy of which the editor will generally provide). In addition to typographical errors, the proofreader corrects obvious stylistic errors missed by the copy editor and points out to the editor or author any other possible problems.

In a second reading, the proofreader may focus on the grammar and sense of the material. However, most editors expect the proofreader to concentrate narrowly on discrepancies between manuscript and proofs and on the most basic issues of style and punctuation, and to ignore potential problems of any other kind if they were not noticed on a first reading.

As mentioned, the proofreader is responsible for knowing and applying the most standard rules of style and punctuation. Thus, if the copy editor failed to notice that a period was typed outside closing quotation marks, the proof-reader would be remiss not to catch the error and automatically correct it (without bothering to ask "Ed:OK?" in the margin).

A proofreader's basic tools are minimal: several well-sharpened lead pencils, some editing tags or flags, a good dictionary, and a pica ruler with which to verify conformity to the design specifications. A small opaque ruler or an index card can be used to help the eyes focus on one line at a time.

First or Galley Proofs

Text sent to the typesetter as a manuscript returns to the publisher in the form of *first proofs*, on which the text is set the width of the type page. These proofs are often called *galley proofs* or *galleys,* named for the long strips of paper on which such proofs were usually printed. Traditional galley proofs omit art, captions, tables, and footnotes. However, first proofs today usually closely resemble book pages in almost every respect, having the same length of text block and including tentative folios and running heads or feet, and leaving room for art at the appropriate locations when they do not incorporate copies of the art itself. However, any page numbers and running heads or feet are usually only provisional, and footnotes and tables may all be segregated on separate pages rather than positioned as they will be in the bound book.

First proofs are usually sent out by the typesetter in batches so that proof-reading can begin while typesetting continues on another batch of manuscript. Two or more copies are sent: one copy may be sent to the author for review (see below); another, designated the *master* proof, is the one that will be returned to the typesetter with all corrections marked on it, and is given to a proofreader.

Whenever more than one person works on a set of proofs, each should use an identifiable color of pencil or pen. Before the master copy is returned to the typesetter, the editor or proofreader must take special care that all revisions and instructions from all those who examined the proofs are properly transferred, or *carried,* to the master.

Most type proofs are merely photocopies; thus they will sometimes slightly distort the printed image and will often have physical flaws, such as faint type and small specks, which should not concern the proofreader.

Revisions to proofs should be kept to a reasonable minimum, because it is expensive to make changes in typeset text. (The cost of alterations, usually stated in terms of the hourly cost of the typesetter's work, should be stated as part of the typesetter's job estimate.) For this reason, a proofreader is usually expected only to compare the proof with the manuscript copy and mark any necessary corrections but not to make other revisions. A proofreader who is concerned about some larger aspect of the typeset text should query the editor about it.

Author's Revisions

A fresh set of first proofs or a set of proofs that has already been proofread is usually sent to the author along with a request to proofread it and particularly to verify such details as the spellings of proper names, the accuracy of numerical data, and the content of bibliography and footnote items—things easily missed by a copy editor. A copy of the edited manuscript is included with the galleys to make comparison and checking easier. Authors are asked to keep new corrections to a minimum and are reminded about the cost of revision, which will often be charged to them. (Their contract will usually state that all author's alterations beyond a stated amount will be billed to the author.)

The proofreader's queries are usually written in the margin, preceded by "Au:" (for "Author")—assuming the proofreader has been told that the author will be seeing the proofread set—or "Qu:" (for "Query") or simply a question mark, and circled. When suggesting a correction that goes beyond a typographical error, the proofreader normally makes the correction and asks for confirmation in the margin by means of a simple note such as "Ed:?" or "Au: OK?" The author is instructed, in a cover letter or a printed instruction sheet, to cross out such question marks and let the correction stand if it is acceptable. If it is not, the author is told to cross out the whole query, including the suggested change, and either write "OK as set" or provide an alternative revision. ("OK" by itself should be avoided, because it may not be obvious whether this applies to the original or the revision).

The author should be instructed not to erase any marks written on the galleys. Instead, an X drawn over a notation will indicate that it is unacceptable without obliterating it.

Proofreaders' Duties and Proofreading Marks

The correction marks used by proofreaders are shown in Table 12.1 on pages 291–293. All proofreader's marks are written in the margin opposite the affected line rather than above the line, with only a corresponding caret, deletion strike-through, circle, or underscore in the text itself to show where the correction should be made. (All proofreading marks are traditionally written in the margin because typeset lines are single-spaced, leaving no room for the interlinear marks used by copy editors. Consequently, typesetters look for them only in the margins.) When two or more corrections occur in a single line, slash marks separate the symbols in the margin; the symbols are written in the same sequence as the errors in the line, reading from left to right. Proofreading symbols may be written in either margin. If several corrections must be made in a single line, they may begin in the left margin and continue to the right margin; however, a line with many errors should be deleted and rewritten correctly in the margin.

On first proofs, the proofreader's duties include confirming, at a minimum, the following aspects of the text:

1. Precise reproduction of every character in the edited manuscript, except where the copy editor failed to catch a standard error
2. Precise conformity of every element to the design specs throughout
3. Numerical and alphabetical sequences
4. Vertical and horizontal alignment of set-off text
5. Acceptable end-of-line word breaks

If first proofs arrive in the form of made-up pages with running heads and folios, the proofreader should additionally check the latter for correctness and sequence. (The specs should stipulate the content as well as the design of the running heads.) However, if the book will include art but no holes have yet been left for it, there is no point in checking the folios and running heads since addition of the art will alter the page makeup.

Any text references to missing tables or art of any kind should be repeated in a marginal note ("Fig. 8.1," "Einstein portrait," etc.).

Queries, as mentioned above, are usually kept as brief as possible and written right in the margin. A tag or flag, with the page number on it, may be used for longer queries.

In order that the publisher may allocate the costs of typesetting changes at the proof stage, the proofreader is traditionally (but not always) asked to assign responsibility for each marked alteration. These are classified as one of three types: (1) *printer's errors* (really *typesetter's* errors), errors that result from the typesetter's misreading of copy, careless keyboarding, or careless misunderstanding of design specs; (2) *author's alterations,* changes requested by the author as a result of discovering errors made in the manuscript or late changes in desired wording; and (3) *editor's alterations,* corrections that the copy editor failed to make or other changes requested by the proofreader. The proofreader identifies these alterations by writing and circling the abbreviation "PE," "AA," or "EA" in the margin by each requested change. If the proofreader is not reading proofs that the author has already marked up, only "PE" and "EA" will be needed; assigning the author's responsibility may be left to the in-house editor as one of the tasks of conflating the author's and proofreader's marks onto a single set of proofs. The proofreader should never label an error "PE" unless the copy and the instructions were absolutely clear; the typesetter should not be held responsible for misspelling a name as a result of an editor's bad handwriting or styling a text element wrong as a result of an ambiguously worded spec.

If the publisher will be absorbing the costs of the author's changes (this will generally be stipulated in the author's contract), only "PE" and "EA" need be used at all. The proofreader should always be told at the outset of each project what the PE (AA, EA) policy will be.

The following paragraphs describe (in alphabetical order) the standard proofreading marks, most of which are shown in Table 12.1.

Align   Use the symbol in the text to show where type (usually in tables or lists) should be aligned. In the margin, write "align" or provide a specific instruction such as "Align col heads."

Boldface   Draw a wavy line below the text, and write and circle "bf" in the margin.

Capital letter   Draw three lines under lowercase type in the text, and write "cap" or "uc" in the margin.

Center   Enclose the text to be centered between reverse brackets. Repeat the symbols in the margin, or write and circle "ctr." If clarification seems necessary, include an instruction such as "Ctr below head of col 1."

Centered dot   In the text, put a caret above the dot and an inverted caret below it, and draw the dot with both carets in the margin.

Change or add punctuation To change punctuation, draw a slash through the incorrect punctuation mark and write the correct mark in the margin. To add punctuation, draw a caret at the text insertion point and write the punctuation in the margin, using the punctuation symbols in the table.

Close up Place a close-up sign at the appropriate point in the text, and repeat it in the margin.

Deletion Cross out the word or passage (use a slash to delete a single letter), and draw a delete sign in the margin. To substitute new text for deleted text, line out the deleted text and write the new text in the margin but omit the delete sign. To delete a paragraph or more, draw a box around the section, drawing a large X through it, and put a delete sign in the margin. To delete letters from the middle of a word, line them out (for a single letter, use a slash) and draw the delete sign within a close-up sign in the margin.

Em or en dash Indicate the insertion point with a caret, and draw the appropriate symbol in the margin.

Em space Draw the symbol or a caret in the text, and draw the symbol in the margin. To indicate more than one em, insert a 2 (3, 4, etc.) within the square or repeat the symbol for each em space required. To extend the indention downward, draw a vertical line descending from the em quad.

Hyphen Indicate the insertion point with a caret, and draw a double hyphen in the margin.

Imperfect character To mark an imperfectly printed character, circle it and put a circled X in the margin.

Insertion Use a caret to show the insertion point in the text, and write the text for insertion in the margin.

Italic Underline the text, and write and circle "ital" in the margin.

Lowercase Draw a diagonal line through the capital letter in the text, and write and circle "lc" in the margin.

Move left or right Draw the move-left or move-right mark in both text and margin.

Paragraph To indicate a new paragraph, draw either a paragraph symbol or a line-break symbol (or both) in the text and put the paragraph symbol in the margin. To join two paragraphs into a single paragraph, connect the end and beginning of the separated paragraphs with a curving line and write "no ¶" in the margin.

Question mark Indicate the insertion point with a caret, and write and circle "set ?" in the margin.

Roman Circle italicized text, and write and circle "rom" in the margin. Circle boldface text, and write and circle "lf" ("lightface") in the margin.

Slash Indicate the insertion point with a caret, and write and circle "set slash" in the margin.

Small capitals Mark the text with a double underscore, and write and circle "sm cap" or "sc" in the margin.

Space Use a caret or a slash in the text to show where space should be added, and write the space symbol in the margin. This symbol may also be used to ask for added space between lines. To separate two letters that are crashing, specify "hair #" in the margin.

Spell out Circle the typeset number or abbreviation, and write "sp" in the margin. To avoid possible ambiguity, spell out the number or abbreviation in the margin instead.

Stet Place dots below inadvertently deleted material in the text, and write "stet" in the margin.

Subscript Circle the affected number in the text, and write the number with a caret above it in the margin. To add a superscript number (or change a number to a subscript), place a caret in the text (or circle the affected number) and write the number in the margin with a caret above it. To add a comma, use a caret in the text and draw a comma with a caret above it in the margin.

Superscript To add a superscript number (or to change a larger number to a superscript), place an inverted caret in the text (or circle the affected number) and write the number in the margin with an inverted caret below it. Add quotation marks and apostrophes by means of an inverted caret in the text and the appropriate mark with an inverted caret below it in the margin.

Transpose Use the curving line within the text, and write "tr" in the margin.

Figure 12.4 shows a page of text on which a number of the marks listed above are illustrated.

Word division Computer typesetting systems break words as commanded by their own internal dictionaries; these usually produce acceptable breaks, but may not be able to deal with names, odd punctuation, symbolic language, or unusual, technical, or foreign words. To correct any faultily divided words, insert a line-break symbol within the word (or between words) and repeat the symbol or write "bb" (for "bad break") in the margin.

Paragraph endings Most publishers and typesetters avoid dividing the last word of a paragraph at the end of the line or allowing a very short word to appear by itself on the last line of a paragraph. To correct any such runovers that may have been typeset, the proofreader may simply insert a line-break symbol near the end of the preceding line to force a word or part of a word to run over. If this would produce an awkward result, the editor may instead insert a word or two in the next-to-last line, but will probably simply choose to ignore the problem.

Headings Runover lines in a heading should break at a logical point when possible. Words within headings should not be divided except where it is unavoidable. (The design specs should have stipulated this.)

Figure 12.4 Proofread Text

John Wallis, a mathematician and Member of the Royal Society, published in 1658 a grammar, written in Latin, for the use of foreigners who wanted to learn English. Wallis, according to George H. MacKnight, abandoned much of the method of Latin grammar. Wallis' grammar is perhaps best remembered for being the source of the much discussed distinction between *shall* and will. Wallis's grammar is also the one referred to by Samuel Johnson in the front matter of his 1755 dictionary. Dryden deserves mention too. He defended the English of his time as an improvement over the English of Shakespeare and Johnson. He is the first person who worried about the preposition at the end of a sentence we know of. He eliminated many such prepositions his own writings when revising his works for a collected edition. He seems to have decided the practice was wrong because it could not happen in Latin.

C. C. Fries tells us that 17th century grammars in general were designed for foreigners or for school use, in order to lead to the study of latin. In the 18th century, however, grammars were written predominately for English speakers, and although they were written for the purpose of instructing, they seem to find more fun correcting. A change in the underlying philosophy of grammar had occurred, and it is made explicit in perhaps the first eighteenth century grammar, A Key to the Art of Letters . . . , published in 1700 by a schoolmaster named A. Lane. He though it a mistake to view grammar simply as a means to learn a foreign language and asserted that "— the true End and Use of Grammar is to teach how to speak and write well and learnedly in a language Already known, according to the unalterable Rules of right Reason." Gone was Ben Jonson's appeal to custom.

The 18th-Century Grammar
There was evidently a considerable amount of general interest in things grammatical among men of letters, for Addison, Swift and Steele all treated grammar in one way or another in The Tatler and The Spectator in 1710, 1711, and 1712. In 1712 Swift published yet another proposal for an English academy (it came within a whisker of succeeding); John Oldmixon attacked Swift's proposal in the same year. Public interest must have helped create a market for the grammar books which began appearing with some frequency about this same time. And if controversy fuels sales, grammarians knew it, they were perfectly willing to emphasize their own advantages by denigrating their predecessors, sometimes in abusive terms.

Footnotes, tables, and illustrations If the text will have footnotes (rather than endnotes), note where the footnote references occur, write a note in the margin ("fn 1," "fn 2," etc.) next to where a footnote reference occurs. Any notations in the margins of the manuscript that concern tables and illustrations ("Insert Islands chart about here," "fn 2 here," "Fig. 3.1," etc.) must be carried to the galley margins by the proofreader.

Lengthy insertions The proofreader will occasionally have to insert lengthy material that the typesetter has inadvertently omitted or will have to carry to the master proof some addition from the author. In the case of omitted material, the typesetter can simply be instructed to "Set omitted text on msp. 133." Added material that does not fit at the bottom of the proof may be typed or photocopied on a separate page and identified as "insert A," "insert B," and so on. The point of insertion should be marked with a caret, and a note such as "insert A attached; run in" should be written in the margin.

Carryover instructions All instructions from the editor to the typesetter that remain pertinent at this stage must be carried from the manuscript to the proofs.

If the galley proofs are of the traditional long kind that do not resemble finished pages, it may be necessary to include instructions about how to handle elements that present page-makeup problems—for example, long tables that could extend onto a second page (e.g., "Comp: Repeat title and col heads on new page")—but only if such instructions are not included in the specs, as they should have been.

For all cross-references that include page numbers (the number 000 or an eye-catching symbol will normally have been set in place of any actual numbers at this stage), the proofreader should carry over in the margin the number of the manuscript page where the discussion appears (e.g., "msp.47"), so that at the page-proof stage the proper text material can easily be located and confirmed by comparing the manuscript and the page proofs before writing in the final page reference. To make the task still easier at the future page-proof stage, the proofreader may provide both the manuscript page number and the corresponding galley page number (e.g., "msp.47, galley p.31"). If the first proofs are in page-proof form, the author may have been asked to insert the correct page references on his or her copy of the proofs.

Checking Proofs against Design Specs

In addition to reading the proofs against the manuscript, the proofreader or in-house editor should make a special pass through the proofs to see that every element conforms to the design specifications, which the proofreader should normally have been given. (See Chapter 13, "Design and Typography.") This entails taking various measurements—the width of the text block (and its length, if the first proofs take the form of made-up pages), the spacing around various levels of headings and around lists and other set-off material, the indention of extracts, and so on—as well as checking the size, face, and style of the type in headings, captions, tables, and other elements. After verifying conformity with the specs at the initial appearance of each element, all its subsequent appearances can generally be checked merely visually.

Typesetters usually require some latitude in spacing in order to make up visually acceptable pages; therefore, the spacing above heads (particularly at the second-proof stage) will not invariably be identical throughout. The proofreader must use some personal judgment about how much variation is acceptable.

Sometimes variations also occur in the density of the typesetting—that is, the amount of spacing between letters—and in the heaviness or darkness of the type itself. Typesetting machines allow for various density settings, or *tracks,* and the overall density setting is called the *tracking.* The proofreader should mark any striking examples of variable density on a given line (e.g., "Line set too tight" or "Line set too loose") or larger passage ("Match tracking density of earlier text") and should query the typesetter about any marked variation in heaviness, which will sometimes be merely the result of bad photocopying.

Second or Page Proofs

The master set of marked-up first proofs is returned to the typesetter, along with the camera-ready artwork and instructions as to where and how to insert the illustrations into the text. (For highly designed books, the editor may have had a dummy made from the proofs, which will be enclosed with them when they are returned to the typesetter. See Chapter 13, "Design and Typography.")

After the typesetter makes the requested revisions, the revised text is re-output as *second proofs,* traditionally known as *page proofs,* which show just what each page of the book will look like. (Since first proofs today usually take the form of pages, the term *page proofs* has become somewhat ambiguous, and *second proofs* is now the preferred name.) If the book contains artwork, it is normally at this stage that film or proofs of the illustrations, which have been photographed from the camera-ready artwork, are combined with film or proof of the text.

The typesetter sends back the marked-up first proofs along with copies of the new second proofs, including a master proof for the editor and a copy for the indexer. The indexer should be sent copies of each batch as it arrives, since there will usually be minimal time in the schedule for creating the index.

Second proofs present a much easier proofreading job than first proofs, since there will be many fewer errors and the proofreader need not even reread sections of material for which no corrections were requested. The task will therefore often be assigned to an in-house proofreader rather than a free-lancer, or the in-house editor may even personally proofread the second proofs.

The proofreader compares the marked-up first proofs with the new second proofs to confirm that all the requested alterations were carried out. Wherever a correction was made, the proofreader must check not only the line with the correction but any subsequent lines that were altered by the correction; though computer typesetting hardly ever introduces actual errors when text is simply repositioned because of changes elsewhere in the paragraph, undesirable character spacing and bad end-of-line breaks may sometimes result. The proofreader should also *slug* the second proofs against the first proofs—that is, hold corresponding sections of first and second proofs next to each other as a quick check that no lines were unintentionally deleted between the two stages. If so instructed, the proofreader again labels any new changes "PE" or "EA." As at the first-proof stage, the proofreader will only use "AA" when consolidating the author's marks on proofs that the author has already reviewed. Any errors marked in the first proofs (whether as "PE," "EA," or "AA") but not corrected by the typesetter is marked "PE" at this stage; however, any error noticed for the first time only in the second proofs should not be marked "PE."

The conscientious proofreader may want to make a series of quick passes through the second proofs, each devoted to a separate aspect of the text. A checklist would include at least the following items.

Corrections Examine every correction marked on the galley to be sure that the copy has been corrected as requested without introducing unwanted alterations. Examine the copy that surrounds the correction, especially the lines below it, to be sure that no undesirable spacing or end-of-line breaks have been introduced.

Typesetting instructions Be sure that all other instructions to the typesetter written on the first proofs, in the design specs, or in a cover letter have been carried out.

Cross-references Check each cross-reference to see that it refers the reader to the correct place. If the cross-reference is to the title of a chapter or section, be sure the wording matches. If the reference is to a page number (probably typeset as "page 000"), insert the correct number. (Ideally this will be done by the author, who will usually have been sent a set of second proofs and asked to provide missing cross-references.) If the cross-reference is to a passage that has not yet been set in pages, make a note in the margin to insert the reference later.

Tables and illustrations If tables and illustrations are not referred to by number in the text, read the text carefully for phrases like "the figure above" and make sure each figure has been positioned accordingly. If there is a discrepancy, revise the phrase (e.g., to "the figure below") rather than asking that the figure be moved. Check that each illustration or table matches its text reference and is complete, properly oriented and positioned, and correctly identified by caption. When a table continues to a second page, check that its headings have been repeated on the new page and that any continuation line required by the specs has been set.

Notes Check the sequence of footnote or endnote numbers, and match each superscript number in the text with its note. Each footnote must begin on the same page with its text reference; a long footnote may run over to the following page, as long as two lines or more are carried over. Check the footnotes for conformity to design specifications.

Running heads and folios Read the running heads on each page to confirm that they are correct. If a long running head has not been shortened so as to fit comfortably on its line (any necessary shortened forms should have been specified by the editor before the manuscript was sent out), the editor must abridge it at this point. Remove any running heads mistakenly set on chapter-opening pages or on any other pages where the specs require that they be omitted (e.g., pages with full-page illustrations or tables). Check that the folios are complete and sequential.

Facing pages Make sure that the last line of type on each page aligns with that on the opposite page. If not, draw double horizontal lines to indicate alignment and write in the margin "Align bottom of page."

Top of page Avoid beginning a page with the short final line of a paragraph, known as a *widow,* or any single short indented item such as the final item in a list. Either instruct the typesetter to remake the page or add words to the widow to fill it out. (Typesetters usually automatically avoid widows even when the specs fail to mention them.)

Bottom of page A heading should never be set at the bottom of a page without at least two lines of text below it. Most typesetters will observe this rule even if the specs do not include it, but the designer should have specified it nonetheless. To fix a mispositioned head, use the techniques described below either to add lines below the head and cut some above, or to add lines above the head in order to move it to the next page.

Chapter-ending pages Make sure the last page of each chapter contains at least five lines of text. (Again, the typesetter will generally do this without being told.)

It is generally expensive to make corrections on second proofs, so only essential changes should be made, and only in places and in ways that will cause the fewest lines to be reset. If possible, every line added to or deleted from a page must be compensated for in some way on that page, either by deleting or adding another line or by reducing or expanding space somewhere, such as above or below a heading or list.

While it is generally acceptable to shorten or lengthen the text block by one line, a similar change should usually be made on the opposite page to balance the alignment. If an illustration or table is set at the bottom of a page, strict facing alignment is unnecessary. Whenever the editor chooses to alter the bottom margin, the typesetter should be notified that the change is intentional by means of a note such as "1 li short OK." The editor can suggest ways to alter the spacing in such situations—for example, by asking in a marginal note that space be added or deleted around illustrations, tables, footnotes, or displayed passages. Deleting or adding text may prove awkward, and usually requires approval from the author.

Since the typesetter may charge extra for every line affected by an author's or editor's alteration, the least costly way to gain a line is to extend the last line of a paragraph over to a new line by adding words. When lines must be cut, the cuts should ideally be made near the end of a paragraph.

When the marked-up second proofs return from the publisher, the typesetter makes the final corrections. The typesetter confirms any requested corrections by sending (often faxing) copies of the individual corrected pages to the editor, who calls back to approve them.

Printers' Proofs

At this point the typesetter will finally produce the pages in the form the printer will receive them. These often take the form of *reproduction* (or simply *repro*) *proofs*—high-quality, camera-ready positive prints on specially coated paper, which will be photographed to make film negatives, from which the book plates will be created. The typesetters may make the film themselves from their own repro proofs. Whether repro or film, it will usually be sent directly to the printer, though it may instead be sent to the publisher to be forwarded to the printer. The editor should check that all the pages are included, and may want to look them over for specks and other imperfections.

A third possibility is that the typesetter will send the printer nothing but an electronic version of the pages, and the printer will create any necessary media directly from it.

After a period of usually one to four weeks, the printer sends the publisher a last set of proofs, produced from the film itself. These *film proofs* are commonly known as *bluelines* or *book blues*—or simply *blues*—because they are usually printed in blue ink. They arrive already folded into signatures matching the signatures in the book-to-be.

Checking the blues is an extremely important task, since any errors the editor misses at this stage will almost certainly show up in the bound book itself. Thus, the following steps are essential:

1. Check that the correct identifying mark appears on the spine of each signature. The signatures should either be numbered sequentially or have a distinctive mark that indicates the signature's order, generally by being lower on the spine than those that precede it and higher than those that follow it, or vice versa.

2. Check that all the pages are present and in order. Scan every page—spend at least five seconds apiece—for specks, blotches, obscured type, and the like. If an entire page or part of a page has printed light, this likely will not reflect the way the actual page will print, but it may be safer to mark such pages anyway. Circle each error prominently in ink; if the printer might be unsure what is wrong, describe the error in a note on the page itself.

3. Page through the set again, this time spot-checking the page backup. Hold up to the light a reasonable sample of the pages to see whether the running head, folio, and text block align with those on the reverse side. Wherever they do not, note this on the page itself; if the problem is common, instruct the printer to "Check page backup throughout."

4. Check that all art is in its correct place and has printed clearly with sharp outlines. Check that none of the art has been flopped (reversed in orientation so that it reads backwards). If any late-arriving art has not been sent to the printer, it must be included in the package with the returned blues, along with any necessary sizing or other instructions. Likewise, if the index was typeset too late to be included in the blues, its film or repro must be sent back with them, along with any necessary instructions.

5. If the CIP data has not yet been added on the copyright page, it must be returned with the blues.
6. On the first page of blues, list all the pages where errors, changes, or omissions have been marked. The list may be repeated in a cover letter.

Because printers' schedules tend to be tight, blues usually have to be returned quickly, sometimes on the same day they arrive.

The very last form in which an editor sees a printed text before the bound books arrive is known as *folded and gathered sheets,* or simply *F&G's.* F&G's are a complete set of the actual signatures that will be bound—that is, with the actual ink color and on the same paper stock. F&G's are sent immediately to the publisher as soon as the print run begins; they often arrive on an editor's desk while the run is under way. (They need not be returned to the printer.) If the print run is a short one, there may be no time to halt it even if a serious error is discovered in the F&G's, though even if the printing cannot be stopped the binding often can be. Any interruption at this stage will always be disruptive and costly, however, and is rarely resorted to except when a disastrous error is discovered.

If all the previous stages have been properly checked, the bound books themselves should contain no unpleasant surprises—or at least none that the editor can be held responsible for. Sometimes part of a print run will be trimmed badly, so that the type block comes too close to the edge of the page. Occasionally a signature will be omitted. The editor should take a few minutes to examine an advance copy before sending one off to the author, and should alert the manufacturing manager about any faults. (See Chapter 14, "Typesetting, Printing, and Binding.")

Parts of a Book

All books contain several pages of front matter preceding the main body of text, and nonfiction books also usually contain some back matter following it. In addition, creation of the book's jacket or cover almost always requires the participation of the editor.

Jacket or Cover

In standard terminology, a book's *jacket* is a removable paper covering, whereas a book *cover* is the binding itself. (*Cover* is often used for both; the confusion is understandable, since a paperback cover will often mimic the jacket of its preceding hardcover version.) Jacket and cover materials are dealt with in Chapter 14.

Jacket or cover design is primarily the province of the design and marketing departments, but responsibility for their text content is usually shared with the editor. *Jacket* or *cover copy* is divided into *front-cover copy, back-cover copy, spine copy,* and, in the case of jackets, *flap copy* (the text written on the two folded flaps). A glance at a few current books will reveal how these normally differ. At the very least, the editor will provide the information with which a copywriter will produce the jacket or cover copy and will review the copy before it is sent out for typesetting. Jacket copy for serious books is often actually written by the editor.

Bar codes Almost all books published in the United States today display on their covers at least one *bar code,* a familiar computer-scannable rectangular symbol consisting of thick and thin vertical lines, along with the numerals they encode. The code may be stuck onto the jacket or cover after the latter has been printed (often done by publishers to accommodate the needs of specific retailers), or (more commonly) printed as part of the jacket or cover. Publishers now usually have their own machines for producing adhesive-backed bar codes, though these can also be purchased from suppliers. They can be made less obtrusive by printing their background in a light color other than white, though the background color may never include any black or blue component. High-quality reproduction and proper positioning are necessary to ensure proper scanning; achieving adequate quality may require the cooperation of the designer, manufacturing manager, and printer.

Two bar codes are now in common use among publishers and booksellers. The *Bookland EAN* (for "European Article Number") code encodes the book's ISBN (see "Copyright page" below) or a periodical's ISSN, but with a new final "check digit." The ISBN follows three digits that identify the product as either a book (978) or a periodical (977). The line pattern may also encode the book's price (usually preceded by 5, the symbol for "U.S. $" or "United States"), though this is optional and the placeholding digits 90000 may appear instead. Books also sold in venues that are not primarily booksellers (office-product stores, drugstores, supermarkets, gift shops, etc.) often also include the *Universal Product Code (UPC),* a bar code used on a much wider range of merchandise. The UPC does not encode the price. On mass-market books, the back cover will often carry the UPC alone and the EAN will appear only on the inside front cover.

Front Matter

A book's front matter traditionally comprises all the opening text whose folios are printed as lowercase Roman numerals (i, ii, iii, iv, etc.). (In the front matter, folios are in fact usually absent from all the pages except the continuation pages of the longer elements—table of contents, foreword or preface, etc.—but those that appear are reckoned exactly as if a folio had appeared on every page.) This pagination prevents late changes in this material from disrupting the numbering of the main part of the text, which traditionally begins with an arabic 1. The length of the front matter must often be adjusted after the entire main body of the text has been set, since the entire volume must generally be fit into a set of signatures, and thus the total number of pages must generally be divisible by 16, sometimes by 32, and occasionally by only 8. The adjustment can often be divided between the front and back matter (particularly the index). In order to expand or shrink the material as necessary, the front matter and the index must be designed or adjusted at the last stage.

When the final page proofs have arrived and the index's precise length has been determined, the editor will need to determine the precise pagination of the front matter by drawing up a list such as the one below (a somewhat improbable list intended to show most of the possible front-matter elements).

i–iv	blanks or advertisements
v	half-title
vi	list of author's other titles [other works in the series, frontispiece, etc.]
vii	title page
viii	copyright page
ix	list of contributors
x	blank
xi	dedication
xii	blank
xiii–xiv	table of contents
xv–xvi	table of illustrations [of tables, etc.]
xvii–xix	foreword
xx	blank
xxi–xxii	preface
xxiii–xxiv	acknowledgments and credits
xxv–xxviii	explanatory notes w/lists of terms and abbreviations
xxix	half-title
xxx	blank

The ordering of several of these elements has never been standardized. In particular, the foreword, preface, and acknowledgments may precede the table of contents. Note that it is traditional for many front-matter elements to occupy recto pages; only when space requirements are extremely tight may a foreword or preface begin on a verso, and a title page or half-title is never set as a verso.

Obviously front-matter elements will vary greatly from book to book. A novel might need no more than a title page and a copyright page, whereas a complex reference work might require even more elements than are listed above.

Endpapers Though a book's endpapers do not officially form part of its front matter, the front matter may effectively begin with printed endpapers. The front and back endpapers are perhaps the handiest location for quick-reference material that may be sought repeatedly by the reader. If the endpapers will contain typeset material, the manufacturing manager must be notified well in advance and may ask for the endpaper film or repro by an early date.

Blanks and advertisements A single blank leaf, or even two, may begin the page sequence. In paperbacks, one or more leaves may be devoted to reviewers' blurbs or to advertisements for other books.

Half-title and its verso In past centuries, when most books were bought unbound and the buyer himself had to have covers put on them, the title page was protected by a *half-title page* that only minimally identified the book, often omitting not only the author's and publisher's names but even the subtitle (if any). Today a half-title is rarely required but is always available as an option.

Even when a half-title leaf serves no other purpose, it is often felt to add a suggestion of dignity or luxury to a volume and is thus very commonly seen. It is often used to fill extra pages of a partly filled signature when the editor wants to avoid leaving more than a given number of blanks at the end of the book.

A half-title normally contains only the book's simple title (lacking any subtitle or edition number), set somewhat above the middle of the page in type smaller than on the title page.

Its obverse side is often left blank, but it may also be used for other purposes, particularly for listing other works by the same author, the contributors to the volume, or other works in the series to which the present book belongs, or for a *frontispiece*—a photograph, artwork, or map that is often somehow emblematic of the book as a whole. Occasionally the title page itself will be designed to extend onto the half-title's verso.

Another identical half-title may, less commonly, follow the front matter and immediately precede page 1 of the main text. Second half-titles generally have blank versos, though the verso may be used for an epigraph or even an illustration.

Title page The title page either begins the front-matter sequence or follows the half-title leaf. It displays the book's full title and subtitle, its edition (if other than the first), its author or editor (with any translator), and its publisher's name and city (and sometimes its logo). The subtitle is almost always distinguished from the main title typographically, if only by being set on a new line, and thus is not preceded by a colon. The author's name is given in his or her preferred style; it may be followed by an affiliation, but rarely by an academic degree. Like a half-title, the title page always falls on a recto (though it may occupy a full spread).

Copyright page The copyright page is frequently the most complicated piece of the front matter. It contains more standard elements than any other page, and may have to accommodate many others that vary from book to book.

Its most essential element is the copyright line. (This is no longer required to appear on the copyright page, but almost invariably does.) This must reflect copyright ownership as stated in the publishing contract. (See "Copyright and Permissions" beginning on page 319.)

For the sake of librarians and others who may need to catalog books for any reason, most books published in the United States print the Library of Congress's *Cataloging-in-Publication Data*—usually known simply as *CIP data*—on the copyright page. This data is basically identical to the Library of Congress's own catalog entry for the book; it is now used by most American libraries when they acquire their own copies of new books. Books too ephemeral or trivial to be acquired and cataloged by libraries (including the Library of Congress) usually are not given CIP data.

The data should be typeset in the same format as it is typed by the Library. However, it should be checked for errors; any errors found (or any changes made subsequent to the filing of the application) should be fixed and the Library should be notified.

Application forms for CIP data can be obtained by writing to: Cataloging in

Publication Division, Library of Congress, COLL/CIP (4320), Washington, DC 20540-4320. The Library formerly requested that a complete set of book proofs or the complete manuscript accompany the completed form; now it usually requires only a typeset or manuscript copy of the book's title page, copyright page, table of contents, and preface, along with a sample chapter if possible. The Library may take as long as three weeks after receiving the application materials to return the CIP data; thus, the process should not be left until the last minute. (CIP data is sometimes not added to books until the blues stage. When a schedule is extremely tight, the data is sometimes "typeset" by the editor on a word processor, returned with the book blues, shot by the printer, and stripped into the space left for it on the copyright page.)

The copyright page always includes the *International Standard Book Number,* or *ISBN.* American ISBNs are maintained and assigned by the publisher R. R. Bowker (New Providence, N.J.); Bowker provides each participating publisher with a printout of thousands of its own ISBNs, which the publisher itself assigns to its books in sequence as needed.

The ISBN is a string of digits segmented by three hyphens. The first component identifies the language of the country of publication (0 is used for the English-speaking countries). The second component, which may range from one to five digits, identifies the publisher and always remains the same. The third component identifies the book itself; for a given publisher, this number may be as short as one digit (for its earliest publications) or as long as six; shorter numbers in this position may or may not begin with zeros. The final component is a single digit, the so-called "check digit," which is calculated electronically and is not part of a sequence; when an ISBN printed on a book is run through a computer check, the check digit will reveal whether the preceding digits are incorrect as printed.

The ISBNs of a hardcover book and its subsequently (or simultaneously) published paperback version will be different. (Both may be listed on the copyright page; if so, however, each must be identified by a tag such as "hardcover" or "paper.") A second edition takes a new ISBN. A multivolume work whose volumes will never be sold separately may use a single ISBN. (An *International Standard Serial Number,* or *ISSN,* is assigned once only to a given periodical and does not change from issue to issue.)

A standard statement regarding reservation of rights (usually beginning "All rights reserved") is frequently included on the copyright page, though it is not legally necessary.

A line such as "Made [*or* Printed] in the United States of America [Hong Kong, Italy, etc.]" is no longer legally required but is often included.

A printing line, which cryptically records the number and year of the latest printing, is frequently displayed as well. Such a line might be set as "97989900QP/M7654321"; the outer numbers, 97 and 1, indicate that this is the first printing and took place in 1997. (The optional letters at the center indicate that the printer was Quebecor Printing in Martinsburg.) If the second printing occurs in 1998, the printer simply opaques the outer numbers on the film to make the line read "989900QP/M765432."

A small number of credits may be listed on the copyright page. If permission to use three or four literary excerpts was obtained, for example, the credit lines may be gathered here, and can be run in together to save space. However, a lengthy list of credits either requires a page of its own or should be included in an "Acknowledgments" section.

If the book has been printed, for the sake of longevity, on acid-free paper that meets standards set by professional groups, that fact should be stated on a line of its own.

Other optional elements might include the publisher's precise address, the publishing history, credits to the book's designer and printer, and a publisher's standard statement about quality.

Dedication A dedication is ideally given a page to itself; the page's verso is usually blank. If space is lacking, the dedication may appear on a verso or on the copyright page.

Sometimes an epigraph will appear in addition to or in place of a dedication. A quotation that relates to the dedicatee will appear on the same page as the dedication.

Table of contents A table of contents (usually headed simply "Contents") provides the names and page references of chapters and often of section headings (A-heads) within the chapters as well. These must naturally match the actual headings precisely.

The best tables of contents will usually be short—preferably no more than three pages—so as to make them easy to survey. Since they lack the alphabetical arrangement that makes indexes so accessible, anything longer can become difficult to scan. An effective shortening technique is to run in the A-heads together rather than list them vertically.

Page references are often easier to match with their corresponding headings when they are kept close to the headings rather than set in a column at the right margin.

Lists of illustrations or tables The table of contents may be supplemented by a list of illustrations, tables, maps, or other categories of graphic material. The decision as to whether to include such a list should depend on the author's or editor's expectation of its usefulness to the expected reader.

Foreword and preface An author's prefatory remarks are usually titled "Preface." When another person writes an introductory essay, it is normally called a foreword; the author's preface, if any, follows it. The preface often closes with acknowledgments of those who assisted in the project. A preface is usually signed (and the date and place of writing often follow the typeset signature); a foreword by another person always is. Information essential to the main text should generally be placed in a set of explanatory notes, or perhaps in an "Introduction" that may be paginated in arabic numerals with the main text, rather than in a preface.

Acknowledgments Acknowledgment of people or institutions who assisted in the writing of a book is usually done at the end of a preface. If the list is lengthy, and especially if it will include a number of credits for use of material, it is better accommodated as a separate "Acknowledgments" section.

Back Matter

Back matter includes everything that follows the main text. This may comprise endnotes, a glossary, appendixes, a bibliography, and indexes. All back-matter elements ideally begin on recto pages. As for front matter, the order of some elements is not standardized, though notes always precede their bibliography and the index always follows all the other standard sections.

The definition of back matter is less technically critical than that of front matter, since none of its components will affect the pagination of the rest of the book; the arabic pagination continues to the end of the book.

Endnotes   Any endnotes often immediately follow the main text, in a section headed "Notes" or "Endnotes." The endnotes for each chapter should be preceded by the appropriate chapter heading, and the section's running heads should serve as an efficient guide to the reader. See Chapter 10, "Notes and Bibliographies."

Glossary   A glossary will begin with a headnote describing its scope or method. Glossaries are set with hanging indention—that is, with each headword set flush left (usually in boldface) and the subsequent lines of each entry indented. A book will occasionally need more than one glossary, each devoted to a given subject.

Appendixes   Auxiliary matter that forms a cohesive whole is often relegated to an appendix. A book may have a single appendix or half a dozen (which will usually be headed "Appendix A," "Appendix B," etc.). An appendix may consist entirely of the author's prose, just like the main text, or it may be devoted to a table, a list, a document, or something else.

Bibliography   Like glossaries and indexes, bibliographies are usually set with hanging indention. Unlike glossaries, they generally do not use boldface type. See Chapter 10, "Notes and Bibliographies."

Index   The index is almost always the final element in an indexed book, apart from any blank pages (sometimes replaced with advertisements in paperback books). Its design often critically depends on the number of pages available in the final signature of the page proofs. See Chapter 11, "Indexes."

Copyright and Permissions

Copyright

The issue of copyright affects publishers in at least two ways. First, they must ensure that their own works receive maximum copyright protection. Second, they must be careful not to trespass on material copyrighted by others.

U.S. copyright law has been considerably altered by two events in recent years. In the mid-1970s the U.S. copyright law (dating from 1909) was substantially revised; the changes took effect on January 1, 1978. And on March 1,

1989, the United States finally became a party to the international Berne Convention.

Copyright law protects intellectual works, both published and unpublished. These include not only written works but also such artistic media as music, dance, and film.

Copyright protection actually begins as soon as a work is created in fixed form; that is, the work need not be printed or stamped with a copyright notice. (Before 1978, publication with copyright notice was required before a work could gain copyright protection.) However, authors may want to place copyright notices even on their manuscripts to prevent any innocent infringement of their rights to the material.

Though a copyright notice on a published work has been technically optional since 1989, it is highly recommended. Such a notice tells readers that the work is protected and thus makes it difficult for any potential infringer of the law to later claim not to have realized the work was copyrighted. The notice should contain (1) the symbol © or the word "Copyright" or both, (2) the year of first publication, and (3) the name of the copyright owner. If the work is a compilation of previously published material, the publication year of the compilation itself is all that is necessary. Later editions of a work will often include the dates of the earlier editions as well, though this is not strictly necessary.

Any work created on or after January 1, 1989, is automatically protected from the moment of its creation. This protection normally lasts for 50 years after the death of the author (or the last surviving author). Works done for hire are normally protected for 75 years after publication.

Any work created before 1989 may be protected for a maximum of 75 years after the date of publication. The initial copyright protects such works for 28 years, at which time the copyright holder was originally obliged to renew the copyright for another 28 years, after which it would lapse forever. Under the 1978 copyright law, this renewal period was extended to 47 years (for a total of 75 years), and for any works whose 28-year renewal was still in force the renewal period was automatically extended to 47 years.

International copyright The United States now belongs to the two major international copyright treaties.

The Universal Copyright Convention (UCC), which took effect in 1955, protects all member states within all other member states. The traditional copyright notice described above generally guarantees protection under the UCC.

The United States only joined the much older Berne Convention in 1989. The term of protection under the Convention extends for fifty years after the death of the author; there is no provision for copyright renewal. However, this applies only to works published from 1989 on.

Copyright registration As mentioned, copyright registration is not generally necessary in order to secure copyright protection. However, registration does establish a public record of the copyright and will make any eventual infringement suit considerably easier to pursue. For this reason, all publishers routinely apply for copyright registration for any works published.

Registration requires sending in a completed registration form, a modest registration fee, and either one or two copies of the work to the Register of Copyrights, Copyright Office, Library of Congress, Washington, DC 20559. Complete information on copyright requirements is available from the office by mail or at the U.S. Copyright Office's World Wide Web site.

Use of copyrighted materials The intention of copyright law is to prevent unauthorized use of protected material. However, some limited uses of copyrighted material are considered "fair use," which is permitted because it serves a constructive purpose and does not seriously infringe its owner's interests.

There are no hard-and-fast rules as to what constitutes fair use, but four factors must be taken into account, according to the present law: (1) the purpose and character of the use, (2) the nature of the copyrighted work, (3) the relative amount of the work reproduced, and (4) the effect of the reprinting on the market for the reproduced work. A pirated work that its publishers are attempting to sell in place of the original, or a work that borrows much of the language of the original so as to make the writing job simpler for the second author, are perhaps the two situations the law is principally intended to prevent. Quoting three or four paragraphs from a published work, with proper attribution, will hardly ever be regarded as infringing on the original author's rights. To be safe, however, some publishers recommend that permission be obtained for any excerpt longer than 250 words or combined excerpts totaling more than 250 words, and are much stricter when the material represents more than 5 percent of a work or if the material is music, poetry, or drama.

The factor of relative amount may rule out certain brief borrowings, since 50 percent of even a brief work is obviously a very large relative amount. Thus, quoting a complete poem—even a four-line poem—may in certain instances exceed the bounds of fair use, as will a complete song or lyric, and reprinting a complete short story or essay still protected by copyright unquestionably exceeds such bounds.

Art is governed by the same copyright laws as written material, and reproducing an artwork (a painting or a photograph, for example), or even a detail from an artwork, will frequently require permission. A great many older artworks are no longer protected, though photographs of such works may indeed be protected.

Commercial photo archives usually claim rights to their photos, including previously published images on which copyright has expired, in language that makes it seem as though the rights are exclusive. However, an identical image, when obtained from another source, may in fact be completely unprotected. Thus, what the archive may actually be providing is simply wide selection, convenience, and high-quality prints.

Not many infringement suits are filed, since publishers generally give each other considerable leeway. A credit line or a citation in the running text is all that is needed in many cases; since such an acknowledgment can represent a kind of advertisement, the author or publisher of the original is unlikely to object in most cases. However, works from the realm of popular culture—songs, comic strips, iconic images of celebrities, and so on—are often fiercely guarded and monitored.

Permissions

The job of obtaining permissions to use copyrighted material is usually left to the author. Any permission fees charged by copyright holders must often also be paid by the author; however, if the sum seems likely to be substantial, the author may ask the publisher to share the burden of payment. (Any such agreement will normally take the form of a clause in the publishing contract.)

The publisher may explain the permissions procedure in a guide prepared for its authors, and will usually provide the author with a batch of blank permission forms. On each form the author fills in a description of the book being written and the material that will be reprinted, along with a proposed credit line, before sending it out to the copyright holder. (Such responsibility is usually stated in the author's contract, which may provide for full reimbursement of permissions fees, or for reimbursement up to a stated amount, or for no reimbursement at all.) These forms usually describe the new publication and ask (rather hopefully) that permission be granted in return for nothing more than a credit line. (Model language for such forms is provided in such sources as Alexander Lindey's *Lindey on Entertainment, Publishing & the Arts;* see Bibliography.)

The copyright holder may simply sign the form and return it, thereby granting permission on the author's terms—that is, forgoing any fee and accepting the author's credit line and placement. However, the response may instead come on its own form, with any of various stipulations: a fee (sometimes higher than the author will want to pay) may be requested, the credit line may be worded differently and its placement strictly specified, permission may be limited to the first edition of the book only, or free copies of the book may be requested on its publication.

All the permissions will ideally have been obtained by the time the finished manuscript is delivered to the publisher. To ensure that they are, it is important that the author begin the process as soon as possible, since publishers can be very slow to respond to such requests and may have to be prodded by follow-up letters or phone calls.

As mentioned earlier, the in-house editor may send the permissions file—that is, all the completed permission forms—to the copy editor, though probably more often the credit lines and permission status will be checked in-house. The copy editor is generally responsible only for flagging material that seems likely, on the face of it, to be protected by copyright, leaving the checking of its actual status to the author and publisher.

13   Design and Typography

Letters, Type Styles, and Typefaces   323
Page-Design Elements   336
Writing the Design Specifications   343

Graphic design entails the selection, styling, and arrangement of elements on the printed page—the choice of type sizes and styles, line length and spacing, table layout and typography, and illustration sizing and positioning, among other things. Though books, magazines, and other printed materials are often designed by professional graphic designers, especially when they are highly illustrated, editors often work in consultation with designers, and book editors frequently have sole responsibility for designing their books' interiors.

A book's design is expressed in its *design specifications,* or *specs,* a set of highly technical instructions from the designer to the typesetter describing precisely how each element is to be set. A complete set of specs is provided near the end of the chapter, and references to the writing of specs will occur throughout. The design of tables and indexes are discussed in their respective chapters. Coding and typemarking are discussed further in Chapter 12, "Production Editing, Copyediting, and Proofreading," and Chapter 14, "Typesetting, Printing, and Binding."

Graphic design is a large topic that has been the subject of many excellent books. This chapter deals primarily with book design, though most of the principles it discusses are more broadly applicable. Magazine designers today are often given great liberty, however, and the scope of magazine design possibilities is larger than can be discussed here. (See the Bibliography for useful books on design.)

Letters, Type Styles, and Typefaces

When analyzing typefaces, it can be helpful to be able to refer to the various parts of individual letters. An *uppercase* letter is more commonly known as a *capital* letter; a *lowercase* letter is a "small" or noncapital letter. A letter's *cap height* is the height of the capital letter. A letter's *x-height* (meaning literally the height of a lowercase *x*) is the height of the main body—that is, the part of a letter that does not include any ascender or descender—of the lowercase letter. The *baseline* is the imaginary line on which the main body of the letter rests. An *ascender* is the part of some lowercase letters that rises above its main body or x-height. A *descender* is the part of some lowercase letters that descends below the main body or baseline. A *stroke* is one of the lines of a letter; a *thick* is a thick stroke, and a *thin* is a thin stroke. A *serif* is a tiny, trailing, curving or angled line that stems from the upper or lower end of a stroke. A *counter* is a wholly or partly enclosed area within a letter.

Type Styles

A given typeface or type family (see "Typefaces" on page 328) normally includes at least three different type styles: roman, italic, and boldface.

Roman type, the style of the text you are reading, is the most common letter style.

Italic type is type in which the letters slant upward to the right and also often have prominent curving serifs, in quasi-imitation of cursive handwriting. Its standard use is to provide contrast with text set in roman type.

Boldface type has thicker strokes than standard roman or italic type. It is used for setting headings, captions, and glossary entries, among other things. *Boldface italic,* though used infrequently, is sometimes useful for providing contrast within nonitalic boldface contexts, or as an alternative to nonitalic boldface in headings.

Many typefaces are also available in various other styles. *Lightface* type has thinner strokes than standard roman type. (The word *lightface* or its abbreviation, *lf,* is also often used, somewhat confusingly, to mean simply "non-boldface"—that is, standard roman type—especially when specifying that a passage already set in bold should instead be set in normal roman.)

The type style often called *extra bold, ultra bold,* or *black* has still thicker strokes than standard boldface, and is used exclusively as display type and for headings. The style often called *demibold* is somewhat lighter than a genuine boldface.

Typefaces are today almost always available in *condensed* and *expanded* (or *extended*) versions—that is, horizontally "squeezed" or "stretched." Condensed faces are used for data and text in books where space is at a premium and users will not need to read extended passages, such as directories. Expanded faces are used for isolated design elements rather than for lengthy passages of text. Character height can also be manipulated independently of its width (which actually produces letter forms identical to those produced by condensing or expanding) in order to permit text originally fitted into a given horizontal space to be altered without otherwise changing the design. In computer layout programs, horizontal and vertical scale can be manipulated within each type style.

Small capitals are often no higher than the x-height of lowercase letters. Since they are now usually merely roman capitals at a smaller point size, they should perhaps not be regarded as a separate type style. Small caps (as they are usually called) are often combined with regular capitals.

Several of these type styles are shown below.

Roman:	Page Design
Italic:	*Page Design*
Boldface:	**Page Design**
Extra bold:	**Page Design**
Condensed:	Page Design
Expanded:	Page Design
Caps and small caps:	PAGE DESIGN

Type Size and Spacing

In discussing type, designers and typesetters use special units of measure. A *pica rule*—a broad, transparent ruler (or plastic sheet) marked with various measures, most of them multiples of points—is therefore an essential tool for editors and designers.

Of the units of measure used in typography, only the pica and the point always represent a fixed amount of space. The other units vary according to the size of type being used.

A *pica* is approximately equal to one-sixth of an inch. Picas are commonly used to measure the length of a line of type, the dimensions of an illustration, or the depth of a page. The lines of type in this book, for instance, are 29 picas long—or, to put it another way, the text block is 29 picas wide.

A *point* is one-twelfth of a pica. Points are most commonly used when referring to type size or the space between lines of type. Half-point type sizes and spacing measures (7½-point, 8½-point, etc.) are also available.

An *em space* (sometimes called an *em quad*) is approximately as wide as the point size of the type being used; thus, in 10-point type an em space is about 10 points wide. A *hair space* is the thinnest possible space, usually about one-half point wide. Other traditional space measurements include the *en space* (half of an em space), the *thick space* (one-third of an em), and the *thin space* (one-fourth or one-fifth of an em).

Type size The specified size of a typeface is based on the distance from the top of the tallest ascender to the bottom of the lowest descender, measured in points. However, it will not always match that distance precisely, and in some typefaces and styles the distance from top to bottom is less than the stated point size, though in no case will it be greater. The illustration below demonstrates the variety of actual sizes that correspond to a single stated point size for four different typefaces. Note how much the x-height itself varies from face to face, a factor to consider when specifying line spacing. (In the following examples the four typefaces are, left to right, Garamond, Times Roman, Bodoni, and Helvetica.)

hij hij hij hij

Only five lowercase letters have descenders *(g, j, p, q, y)*. Typefaces with short descenders (including Times Roman, Caslon, and Century Schoolbook) retain their legibility particularly well with compact line spacing.

Type also has a horizontal dimension, which varies from letter to letter. The capital *M* and *W* are usually the widest letters, the lowercase *i* usually the narrowest. The width of characters in a typeface is generally expressed in terms of the average number of characters per pica. Typeset text (unlike typewritten text) almost always employs *proportional spacing*, which leaves less space for narrow letters than for broad ones.

Line spacing All typefaces are designed to include space above and below so that the descenders on one line do not touch the ascenders on the following line (known as *crashing*). However, this space varies widely. When set with no extra space between lines, Helvetica leaves almost no space between the descenders of one line and the ascenders of the next, whereas Times Roman leaves a good deal of space.

> The word *design*, when used in connection with books, magazines, and other printed materials, refers to the arrangement of elements on the printed page. In addition to the typographical elements, such as the size and style of type, the length of lines, and the space between

> The word *design*, when used in connection with books, magazines, and other printed materials, refers to the arrangement of elements on the printed page. In addition to the typographical elements, such as the size and style of type, the length of lines, and the space between lines, the design of the page often

Whatever face is being used, designers usually add extra space between lines to improve the text's appearance and legibility. This additional space is traditionally called *leading* (pronounced "ledding"); the term dates back to the time when typesetters added spacing with thin strips of lead. Outside of professional typesetting, it is usually referred to simply as *line spacing*. The distance from the baseline of one line of text to that of the next is referred to as the *base-to-base* measurement.

The appropriate amount of leading will vary with the typeface, the type size, the length of the line, the intended audience, and the desired length of the book. In general, the smaller the type and the longer the line, the greater the line spacing ought to be in relation to the type size. Books for young children usually require very wide leading, and readers over the age of 70 or so appreciate a more modest amount of additional leading.

The greater the x-height in relation to the point size, the denser the type will appear. Adding space between the lines can alleviate that density. Helvetica, with its high x-height, is almost always set with extra line spacing; Times Roman can be set without extra spacing, although most designers add a point of leading.

Ten-point type set with two points of leading is referred to as "10 on 12" or "10/12" type. When type is set with no extra space between the lines (e.g., 10/10), it is said to be *set solid*. (The "auto" leading on computer layout or word-processing programs usually provides 10/12.)

Letterspacing The horizontal space between letters, or *letterspacing*, can be manipulated by the typesetter. This is occasionally done to fill out a *justified* (or *right-justified*) line of type—one whose spacing has been adjusted so that it runs exactly the same length as the lines above and below it.

Letterspacing and word spacing are normally closely linked, and both are automatically controlled by means of the typesetting system's *tracking* function. A typical system may have five different tracks, of which the first two are tight, the next two are standard, and the last is loose. Where space is seriously limited, "tight letterspacing" can be requested in the design specs; however, sample pages showing any unusual letterspacing should always be obtained and approved beforehand.

If a typesetting system sets type unattractively tight or loose—whether the type in a given line or all the type on a page or more—the editor or proofreader should request that it be adjusted.

> The word *design*, when used in connection with books, magazines, and other printed materials, refers to the arrangement of elements on the printed page. In addition to the typographical elements, such as the size and style of type, the length of lines, and the space between lines, the design of the page often includes tables, illustrations, and

> The word *design*, when used in connection with books, magazines, and other printed materials, refers to the arrangement of elements on the printed page. In addition to the typographical elements, such as the size

Extra letterspacing will often be desired in particular design elements. It is particularly common in running heads set in all-capitals. It is also used for chapter and text headings (again, especially those in capitals or small caps). In the specs, the designer may simply ask for "extra letterspacing," or, preferably, for a more precise result such as "½-pt letterspacing," which requests an additional half-point of spacing between each pair of letters. (The visual effects of the various spacings can be tested on a desktop computer.)

The term *kerning* is often used as a synonym for *letterspacing*. However, designers often use it to refer only to the adjusting of space around selected individual letters, usually in decorative display type.

The amount of space between words, or *word spacing*, varies according to the type size and whether or not the lines are justified. Occasionally the editor or proofreader will have to ask the typesetter to equalize a line's word spacing ("eq #") or otherwise adjust it.

Typefaces

The terms *typeface, type font,* and *type family* are often used confusingly today. A given *typeface* usually includes a complete alphabet of uppercase and lowercase letters, with all the numerals, standard punctuation, and other type symbols, in several styles (roman, italic, etc.). A *type font* is usually an alphabet (with punctuation, etc.) in a given style and size—for example, 11-point Garamond Italic. These two terms are not always distinguished, however; *typeface* is sometimes used to mean a single style (e.g., Caslon Bold), and *font* is often used to mean all the alphabet designs under a given proper name (e.g., Palatino). *Type family,* however, will always include all available weights, styles, and sizes of the named type.

The subject of typefaces is a large and interesting one, but the fundamentals can be stated fairly briefly. Thousands of different typefaces have been designed over the years. Palatino, Garamond, Baskerville, Century, Caslon, Times Roman, Caledonia, Helvetica, Bodoni, Futura, Bookman, Electra, Univers, and Goudy are among the most familiar and well established. Many others are quite new, and more are being designed every year. Different typesetting systems often use faces that differ subtly from faces with the same name used by other systems. (Typefaces cannot be patented or trademarked; new typeface names may be trademarked, but traditional names such as Bembo, Granjon, Baskerville, Bodoni, Caslon, and Palatino date back centuries and have long been in the public domain.) And some systems use faces that are virtually identical to various standard faces but have been given new names.

Many typefaces are intended only as *display type*—that is, type to be used in large, eye-catching headings, usually for advertising purposes. These highly individual faces must be distinguished from proper *text type,* which is intended for setting large amounts of prose and thus is designed to be highly legible rather than highly distinctive. Though some text faces are widely used as display type, display faces are never appropriate for standard text (and many even lack lowercase letterforms).

Large display type often evokes conscious responses in the reader. Different typefaces carry connotations of solidity, frivolity, austerity, warmth, dignity, liveliness, aggressiveness, elegance, playfulness, or sweetness; they may look antique, old-fashioned, modern, or futuristic; they can suggest business, electronics, entertainment, school, or the home; and they may conjure up the Renaissance, colonial America, Victorian England, the Wild West, the fin de siècle, the Twenties, the Third Reich, or the Sixties.

Old Towne

Old English

Peignot

Park Avenue

Broadway

Caslon Antique

Text type, on the other hand, is not intended to evoke specific reactions and is generally set too small to produce pronounced reactions in any event. As a result, readers may not agree on the psychological effect of a text typeface, and the designer's preference for one text face over another may thus be highly subjective.

Anyone designing a publication should begin only after examining a type catalog, preferably one from the typesetter that will be doing the work. This not only will suggest interesting type possibilities but will show the precise appearance of the type used by the particular typesetting system.

If the text will employ italic or boldface frequently, the legibility of the italic or boldface type and especially the quality of the contrast between it and the normal roman type should be taken into account.

Most books on typography attempt to categorize typefaces on the basis of not only their most obvious visual aspects but also their historical development. Such attempts usually end up being more confusing than helpful to the beginner. Therefore, this section simply describes several visual characteristics that are particularly prone to variation, and provides samples of twelve different typefaces to illustrate how these vary from typeface to typeface.

A primary aspect of any typeface is whether or not its letters have serifs. Typefaces that lack serifs are called *sans-serif* faces. (In the samples that follow, Helvetica, Optima, and Univers are sans-serif faces.) Since serif faces are somewhat easier to read in blocks or paragraphs of text than sans-serif faces, the main text of books and magazines is rarely set in sans-serif, which is instead generally reserved for short elements such as headings and captions. (For captions and labels in small type, sans-serif type can be optimally readable.)

Among serif faces, the shape of the serif varies considerably. Most serif faces have *bracketed serifs*, serifs joined to the strokes with a curved line. (In the following samples, Baskerville, Caledonia, Garamond, and Times Roman have bracketed serifs.) Other serifs include the thin *hairline serif* (used in Bodoni) and the pronounced and sharply angled *square serif* (used in Clarendon).

Another noticeable type feature is the contrast between thick and thin strokes. In the samples that follow, Garamond shows relatively little contrast between thicks and thins; Baskerville and Bodoni show more. Most sans-serif faces show no contrast between their strokes; Optima is an exception.

When attempting to match the type of an earlier edition, or when analyzing the design of a book or magazine from another publisher, the editor or designer will sometimes need to identify an unfamiliar typeface or distinguish two typefaces. Certain characters tend to be particularly distinctive from one typeface to another.

The lowercase *g* may have a simple curved tail or a loop instead; among two-loop *g*'s, the shapes of the two loops will vary, as will the angle and thickness of the stroke connecting them and the shape of the "ear" attached to the upper loop. The lowercase *t* in most serifed faces is short and has a pointed top; in others, it has a square top and may extend to full capital height. Lowercase *y*'s vary in whether their descenders have a rounded thickening at the bottom and in how far they curve to the left. In uppercase *E*'s and *F*'s the crosspieces vary in their relative length; they may be of nearly equal length, the middle piece may be much shorter than the other(s), or all three of the *E*'s pieces may be of different lengths. The capital *J* in some typefaces extends below the baseline. The uppercase *Q* is often the most distinctive letter; the tail may cross the loop at an angle, perhaps first making a little loop itself, or it may only touch the loop. Uppercase *R*'s vary in whether their right leg joins the loop at its lower right corner or joins the left leg instead. In some serifed faces, the capital *T* has pointed serifs that extend above the crossbar.

Quotation marks, question marks, and commas all vary from typeface to typeface. Opening and closing quotation marks usually are distinctively curved, but in some faces they are identical and consist of straight strokes. Question marks vary in shape and in the relative weighting of thick and thin parts of the stroke. The comma may resemble a period with a curved tail or may simply be a short angled stroke.

Each of the samples on pages 331–334 includes alphabets in roman, italic, and boldface. The roman, italic, and boldface samples are set in 11-point type; the text passages are set in 10/11 type.

Mixing typefaces in page design A standard rule of typography is that a book design should use no more than two typefaces (including their roman, italic, and bold styles). Designers very frequently employ two faces: a sans-serif face for headings and a serif face for running text, which produces a contrast that readers generally accept as appropriate. When two different serif faces are used instead, the near-identity of the faces may produce the impression of "clashing."

More austere designers often prefer to use a single face throughout, and have produced beautifully integrated designs by thus limiting their palette. Sticking to a single face can help assure that a design remains within tasteful boundaries. It does not by itself guarantee tastefulness, however; headings in large boldface capitals will dwarf the surrounding text, use of an "ultrabold" style of the typeface will usually result in ugly contrasts, and the many other elements of page design can also contribute to inept and graceless layouts.

A substantial private file of photocopies of good designs, continuously updated, will provide the designer with numerous ideas to fall back on when imagination flags. (A file of *bad* designs may also be instructive.) It may be divided into separate files for tables of contents, tables, captions, bibliographies, sidebars, indexes, and so on. Each face and its size and leading should be identified on the margins of the photocopied pages, by means of a typesetter's catalog and a pica rule.

Legibility

Legibility is a product of several factors—typeface and style, type size, leading, line length, and contrast between ink and paper color.

As mentioned above, studies of typeface legibility have tended to demonstrate that standard serif typefaces can be read somewhat more easily and quickly than standard sans-serif faces, and thus the vast majority of books and magazines use serif type for their text face. Designers nevertheless claim that sans-serif type can be made as legible as serif type by simply keeping the line length short and increasing the leading. And since certain sans-serif faces are

Baskerville

abcdefghijklmnopqrstuvwxyz
ABCDEFGHIJKLMNOPQRSTUVWXYZ

abcdefghijklmnopqrstuvwxyz
ABCDEFGHIJKLMNOPQRSTUVWXYZ

abcdefghijklmnopqrstuvwxyz
ABCDEFGHIJKLMNOPQRSTUVWXYZ

The word *design*, when used in connection with books, magazines, and other printed materials, refers to the arrangement of elements on the printed page. In addition to the typographical elements, such as the size and style of type, the length of lines, and the space between lines, the design of the page

Bodoni

abcdefghijklmnopqrstuvwxyz
ABCDEFGHIJKLMNOPQRSTUVWXYZ

abcdefghijklmnopqrstuvwxyz
ABCDEFGHIJKLMNOPQRSTUVWXYZ

abcdefghijklmnopqrstuvwxyz
ABCDEFGHIJKLMNOPQRSTUVWXYZ

The word *design*, when used in connection with books, magazines, and other printed materials, refers to the arrangement of elements on the printed page. In addition to the typographical elements, such as the size and style of type, the length of lines, and the space between lines, the design of the page often includes

Caledonia

abcdefghijklmnopqrstuvwxyz
ABCDEFGHIJKLMNOPQRSTUVWXYZ

abcdefghijklmnopqrstuvwxyz
ABCDEFGHIJKLMNOPQRSTUVWXYZ

abcdefghijklmnopqrstuvwxyz
ABCDEFGHIJKLMNOPQRSTUVWXYZ

The word *design*, when used in connection with books, magazines, and other printed materials, refers to the arrangement of elements on the printed page. In addition to the typographical elements, such as the size and style of type, the length of lines, and the space between lines, the design of the page often includes tables,

Century Schoolbook

abcdefghijklmnopqrstuvwxyz
ABCDEFGHIJKLMNOPQRSTUVWXYZ

abcdefghijklmnopqrstuvwxyz
ABCDEFGHIJKLMNOPQRSTUVWXYZ

abcdefghijklmnopqrstuvwxyz
ABCDEFGHIJKLMNOPQRSTUVWXYZ

The word *design,* when used in connection with books, magazines, and other printed materials, refers to the arrangement of elements on the printed page. In addition to the typographical elements, such as the size and style of type, the length of lines, and the space between lines, the de-

Clarendon

abcdefghijklmnopqrstuvwxyz
ABCDEFGHIJKLMNOPQRSTUVWXYZ

abcdefghijklmnopqrstuvwxyz
ABCDEFGHIJKLMNOPQRSTUVWXYZ

abcdefghijklmnopqrstuvwxyz
ABCDEFGHIJKLMNOPQRSTUVWXYZ

The word *design,* when used in connection with books, magazines, and other printed materials, refers to the arrangement of elements on the printed page. In addition to the typographical elements, such as the size and style of type, the length of lines, and the space

Garamond

abcdefghijklmnopqrstuvwxyz
ABCDEFGHIJKLMNOPQRSTUVWXYZ

abcdefghijklmnopqrstuvwxyz
ABCDEFGHIJKLMNOPQRSTUVWXYZ

abcdefghijklmnopqrstuvwxyz
ABCDEFGHIJKLMNOPQRSTUVWXYZ

The word *design,* when used in connection with books, magazines, and other printed materials, refers to the arrangement of elements on the printed page. In addition to the typographical elements, such as the size and style of type, the length of lines, and the space between lines, the design of the page often includes tables, illustrations, and

Goudy Old Style

abcdefghijklmnopqrstuvwxyz
ABCDEFGHIJKLMNOPQRSTUVWXYZ

abcdefghijklmnopqrstuvwxyz
ABCDEFGHIJKLMNOPQRSTUVWXYZ

abcdefghijklmnopqrstuvwxyz
ABCDEFGHIJKLMNOPQRSTUVWXYZ

The word *design,* when used in connection with books, magazines, and other printed materials, refers to the arrangement of elements on the printed page. In addition to the typographical elements, such as the size and style of type, the length of lines, and the space between lines, the design of the page often includes tables, illustrations, and

Helvetica

abcdefghijklmnopqrstuvwxyz
ABCDEFGHIJKLMNOPQRSTUVWXYZ

abcdefghijklmnopqrstuvwxyz
ABCDEFGHIJKLMNOPQRSTUVWXYZ

abcdefghijklmnopqrstuvwxyz
ABCDEFGHIJKLMNOPQRSTUVWXYZ

The word *design,* when used in connection with books, magazines, and other printed materials, refers to the arrangement of elements on the printed page. In addition to the typographical elements, such as the size and style of type, the length of lines, and the space between lines, the design of the page

Optima

abcdefghijklmnopqrstuvwxyz
ABCDEFGHIJKLMNOPQRSTUVWXYZ

abcdefghijklmnopqrstuvwxyz
ABCDEFGHIJKLMNOPQRSTUVWXYZ

abcdefghijklmnopqrstuvwxyz
ABCDEFGHIJKLMNOPQRSTUVWXYZ

The word *design,* when used in connection with books, magazines, and other printed materials, refers to the arrangement of elements on the printed page. In addition to the typographical elements, such as the size and style of type, the length of lines, and the space between lines, the design of the page

Palatino

abcdefghijklmnopqrstuvwxyz
ABCDEFGHIJKLMNOPQRSTUVWXYZ

abcdefghijklmnopqrstuvwxyz
ABCDEFGHIJKLMNOPQRSTUVWXYZ

abcdefghijklmnopqrstuvwxyz
ABCDEFGHIJKLMNOPQRSTUVWXYZ

The word *design,* when used in connection with books, magazines, and other printed materials, refers to the arrangement of elements on the printed page. In addition to the typographical elements, such as the size and style of type, the length of lines, and the space between lines, the design of the page

Times Roman

abcdefghijklmnopqrstuvwxyz
ABCDEFGHIJKLMNOPQRSTUVWXYZ

abcdefghijklmnopqrstuvwxyz
ABCDEFGHIJKLMNOPQRSTUVWXYZ

abcdefghijklmnopqrstuvwxyz
ABCDEFGHIJKLMNOPQRSTUVWXYZ

The word *design,* when used in connection with books, magazines, and other printed materials, refers to the arrangement of elements on the printed page. In addition to the typographical elements, such as the size and style of type, the length of lines, and the space between lines, the design of the page often includes tables, illus-

Univers

abcdefghijklmnopqrstuvwxyz
ABCDEFGHIJKLMNOPQRSTUVWXYZ

abcdefghijklmnopqrstuvwxyz
ABCDEFGHIJKLMNOPQRSTUVWXYZ

abcdefghijklmnopqrstuvwxyz
ABCDEFGHIJKLMNOPQRSTUVWXYZ

The word *design,* when used in connection with books, magazines, and other printed materials, refers to the arrangement of elements on the printed page. In addition to the typographical elements, such as the size and style of type, the length of lines, and the space between lines,

extremely compact, they are always useful for data that will not have to be read in quantity but must fit into a limited space.

One of the most legible of all standard text faces is Baskerville, a fairly spacious face. Times Roman, being considerably more compact than Baskerville while still remaining highly legible, is for that reason very popular—perhaps more widely used than any other typeface.

Roman type is more legible than boldface type and far more legible than italic. Lowercase letters are more legible than capital letters, since their shapes are more varied vertically; therefore, all-cap and small-cap setting is generally appropriate only for headings, running heads, labels, short captions, and the like.

Proper type size is naturally essential to legibility. The main text in books today is usually set in 10-point type, less frequently in 9-point or 11-point, and still less frequently in 8-point or 12-point. Dictionaries and indexes may use type as small as 6-point, while the type in children's books ranges up to 20-point and larger. In general, reference books can employ small type because readers will only be reading short passages at a time (though even so, older users may find such type unreadable without a magnifying glass). Magazines and newspapers, with their narrow columns, often employ 8- and 9-point type.

Added leading can enhance legibility by making it easier for the reader to rapidly find the beginnings of successive lines of text. The longer the line, the more desirable extra leading becomes. Additional leading up to at least half the point size of the text (e.g., 10/15) continues to enhance readability. However, space limitations rarely permit such generous leading, except in special layouts such as the decorative openings of magazine articles.

The ideal line length for legibility seems to be short enough that the eye does not move in scanning the line—about 40 characters, a length frequently seen in three-column magazines and in five- and six-column newspapers. Shorter lengths tend to result in frequent hyphenation at the end of right-justified lines, which interferes with rapid comprehension. Books rarely employ such narrow columns, however; even on double-column pages (often seen in reference books), the lines tend to run longer. Most book designers limit their line lengths to about 75 characters (in 10-point Baskerville, about 30 picas long; in 10-point Times Roman, about 25 picas), though extra leading permits longer lines to be read comfortably.

Maximum contrast is represented by black print on a pure-white background. Since pure-white paper can in fact be tiring for the eyes, however, off-white shades are normally preferred. Colored type reduces contrast and is rarely used except in advertising. Colored paper and gray backgrounds likewise reduce contrast; thus, using screens to shade the backgrounds of headings or boxed text, even if it looks fancier and makes the page more graphically interesting, is not necessarily a kindness to the reader.

Some typefaces and styles tend to print particularly poorly on the more absorbent paper stocks; printing on inferior stock may cause the strokes to thicken and impair the characters' legibility.

Compromises will often be necessary when balancing legibility needs against the need to save space. Increasing the width of the text block from 28 to 30 picas, for example, may reduce the length of a 400-page book by 25 pages. Removing a point of leading throughout could decrease the length of the same book by almost 40 pages. Simply changing the book's text face from Electra (a very compact face) to Clarendon (a spacious face) could increase its length by 80 pages.

Page-Design Elements

Running Heads, Running Feet, and Folios

Running heads and feet   *Running heads* are the headings that run along the top of the page in most books. *Running feet* are identical headings that run along the bottom of a page instead. (In computer programs these are usually called *headers* and *footers*.) Since running heads and feet observe the same principles of design and content, any references here to running heads should generally be understood to include running feet as well.

Books, as mentioned, usually employ running heads. Popular magazines generally employ a running foot (or *foot line*) that consists of the magazine's name and the issue's date. Scholarly and professional journals more often use running heads; the verso head often identifies the magazine, while the recto head identifies the article.

In books, the running head that appears on each left-hand or *verso* page (i.e., the page on the left when the book is lying open) is often the work's title, sometimes in shortened form. The running head on the right-hand or *recto* page is often the chapter title or a shortened form of it. In novels, which lack headings and usually even chapter titles, the author's name may appear on every verso and the book title on every recto. In books in which the chapters have subdivisions, the running head on the verso page is usually the chapter title, and that on the recto is an A-head (see "Headings" below). In reference books especially, running heads can be very useful and should be chosen to provide useful information to the reader. (A book's title and author's name obviously are not highly informative to someone already reading the book.)

Running heads may be centered, set flush inside (flush right on verso pages and flush left on recto pages), or set *flush left and right* or *flush outside* (flush left on versos and flush right on rectos). They are most often set just "inside" the folio, which is set flush outside.

Though most books with running heads put them on both recto and verso pages, running heads may instead be set on either rectos or versos only.

Running heads often use the same typeface as the main text. They may be set in roman, boldface, or italic, and in all-capitals, capitals and lowercase, or capitals and small capitals. When set in capitals, they often employ wide letterspacing. They are sometimes set in type much smaller than the text type; however, for books in which the running heads are meant to be highly practical rather than primarily formal or decorative, they are usually set larger than the text type.

Running heads are often omitted from books in which they would serve no useful purpose, such as novels and poetry collections.

Folios Page numbers, or *folios,* may be prominent or unobtrusive. Folios set flush left and right (in the left corner on verso pages, the right on rectos) are easy to scan for a reader fanning the pages and for that reason are the most common. Folios are less conspicuous when placed at the bottom of the page than at the top, and when placed at the gutter margin rather than the center or the outside margin. Practically speaking, only folios that will actually be frequently referred to by the reader (primarily in books with tables of contents, indexes, and cross-references) need be conspicuous.

Odd folios always appear on recto pages, even folios on verso pages.

The folio generally accompanies the running head (or foot) on the same line. A symbol such as a slash or bullet may separate the two elements, but space alone is usually adequate. Alternatively, the running head may stand at the top of the page and the folio at the bottom.

The folio is often set in boldface or set larger than the running head, even when it sits on the same line. Outsize folios can be ornamental, though folios should never be distractingly large.

Designers will sometimes set folios in highly decorative ways—in reverse type in solid-color boxes, framed by ornate ornaments, and so on. Except in very playful books, this may give the impression of inappropriately exalting the folios' importance.

Old-style numerals with ascenders and descenders—1234567890—are often used for folios because of their decorative quality.

If the running heads include the numbers of the sections into which the book is divided, the folios will often be moved to the bottom of the page so that the numbers do not war with each other.

Folios are often omitted on pages with full-page illustrations or tables.

On chapter-opening pages, folios that would normally appear at the top of the page are generally moved to the bottom, where they are called *drop folios.* (The running head is usually omitted on such pages, since the chapter title is already there.) When "speccing" drop folios, the designer must be sure there is an adequate bottom margin and that the folio will not risk being set dangerously close to the edge of the page if the text block runs long.

The Text Block

The length of the lines on a page of type is usually related to the type size, as observed above. Lines of type with more than approximately 75 characters become difficult to read. The 10-point Baskerville you are reading averages about 2.55 characters per pica; set on a 29-pica line as here, it averages 74 characters per line. If this book had been set in 10-point Times Roman, with its 2.85 characters per pica, the 29-pica line would have averaged 83 characters per line, more than optimal for comfortable legibility. Added line spacing, as mentioned, can enhance the legibility of an otherwise overlong line.

Margin width will obviously vary in inverse proportion to the width of the text block. (Note that *text block* is sometimes used confusingly along with the terms *type page* and *type block.* The type page, or *type area,* includes the entire area from the running head and folio to the last line of type. *Text block* often excludes the running head or foot and folio.) Narrow margins can cramp an otherwise well-designed page, whereas wide margins can contribute to a generous and spacious impression. Larger pages generally require larger margins for a harmonious design.

Since printers are often imprecise in their trimming of pages, enough space must be provided on all sides to allow for trimming errors of up to ¼". The *inside* or *gutter margin*—the margin by the spine—must always be wide enough to permit the innermost text to be read easily when the book is bound in the intended way.

The amount of horizontal space between words varies according to the type size and whether or not the lines are *justified*—set to exactly the same length by adjusting the space between the words, and sometimes also the letterspacing (as in the text you are reading). In *ragged-right* setting, the word spacing is identical throughout, resulting in an uneven right margin.

Ragged-right setting is common in magazines but rare in books (except in their indexes). The principal reason is that, in narrow columns such as those standard in magazines, right-justification can easily result in either excessively wide word spacing (and sometimes even wide letterspacing) or excessive end-of-line hyphenation, or both. In the longer lines seen in books, by contrast, spacing adjustments can almost always be apportioned so evenly as to be unnoticeable.

Nevertheless, a few books continue to employ ragged-right margins for the sake of a relaxed, natural appearance. One attraction of ragged-right lines is that they make most end-of-line hyphenation unnecessary. However, a long word that won't fit and must be moved in its entirety to the next line will leave an unattractively wide space. Therefore, most ragged-right setting is in fact designed to produce a "soft rag," or moderately curving right edge, rather than a "hard rag," or severely jagged edge, by means of a spec stipulating that words should be broken whenever any line would otherwise run shorter than a stated length.

Headings   *Headings,* or *heads,* are words or phrases used to introduce and identify text passages. The fundamental principle of heading design is that ascending importance should be reflected in ascending typographic prominence.

The most obvious kind of heading is the chapter title. When chapters are divided into main sections, their headings are usually called *A-heads* or *1-heads*. (See, e.g., the heading "Page-Design Elements" above.) If these sections are themselves divided, the subdivisions may be headed with *B-heads,* or *2-heads* (such as "The Text Block" above). Still smaller subdivisions may be indicated by less prominent headings called *C-heads* or *3-heads* (see "Headings" above) and *D-heads* or *4-heads* (see "Corrections" on page 310).

A-heads and B-heads are generally set flush left in large type, with extra space above and below (usually more space above than below). Flush-left setting permits the reader to scan the beginnings of successive heads rapidly. Less frequently, one or both may be centered on the page. Rarely, A-heads are set flush outside (flush left on verso pages and flush right on rectos). If A-heads are set in all-caps, B-heads will commonly be set in caps and lowercase. C-heads and D-heads are almost always set flush left, and the following text usually is *run in*—that is, it follows immediately on the same line. If the C-heads are boldface, the D-heads will commonly be italic. If C-heads are capitalized headline-style (cap/lowercase), D-heads will commonly be lowercased except for the single initial cap.

A few texts employ *margin heads*, headings set in the outside margin. Since margin heads may be slightly expensive to set and the wide margins they require can be wasteful of space, they tend to be employed only when the margin is also being used for illustrations or when the designer desires to produce a luxurious impression by leaving ample white space.

Lists Lists are frequently set in vertical format for the sake of clarity, as numbered, unnumbered, or bulleted lists. The choice among these alternatives should not be random; the author (and copy editor) should aim for logic and consistency throughout the text when choosing list styles.

Lists are generally set in the same typeface as the rest of the text but often one point smaller. They are usually set off from the surrounding text above and below by a line space.

Turn lines (lines following the first line of a given item) in a numbered or bulleted item usually align under the item's first word rather than under the number or bullet. Unnumbered lists often use hanging (flush-and-hang) indention to make the items easier to scan.

Single-column lists are almost always aligned on an indention, usually at least as large as that of the paragraph openings. Within a given text, single-column numbered, unnumbered, and bulleted lists should generally be indented the same amount.

One or two points of extra leading between list items (in addition to any leading between the turn lines in an individual item) is common.

Various symbols (☞, ★, ■, ➤, etc.) have traditionally been employed as bullets, but today the simple round black bullet (•) is almost universally used. The latter has in fact become very popular in recent years, perhaps because it is available in automatic list formats on desktop computers. Nevertheless, many readers continue to regard bulleted lists as somewhat undignified. Such readers may associate bullets with advertising, which is always striving to catch the reader's attention, and both in advertising and elsewhere bullets often highlight items that are already set off and do not truly require further emphasis. Thus, more serious books and journals rarely use bullets. Note that the prominence of bullets depends on their size, and it is best to specify their diameter in the design specs (e.g., "set 2-pt bullets").

Lists of short items generally employ double-column or multicolumn format. Such formats may be given their own separate spec. It will often be helpful to test a proposed multicolumn design by formatting one of the text's lists on a desktop computer.

Sidebars *Sidebars* are textual features usually set off inside box rules, generally consisting of ancillary information that is not essential to the text it accompanies. Despite their name, they may extend the full width of the page. Sidebars have long been used in magazines; in recent decades they have become popular in books as well, particularly textbooks and coffee-table books, which they are felt to make more inviting and pleasanter to browse.

Sidebars frequently use background shading (either gray or another color) to set them visually apart from the rest of the text. However, shading can reduce print/background contrast and thus legibility; a distinctive heading style, typeface, ornament, or box style can usually serve just as effectively to set off the sidebar from the normal text.

The positioning of sidebars is often less critical than that of illustrations or tables, since sidebars are generally more loosely connected to the main text, and this permits the typesetter considerable liberty in page makeup. If a given sidebar must appear near its text reference, a note in the manuscript margin from the editor or author can request that it do so.

A sidebar spec might read as follows:

> Set double box rule consisting of 1-pt box rule with ½-pt box rule 2 pts inside it. Set box column-width or page-width, as indicated on manuscript for each box. Allow 18 pts from top of box to base of sidebar head. Set head in 12-pt Sabon Bold; set ornaments, as shown on samples, 6 pts to either side of head. Allow 14 pts b/b to top of sidebar text, set in 10/12 Sabon. Allow 1 pi bet. text and box at left, right, and bottom.

Pullquotes A very common feature of magazine layout is the *pullquote*, also known as the *breakout, callout*, or *liftout*—an interesting sentence (or sometimes more than one) pulled out of the text and set in large type by itself somewhere on the page. The purpose of pullquotes is to grab the attention of a browsing reader and entice him or her into the article. Since readers rarely browse books in the same way as magazines, pullquotes are hardly ever used in books.

To make pullquotes conspicuous and arresting, designers employ such devices as fanciful typefaces, large initial caps, color, rules, boxes, background shading, added leading, outsize quotation marks, ornaments, and odd-shaped outlines. With such resources, pullquotes can easily overwhelm a page of text— and indeed many magazines today convey the impression that the designer has been given precedence over the writers.

Pullquote design permits almost infinite variation, and can best be approached by critically studying page designs in a variety of magazines along with books devoted to design (see Bibliography).

Ornaments Book designers have traditionally employed little ornaments, or *dingbats*, for any of various functions. They may decorate the openings or ends of chapters, or of poems in a book of poetry; they may separate aphorisms, paragraphs, or other short passages in a book composed of such passages; they may form part of the running head or foot, or flank a lone folio.

Since they derive from older woodcuts and engravings and are intended to be as universally useful as possible, they are always drawn as line art. Below are a few of the thousands of text ornaments that have been used through the years.

Simple bullets (•)—which, like other types of bullets such as arrows (➤) and fists (☞), usually serve to highlight set-off items, especially in lists—are perhaps the most common form of ornament today.

In magazines, articles frequently end with a tiny square (□, ▪) or diamond (◆, ❖) at the end of the last line of text.

Though dingbats may reflect the text they ornament (as when the comic-tragic masks are used to decorate a book on theater), they more often bear no meaningful relation to the text.

Dingbats are less common today than in the last century, and most books now contain no element more decorative than a few plain rules. However, discreet ornaments can still provide an attractive touch to a well-designed book. Many are readily available on typesetting systems (and even on desktop computers); a designer desiring something more fanciful or distinctive can design a new symbol using a computer art program, or scan in an original hand-drawn design or a design found in an older source (or send it to the typesetter for scanning).

Rules Though vertical rules are uncommon except in tables, horizontal rules are commonly employed as design elements. Horizontal rules are frequently set below running heads, under chapter titles, above or below A-heads, and above sets of footnotes. They should be used sparingly within a given text, however, to avoid cluttering the page and confusing the reader.

Rules vary in thickness and are usually referred to in terms of their point size.

hairline	————————————
½-point	————————————
1-point	————————————
1½-point	————————————
2-point	————————————

Ornamental rules can sometimes be used in place of plain rules.

Miscellaneous elements The first lines of paragraphs are generally indented in published text. The amount of indention is often specified by the designer; if not, the compositor will choose a standard indention. The first paragraph following a heading usually omits any indention. A very few publications—mostly elaborately designed magazines—use *block-style paragraphs,* which are not indented at all but instead are separated by extra line spacing. *Hanging indention* (also known as *flush-and-hang* or *reverse indention*), in which the first line of a paragraph or entry sets flush left and the following lines are indented, is used in bibliographies, glossaries, indexes, and other alphabetical listings where the first word of each entry must catch the reader's scanning eye. It is hardly ever used for standard prose.

Drop capitals, or *drop caps,* are large initial letters, generally used to begin a chapter or article, that extend well below the baseline, usually taking up the beginning of the next line or two of type below. (The design spec may read simply "Initial cap drops 3 lines"; for safety's sake, each initial should also be marked on the manuscript.) Alternatively, an outsize initial capital letter may instead ascend two or three lines above its baseline. The initial capital may be from a decorative typeface different from the text face.

Following a drop cap or a large ascending capital, a portion of the first line of text is often set entirely in small caps. The small-cap passage should constitute a coherent phrase rather than ending with a preposition, article, or conjunction.

Drop-out or *reverse* type—type that prints white against a black or colored background—is often employed in magazines and newsletters, less often in books. A heading printed white on a solid black band across the text page can make a striking effect but will usually be too strong for anything but chapter or article openings.

Layout

When the design of a particular page is complex, the typesetter should also be sent a *layout* of the page—a drawing that shows the approximate size and position of each element and that includes additional instructions, dimensions, and specifications to help the typesetter understand the designer's wishes.

Highly illustrated texts and texts with complicated designs have traditionally required that a *dummy* of the final pages be created from the galleys. A complete dummy provides a layout of each set of facing pages (or *spreads*) for an entire publication. Often a dummy will only be needed for individual pages or sections; books with straightforward designs such as novels do not require dummies at all.

A proper dummy is a precise, line-for-line model of the final pages. Dummies are made by cutting up the text galleys and mounting them—along with proofs or photocopies of illustrations, footnotes, and any other necessary elements—onto *boards*, pieces of heavy paper at least the size of two facing pages. Dummy boards have printed lines that outline the type area and may indicate every single line of text, including folios and running heads. Thus, specially printed boards must usually be ordered for each design project.

Wherever a photocopy of an illustration is not available, a measured blank space, or *hole*, is left, and the illustration's identity is indicated by either the caption or a name or number written in the hole.

A layout or dummy of the book may precede the selection of an artist or photographer, and the precise dimensions of the art in the printed book will thus have been specified. This will generally only be done for lavishly illustrated books (but much more often for magazines). Books will frequently instead segregate all their illustrations into galleries or inserts, one or more signatures of higher-quality paper devoted exclusively to graphic material.

Before desktop layout programs became common, actual mechanicals were created with cut-and-pasted repro-quality galleys. The final boards were then shot by camera to produce negatives.

The dummy is typically created by the publisher's layout artists and sent to the typesetter along with the corrected galleys. (Since any large corrections will require revision of a layout, the editor must check that any layout prepared from uncorrected galleys remains usable.) However, dummies are often made up by the typesetters themselves; these may be submitted to the editor for approval or simply used internally and never seen by the editor.

The editor or designer will often have to prepare a *castoff* of the manuscript—an estimate of the number of pages it will require. If a manuscript is in electronic form, casting off becomes considerably easier. As the computer files of the manuscript are edited and reformatted, the program will keep track of word-count totals and the number of printed pages that will result from different format designs.

Today desktop publishing (DTP) functions extend personal computers beyond the realm of word processing and allow the user to produce sophisticated layouts for newsletters, handouts, manuals, reports, brochures, flyers, newspaper and magazine ads, catalogs, forms, price lists, posters, diagrams, business cards, letterheads, transparencies and even books without leaving the office. By bypassing the services of a typesetter and often a professional printer, desktop publishing can save companies and organizations considerable money (once an initial investment of several thousand dollars has been absorbed) while often speeding the production of such materials.

A DTP system will include a computer with enough memory to display graphics, a high-resolution monitor, a scanner, a laser printer, and a special drive with removable disks or cartridges for storing and transporting large files and graphics. With sophisticated graphics software for creating digital artwork (such as Adobe Photoshop, Illustrator, or Freehand) and layout programs that incorporate all the elements of the page (such as Quark XPress or Page-Maker), an editor or designer can create final layouts that can be output to film at a service bureau or exposed directly to the plates at the printer.

Page-layout software lets the user turn word-processed text and electronically prepared graphics—including text and graphic files imported from a variety of sources—into formatted pages. Draft layouts are easily manipulated and edited on the computer, allowing great flexibility for editors and art directors. In fact, designers and editors often find that the greatest boon of such software is not that it saves time or even money but rather that it permits almost infinite adjustment of both design and content until they meet the approval of everyone concerned.

When using a personal computer to design and lay out books or magazine pages that will eventually be output to film through an imagesetter (see Chapter 14), it is important to be aware of different type systems. Type 1 digital-format fonts (*font* is the preferred general term among software companies) are a worldwide standard and are those used most often by professional designers. Most imagesetters support only Type 1 fonts. They have two software parts: a screen font, which renders the letter on the monitor, and a PostScript or printer font. (PostScript, developed by Adobe Systems, is widely used software that reads and interprets graphic elements and type.)

TrueType, a system developed as an alternative to PostScript, is the more useful system for printing on personal printers, since it is the system most frequently sold with them. It provides a large variety of both classic and decorative fonts. When a personal computer is to be used as a desktop-publishing system, it is generally advisable to switch the TrueType fonts that may have come with the computer to Type 1 fonts.

Writing the Design Specifications

The design specifications are the means by which the designer communicates a book's design to the typesetter. The writing of design specifications, especially for a complex book, can be an exacting task; however, though "speccing" always requires concentration and precision, the rudiments of spec writing are not hard to learn.

Though design choices can be tested on an office computer, it may still be hard to recognize when one's own specs have been incorrectly written so that a typesetter may understand them in unintended ways. Since an improper specification may result in expensive typesetting charges for corrected galleys, designers always have the typesetter prepare a set of sample pages based on the initial specs, pages that show all the elements of a given design. Sample pages also permit any interested editors or the publishing board to consider the quality of the design and offer suggestions for improvement. In addition, setting samples permits the typesetter to preset the design into the system, which may permit speedier completion of the actual typesetting job subsequently.

Specifications are written in different ways by different designers, and typesetters learn to understand a variety of styles. Nevertheless, various conventions have become standard, and in particular the following abbreviations are widely used. The design specifications shown as Figure 13.1 include most of the specs used for the present book. Note that there are no entries for the front matter or index, since these are typically left until the rest of the book has been set in pages and then designed so as to fit to fill out any partly filled signature (or one or more signatures in addition to the partly filled one).

pt	point	b/b	base-to-base
pi	pica(s)	col	column
caps, c, uc	capitals	x	by
lc	lowercase	MS	manuscript
C/lc, c&lc,	caps/uppercase and	turns, t.o.'s	turn lines, turnovers
u/lc	lowercase (headline-style)	li	line(s)
initial C/lc	initial cap followed by	w/	with
	lowercase (sentence-style)	w/o	without
sm caps, sc	small caps	max	maximum
C/sc	caps and small caps	min	minimum
#	space	horiz	horizontal
ital	italics	vert	vertical
bf	boldface	RH	running head
rom	roman	RF	running foot
fl	flush	FPO	for position only
ctr	center		

The specs usually begin with the measurements and elements that will apply or appear throughout the book and will not be marked on the manuscript: the book's dimensions or trim, the page margins, the page folios and running heads or feet, and the main text itself. These will be followed by the elements that will be signaled by their own typemarking codes or tags in the manuscript. The codes will usually appear in their own left-hand column for ease of scanning.

The size of the final printed page is referred to as the *trim size*. The top of the type page is specified in terms of its drop from the top of the page itself, commonly referred to as the *top of the trim*, or simply the *trim*. The drop is measured either to the top or base of the running head (or folio) or to the top or base of the first line of text.

Figure 13.1 Sample Design Specifications

Specifications for *Merriam-Webster's Manual for Writers and Editors*

Trim: 6½" x 9¼"

Margins: top: 11/16" from top of trim to base of folio and RH
bottom: 11/16"
outside: 3/4"
inside: 13/16"

Text: 10/11 Baskerville. Text block 29 x 44 pi (excl. RH and folio); may run one line long or short if necessary, but facing pages must align. Indent 1st line of paragraphs 18 pts, but no indention following heads.

Folios: 10-pt Helvetica Bold, fl outside. No folio on chapter-opening pages.

Running heads: 9-pt Helv. caps, aligned at base w/folio. Set 1/2-pt rule x 29 pi 4 pts below base. Allow 10 pts # from folio to 2-pt bullet, 10 pts # from bullet to RH. Set chapter title on verso, A head on recto. Allow 24 pts b/b to first line of text block.

Tag	Description	Typography
CN	Chapter Number	24-pt Helv. Set fl left, sunk 8 pi from top of trim to baseline.
CT	Chapter Title	24-pt Helv., C/lc. Align at base w/CN; allow 24 pts # bet. no. and title. Turns align on 1st word.
CC	Chapter Contents	11/13 Helv., C/lc. Indent 3 pi from fl left. Allow 12 pts # bet text and page no. Allow 30 pts b/b from last line of CT above and 36 pts b/b from last line of CC to normal text below. Set 1-pt vertical rule x depth of CC indented 18 pts from fl left.
A	A-head	16-pt Helv., C/lc. Set fl left; set 1-pt rule x 29 pi 7 pts below base. Allow 36 pts b/b from text above and 20 pts from rule to base of 1st line of text below.
B	B-head	12-pt Helv. Bold, C/lc. Set fl left. Allow 24 pts b/b from text (or rule) above and 16 pts b/b to text below.
C	C-head	10-pt Helv. Bold, initial C/lc. Allow 20 pts b/b from text above. Set fl left, followed by 10 pts # and text run in.
D	D-head	10-pt Helv. Italic, initial C/lc. Set fl left, followed by10 pts # and text run in.Allow 20 pts b/b from text above. If EX text follows, allow 14 pts b/b to 1st line of EX text.
NT	Numbered Text Paragraph	10-pt Helv. Bold for numeral and period, set fl left and cleared for tens. Allow 6 pts # from numeral period to 10/11 Bask. text (approx. 20 pts from fl left). Turns align on 1st word, as do subsequent NTO paragraphs under same numeral. Allow 20 pts b/b from normal text above and 14 pts to EX text below.
NTO	Paragraphs within NT but w/o Numeral	10/11 Bask. Indent 20 pts from fl left; align under NT paragraph above. Turns align on 1st word. Allow 18 pts from text above and 14 pts to EX text or 20 pts to normal text below.
EX	Example	9/10 Bask. Indent 3 pi to 1st word. For 2-col EX, 2d col indents 15 pi; for 3-col EX, 2d col indents 11 pi and 3d col indents 19 pi; allow 12 pts min. # bet. cols. For EX with more than 3 cols, space evenly. Turns indent 6 pts on col. Add 1-pt. leading bet. examples. Allow 14 pts b/b from text above and either 18 pts b/b to NTO paragraph or 20 pts b/b to normal text below.

Figure 13.1 *(continued)*

Tag	Description	Typography
EXI	Example w/Italic Sideheads	9/10 Bask. Indent 3 pi to ital sidehead. Set sideheads to max. width of 7 pi. Set sideheads that turn at 9/9½. Turns indent 6 pts on col. Examples within a single list align left, 12 pts after longest sidehead; 1st word of right-hand col aligns horiz. with last word of sidehead. 2d example in right-hand col aligns under 1st example. Add 2 pts leading above subsequent ital sideheads. Allow 14 pts b/b from normal text above and 20 pts b/b to normal text below.
QX	Set-off Quotation below Example	8/9 Bask. Indent 4 pi to 1st word; turns either align under 1st word or, where indicated, indent 10 pts. Where marked, new paragraphs indent 12 pts. Add 2 pts above and below extract to EX text or 20 pts b/b to normal text below.
LE	List in Even Columns	9/11 Bask. 1st col indents 18 pts. For 2-col list, 2d col indents 15 pi. Turns indent 6 pts on col. Allow 12 pts min. # bet. cols. Allow 14 pts b/b from normal text above and 20 pts b/b to text below.
NL	Numbered List	10/11 Bask. Indent 18 pts to numeral with period, cleared for tens, followed by 6 pts # to 1st word. Turns align on 1st word. Add 2 pts bet. subsequent NL entries. Allow 14 pts from text above and either 14 pts b/b to NLX text or 20 pts b/b to normal text below.
FC	Figure Caption	9-pt Helv. Bold, C/lc. Set fl left; allow 10 pts bet. numeral period and caption. Allow 24 pts b/b from text above and 14 pts to art below.
TBL	Table (chaps. 6 and 9)	*Table Title:* 10-pt Bask. Bold, C/lc, fl left. Allow 6 pts # below to 1-pt rule x 29 pi, line # above to last text line. (If at top of page, position fl top on text block.) Allow 14 pts b/b from normal text above and to top of table below. *Heads:* 9/9 Bask. Bold, initial C/lc. Turns align under base of first word. Allow 6 pts from base of last line to ½-pt rule x table width. *Table Body:* 9/10 Bask. 1st col aligns fl left; for 2-col table, 2d col indents 15 pi; for 3-col table, 2d col indents 10 pi, 3d col indents 20 pts; for more than 3 cols, space evenly with 12 pts min. # bet. cols. For tables with 2 sections, allow 12 pts # bet. col subheads and 24 pts # bet. sections; repeat col titles in each section. Align cols left under heads. Turns indent 6 pts on col. 1-pt rule x 29 pi sets 6 pts below last entry. Follow copy for other specs.
TC	Table Caption	9-pt Helv. Bold, C/lc. Set fl left; allow 10 pts # bet. numeral period and caption. Allow 24 pts b/b from text above and 14 pts to table below.
G	Glossary	10/11 Bask. Set double col; 1st col sets fl left, 2d col indents 16 pi; allow 2 pi # bet. cols. Set headword in bold lc, followed by 10 pts # and text run in. Turns indent 10 pts. Add 6 pts leading bet. entries.
BB	Bibliography	10/11 Bask. 1st line of each entry sets fl left; turns indent 18 pts. Add 6 pts leading bet. entries. Allow 14 pts b/b to entry text from head above, 20 pts b/b from entry text to head below.

The location of every element on the page can be described by reference to either the edge of the printed page or the edge of the text block (the area that the main text fills). Thus, the dimensions of both the book page and the text block must be specified. The terms *sink* and *sinkage* refer to the amount of vertical space from a given point—often the top of the trim—to a given element.

The width of the text block is equal to the length of the longest line. Its horizontal positioning is described in terms of its distance from the outer edge of the page (also often called simply the *trim*).

The measurement of the page trim and margins is traditionally given in inches, while the rest of the specs are given in picas and points. The reason is that printers, who must impose the image of the type page on the actual paper, use only inches for measurement; expressing the relevant measurements in terms of inches from the outset will ensure that no errors are made when the time comes to communicate these measurements to the printer.

A number of the elements itemized in the sample specs are discussed in Chapter 12, "Production Editing, Copyediting, and Proofreading." See Chapter 14, "Typesetting, Printing, and Binding" for a discussion of typesetting codes and generic coding of manuscripts.

14 Typesetting, Printing, and Binding

Typesetting 348
Typesetting Codes and Generic Markup 350
Platemaking and Printing 355
Paper 358
Binding 361

The subject of typesetting is always of significant concern to writers and especially editors. The printing and binding processes are usually considerably more remote for both; however, most editors will from time to time find that a basic knowledge of printing and binding can become quite helpful. This chapter gives an overview of all three processes and some of their special vocabulary. Three earlier chapters—"Production Editing, Copyediting, and Proofreading," "Tables and Illustrations," and "Design and Typography"—encroach on the subject matter of this chapter, and all three should be reviewed for a full overview of its subjects. For further reading on each process, see the Bibliography.

Book manufacturing typically involves first a *typesetter* or *compositor*, which takes the edited manuscript and the design specifications and from them creates a high-quality image of each page of the book exactly as it will appear in its final form. Through a series of steps, some of which may be carried out at the typesetter but most of which are done in the printing plant, each page image is transferred to a printing plate. The plate is mounted on a printing press and inked, and the ink is transferred to a paper sheet by pressing the plate against the paper. After the sheet has been printed on both sides, it is folded, trimmed, and bound.

Though typesetting, printing, and binding can take place within one shop, a book will far more commonly be typeset by one company and printed and bound by another (and occasionally the binder may even be separate from the printer). No matter how the actual work is handled, the processes can be divided into the distinct stages of typesetting, platemaking, printing, and binding—or *prepress* (which includes typesetting and platemaking), *on-press* (or printing), and *postpress* (binding).

Typesetting

The history of typesetting from Gutenberg to the 1950s is an interesting one that can hardly be alluded to here. Suffice it to say that the changes over hundreds of years up to the middle of this century were largely incremental, whereas those in the last few decades have been revolutionary. Three technologies have been principally employed in these recent decades, two of which, though described briefly below, have all but vanished today.

Phototypesetting, also called *photocomposition* or *filmsetting,* sets type by photographing characters on film or light-sensitive paper from a negative master containing all the characters. In a phototypesetting system at its simplest, type is set by shining a light through a cutout the size and shape of a letter onto film or paper. The phototypesetting machine includes drums or discs on which cutouts for all the characters in a font are included, along with prisms and mirrors that aim the letters in the precise size at the precise spot on the film or light-sensitive paper to produce properly aligned lines of type. After the paper or film has been exposed to the letters, it is developed like any other photograph. The output of the phototypesetter is of repro quality, but often not in page format. Phototypesetting has now been largely displaced by computerized typesetting systems.

CRT typesetting is so called because it makes use of a cathode-ray tube, similar to a television picture tube but with much sharper resolution. CRT systems differ from phototypesetting systems in that all the characters used in a CRT system exist simply as digital information stored within the system. CRT systems eliminate the phototypesetter's turning disc or drum, which can stick, jump, or misalign, introducing new errors into typeset lines when material is being recomposed. Like a phototypesetter, the CRT system reads characters from a typesetting tape; but unlike the phototypesetter, the CRT system translates the characters and electronically assembles them into a picture of the typeset lines and projects that picture by means of a stream of electrons at the cathode-ray tube's screen. The image of the typeset lines displayed on the screen is transferred to photosensitive paper, which becomes the repro.

Phototypesetting and CRT typesetting are now rarely used except for the maintenance and revision of texts originally created in such systems. In their place, systems incorporating imagesetters, as described below, have become the standard.

Most typesetters today use desktop computers with software applications that perform typography. The software chosen depends on the requirements of the job at hand. Some applications' strengths lie in the highly automated pagination and formatting capabilities often required by reference books, while others are better with the complicated page layouts of highly illustrated books. The final result of these applications is an electronic file in the almost universal page-description programming language called PostScript (created by Adobe Systems).

PostScript provides commands that may be output by any device having a PostScript interpreter. The device, called an *imagesetter,* translates the description into a rasterized image that it may transfer to paper, film, or plate (depending on the imagesetter). *Rasterizing* is the process of converting *object-oriented* or *vector graphics,* in which the image or type is composed of collections of lines, into *bitmapped graphics,* which are composed of tiny dots and suitable for printing. The interpreter is thus known as a *raster image processor,* or simply a RIP.

Imagesetters differ most notably from earlier typesetters in that (as their name implies) they can set images along with type in complex layouts. Some imagesetters can now expose the computer file directly onto printing plates—

in the so-called *direct-to-plate* system—for offset printing, or etch directly onto a copper cylinder for gravure printing. Although direct-to-plate printing eliminates the cost of creating film, one disadvantage is the inability to create the kind of high-quality proofs (such as bluelines or color Matchprints) that are made from film. A digital proof can be produced from an early RIP, but there may be problems in producing such proofs from the later RIP that creates the plates, and requiring press proofs (actual printed sheets) can be very expensive if a problem is discovered at that late stage.

The essential elements of all typesetting systems are similar: (1) an input method, by which the typesetter's operator either keyboards the manuscript or downloads the publisher's coded manuscript on disk; (2) a processing component, in which an application performs the formatting and pagination of the data; (3) a storage component, in the form of a computer that contains the keyboarded, machine-readable version of the manuscript or in the form of a disk, magnetic tape, or CD-ROM; and (4) an output component, the typesetting machine that produces the proofs, repro, and film by means of one of the systems described above. The input method is most directly related to the editorial process.

In one form of input, the typesetter's keyboard operator turns the author's edited and marked-up manuscript into machine-readable form by keyboarding it directly into the computer, creating a file that includes not only the manuscript text but also all the codes necessary to instruct the typesetting application how to set the type in accordance with the design specifications. Editors today generally oversee the creation of their own master files and submit a computer file on diskette along with the design specifications. The manuscript will frequently have already been electronically coded by the time it reaches the typesetter (see below). The typesetter converts the publisher's master file, principally by adding the application-specific typesetting codes needed to operate the typesetting machine or imagesetter and then adjusting elements as necessary to make up the pages.

Another form of input is the *optical character recognition* (OCR) system, which scans copy, records the characters, "reads" them, and converts them into a standard word-processing file. Although accuracy is steadily improving, even the best OCR systems are prone to introducing errors, and they are generally used only for special projects such as the conversion of previously published text.

Once the input file, or *master file*, is complete, other design specifications are entered into the computer—size and style of type, line length, line spacing, page depth, and so on. The master file and the design specifications are combined, and the result is a typesetting file complete with all the instructions necessary for running the typesetting application, such as where to break words at the end of lines and how much word spacing to insert to justify the lines.

Typesetting Codes and Generic Markup

As word processing has become the standard means of producing manuscripts, electronic markup has become a duty of many authors and editors working at personal computers. Though manual typemarking in pen or pencil in the margins of the printed manuscript is still very common, it has also become common for such marks to be keyboarded directly into the computer file by the author, the copy editor, or an in-house editor or typist. (See also "Typemarking" on pages 296–297.)

When manuscripts were produced on typewriters and editorial changes were marked on paper, typemarking tags were only required for communication between the designer and the typesetter. But with the ascendance of electronic manuscripts—often produced by different authors using different computers or systems—and the heightened expectations of the useful possibilities of capturing text and art electronically, general consistency has become everyone's concern. Works owned by one publisher may be licensed for publication by others; later versions of the material may include not only printed books and magazines but also CD-ROMs and on-line publishing. Each medium has its own presentation requirements, and the possibility of such republication and repurposing calls for coding data elements and special characters in a way that makes them readily available to these subsequent users.

In a typical word processor or typesetting system, any text that must appear different from the normal text—large or smaller type, italic or boldface text, special indentions, and so on—is indicated in the system by a set of codes recognized by the computer as indicating the particular font, indention, type size, or position. An author desiring to switch to italics need only hit the appropriate keys or click on the proper on-screen button and then employ the same keys or button to switch back. However, within the word-processing program, "turn on italics" is accomplished by one set of codes and "turn off italics" by another. And since different programs use different code patterns for these options, any transporting of files from one system to another suggests the desirability of generic tagging.

Generic tagging is not computer- or program-specific, and the tags used are usually mnemonic and understandable by humans as well as processible by computer program. A generically tagged manuscript can be easily transported to any system or any kind of distribution channel, allowing for multiple uses of the same document: "Write once, publish many times." Generic tagging may be regarded as markup that indicates the general nature of the content rather than its specific typographical representation. Thus, like normal typemarking, it permits a second-level heading to be identified as such rather than with its font, size, and position; and an item to be italicized—such as a book title or a new term—could be marked to indicate its nature rather than just its appearance. A word or phrase that may appear in the text without any special typographical distinction but is to be included in an index might be coded with an "index" tag so that it can be found by an automatic retrieval process later on. Each of these items or structures can be regarded as a text element and marked by a unique code or tag.

Generic markup requires establishing a set of data tags that will be understandable and will uniquely describe each element. As mentioned, mnemonic tags indicating the text element in a spelled-out or abbreviated form are common. For example, quotations may be mnemonically tagged "quote" (or just "q"), the table of contents may be tagged "toc," and a numbered list may be tagged "nl."

The tags must be distinctive in order to be mechanically recognizable; the standard method is to enclose them in angle brackets < >, though curly braces { } or square brackets [ ] may be used instead. (This means that the chosen brackets or braces must *only* be used for enclosing tags; any that will be needed in the printed text must themselves be given a special-character code.) It is essential that the opening delimiter of the tag be distinct from its closing delimiter (as in <tag>); using one symbol for both (as in \tag\) will likely cause processing problems.

In addition to allowing portability, generic markup or tagging of text elements allows for flexibility in the manipulation of the data. Take, for example, a chapter in a textbook or technical manual in which italics are used in various ways—for book titles, for highlighting new terms, for cross-references, and so on. In checking the electronic manuscript, the editor may want to gather together all references to book titles to ensure that they are consistently styled, to gather all the glossed terms to create a glossary, or to gather all cross-references for ease in checking them against their targets. If each discrete text element is tagged according to its content rather than its typographical presentation, each element can be accessed as needed with the help of a simple extraction program, yet each will appear in identical italics in print.

Generic typemarking of the kind done by copy editors and reflected in the design specs must always be translated at some point into the more complex typesetter's codes—codes that the typesetting system will recognize and interpret to produce each text element to the designer's specifications—and entering these codes represents a significant part of the typesetter's job. Typesetting codes, which may be highly specific to a given typesetting system, tend to be long and complex; a typical code marking a heading might read "\cj12,15,18″\ ci\fy76″\cc25,1,24,28″\xr\tr24,1″Preface." (Publishers today usually retain a copy of the generically coded file. If the file was sent to the typesetter with no electronic coding in place, the editor will frequently ask the typesetter to return a generically tagged file when the typesetting is finished, which may require that the typesetter translate the specific typesetting codes back into the generic tags that appear on the design specs and in the manuscript margins.)

One approach to standardization has been developed by Microsoft Corp. in the form of Rich Text Format (RTF), which can be used by any number of word-processing programs and has readily available conversion programs to allow typesetters to convert RTF manuscripts into their own proprietary typesetting codes. But while Rich Text Format is indeed rich with text formatting (typeface, type size, indentions, etc.), it is not generic tagging.

A given instance of generic tagging will not necessarily be universal in its application, since each publisher may employ a unique set of codes. The international standard for generic tagging is Standard Generalized Markup Language, or SGML, a system that is being increasingly widely adopted. SGML is unique in that it not only allows generic tagging of data elements and special characters within the text itself but provides for a document description that defines the data elements and how they are arranged in the individual document. This description, called a *document type definition* or DTD, represents the rules or "grammar" of the document's structure, showing which elements may follow other elements, which may repeat, which may be contained in larger elements, and which are required and which optional. The DTD is readable both by humans and by a computer program called a *parser*. The parser checks the text (or *document instance*) against the DTD to ensure that all the tags and required elements are in place and that all the rules of sequence and structure have been followed. For authors and editors working with SGML, there are SGML editing systems that work much like word processors but also read the DTD and indicate to the user which elements are permitted at certain places in the document and prevent the placing of elements where they are not permitted. SGML editing systems permit WYSIWYG editing while they insert the appropriate tagging automatically and invisibly.

HTML (HyperText Markup Language) is the language of World Wide Web browsers. It is essentially a subset of SGML, with certain limitations on what data can be presented (often depending on what browser is being used). With advances in development, browsers will soon be making use of all the richness of SGML coding.

At the computer-processing stage, the processor will recognize each marked element as a data tag and process the tagged material according to instructions that apply at the time. For example, a first-level section heading labeled <h1> may in one publishing environment (such as a book) be processed to appear as 18-point Bold Helvetica type, centered, with a one-point rule underneath; in another publishing environment (such as on-line), it may appear flush left in 30-point magenta Bold Times.

A text element should have not only a beginning tag but an ending tag. (Since the beginning of a new tagged element often implies the end of the previous one, manuscripts actually frequently forgo ending tags for those elements that do not require them.) The conventional method of designating an ending tag is to prefix the mnemonic with a forward slash /. Thus, the opening tag <h1> would be paired with the ending tag </h1> at the end of the heading. Sections might use the tags <sect1> . . . </sect1>, <sect2> . . . </sect2>, and so on; incidental italics could use the tags <i> . . . </i> or <it> . . . </it>. Since many typesetting systems will not recognize carriage returns, paragraphs need their own tags, usually <p> . . . </p>, to instruct the typesetting system to set a prescribed indention. A bulleted list might be tagged <bl> (and a numbered list <nl>), and every item in the list <item>; the bullets (or numbers) themselves would not be keyboarded but would only be inserted at the typesetting stage. Superscripts and subscripts are usually treated as data elements. Some systems use <sup> for a single-character superscript and <sub> or <inf> for a single-character subscript (e.g., x² for x^2, and H₂O or H<inf>2</inf>O for H_2O), and may or may not require a separate tag for each of a series of such characters (e.g., for 3^{xy}, either 3^x ^y </sup> or 3 ^{xy}).

Here are some examples of generic data-element tags and their meanings:

<chap>	chapter text (enclose chapter contents)
<cn> *or* <chapnum>	chapter heading and number
<ct> *or* <chaptitl>	chapter title
<cc> *or* <chapcont>	chapter contents (list of items and page numbers)
<list>	list
<item>	list item
<page>	page number in contents list
<p>	new paragraph with normal indention

<p0>	new paragraph with no indention
<h1>, <h2>, etc.	heading level 1 (A-head), 2 (B-head), etc.
<i> or <it> or <ital>	italics
<sc>	small caps
<sup>	superscript
<sub> or <inf>	subscript/inferior
<nl> or <numlist>	numbered list
<tx> or <text>	text that follows another coded item such as a run-in heading or a list
<ex> or <examp>	set-off example
<bq> or <quote>	block quotation or extract
<po> or <verse>	poetry, verse
<newline> or <break>	new line
<bl> or <bullist>	bulleted list

Comments not intended to be printed may be typed between unique markers; for example, <!—Editor: Permission needed here?—!>.

Special Characters

Special characters—including such standard characters as the cents sign, such math symbols as the division sign, letters with accent marks or diacritics, and Greek and Cyrillic letters—generally require their own markup. Though most such characters are available as special symbols in word-processing programs; some of the system-specific special characters will be lost when files are translated to a different system, so it is best to use special-character codes for everything that does not appear on the computer keyboard.

Since the special character is a single printed item, it can be represented by a single code rather than as a character with opening and closing tags surrounding it. These special-character codes may be enclosed in angle brackets; for example, *cliché* might be typed "clich<eacute>." Publishers wishing to distinguish special-character codes from text-element tags may enclose the former in curly braces ("clich{eacute}"). In SGML, a special-character code begins with an ampersand and ends with a semicolon ("cliché"). (As mentioned, if angle brackets and curly braces are used for tag delimiters, they must not be used as literals in the text itself. A solution is to use generic tagging for brackets and braces that will actually be printed: for example, {lang} and {rang} for left and right angle brackets, and {lcub} and {rcub} for left and right curly braces. Since some typesetting systems make a distinction between angle brackets and the mathematical "less than" and "greater than" signs, the latter may be coded as {lt} and {gt}.)

The examples given here are shown inside curly braces, but could instead be enclosed in angle brackets, square brackets, or (as in SGML) ampersands and semicolons. For more information on SGML special-character markup, see the Bibliography.

{copy}	© (copyright symbol)
{trade}	™ (trademark symbol)
{ccedil}	ç (c with cedilla)
{eacute}	é (e with acute accent)
{Eacute}	É (E with acute accent)

{egrave}	è (e with grave accent)
{ntilde}	ñ (n with tilde)
{ocirc}	ô (o with circumflex)
{uuml}	ü (u with umlaut)
{emsp}	em space
{ensp}	en space
{thinsp}	thin space
{numsp}	number space (used to align single and double digits)
{mdash}	— (em dash)
{ndash}	– (en dash)
{equals}	= (equals sign)
{times}	× (times or multiplication sign)
{minus}	− (minus sign)
{plus}	+ (plus sign)
{prime}	′ (single prime)
{frac12}	½ (case fraction one-half)
{ldquo}	" (left double quotation marks)
{rdquo}	" (right double quotation marks)
{lsqb}	[(left square bracket)
{rsqb}	] (right square bracket)
{agr}	α (Greek alpha)
{Agr}	A (Greek Alpha)
{bgr}	β (Greek beta)
{Bgr}	B (Greek Beta)

Platemaking and Printing

There are at least three ways in which a printing plate can be made to transfer ink to paper. In *letterpress printing,* the plate has raised surfaces that are inked and pressed against paper. In *gravure printing,* the plate is etched and the ink settles into the etched recesses. In *offset lithography,* the plate has neither raised nor engraved surfaces but specially treated areas to which ink will adhere, in patterns which are transferred to a rubber roller and from there onto paper. *Offset lithography* (which, despite its name, does not involve stone at all) is by far the most common method for printing books and magazines today, and it is described in more detail below.

Platemaking

Printing plates are large sheets of very thin and flexible aluminum, plastic, or even paper, which are imprinted with the image of several pages, attached to cylinders on the printing press, and inked to transfer the image to paper sheets passed through the press and over the cylinder's surface. Each plate of the type used in offset lithography holds a *signature* of (usually) 8, 16, or 32 pages—a grouping of pages printed on a single sheet, which, when folded and trimmed, will be sequenced in proper order.

The process of making the printing plate usually begins with full-size film of the repro page or the digital file. The film is opaque for those portions of the page that will not print and transparent for those that correspond to the letter images or other text or art elements meant to print.

If the films are made by the typesetter, they must be ordered in the form in which the printer needs them. These are usually ordered as negatives which are "opaqued, right-reading, emulsion side down." *Opaqued* means that any scratches or other defects on the negatives that have left transparent marks have been painted over manually. The *emulsion side* is the side of the negative with the photographically sensitive coating. *Right-reading, emulsion side down* means that the text of the negative can be read normally when the negative is positioned with its emulsion side down. Occasionally a printer will require a positive film, on which the dark and light areas are the reverse of a negative.

In the traditional method, the individual page negatives are taped down onto a sheet big enough to hold all the negatives for the pages that will be printed from a single plate. The sheet, or *flat*, is itself opaque but has cutouts the size of the page area on the negatives, into which the latter are *stripped* or *imposed*. The imposition must be done with extreme precision, since this will determine the position of the text block on the eventual printed pages. This traditional manual stripping is increasingly being replaced by computerized stripping; in the direct-to-plate process, the computer positions all the images electronically and then projects them onto the plate.

A proof of each flat—called *bluelines* or *blues* for the color of the light-sensitive paper and ink used to print it—is folded and trimmed into book signatures and sent to the editor so that he or she can confirm that the pages are in order and properly printed and positioned. A blueline proof gives the publisher a last chance before the actual printing begins to check for such flaws as scratches, specks, and bad alignment.

Plates are today often produced directly from the digital file, in a direct-to-plate process, whereby computer-driven lasers engrave the images onto the plate.

Printing Processes

As mentioned, offset lithography is the predominant printing process today. The relatively low cost and overall speed of preparing offset plates have made offset printing the choice for most printing projects, though paperback books are often printed by letterpress on a press that performs the printing and binding operations in one pass.

Offset printing is based on the principle that oil-based ink will not stick to a surface wet with water. As in any photographic developing, the transference of the film image to the plate is a chemical process. The developing process produces a surface on which the areas where the image appears attract the grease-based ink and repel the mixture of water, alcohol, and other ingredients with which the plate is constantly being wetted during the printing process, while the blank areas repel the ink but attract water. The plate, wrapped around a cylinder, is rolled against another cylinder with a rubber coating, called a *blanket cylinder*. The ink is transferred, or *offset*, to this second cylinder—on which the image is thus reversed or "wrong-reading"—and the blanket cylinder in turn rolls against the paper and lays down a "right-reading" image.

The paper may be fed through its press either as individual sheets the size of the printing plate, or in a continuous roll called a *web;* the presses designed for each type are called respectively *sheetfed* and *web* presses. Sheetfed presses are generally used for small print runs and for printing on specialty papers. Web presses are employed for most large jobs but increasingly for small runs as well.

Color Printing

Pages printed in process color are generally printed on presses with four different printing plates that are inked from four different ink supplies. Each plate lays down tiny dots of a single color: one lays down dots of yellow, another dots of greenish blue (called *cyan*), another dots of purplish red (called *magenta*), and another dots of black. (See also "Color Art" on pages 197–199.)

The four printing plates are made from four different negatives. To make these negatives, the colors in the original artwork are broken up electronically or through a series of filters into the four printing colors. This process is referred to as *color separation*, and it is usually done by the typesetter or in a special color-separating shop. Most color separations done today use a laser scanner or electronic color imaging system.

After the color separation, publishers receive proofs to show the result of the color corrections. These may be produced as an acetate overlay of four proofs (called a *color key*), one for each negative, or, more commonly, as a laminate, which gives a more accurate proof of the finished print. If the file will go direct-to-plate, with no repro or film stage, a digital proof is generated earlier in the process.

The editor or designer may also ask for a *press proof*—a proof made on the printing press before the complete run is begun—for a final review to check that the colors are printing as expected. This proofing stage is usually done at the printing plant, in order to avoid stopping or slowing the printing job. This stage can often be left to the printer, who can then alert the editor if problems arise.

Four-color illustrations are normally printed on a four-color press, requiring only a single pass which runs it over four cylinders each with its own color. Alternatively, four-color work can be printed on a one- or two-color press by running a sheet through in multiple passes.

Some books are printed partially in color, often succeeding in giving the impression that color has been used throughout. This can be done in various ways to produce various patterns and percentages of color pages. Color illustrations can also be limited to separate signatures (usually signatures of high-quality paper) printed on a separate press. Individual color illustrations are even occasionally *tipped in,* glued to individual sheets by hand—an expensive process rarely used today.

Printing Inks

Ink is composed primarily of *pigment* (black or color solid particles, organic and inorganic), *vehicle* (the liquid carrying the pigment, usually petroleum-based), and miscellaneous ingredients such as drying agents. These ingredients are altered according to the type and speed of the printing process, the ink-drying system used, and the type of paper chosen.

One common problem occurs when a given ink is used on paper stock that is too absorbent for it, which causes the type to blur and run together (*dot gain* being the technical term for the undesirable expansion of dots that can result in fuzzy printed images). Ink is also affected by a paper's finish. Coating results in the ink being held on the paper's surface (called *ink holdout*) rather than being absorbed. Optimal holdout produces precise dot reproduction, bright colors, and sharp images. (Too much holdout, however, can cause ink *setoff*, transfer of ink to an adjacent sheet.)

Though the choice of ink is important in all types of printing, inks are not often of concern to the editor, who will be unlikely to see their effect until the printing process is completed.

Paper

Outside of the smallest publishing houses, the editor is rarely required to be knowledgeable on the subject of paper, which is primarily the province of a manufacturing manager. However, since the editor is presumably the person most attuned to the book's audience, he or she should be sensitive to the acceptable tradeoffs between optimal production quality and desirable pricing and will sometimes want to take part in discussions of paper.

Various issues can affect the choice of a particular paper for a printing project.

Characteristics

The distinctive characteristics of a sheet of paper include its grain, weight, bulk, opacity, color, brightness, and finish.

Grain refers to the direction in which most of the fibers (generally wood fibers) of a sheet are aligned during the papermaking process. Grain affects the tendency of paper to fold easily; the terms *against the grain* and *cross-grain* refer to folding or feeding paper into the press at right angles to the normal grain direction of the paper. In order that a book will lie open properly, its paper should be *right-grained*—that is, the grain should run parallel to the spine. (Only rarely is *wrong-grained* orientation necessary.)

The paper's *basis weight* is the weight of 500 sheets of paper (a *ream*) in the standard size for that grade of paper. Standard sizes can vary from one type of paper to another (bond paper is 17″ x 22″, newsprint is 24″ x 36″). Tables of equivalent weights compare various types of paper by size and weight. Paper is identified by ream weight ("20-pound bond," "70-pound book," etc.). Book paper varies from about 30- to 120-pound, the commonest being perhaps 50-pound. Standard cover stock for paperbacks is about 65-pound—which is far heavier than 50-pound text stock, since the basis weight of cover stock is calculated with reference to smaller sheets. Mass-market paperbacks generally use 35-pound newsprint. (Newsprint's basis weight is calculated similarly but not identically to that of book papers.)

Bulk refers to the thickness or *caliper* of a sheet of paper, and is measured either in thousandths of an inch (*mils* or *points*) or in pages per inch (*ppi*); the ppi bulk measurement is used mainly for book papers in book publishing. The thickness of a bound book is perhaps largely of concern for its effect on the prospective buyer, who may regard thickness as evidence of value, but will also affect the number of copies that will fit in a given size of box for shipping. For a book with a very high page count, the publisher may desire to keep the bulk down to prevent the book from becoming unwieldy. Standard book papers vary in bulk from about 200 to 900 pages per inch; thus, a very high-bulking paper may be four times as thick as an extremely thin paper. Since paper bulk affects the size of the book's spine, the designer of the book's jacket or cover must always know the expected total bulk.

Opacity refers to the ability of the paper to resist show-through from the reverse side of a page. Opacity is naturally influenced by the bulk and weight of the paper, but it is not simply a function of bulk, since very thin bible paper can be highly opaque. Inadequate opacity can make any book a trial to read; high opacity is especially important for illustrated books.

Color or *shade* describes the tones of paper stock, particularly those of white paper, which range from cream-white to blue-white. (Actual colored stock, which is generally more expensive than white paper, is rarely seen in books but is occasionally used for a separate section of special reference material.) The higher white tones—those tending toward blue-white—are desirable for reproduction of continuous-tone art, and particularly color art. *Brightness* refers to the reflective quality of a sheet of paper, which is measured by mechanical means. The brightest papers are rated around 95 percent (100 percent is represented by a sheet of zinc oxide). Brightness affects contrast and, like shade, brightness is an important consideration when printing color illustrations. Both color and brightness also affect the comfort with which text can be read; paper with a high white sheen may be thought aesthetically attractive but actually tends to produce eyestrain.

Finish describes the treatment given to the paper surface in the papermaking process. Paper may be either *uncoated* or *coated*. Coating is a clay solution that, when applied to a paper surface in the manufacturing process, keeps ink from being absorbed deeply before it dries. Keeping the ink on the paper's surface helps preserve an image's sharp outlines and bright colors. Optional treatments of coated papers can produce a variety of coating types with names such as *film-coated* and *glossy*. A *matte* finish is a flat coating, used mainly for text pages without illustrations; an *enamel* finish is very shiny and is often used for high-quality halftones and color reproductions. Books printed primarily on standard text paper may have one or more inserted signatures of illustrations printed on coated stock.

Uncoated finishes range from *antique* to *eggshell*, *vellum*, and *English finish*. These are distinguished by the amount of *calendering*, or "ironing," the paper receives. Antique papers receive the least and thus are the bulkiest and the dullest of the uncoated papers; English-finish papers are thin (though not necessarily light) and relatively shiny. The smoother papers produce greater ink holdout and sharper dot reproduction.

Paperback covers are normally of heavy stock *coated one side only* (often abbreviated *CIS*).

Paper Grades and Quality

Papers are further classified into one of several *grades: newsprint, text papers, bond* or *writing papers, cover papers, book papers, coated book papers, board,* and various *specialty papers.* Grade primarily refers to the ways in which a paper is used; what qualities are regarded as desirable obviously depend on the paper's intended use.

Book papers include the widest range of choices. Because of the predominance of offset printing, book papers are prepared or sized to resist the wetting solution used in that process; thus, these papers are also called *offset papers.* Certain grades of paper are more appropriate for sheetfed printing than for web presses. General sturdiness and durability are obvious considerations for the paper in children's books. Though high bulk does not translate automatically into sturdiness, the strongest papers tend to be somewhat bulky.

The best book papers are required for exacting reproduction of color art. The cheapest are capable of both color and halftone reproduction (as in newspapers) but the quality of reproduction may be painfully low, and these are best reserved for books with no significant graphic component. An expensive book paper can cost many times as much as a cheap paper.

Mass-market paperbacks are usually printed on either newsprint or *groundwood* (a slightly better paper). Trade or quality paperbacks are often printed on paper of the same good quality as the hardcover books that preceded them. Higher grades of paper (usually coated) that are free of groundwood content are called *free sheets.*

Recycled paper has become widely available as a result of environmental concerns and legislation. Recycled papers tend to be somewhat weaker than virgin papers, but their strength may depend on various factors, including the percentage of recycled fibers in the paper. Such papers should be considered for any appropriate projects, particularly those for which permanence may not be a central concern.

Acid-free paper is recommended by the American National Standards Institute and the American Library Association (librarians have watched millions of older books turn to dust as a result of paper acidity), and most publishers now comply with the recommendations, at least for hardcover books and books generally felt to have some permanent value. Acid-free paper costs somewhat more than acidic paper, and the cheapest papers are always high in acid. (A statement that a book has been published on acid-free paper is generally printed in the book, usually on the copyright page.)

Since page-size sheets are always cut from larger standard-size sheets, a given book size will sometimes result in a significant amount of wasted paper—paper that must be thrown away or recycled by the printer—and the publisher will normally be charged for such wastage. The manufacturing manager, consulting with the printer, will be alert to such problems and will sometimes favor certain sizes over other slightly different sizes for this reason. But, as a brief tour of a bookstore will confirm, American publishers have generally refused to adopt truly standard book sizes. Even mass-market paperbacks, which must fit into standard jobbers' racks in stationery stores, drugstores, and supermarkets, vary in size from one publisher to another.

Binding

After the sheets have been printed, they are sent through another set of machines that fold the sheets into signatures and trim the signatures down to the size in which they will be bound. Stacks of folded and trimmed signatures are then loaded onto a gathering machine, which takes a signature from each stack and assembles new stacks, each corresponding to an individual book.

These gathered and collated signatures are then checked for their correct sequence; small collating marks or numbers printed at the signature fold show their correct order, usually forming a diagonal series across the backs of the folds when the signatures are properly assembled. One set of the collated signatures—called *folded and gathered sheets*, or *F&G's*—is sent quickly to the publisher, who may check it quickly for any disastrous errors even as the binding process is proceeding.

Hardcover and Paper Binding

Hardcover or *case binding* is perhaps the oldest binding method still in use.

The book's hard cover, or *case,* is completely assembled before being attached to the book. The case itself consists of a back board, a front board, and a spine, all usually made of laminated cardboard. These are covered with woven fabric (usually cotton, linen, vellum, or a synthetic), paper, plastic, or leather, which folds over the inside edges. Nonwoven synthetic materials are more widely used than cloth today. They are less expensive, can be printed in more than one color, are tough enough that they often eliminate the need for a jacket, and are often manufactured to school or library specifications that require them to withstand rough treatment.

An *endpaper* or *endsheet*—a single sheet of heavy paper as large as two normal pages—is glued at its center to the gutter margin of the first and the last page of the book so that half of each sheet is hanging free. Glue is applied to the spine; the *super* or *crash*—a piece of heavy gauze wider than the spine—is attached; and a *back strip* of heavy paper the width of the spine is glued over the super. *Headbands*—tiny decorative strips of cloth positioned at the inside top and bottom of the spine on well-bound books for reinforcement and ornamentation—may be glued to the ends of the super.

The case is attached to the pages by applying glue to the free halves of the endpapers and then folding the case around them. The ends of the super are thus glued between the endpapers and the boards so as to function (with the endpapers themselves) as hinges for the covers. The endpapers extend almost to the edges of the two covers, hiding the glued-down edges of the applied fabric or synthetic surface covering the exterior.

The case always carries some text itself, generally on the spine and frequently on the front as well. This type is usually stamped or embossed by means of a specially cast metal die, leaving a shallow impression. The die itself is created from a design sent by the designer. It usually applies either ink or foil (which may look just like ink) to the cover. Cover stamps may use two or more colors, but continuous-tone effects are not possible on fabric covers. The cases of books that will not have jackets—such as textbooks and children's books—usually have coated paper surfaces brightly printed in four colors, often with continuous-tone art.

Paper covers represent a simpler and cheaper alternative. They consist of sheets of heavy cover stock (usually 80 or 100-pound), generally coated on the outside *(coated one side,* or *C1S)* and sometimes on the inside as well, and printed in color, which are glued directly to the spine edge of the book pages. (Well-bound paperbacks may incorporate super for sturdiness.) The heaviness of the stock and such options as plastic lamination and texture (often simulating fabric or leather) affect their strength and appearance. The pages of paperbound books may be held together by various methods, including several of those discussed below.

Smyth sewing Hardcover books often employs the technique known as *Smyth sewing,* in which the pages within each signature are sewn together directly through the signature's fold, and then each signature is attached to the next by its threads. Smyth-sewn bindings, being durable and allowing the pages of an opened book to lay flat rather than partially shutting, are traditionally used for high-quality books. Paperbacks use it more rarely.

Adhesive bindings In *perfect binding,* the signatures are trimmed in such a way that the fold itself is cut off after the signatures have been collated, producing a stack of separate pages. The trimmed inside edges are roughened and coated with flexible glue. This type of binding, long standard for paperback books, is now common also for hardcover books and for magazines. Its dubious reputation—resulting in part from the cheap older paperbacks whose pages were highly prone to detach themselves individually or in clusters—has improved with developing technology.

Two related forms of adhesive binding are becoming steadily more popular with publishers. In *notch binding,* the signature fold is preserved rather than being trimmed off, and a series of vertical notches is cut deep into each fold, permitting the glue to penetrate. In the very similar *burst binding,* the length of the fold is perforated instead. Both techniques can produce sturdily bound books which lay satisfactorily flat when opened.

Mechanical bindings In *mechanical binding,* the pages are trimmed on all four sides and have round holes or slots punched or drilled through them near the inside margin. In a book with a *spiral binding,* the pages are held together by a wire or plastic spiral coiled through the holes. A *plastic-comb binding* consists of a plastic spine with a series of protruding plastic tongues that curve around through the punched holes to form circles that hold the pages in place. Spiral and comb bindings are often used for notebooks, cookbooks, practical manuals, and other books that must lie flat when opened. *Loose-leaf* binding uses two or more split rings that hold sheets with punched holes together but also allow them to be removed and replaced. All such mechanical binding methods require an inside margin wide enough to accommodate the punched holes and fasteners (usually at least ½″).

Wire stitching *Wire stitching* employs wire staples to attach the pages, which are not gathered as signatures but rather form a single gathering held together by a single set of staples. *Saddle wiring* (and the similar *saddle stitching,* which employs thread rather than staples) is used for smaller publications—usually up to about 112 pages long, but sometimes over 150, depending on the paper's bulk—such as pamphlets and magazines. The staples (usually two or three) are run through the cover and the pages from the outside at the fold. The staples are exposed on the outside and between the two middle pages; like spiral and comb-bound books, saddle-wired publications lack a square spine that can be read when shelved normally.

Side-wired books, by contrast, consist of signatures with trimmed-off folds. The staples go through the pages from the front of the book to the back. (In *side-stiched* or *side-sewn* books, thread replaces the staples.) Side-wired books have square spines, and a glued-on cover usually covers the staples. The bindings are very sturdy, but the open book will not lie flat. Side wiring is standard for library bindings.

Jackets

Book jackets, or *dust jackets,* are paper wrappings originally intended simply to protect a casebound book's cover. Today, with color, elaborate graphic design, and inviting copy, they are regarded as essential to the presentation, advertising, and marketing of the hardbound book. They are printed on somewhat heavy stock which is coated, plastic-coated, or varnished on one side. The jacket may be printed by the same printer as the rest of the book.

Grammar Glossary

This glossary provides definitions, and sometimes discussions, of grammatical and grammar-related terms, many of which appear in the text. Examples are enclosed in angle brackets. Cross-references to other glossary entries are shown in boldface.

abbreviation A shortened form of a written word or phrase used in place of the whole (such as *amt.* for *amount,* or *c/o* for *care of*).

Abbreviations can be used wherever they are customary, but note that what is customary in technical writing will be different from what is customary in journalism or other fields. See also **acronym**.

absolute adjective An adjective that normally cannot be used comparatively <*ancillary* rights> <the *maximum* dose>.

Many absolute adjectives can be modified by adverbs such as *almost* or *near* <an *almost fatal* dose> <at *near maximum* capacity>. However, many adjectives considered to be absolute are in fact often preceded by comparative adverbs <a *more perfect* union> <a *less complete* account>. In such cases, *more* means "more nearly" and *less* "less nearly."

absolute comparative The comparative form of an adjective used where no comparison is implied or stated, although in some cases comparison may be inferred by the reader or hearer <*higher* education> <a *better* kind of company> <gives you a *brighter* smile> <an *older* woman>. See also **absolute adjective; comparison; double comparison; implicit comparative**.

acronym A word or abbreviation formed from the initial letter or letters of each of the major parts of a compound term, whether or not it is pronounceable as a word (such as *TQM* for *Total Quality Management,* or *UNPROFOR* for *United Nations Protection Force*); also called *initialism.*

active voice A verb form indicating that the subject of a sentence is performing the action <he *respects* the other scientists> <a bird *was singing*> <interest rates *rose*>; compare **passive voice**.

adjective A word that describes or modifies a noun <an *active* mind> <this is *serious*> <*full* and *careful* in its attention to detail>.

An adjective can follow a noun as a complement <the book made the bag *heavy*> and can sometimes modify larger units, like noun phrases <the *celebrated* "man in the street"> and noun clauses <it seemed *incomprehensible* that one senator could hold up the nomination>.

Adjectives can be described as *coordinate adjectives* when they share equal relationships to the nouns they modify <a *concise, coherent* essay> <a *soft, flickering, bluish* light>, and as *noncoordinate adjectives* when the first of two adjectives modifies the second adjective and the noun together <a *low monthly* fee> <the *first warm* day>.

An *indefinite adjective* designates unidentified or not immediately identifiable persons or things <*some* children> <*other* hotels>.

An *interrogative adjective* is used in asking questions <*whose* book is this?> <*which* color looks best?>.

A *possessive adjective* is the possessive form of a personal pronoun <*her* idea> <*its* second floor>.

A *relative adjective (which, that, who, whom, whose, where)* introduces an adjectival clause or a clause that functions as a noun <at the April conference, by *which* time the report should be finished> <not knowing *whose* lead she should follow>. See also **absolute adjective**; **attributive**; **demonstrative adjective**; **predicate adjective**.

adverb A word that modifies a verb, adjective, adverb, preposition, phrase, clause, or sentence.

Traditionally adverbs indicate time, place, or manner <do it *now*> <*there* they remained> <she went *willingly*>. They can connect statements <a small bomb had been found; *nevertheless,* they were continuing their search> and can tell the reader what the writer thinks about what is being said in the sentence <*luckily* I got there on time>. They can modify verbs <ran *fast*>, adjectives <an *awfully* long speech>, participles <a *well*-acted play>, adverbs <doing *fairly* well>, particles <woke *right* up>, indefinite pronouns <*almost* everyone>, cardinal numbers <*over* 200 guests>, prepositional phrases <*just* out of reach>, and more. Sometimes they modify a preceding noun <the great city *beyond*>, and some adverbs of place and time can serve as the objects of prepositions <since *when*> <before *long*>.

The notion that adverbs should not separate auxiliaries from their main verbs <you can *easily* see the river from here> <they should be *heartily* congratulated> is a false one, apparently based on fear of the split infinitive. See also **auxiliary verb**; **sentence adverb**; **split infinitive**.

adverbial genitive A form, or case, of some nouns used as adverbs of time, normally formed by adding *-s* <he worked *nights*> <the store is open *Sundays*>.

agreement A grammatical relationship that involves the correspondence in number either between the subject and verb of a sentence or between a pronoun and its antecedent; also called *concord*.

Subject-verb agreement for compound subjects joined by <u>and</u>: When a subject is composed of two or more singular nouns joined by *and,* the plural verb is usually used <*the sentimentality and lack of originality* which *mark* his writing> <*the bitterness and heartache* that *fill* the world>. Occasionally when the nouns form a single conceptual unit, the singular verb can be used <*the report's depth and scope demonstrates*> <*her patience and calm was* remarkable>. See also **notional agreement**.

Compound subjects joined by <u>or</u> (or <u>nor</u>): When singular nouns are joined by *or,* the singular verb is usually used <*the average man or woman was* not interested>; when plural nouns are so joined, the plural verb is used <*wolves or coyotes have* depleted his stock>. When the negative *neither . . . nor* is used with singular nouns, it usually takes a singular verb <*neither she nor anyone else is* fond of the idea>; when used with plural nouns, it takes a plural verb <*neither* *the proponents nor their adversaries are* willing to accept>. But when *neither . . . nor* is used with nouns of differing number, the noun closest to the verb usually determines its number <*neither he nor his colleagues were* present> <*neither the teachers nor the principal was* interested>. Similar rules apply to *either . . . or.*

Compound subjects joined by words or phrases like <u>with</u> or <u>along with</u>, or by punctuation: When a singular noun is joined to another by a word or phrase like *with, rather than,* or *as well as,* a singular verb is generally used <*that story, along with nine others, was* published> <*the battleship together with the destroyer was* positioned three miles offshore>. Parenthetical insertions set off by commas, dashes, or parentheses should not affect agreement <*this book, as well as various others, has* achieved notoriety> <*their management—and the company's balance sheets—has* suffered>.

Subject formed by a collective noun phrase: In constructions like "a bunch of the boys were whooping it up" or "a fraction of the deposits are insured," which make use of a collective noun phrase (*a bunch of the boys, a fraction of the deposits*), the verb is usually plural, since the sense of the phrase is normally plural. See also **collective noun**.

Subject expressing money, time, etc.: When an amount of money, a period of time, or some other plural noun phrase of quantity or measure forms the subject, a singular verb is used <*ten dollars is* all I have left> <*two miles is* as far as they can walk> <*two thirds of the area is* under water>.

Subject formed by <u>one in (out of)</u> . . . : Phrases such as "one in five" or "two out of three" may take either a singular or a plural verb <*one in four union members was* undecided> <*one out of ten soldiers were* unable to recognize the enemy>, though grammarians tend to favor the singular.

Pronoun-antecedent agreement for nouns joined by <u>and</u>, <u>or</u>: When antecedents are singular nouns joined by *and,* a plural pronoun is used <*the computer and the printer* were moved because *they* were in the way>. But singular nouns joined by *or* can use either a singular or a plural pronoun, whichever sounds best <either *Fred or Marianne* will give *their* presentation after lunch> <*each employee or supervisor* should give what *he or she* can afford>.

Agreement for indefinite pronouns: The indefinite pronouns *anybody, anyone, each, either, everybody, everyone, neither, nobody, none, no one, somebody,* and *someone,* though some of them are conceptually plural, are used with singular verbs <*everyone* in the company *was* pleased> <*nobody is* responsible>, but are commonly referred to by *they, their, them,* or *themselves* <*nobody* could get the crowd's attention when *they* spoke> <*everybody* there admits *they* saw it>. Writing handbooks prescribe *he, she,* or *he or she,* or some other construction instead of the plural pronouns, but use of the plural *they, their,* or *them* has long been established and is standard.

antecedent A word, phrase, or clause to which a subsequent pronoun refers <*Judy* wrote to say *she* is coming> <they saw *Bob* and called to *him*> <I hear that *he* is ill and *it* worries me>.

appositive A word, phrase, or clause that is equivalent to an adjacent noun <a biography of *the poet Robert Burns*> <sales of *her famous novel, <u>Gone with the Wind</u>,* reached one million copies in six months> <*we grammarians* are never wrong>.

Restrictive and nonrestrictive appositives play different roles in a sentence and are traditionally distinguished by their punctuation. A nonrestrictive appositive <*his wife, Helen,* attended the ceremony> is generally set off with commas, while a restrictive appositive <he sent *his daughter Cicely* to college> uses no commas and indicates that one out of a group is being identified (in this case, one daughter from among two or more). Exceptions occur where no ambiguity would result <his wife Helen>. See also **nonrestrictive clause**; **restrictive clause**.

article   One of three words *(a, an, the)* used with a noun to indicate definiteness <*the* blue car> or indefiniteness <*a* simple task> <*an* interesting explanation>.

attributive   A modifier that immediately precedes the word it modifies <*black* tie, *U.S.* government, *kitchen* sink, *lobster* salad>.

Nouns have functioned like adjectives in this position for many centuries. In more recent years, some critics have objected to the proliferation of nouns used to modify other nouns: e.g., *language deterioration, health aspects, image enhancement.* While long or otherwise unexpected strings of this sort can occasionally be disorienting to the uninitiated (e.g., *management team strategy planning session*), the practice is flourishing and usually serves to compress information that the intended audience need not always have spelled out for it. Be sure, however, that the context and audience will allow for such compression.

A fairly recent trend toward using plural attributives has been attacked by some critics. There always had been a few plural attributives—*scissors grinder, physics laboratory, Civil Liberties Union, mathematics book*—but is it proper to use the more recent *weapons system, communications technology, operations program, systems analyst, earth-resources satellite, singles bar, enemies list?* The answer is that such plural attributives are standard. The plural form is chosen to stress plurality—more than one weapon, operation, enemy, etc.—or to otherwise distinguish its meaning from whatever the singular attributive might connote.

auxiliary verb   A verb that accompanies another verb and typically expresses person, number, mood, or tense (such as *be, have, can, do*) <they *can* see the movie tomorrow> <she *has* left already>. See also **verb**.

cardinal number   A number of the kind used in simple counting <*one, 1, thirty-five, 35*>; compare **ordinal number**.

case   In English, a form of a noun or pronoun indicating its grammatical relation to other words in a sentence. See **nominative**; **objective**; **possessive**. See also **genitive**.

clause   A group of words having its own subject and predicate but forming only part of a compound or complex sentence. A *main* or *independent clause* could stand alone as a sentence <*we will leave* as soon as the taxi arrives>; a *subordinate* or *dependent clause* requires a main clause <we will leave *as soon as the taxi arrives*>.

There are three basic types of clauses—all subordinate clauses—that have part-of-speech functions. An *adjective clause* modifies a noun or pronoun <the clown, *who was also a horse trainer*> <I can't see the reason *why you're upset*>. An *adverb clause* modifies a verb, adjective, or another adverb <*when it rains*, it pours> <I'm certain *that he is guilty*> <we accomplished less *than we did before*>. A *noun clause* fills a noun slot in a sentence and thus can be a subject, object, or complement <*whoever is qualified* should apply> <I don't know *what his problem is*> <the trouble is *that she has no alternative*>. See also **sentence**; **subordinate clause**.

collective noun A singular noun that stands for a number of persons or things considered as a group (such as *team, government, horde*).

Subject-verb agreement: Collective nouns have been used with both singular and plural verbs since Middle English. The principle involved is one of notional agreement. When the group is considered as a unit, the singular verb is used <the *government is* prepared for a showdown> <his *family is* from New England> <the *team has won* all of its home games>. When the group is thought of as a collection of individuals, the plural verb is sometimes used <her *family are* all staunch conservatives>. Singular verbs are more common in American English and plural verbs more common in British English, though usage remains divided in each case. See also **agreement**; **notional agreement**.

A collective noun followed by *of* and a plural noun follows the same rule as collective nouns in general. When the notion is that of plurality, the plural verb is normally used <an *assemblage of rocks were* laid out on the table> <a *group of jazz improvisers were* heard through the window>. When the idea of oneness or wholeness is stressed, the verb is generally singular <this *cluster of stars is* the largest yet identified>.

Pronoun agreement: The usual rule is that writers should take care to match their pronouns and verbs, singular with singular <the committee *is* hopeful that *it* will succeed>, plural with plural <the faculty *are* willing to drop *their* suit>. But in fact writers sometimes use a plural pronoun after a singular verb <the audience *was* on *their* way out>. (The reverse combination—plural verb with singular pronoun—is very rare.)

Organizations as collective nouns: The names of companies and other organizations are treated as either singular <*Harvard* may consider *itself* very fortunate> or, less commonly, plural <the *D.A.R. are* going to do another pageant>. Organizations also sometimes appear with a singular verb but a plural pronoun in reference <*M-G-M hopes* to sell *their* latest releases> <*Chrysler builds their* convertible in Kentucky>. This usage is standard, though informal.

colloquial An adjective describing usage that is characteristic of familiar and informal conversation.

While not intended to carry pejorative overtones, the label *colloquial* often implies that the usage is nonstandard. See also **dialect**; **nonstandard**; **standard English**.

comma fault (comma splice, comma error) The use of a comma instead of a semicolon to link two independent clauses (as in "I won't talk about myself, it's not a healthy topic"). Modern style calls for the semicolon, but comma splices are fairly common in casual and unedited prose.

comparison Modification of an adjective or adverb to show different levels of quality, quantity, or relation. The *comparative* form shows relation between two items, usually by adding *-er* or *more* or *less* to the adjective or adverb <he's short*er* than I am> <her second book sold *more* quickly>. The *superlative* form expresses an extreme among two or more items, usually by adding *-est* or *most* or *least* to the adjective or adverb <the cheetah is the fast*est* mammal> <that's the *least* compelling reason> <the *most* vexingly intractable issue>. See also **absolute adjective; absolute comparative; double comparison; implicit comparative.**

complement An added word or expression by which a predicate is made complete <they elected him *president*> <she thought it *beautiful*> <the critics called her *the best act of her kind since Carmen Miranda*>.

compound A combination of words or word elements that work together in various ways (*farmhouse; cost-effective; ex-husband; shoeless; figure out; in view of* that; *real estate* agent; *greenish white* powder; *carefully tended* garden; *great white shark*).

Compounds are written in one of three ways: solid <*workplace*>, hyphenated <*screenwriter-director*>, or open <*health care*>. Because of the variety of standard practice, the choice among these styles for a given compound represents one of the most common and bothersome of all style issues. A current desk dictionary will list many compounds, but those whose meanings are self-explanatory from the meanings of their component words will usually not appear. Most writers try to pattern any temporary compounds after similar permanent compounds such as are entered in dictionaries.

compound subject Two or more nouns or pronouns usually joined by *and* that function as the subject of a clause or sentence <*doctors and lawyers* reported the highest incomes for that period> <*Peter, Karen, and I* left together>. See also **agreement; collective noun.**

concord See **agreement.**

conjunction A word or phrase that joins together words, phrases, clauses, or sentences.

Coordinating conjunctions (such as *and, because, but, or, nor, since, so*) join elements of equal weight, to show similarity <they came early *and* stayed late>, to exclude or contrast <he is a brilliant *but* arrogant man>, to offer alternatives <she can wait here *or* return later>, to propose reasons or grounds <the timetable is useless, *because* it is out-of-date>, or to specify a result <his diction is excellent, *so* every word is clear>.

Correlative conjunctions (such as *either . . . or, neither . . . nor*) are used in pairs and link alternatives or equal elements <*either* you go *or* you stay> <the proposal benefits *neither* residents *nor* visitors> <she showed *not only* perceptive understanding *but also* mature judgment>.

Subordinating conjunctions (such as *unless, whether*) join subordinate clauses to main clauses and are used to express cause <*because* she learns quickly, she is an eager student>, condition <don't call *unless* you're coming>, manner <it looks *as though* it's clearing>, purpose <he gets up early *so that* he can exercise before work>, time <she kept a diary *when* she was a teenager>, place <I don't know *where* he went>, or possibility <they were undecided *whether* to go or stay>.

conjunctive adverb A transitional adverb (such as *also, however, therefore*) that expresses the relationship between two independent clauses, sentences, or paragraphs.

Conjunctive adverbs are used to express addition <he enjoyed the movie; *however,* he had to leave before the end>, emphasis <he is brilliant; *indeed,* he is a genius>, contrast <that was unfortunate; *nevertheless,* they should have known the danger>, elaboration <on one point only did everyone agree: *namely,* too much money had been spent already>, conclusion <the case could take years to work its way through the courts; *as a result,* many plaintiffs will accept settlements>, or priority <*first* cream the shortening and sugar, *then* add the eggs and beat well>.

contact clause A dependent clause attached to its antecedent without a relative pronoun such as *that, which,* or *who* <the key [that] *you lost*> <he is not the person [who] *we thought he was*>.

The predicate noun clause not introduced by the conjunction *that* <we believe [that] *the alliance is strong*> is as long and as well established in English as the contact clause. It is probably more common in casual and general prose than in formal prose. It is also more common after some verbs (such as *believe, hope, say, think*) than others (such as *assert, calculate, hold, intend*).

contraction A shortened form of a word or words in which an apostrophe usually replaces the omitted letter or letters (such as *dep't, don't, could've, o'clock, we'll*).

Contractions involving verbs used to be avoided more than they are today. In fact, many contemporary writing handbooks recommend using contractions to help you avoid sounding stilted.

count noun A noun that identifies things that can be counted <two *tickets*> <a *motive*> <many *people*>; compare **mass noun**.

dangling modifier A modifying phrase that lacks a normally expected grammatical relation to the rest of the sentence (as in "*Caught in the act,* his excuses were unconvincing").

The common construction called the *participial phrase* usually begins with a participle; in "*Chancing to meet them there,* I invited them to sit with us," the subject, "I," is left implicit in the preceding phrase, which modifies it. But a writer may inadvertently let a participial phrase modify a subject or some other noun in the sentence it was not intended to modify; the result is what grammarians call a *dangling participle.* Thus in "*Hoping to find him alone,* the presence of a stranger was irksome," it is the "presence" itself that may seem to be hoping.

Dangling participles can be found in the writing of many famous writers, and they are usually hardly noticeable except to someone looking for them. The important thing to avoid is creating an unintended humorous effect (as in "*Opening up the cupboard,* a cockroach ran for the corner").

dangling participle See **dangling modifier**.

demonstrative adjective One of four adjectives—*this, that, these,* and *those*—that points to what it modifies in order to distinguish it from others. The number (singular or plural) of the adjective should agree with the noun it modifies <*this* type of person> <*that* shelf of books> <*these* sorts of jobs> <*those* varieties of apples>.

demonstrative pronoun One of the words *this, that, these,* and *those* classified as pronouns when they function as nouns <*this* is my desk; *that* is yours> <*these* are the best popovers in town> <*those* are strong words>.

dialect A variety of language distinguished by features of vocabulary, grammar, and pronunciation that is confined to a region or group. See also **nonstandard**; **standard English**.

direct object A word, phrase, or clause denoting the goal or result of the action of the verb <he closed the *valve*> <they'll do *whatever it takes*> <*"Do it now,"* he said>; compare **indirect object**.

direct question A question quoted exactly as spoken, written, or imagined <the only question is, *Will it work?*>; compare **indirect question**.

direct quotation Text quoted exactly as spoken or written <I heard her say, *"I'll be there at two o'clock"*>; compare **indirect quotation**.

divided usage Widespread use of two or more forms for a single entity (such as *dived* and *dove* for the past tense of *dive*).

double comparison Use of the forms *more, most, less,* or *least* with an adjective already inflected for the comparative or superlative degree (such as *more wider, most widest*).

This construction results from using *more* and *most* as intensifiers <a *most* enjoyable meal>. In modern usage, double comparison has all but vanished from standard writing. See also **comparison**; **intensifier**.

Double comparison can also occur by inflection. Though forms such as *firstest, mostest,* and *bestest* are most typical of the speech of young children, the form *worser* (which has a long literary background) still persists in adult speech. You will want to avoid it in writing.

double genitive A construction in which possession is marked both by the preposition *of* and a noun or pronoun in the possessive case.

In expressions like "that song of Ella Fitzgerald's" or "a good friend of ours," the possessive relationship is indicated by both *of* and the genitive inflection (*Fitzgerald's, ours*), even though only one or the other would seem to be strictly necessary. However, this construction, also known as the *double possessive,* is an idiomatic one of long standing and is standard in all kinds of writing. See also **genitive**.

double modal The use of two modal auxiliaries in succession, resulting in such expressions as *might can, might could,* and *might should.*

Today double modals tend to be found in Southern dialect and are unfamiliar to speakers from other parts of the country.

double negative A clause or sentence containing two negatives and having a negative meaning.

In modern usage, the double negative (as in "they did*n't* have *no* children" or "it would*n't* do *no* good") is widely perceived as a rustic or uneducated form, and is generally avoided in both writing and speech, other than the most informal.

A standard form of double negative is the rhetorical device known as *litotes,* which produces a weak affirmative meaning <a *not un*reasonable request>. It is used for understatement, but should not be overused.

double passive A construction that uses two verb forms in the passive voice, one being an infinitive (as in "the work of redesigning the office space *was requested to be done* by outside contractors").

The double passive is awkward and potentially ambiguous (did outside contractors ask for the work to be done, or were they asked to do the work?) and should be avoided.

double possessive See **double genitive**.

double superlative See **double comparison**.

false titles Appositive preceding a person's name with no preceding article or following comma, which thus resembles a title, though it is rarely capitalized <organized by *consumer advocate* Ralph Nader> <works of *1960s underground cartoonist* Robert Crumb>. The use of such titles is sometimes criticized, but it is standard in journalism.

faulty parallelism See **parallelism**.

flat adverb An adverb that has the same form as its related adjective, such as *sure* <you *sure* fooled me>, *bright* <the moon is shining *bright*>, and *flat* <she turned me down *flat*>.

Although such forms were once common, later grammarians saw them as faulty because they lacked the *-ly* ending. Today flat adverbs are few in number and some are widely regarded as incorrect.

formal agreement See **notional agreement**.

gender In English, a characteristic of certain nouns and pronouns that indicates sex (masculine, feminine, neuter) <*he, him, his, she, her, it, its; actor, actress; brother, sister; emperor, empress; heir, heiress; fiancé, fiancée; testator, testatrix*>.

genitive A form, or case, of a noun or pronoun that typically shows possession or source <the girl*'s* sweater> <nobody*'s* fool> <an uncle *of mine*> <some idea *of theirs*> <the company*'s* failure> <a year*'s* salary> <the nation*'s* capital> <a stone*'s* throw>.

The form is usually produced by adding *-'s* or a phrase beginning with *of.* While the possessive is the genitive's most common function, it has certain other functions as well; these include the *subjective* <Frost*'s* poetry>, *objective* <her son*'s* graduation>, *descriptive* <women*'s* colleges>, and *appositive* <the state *of Massachusetts*> <the office *of president*> genitives. See also **double genitive**; **possessive**.

gerund A verb form having the characteristics of both verb and noun and ending in *-ing* (also called a *verbal noun*) <the ice made *skiing* impossible>.

A gerund can be preceded by a possessive noun or pronoun <her hus-

band's *snoring*> <their *filling* the position>. See also **possessive; possessive with gerund.**

hypercorrection The use of a nonstandard linguistic form or construction on the basis of a false analogy to a standard form or construction (as in "*whom* should I say is calling?"; "this is between you and *I*"; "no one but *he* would notice"; "open *widely*").

idiom A common expression that is peculiar to itself grammatically <*it wasn't me*> or that cannot be understood from the meanings of its separate words <I told them to *step on it*> <the newspaper *had a field day*>.

imperative The form, or mood, of a verb that expresses a command or makes a request <*come* here> <please *don't*>; compare **indicative; subjunctive.**

implicit comparative One of a small group of adjectives (primarily *major, minor, inferior, superior*) whose meaning resembles a true comparative but which cannot be used with comparative forms (such as *more, most; less, least*) <a *major* contributor> <an *inferior* wine>.

However, two other implicit comparatives *junior* and *senior* can be used with comparative forms <a *more senior* diplomat> <the *least junior* of the new partners>. See also **comparison.**

indefinite pronoun A pronoun that designates an unidentified person or thing <*somebody* ate my dessert> <she saw *no one* she knew>.

Many indefinite pronouns should agree in number with their verbs. See **agreement.** See also **notional agreement; pronoun.**

indicative The form, or mood, of a verb that states a fact or asks a question <the train *stopped*> <they*'ll be* along> <everyone *is* ravenous> <*has* the rain *begun?*> <who *knows?*>; compare **imperative; subjunctive.**

indirect object A grammatical object representing the secondary goal of the action of its verb <she gave *the dog* a bone>; compare **direct object.**

indirect question A statement of the substance of a question without using the speaker's exact words or word order <the officer asked *what the trouble was*> <they wondered *whether it would work*>; compare **direct question.**

indirect quotation A statement of the substance of a quotation without using the speaker's exact words <I heard her say *she'd be there at two o'clock*>; compare **direct quotation.**

infinitive A verb form having the characteristics of both verb and noun and usually used with *to* <we had *to stop*> <*to err* is human> <no one saw him *leave*>. See also **split infinitive.**

infinitive phrase A phrase that includes an infinitive and its modifiers and complements <we expect them *to arrive by five o'clock*> <he shouted *to be heard above the din*> <*to have earned a Ph.D. in four years* was impressive>.

inflection The change in form that words undergo to mark case, gender, number, tense, person, mood, voice, or comparison <*he, his, him*> <*waiter, waitress*> <*rat, rats*> <*blame, blames, blamed, blaming*> <*who, whom*> <she *is*

careful, if she *were* careful, *be* careful> <like, *likes, is liked*> <wild, *wilder, wildest*>. See also **case**; **comparison**; **gender**; **mood**; **number**; **person**; **tense**; **voice**.

initialism See **acronym**.

intensifier A linguistic element used to give emphasis or additional strength to another word or statement <a *very* hot day> <it's a *complete* lie> <what *on earth* is he doing?> <she *herself* did it>. See also **double comparison**.

interjection An exclamatory or interrupting word or phrase <*ouch!*> <*oh no, not that again*>.

interrogative pronoun One of the pronouns *what, which, who, whom,* and *whose,* as well as combinations of these words with the suffix *-ever,* used to introduce direct and indirect questions <*who* is she?> <he asked me *who* she was> <*which* did they choose?> <I wondered *which* they chose>.
    Who is frequently substituted for *whom* to introduce a question even when it is the object of a preposition <*who* are you going to listen to?> <*who* do you work for?>.

intransitive verb A verb not having a direct object <he *ran* away> <our cat *purrs* when I stroke her>; compare **transitive verb**.

linking verb A verb that links a subject with its predicate (such as *is, feel, look, become, seem*) <she *is* the new manager> <the future *looked* prosperous> <he *has become* disenchanted>.
    Linking verbs such as the so-called "sense" verbs *feel, look, taste,* and *smell* often cause confusion, since writers sometimes mistakenly follow these words with adverbs <this scent *smells nicely*> instead of adjectives <this scent *smells nice*>.

main clause See **clause**.

mass noun A noun that denotes a thing or concept without subdivisions <some *money*> <great *courage*> <the study of *politics*>; compare **count noun**.

modifier A word or phrase that qualifies, limits, or restricts the meaning of another word or phrase. See **adjective**; **adverb**.

mood The form of a verb that shows whether the action or state it denotes is conceived as a fact or otherwise (e.g., a command, possibility, or wish). See **indicative**; **imperative**; **subjunctive**.

nominal A word or group of words that functions as a noun, which may be an adjective <the *good* die young>, a gerund <*seeing* is *believing*>, or an infinitive <*to see* is *to believe*>.

nominative A form, or case, of a noun or pronoun indicating its use as the subject of a verb <three *dogs* trotted by the open door> <later *we* ate dinner>; compare **objective**; **possessive**.

nonrestrictive clause A subordinate or dependent clause, set off by commas, that is not essential to the definiteness of the word it modifies and could be omitted without changing the meaning of the main clause (also called *nonessential clause*) <the author, *who turned out to be charming*, autographed my book>; compare **restrictive clause**. See also **appositive**.

nonstandard Not conforming to the usage generally characteristic of educated native speakers of a language; compare **standard English**. See also **dialect**.

notional agreement Agreement between a subject and a verb or between a pronoun and its antecedent that is determined by meaning rather than form; also called *notional concord*.

Notional agreement contrasts with *formal* or *grammatical agreement* (or *concord*), in which overt grammatical markers determine singular or plural agreement. Formally plural nouns such as *news, means,* and *politics* have long taken singular verbs; so when a plural noun considered a single entity takes a singular verb, notional agreement is at work and no one objects <the *United States is sending* its ambassador>. When a singular noun is used as a collective noun and takes a plural verb or a plural pronoun, we also have notional agreement <the *committee are* meeting on Tuesday> <the *group* wants to publicize *their* views>. Indefinite pronouns are heavily influenced by notional agreement and tend to take singular verbs but plural pronouns <*everyone is* required to show *their* identification>. See also **agreement; collective noun**.

notional concord See **notional agreement**.

noun A member of a class of words that can serve as the subject of a verb, can be singular or plural, can be replaced by a pronoun, and can refer to an entity, quality, state, action, or concept <*boy, Churchill, America, river, commotion, poetry, anguish, constitutionalism*>.

Nouns are used as subjects <the *artist* painted still lifes>, direct objects <critics praised the *artist*>, objects of prepositions <a painting signed by the *artist*>, indirect objects <the council gave the *artist* an award>, retained objects <an artist was given the *award*>, predicate nouns <Petra Smith is this year's *award winner*>, objective complements <they announced Petra Smith as this year's *award winner*>, and appositives <Petra Smith, this year's *award winner*>. See also **collective noun; count noun; mass noun; nominal; proper noun**.

noun phrase A phrase formed by a noun and its modifiers <*portly pensioners* sat sunning themselves> <they proclaimed *all the best features of the new financial offering*>.

number A characteristic of a noun, pronoun, or verb that signifies whether it is singular or plural. See **singular; plural**.

object A noun, noun phrase or clause, or pronoun that directly or indirectly receives the action of a verb or follows a preposition <she rocked *the baby*> <he saw *where they were going*> <I gave *him the news*> <over *the rainbow*> <after *a series of depressing roadhouse gigs*>. See **direct object; indirect object**.

objective A form, or case, of a pronoun indicating its use as the object of a verb or preposition <we spoke to *them* yesterday> <he's a man *whom* everyone should know>; compare **nominative; possessive**.

ordinal number A number designating the place occupied by an item in an ordered sequence <*first, 1st, second, 2nd*>; compare **cardinal number**.

parallelism Repeated syntactical similarities introduced in sentence construction, such as adjacent phrases and clauses that are equivalent, similar, or opposed in meaning and of identical construction <ecological problems of concern *to scientists, to businesspeople,* and *to all citizens*> <he was respected not only *for his intelligence* but also *for his integrity*> <*to err is human, to forgive, divine*>.

Parallelism is mainly used for rhetorical and clarifying effects, and its absence can sometimes create problems for the reader. *Faulty parallelism* is the name given to the use of different constructions within a sentence where you would ordinarily expect to find the same or similar constructions. Very often such faulty parallelism involves the conjunctions *and* and *or* or such other coordinators as *either* and *neither.* Consider the sentence "To allow kids to roam the streets at night and failing to give them constructive alternatives have been harmful." An infinitive phrase (*To allow kids to roam . . .*) and a participial phrase (*failing to give them . . .*) are treated as parallel when they are not. The meaning would be taken in more readily if both phrases were similar; replacing the infinitive with a participle achieves this parallelism (*Allowing kids to roam . . .* and *failing to give them . . .*). When such errors are obvious, they can be puzzling. Often, however, the problem is subtle and hardly noticeable, as in the sentence "Either I must send a fax or make a phone call." Here *or* is expected to precede the same parallel term as *either;* by repositioning *either,* you solve the problem <I must *either* send a fax *or* make a phone call>. Such examples of faulty parallelism are fairly common, but your writing will be more elegant if you avoid them.

parenthetical element An explanatory or modifying word, phrase, or sentence inserted in a passage, set off by parentheses, commas, or dashes <a ruling by the FCC (*Federal Communications Commission*)> <all of us, *to tell the truth*, were amazed> <the examiner chose—*goodness knows why*—to ignore it>.

participial phrase A participle with its complements and modifiers, functioning as an adjective <*hearing the bell ring,* he went to the door>.

participle A verb form having the characteristics of both verb <the noise has *stopped*> and adjective <a *broken* lawn mower>. The *present participle* ends in *-ing* <*fascinating*>; the *past participle* usually ends in *-ed* <*seasoned*>; the *perfect participle* combines *having* with the past participle <*having escaped*>. See also **auxiliary verb; dangling modifier; possessive.**

particle A short word (such as *by, to, in, up*) that expresses some general aspect of meaning or some connective or limiting relation <pay *up*> <heave *to*>.

parts of speech The classes into which words are grouped according to their function in a sentence. See **adjective; adverb; conjunction; interjection; noun; preposition; pronoun; verb.**

passive voice A verb form indicating that the subject of a sentence is being acted upon.

Though often considered a weaker form of expression than the active voice, the passive nevertheless has important uses—for example, when the receiver of the action is more important than the doer <*he is respected* by other scholars>, when the doer is unknown <*the lock had been picked* expertly> or is understood <*Jones was elected* on the third ballot>, or when discretion or tact require that the doer remain anonymous <mistakes *were made*>; compare **active voice**.

person A characteristic of a verb or pronoun that indicates whether a person is speaking (*first person*) <*I am, we are*>, is spoken to (*second person*) <*you are*>, or is spoken about (*third person*) <*he, she, it is; they are*>. See also **number**.

personal pronoun A pronoun that refers to beings and objects and reflects person, number, and often gender.

A personal pronoun's function within a sentence determines its case. The *nominative* case (*I, we, you, he, she, it, they*) is used for pronouns that act as subjects of sentences or as predicate nouns <*he* and *I* will attend> <our new candidate will be *you*>.

The *possessive* case (*my, mine, our, ours, your, yours, his, her, hers, its, their, theirs*) is used for pronouns that express possession or a similar relationship <*our* own offices> <*its* beak>.

The *objective* case (*me, us, you, him, her, it, them*) is used for pronouns that are direct objects, indirect objects, retained objects, or objects of prepositions <he told *me* about the new contract> <she gave *him* the manuscripts> <he was given *them* yesterday> <this is between *you* and *her*>. See also **indefinite pronoun; pronoun**.

phrase A group of two or more words that does not contain both a subject and a verb and that functions as a noun, adjective, adverb, preposition, conjunction, or verb <*the old sinner*> <*stretching for miles*> <*without a limp*> <*in lieu of*> <*as far as*> <*break off*>.

There are seven basic types of phrases. An *absolute phrase* consists of a noun followed by a modifier (such as a participial phrase) and acts independently within a sentence without modifying a particular element of the sentence <he stalked out, *his eyes staring straight ahead*>.

A *gerund phrase* includes a gerund and its modifiers, and it functions as a noun <*eating two doughnuts* is Mike's idea of breakfast>.

An *infinitive phrase* includes an infinitive and may function as a noun, adjective, or adverb <*to do that* would be stupid> <this was an occasion *to remember*> <they struggled *to get free*>.

A *participial phrase* includes a participle and functions as an adjective <*hearing the bell ring*, he went to the door>.

A *verb phrase* consists of a verb and any other terms that either modify it or complete its meaning <he *comes once a month*> <she *will have arrived too late*>. See also **noun phrase; participial phrase**.

plural A word form used to denote more than one <the *Browns*> <the *children*> <these *kinds*> <seven *deer*> <they *are* rich> <*we* do care>.

possessive A form, or case, of a noun or pronoun typically indicating ownership <the *president's* message> <*their* opinions> <*its* meter>; compare **nominative; objective**. See also **double genitive; genitive; possessive with gerund**.

possessive with gerund Use of a possessive form before a gerund.

In "the reason for everyone['s] wanting to join," either the possessive or the common form of *everyone* can be used. Writing handbooks recommend always using the possessive form, but the possessive is mandatory only when the *-ing* word is clearly a noun <*my being* here must embarrass you>. The possessive is quite common with proper nouns <the problem of *John's forgetting* the keys> but rare with plurals <learned of the *bills* [*bills'*] *being* paid>. In most other instances, either the possessive or common form can be used.

predicate   The part of a sentence or clause that expresses what is said of the subject <Hargrove *threw a spitball*> <the teachers from the surrounding towns *are invited to the dinner*> <Jennifer *picked up her books and left to catch the bus*>.

predicate adjective   An adjective that follows a linking verb (such as *be, become, feel, taste, smell, seem*) and modifies the subject <she is *happy* with the outcome> <the milk tastes *sour*> <he seemed *puzzled* by the answer>.

prefix   An affix attached to the beginning of a word to change its meaning <*a*historical> <*pre*sorted> <*anti*-imperialist> <*post*hypnotic> <*over*extended>; compare **suffix**.

preposition   A word or phrase that combines with a noun, pronoun, adverb, or prepositional phrase for use as a modifier or a predication <a book *on* the table> <you're *in* big trouble> <*outside* himself> <*because of* that> <came *from* behind> <peeking *from* behind the fence>.

Despite a widespread belief that a sentence cannot end with a preposition, there is no such grammatical rule. In fact, many sentences require the preposition at the end <what can she be thinking *of*?> <he got the answer he was looking *for*> <there are inconveniences that we must put up *with*> <they haven't been heard *from* yet> and many others are perfectly idiomatic in placing it there <you must know which shelf everything is *on*>.

prepositional phrase   A group of words consisting of a preposition and its complement <*out of debt* is where we'd like to be!> <here is the desk *with the extra file drawer*> <he drove on *in a cold fury*>.

pronoun   Any of a small set of words that are used as substitutes for nouns, phrases, or clauses and refer to someone or something named or understood in the context.

Pronouns can be divided into seven major categories, each with its own function. See **demonstrative pronoun; indefinite pronoun; interrogative pronoun; personal pronoun; reciprocal pronoun; reflexive pronoun; relative pronoun**. See also **agreement**.

proper adjective   An adjective that is derived from a proper noun and is usually capitalized <*Roman* sculpture> <*Jeffersonian* democracy> <*Middle Eastern* situation> <*french* fries>.

proper noun   A noun that names a particular being or thing and is usually capitalized <*Susan, Haydn, New York, December, General Motors, Mormon, Library of Congress, Middle Ages, Spanish Civil War, Reaganomics*>.

reciprocal pronoun   One of the pronouns *each other* and *one another* used in the object position to indicate a mutual action or cross-relationship <chased *each other* around the yard> <fighting with *one another*>.

Reciprocal pronouns may also be used in the possessive <they depend on *each other's* ideas> <borrowed *one another's* sweaters>.

redundancy Repetition of information in a message.

Redundancy is an implicit part of the English language; it reinforces the message. In "Two birds were sitting on a branch," the idea of plurality is expressed three times: by the modifier *two*, by the *-s* on *bird*, and by the plural verb *were*. Many words can be accompanied by small words that give them extra emphasis <*final result*> <*past history*> <*climb up*> <*refer back*>. These are often attacked as needlessly wordy, but in most instances they are harmless, and sometimes they actually promote communication. The use and employment of many more words, phrases, and expressions than are strictly needed, necessary, wanted, or required should be avoided.

reflexive pronoun A pronoun that refers to the subject of the sentence, clause, or verbal phrase in which it stands, and is formed by compounding the personal pronouns *him, her, it, my, our, them,* and *your* with *-self* or *-selves* <she dressed *herself*> <the cook told us to help *ourselves* to seconds> <I *myself* am not concerned>.

relative pronoun One of the pronouns (*that, which, who, whom,* and *whose*) that introduces a subordinate clause which qualifies an antecedent <a man *whom* we can trust> <her book, *which* sold well> <the light *that* failed>.

The relative pronoun *who* typically refers to persons and some animals <a man *who* sought success> <a person *whom* we can trust> <Seattle Slew, *who* won horse racing's Triple Crown>; *which* refers to things and animals <a book *which* sold well> <a dog *which* barked loudly>; and *that* refers to persons, animals, and things <a man *that* sought success> <a dog *that* barked loudly> <a book *that* sold well>.

Whom is commonly used as the object of a preposition in a clause that it introduces <she is someone *for whom* I would gladly work>. However, *who* is commonly used to introduce a question even when it is the object of a preposition <*who* are you going to listen to?> <*who* do you work for?>.

restrictive clause A subordinate clause not set off by commas that is essential to the definiteness of the word it modifies and cannot be omitted without changing the meaning of the main clause (also called *essential clause*) <textbooks *that are not current* should be returned>. See also **appositive**; **nonrestrictive clause**.

sentence A group of words usually containing a subject and a verb, and in writing ending with a period, question mark, or exclamation point. A *simple sentence* consists of one main or independent clause <*she read the announcement in yesterday's paper*>. A *compound sentence* consists of two or more main clauses <*he left at nine o'clock, and they planned to meet at noon*>. A *complex sentence* consists of a main clause and one or more subordinate clauses <*it began to snow before they reached the summit*>. A *compound-complex sentence* consists of two or more main clauses and one or more subordinate clauses <*Susan left for Masters Hall after the presentation; there she joined the new-product workshop, which was already in progress*>. See also **clause**; **subordinate clause**.

A *declarative sentence* makes a statement <*the cow jumped over the moon*>. An *exclamatory sentence* expresses strong feeling <*that's ridiculous!*>. An *interrogative sentence* asks a question <*who said that?*>. An *imperative sentence* expresses a command or request <*get in here now*>.

A *cumulative sentence* is structured so that its main point appears first and is followed by other phrases or clauses expanding on or supporting it. A *periodic sentence* is structured so that its main idea or thrust is suspended until the end, thereby drawing the reader's attention to an emphatic conclusion. A *topic sentence* is a key sentence to which the other sentences in a paragraph are related; it may be placed either at the beginning (as a *lead-in* topic sentence) or the end of a paragraph (as a *terminal* topic sentence.)

sentence adverb An adverb that modifies an entire sentence, rather than a specific word or phrase within the sentence <*fortunately* they had already placed their order>.

sentence fragment A group of words punctuated like a sentence, but without a subject or a predicate or both <*So many men, so many opinions.*> <*Yeah, when you think about it.*>. See also **sentence**; **clause**.

singular A word form denoting one person, thing, or instance <*man*> <*tattoo*> <*eventuality*> <*she* left> <it *is* here>.

split infinitive An infinitive preceded by *to* and an adverb or adverbial phrase <*to ultimately avoid* trouble>.
  Grammarians used to disapprove of the split infinitive, but most now admit that it is not a defect. It is useful when a writer wants to emphasize the adverb <were determined *to thoroughly enjoy* themselves>. See also **infinitive**.

standard English English that is substantially uniform, well-established in the speech and writing of educated people, and widely recognized as acceptable; compare **nonstandard**. See also **dialect**.

subject A word or group of words denoting the entity about which something is said <*he* stopped> <*it*'s clouding up> <*all sixty members* voted> <*orthodoxy on every doctrinal issue* now reigned> <*what they want* is more opportunity> <*going to work* was what she hated most> <*to sing at the Met* had long been a dream of his>.

subject-verb agreement See **agreement**.

subjunctive The form, or mood, of a verb that expresses a condition contrary to fact or follows clauses of necessity, demand, or wishing <if he *were* here, he could answer that> <it's imperative that it *be* broadcast> <they asked that the meeting *proceed*> <I wish they *would come* soon>; compare **imperative**; **indicative**.

subordinate clause A clause that functions as a noun, adjective, or adverb and is attached to a main clause <theirs is a cause *that will prevail*>. See also **clause**; **sentence**.

suffix An affix attached to the end of a word to modify its meaning <editor*s*> <county*wide*> <Hollywood-*ish*> <umbrella-*like*>; compare **prefix**.

superlative See **comparison**.

tense The characteristic of a verb that expresses time present <*see*>, past <*saw*>, or future <*will see*>.
  Aspect involves the use of auxiliary verbs to indicate time relations other

than the simple present, past, or future tenses. The *progressive* tenses express action either in progress <*is seeing*>, in the past <*was seeing*>, or in the future <*will be seeing*>. The *perfect* tenses may express action that began in the past and continues in the present <*has seen*>, that was completed before another past action <*had seen*>, or that will be completed before some future action <*will have seen*>.

transitive verb A verb that acts upon a direct object <she *contributed* money> <he *runs* the store> <*express* your opinion>; compare **intransitive verb**.

verb A word or phrase that is the grammatical center of the predicate and is used to express action, occurrence, or state of being <*leap, carry out, feel, be*>. See also **auxiliary verb; linking verb; mood; voice.**

verbal One of a group of words derived from verbs. See **gerund; infinitive; participle.**

voice The property of a verb that indicates whether the subject acts or is acted upon. See **active voice; passive voice**.

Bibliography

This bibliography lists books on a variety of topics of interest to writers and editors. While the list can only include a fraction of the books on each topic (and some excellent books have had to be omitted), it attempts to include those that are most widely relied on.

Design and Illustration

Bevlin, Marjorie E. *Design through Discovery: An Introduction to Art and Design.* 6th ed. Orlando, Fla.: Harcourt Brace, 1993.

Bringhurst, Robert. *The Elements of Typographic Style.* 2d ed. Point Roberts, Wash.: Hartley & Marks, 1997.

Craig, James. *Designing with Type: A Basic Course in Typography.* 3d ed. New York: Watson-Guptill, 1992.

———. *Production for the Graphic Designer.* 2d ed. New York: Watson-Guptill, 1990.

Evans, Hilary, and Mary Evans. *The Picture Researcher's Handbook: An International Guide to Picture Sources and How to Use Them.* 6th ed. New York: Routledge, 1996.

Graphic Arts Guild Handbook: Pricing and Ethical Guidelines. Current ed. New York: Graphic Artists Guild.

Houp, Kenneth W., et al. *Reporting Technical Information.* 9th ed. Needham Heights, Mass.: Allyn & Bacon, 1997.

King, Jean C., and Tony Esposito. *The Designer's Guide to PostScript Text Type.* 2d ed. New York: Van Nostrand Reinhold, 1993.

Lee, Marshall. *Bookmaking: The Illustrated Guide to Editing/Design/Production.* 3d ed. New York: Norton, 1998.

Parker, Roger C. *Roger Parker's One-Minute Designer.* Indianapolis: Que, 1993.

Parker, Roger C., and Carrie Beverly. *Looking Good in Print: Deluxe CD-ROM Edition.* Chapel Hill, N.C.: Ventana Press, 1996.

Parker, Roger C., and Joe Grossman. *The Makeover Book: 101 Design Solutions for Online and Desktop Publishing.* 2d ed. Chapel Hill, N.C.: Ventana Press, 1996.

Silver, Gerald A., and Myrna L. Silver. *Modern Graphic Arts Paste-up.* 3d ed. Dubuque, Ia.: Business and Educational Technologies, 1992.

Stevenson, George A. *Graphic Arts Encyclopedia.* 3d ed. New York: McGraw-Hill, 1990.

Tufte, Edward R. *Envisioning Information*. Cheshire, Conn.: Graphics Press, 1990.

———. *The Visual Display of Quantitative Information*. Cheshire, Conn.: Graphics Press, 1983.

———. *Visual Explanations: Images and Quantities, Evidence and Narrative*. Cheshire, Conn.: Graphics Press, 1997.

White, Jan V. *Graphic Design for the Electronic Age*. New York: Watson-Guptill, 1988.

———. *Mastering Graphics: Design and Production Made Easy*. New York: Bowker, 1983.

———. *Using Charts and Graphs: 1000 Ideas for Getting Attention*. New York: Bowker, 1984.

Indexing

Lancaster, F. W. *Indexing and Abstracting in Theory and Practice*. Champaign: Univ. of Illinois Press, 1991.

Mulvany, Nancy C. *Indexing Books*. Chicago: Univ. of Chicago Press, 1994.

Wellisch, Hans H. *Indexing from A to Z*. 2d ed. New York: H. W. Wilson, 1996.

Language and Editing

Business Writing

The AMA Style Guide for Business Writing. New York: AMACOM, 1996.

Barry, Robert E. *Business English for the Nineties*. 2d ed. Upper Saddle River, N.J.: Prentice Hall, 1993.

Brusaw, Charles T., Gerald J. Alred, and Walter E. Oliu. *The Business Writer's Handbook*. 5th ed. New York: St. Martin's, 1997.

Keithley, Erwin F., and Margaret H. Thompson. *English for Modern Business*. 6th ed. Burr Ridge, Ill.: Irwin, 1990.

Lesikar, Raymond V., and John D. Pettit. *Report Writing for Business*. 10th ed. Burr Ridge, Ill.: Irwin, 1997.

Poe, Roy W., and Rosemary T. Fruehling. *Business Communication: A Problem-Solving Approach*. 4th ed. New York: McGraw-Hill, 1989.

Editing and Proofreading

Butcher, Judith. *Copy-Editing: The Cambridge Handbook for Authors, Editors and Publishers*. 3d ed. New York: Cambridge Univ. Press, 1992.

Judd, Karen. *Copyediting: A Practical Guide.* 2d ed. Menlo Park, Calif.: Crisp, 1991.

Plotnik, Arthur. *The Elements of Editing: A Modern Guide for Editors and Journalists.* New York: Macmillan, 1982.

Stainton, Elsie Myers. *The Fine Art of Copyediting.* New York: Columbia Univ. Press, 1991.

Tarutz, Judith A. *Technical Editing: The Practical Guide for Editors and Writers.* Reading, Mass.: Addison-Wesley, 1992.

Grammar, Usage, and Composition

The American Heritage Book of English Usage. Boston: Houghton Mifflin, 1996.

Bailey, Edward P., Jr. *Plain English at Work: A Guide to Writing and Speaking.* New York: Oxford Univ. Press, 1996.

Bailey, Edward P., Jr., and Philip A. Powell. *The Practical Writer.* 5th ed. Orlando, Fla.: Harcourt Brace, 1995.

Baker, Sheridan. *The Practical Stylist: With Readings and Handbook.* 8th ed. New York: 1997.

Bernstein, Theodore M. *The Careful Writer: A Modern Guide to English Usage.* New York: Atheneum, 1977.

Day, Robert A. *How to Write and Publish a Scientific Paper.* 4th ed. Phoenix: Oryx, 1994.

Ebbitt, Wilma R. and David R. *Index to English.* 8th ed. New York: Oxford Univ. Press, 1990.

Flesch, Rudolf. *The Art of Readable Writing.* Rev. ed. New York: Macmillan, 1986.

Follett, Wilson. *Modern American Usage.* Ed. Jacques Barzun. New York: Hill & Wang, 1966.

Fowler, H. W. *The New Fowler's Modern English Usage.* 3d ed. Ed. R. W. Burchfield. New York: Oxford Univ. Press, 1996.

Garner, Bryan A. *The Elements of Legal Style.* New York: Oxford Univ. Press, 1991.

Graves, Robert, and Alan Hodge. *The Use and Abuse of the English Language.* 2d ed. New York: Marlowe, 1995.

Greenbaum, Sidney. *The Oxford English Grammar.* New York: Oxford Univ. Press, 1996.

Johnson, Edward D. *The Handbook of Good English.* 2d ed. New York: Washington Square Press, 1992.

Merriam-Webster's Dictionary of English Usage. Springfield, Mass.: Merriam-Webster, 1989.

Quirk, Randolph, Sidney Greenbaum, Geoffrey Leech, and Jan Svartvik. *A Comprehensive Grammar of the English Language.* London: Longman, 1985.

Randall, Bernice. *Webster's New World Guide to Current American Usage.* New York: Simon and Schuster, 1988.

Strunk, William, Jr., and E. B. White. *The Elements of Style.* 3d ed. New York: Macmillan, 1979.

Williams, Joseph M. *Style: Toward Clarity and Grace.* Reprint. Chicago: Univ. of Chicago Press, 1995.

Wilson, Kenneth G. *The Columbia Guide to Standard American English.* New York: Columbia Univ. Press, 1993.

Zinsser, William. *On Writing Well: An Informal Guide to Writing Nonfiction.* 5th ed. New York: HarperCollins, 1994.

Publishing

Appelbaum, Judith. *How to Get Happily Published: A Complete and Candid Guide.* 5th ed. New York: HarperCollins, 1998.

Bailey, Herbert S., Jr. *The Art and Science of Book Publishing.* Austin: Univ. of Texas Press, 1980. Reprint, Athens: Ohio Univ. Press, 1990.

Balkin, Richard. *A Writer's Guide to Book Publishing.* 3d ed. New York: Plume, 1994.

Dessauer, John P. *Book Publishing: The Basic Introduction.* 3d ed. New York: Continuum, 1993.

LMP: Literary Market Place. New York: Bowker. Annual.

Publisher's Trade List Annual. New York: Bowker. Annual.

Publishing Law and Copyright

Crawford, Tad. *Legal Guide for the Visual Artist: The Professional's Handbook.* 3d ed. New York: Allworth, 1994.

Crawford, Tad, and Tony Lyons. *The Writer's Legal Guide.* Rev. ed. New York: Allworth, 1996.

Latman, Alan, et al. *Copyright for the Nineties: Cases and Materials.* 4th ed. Charlottesville, Va.: Michie Butterworth, 1993.

Lindey, Alexander, and Michael Landau. *Lindey on Entertainment, Publishing and the Arts: Agreements and the Law.* 2d ed. 4 vols. New York: Clark Boardman Callaghan, 1980.

Perle, E. Gabriel, and John Taylor Williams. *Publishing Law Handbook.* 2d ed. Upper Saddle River, N. J.: Prentice Hall, 1992.

Sack, Robert D., and Sandra S. Baron. *Libel, Slander, and Related Problems.* 2d ed. New York: Practising Law Institute, 1994.

Strong, William S. *The Copyright Book: A Practical Guide.* 4th ed. Cambridge, Mass.: MIT Press, 1992.

Reference Books

Biography

American Men and Women of Science, 1998–99: A Biographical Directory of Today's Leaders in Physical, Biological, and Related Sciences. 20th ed. 8 vols. New York: Bowker, 1997.

International Who's Who. London: Europa Publications. Annual.

Merriam-Webster's Biographical Dictionary. Rev. ed. Springfield, Mass: Merriam-Webster, 1995.

Who's Who: An Annual Biographical Dictionary. New York: St. Martin's. Annual.

Who's Who in America. Chicago: Marquis. Annual.

Computers

Freedman, Alan. *The Computer Glossary.* 7th ed. New York: AMACOM, 1994.

Microsoft Press Computer Dictionary. 3d ed. Redmond, Wash.: Microsoft Press, 1997.

IBM Dictionary of Computing. 10th ed. Comp. George McDaniel. New York: McGraw-Hill, 1993.

Pfaffenberger, Bryan. *Webster's New World Dictionary of Computer Terms.* 6th ed. New York: Macmillan, 1997.

Dictionaries

Acronyms, Initialisms, and Abbreviations Dictionary. Ed. Mary R. Bonk. 3 vols. Detroit: Gale Research. Annual.

De Sola, Ralph, et al. *Abbreviations Dictionary.* 9th ed. Boca Raton, Fla.: CRC Press, 1994.

Merriam-Webster's Collegiate Dictionary. 10th ed. Springfield, Mass.: Merriam-Webster, 1993. Updated annually.

Webster's Third New International Dictionary. Springfield, Mass.: Merriam-Webster, 1961. Addendum, 1993.

General

Barzun, Jacques, and Henry F. Graff. *The Modern Researcher.* 5th ed. Orlando, Fla.: Harcourt Brace, 1992.

Dictionary of Occupational Titles. 4th ed. Washington, D.C.: GPO, 1991.

Encyclopedia of Associations. 3 vols. Detroit: Gale Research. Annual.

Gates, Jean Key. *Guide to the Use of Libraries and Information Sources.* 7th ed. New York: McGraw-Hill, 1993.

The New Encyclopaedia Britannica. 15th ed. 32 vols. Chicago: Encyclopaedia Britannica. Updated annually.

Ulrich's International Periodicals Directory. New York: Bowker. Annual.

United States Government Manual. Washington, D.C.: GPO. Annual.

Whitaker's Books in Print. London: J. Whitaker. Annual.

World Almanac and Book of Facts. New York: St. Martin's. Annual.

Geography

Merriam-Webster's Geographical Dictionary. 3d ed. Springfield, Mass.: Merriam-Webster, 1997.

Political Handbook of the World. Ed. Arthur S. Banks et al. Current ed. Binghamton, N.Y.: CSA Publications.

The Statesman's Year-Book: A Statistical, Political and Economic Account of the States of the World. Ed. Brian Hunter. New York: St. Martin's. Annual.

Law

Black's Law Dictionary. 6th ed. St. Paul, Minn.: West, 1992.

The Bluebook: A Uniform System of Citation. Current ed. Cambridge, Mass.: Harvard Law Review Assoc.

Literature

Benét's Reader's Encyclopedia. 4th ed. Ed. Bruce Murphy. New York: HarperCollins, 1996.

Merriam-Webster's Encyclopedia of Literature. Springfield, Mass.: Merriam-Webster, 1995.

Merriam-Webster's Reader's Handbook. Springfield, Mass.: Merriam-Webster, 1997.

The Oxford Companion to English Literature. 5th ed. Ed. Margaret Drabble. New York: Oxford Univ. Press, 1995.

The Reader's Adviser. 14th ed. Ed. Marion Sader. 6 vols. New York: Bowker, 1994.

Medicine

Dorland's Illustrated Medical Dictionary. Current ed. Philadelphia: Saunders.

Merriam-Webster's Medical Desk Dictionary. Springfield, Mass.: Merriam-Webster, 1997.

Physicians' Desk Reference. Montvale, N.J.: Medical Economics. Annual.

Stedman's Medical Dictionary. Current ed. Baltimore: Williams & Wilkins.

Quotations

Bartlett, John. *Familiar Quotations: A Collection of Passages, Phrases, and Proverbs Traced to Their Sources in Ancient and Modern Literature.* 16th ed. Ed. Justin Kaplan. Boston: Little, Brown, 1992.

The Oxford Dictionary of Quotations. 4th ed. Ed. Angela Portington. New York: Oxford Univ. Press, 1996.

Science and Technology

McGraw-Hill Dictionary of Scientific and Technical Terms. 5th ed. Ed. Sybil P. Parker. New York: McGraw-Hill, 1993.

Style Manuals

Humanities, Journalism, and General

The Associated Press Stylebook and Libel Manual. 6th ed. Ed. Norm Goldstein. Reading, Mass.: Addison-Wesley, 1996.

The Chicago Manual of Style. 14th ed. Chicago: Univ. of Chicago Press, 1993.

Gibaldi, Joseph. *MLA Handbook for Writers of Research Papers.* 4th ed. New York: Modern Language Association of America, 1995.

Keithley, Erwin M., Marie E. Flatly, and Philip J. Schreiner. *A Manual of Style for Business Letters, Memos, and Reports.* 4th ed. Cincinnati: South-Western, 1989.

The New York Public Library Writer's Guide to Style and Usage. New York: Harper-Collins, 1994.

The New York Times Manual of Style and Usage. Ed. Lewis Jordan. New York: Times Books, 1982.

Sabin, William A. *The Gregg Reference Manual.* 8th ed. New York: Glencoe–McGraw-Hill, 1996.

Turabian, Kate L., et al. *A Manual for Writers of Term Papers, Theses, and Dissertations.* 6th ed. Chicago: Univ. of Chicago Press, 1996.

U. S. Government Printing Office Style Manual. Washington, D.C.: GPO, 1984.

U. S. News and World Report Stylebook for Writers and Editors. 8th ed. Ed. Robert O. Grover. Washington, D.C.: U. S. News, 1997.

van Leunen, Mary-Claire. *A Handbook for Scholars.* 2d ed. New York: Oxford Univ. Press, 1992.

Words into Type. Based on studies by Marjorie E. Skillin and Robert M. Gay. 3d ed. Upper Saddle River, N.J.: Prentice Hall, 1974.

Science and Mathematics

The ACS Style Guide: A Manual for Authors and Editors. 2d ed. Ed. Janet S. Dodd. Washington, D.C.: American Chemical Society, 1997.

American Medical Association Manual of Style. 8th ed. Ed. Cheryl Iverson et al. Baltimore: Williams & Wilkins, 1989.

A Manual for Authors of Mathematical Papers. 8th ed. Providence: American Mathematical Society, 1990.

Publication Manual of the American Psychological Association. 4th ed. Washington, D.C.: American Psychological Association, 1994.

Science and Technical Writing: A Manual of Style. Ed. Philip Rubens. New York: Henry Holt, 1992.

Scientific Style and Format: The CBE Manual for Authors, Editors, and Publishers. 6th ed. New York: Cambridge Univ. Press, 1994.

Swanson, Ellen. *Mathematics into Type: Copy Editing and Proofreading of Mathematics for Editorial Assistants and Authors.* Rev. ed. Providence: American Mathematical Society, 1986.

Typesetting, Printing, and Binding

Aldrich-Ruenzel, Nancy, ed. *Designer's Guide to Print Production: A Step-by-Step Publishing Book.* New York: Watson-Guptill, 1990.

Chicago Guide to Preparing Electronic Manuscripts. Chicago: Univ. of Chicago Press, 1987.

Goldfarb, Charles F. *The SGML Handbook.* Oxford: Clarendon Press, 1990.

Green, Phil. *Quality Control for Print Buyers: How to Get the Best from Your Printers.* New York: Chapman and Hall, 1993.

Lucas, Charles. *Handbook of Printing Processes.* Pittsburgh: Graphic Arts Technical Foundation, 1994.

Lyman, Ralph. *Binding and Finishing.* Ed. Pamela Groff. Pittsburgh: Graphic Arts Technical Foundation, 1993.

Parsons, Bill. *Graphic Arts Prepress: A Hands-on Introduction.* Albany, N.Y.: Delmar, 1994.

Pocket Pal: A Graphic Arts Production Handbook. Current ed. Memphis: International Paper Co.

Potter, Geoff. *The Publisher's Guide to Binding and Finishing.* New York: Chapman and Hall, 1991.

Travis, Brian E., and Dale C. Waldt. *The SGML Implementation Guide: A Blueprint for SGML Migration.* New York: Springer, 1995.

Van Herwijnen, Eric. *Practical SGML.* 2d ed. Boston: Kluwer Academic, 1994.

Von Hagen, Bill. *SGML for Dummies.* San Francisco: IDG, 1997.

Index

A

Abbreviate, copyediting mark, 288–289
Abbreviations, 79–80
   a or *an* with, 83
   of academic degrees, 82, 85, 89
   in addresses, 85–86
   of amino acids, 126
   with ampersand, 84
   with apostrophe, 2
   at beginning of sentences, 81
   of Bible books, 84, 235
   in bibliographies, 226, 228
   capitalization of, 38, 81
   of chemical symbols (illus.), 122
   in compound words, 82–83
   in computer text, 133
   and contractions, 80
   in dates, 85
   in design specifications (illus.), 344
   division of, 79
   of genus and species names, 130
   with hyphen, 23, 82–83
   in indexes, 245, 253, 260, 265
   inflected forms of, 2, 23
   of international system of units, 119
   of Latin words and phrases, 86–87,
      211, 215–216, 234
   in mathematical copy, 113
   of months, 214, 228
   with names, 88
   within parentheses, 24
   with period, 26–27, 79–80
   plural forms, 58–59, 81–82
   possessive forms, 66, 82
   of proper nouns and adjectives,
      38, 81
   punctuation of, 79–80
   of scientific terms, 88
   with slash, 34, 80
   in source notes, 214, 215–216,
      233–234
   in style sheet, 282
   in thermochemistry, 125
   of units of measurement, 90, 107
   variation in styling of, 79
Abstractions, 38

Academic titles, in indexes, 260
Accent marks, alphabetization of,
   257–258. *See also under individual*
   marks
Acid-free paper, 318
Acknowledgments, 318
Acronyms, in computer text, 133
act, 235
Acute accent
   in biology and medical copy, 128
   in classical Greek, 164–165
   in Czech, 163
   in French, 158
   in Italian, 160
   in Pinyin, 170
   in Polish, 162
   in Portuguese, 160
   in Spanish, 156
A.D., 83, 100
Addresses, street
   abbreviations in, 85–86
   capitalization of in French, 157–158
   numbers in, 98
   punctuation of, 14, 15
Adjective-plus-noun compounds, in index
   headings, 241
Adjectives
   capitalization of in Dutch, 153
   capitalization of in French, 157
   capitalization of in German, 151
   compound, 70–74
   in compound words, 68, 69
   in index headings, 241
   nouns used as, 71–72
Administration, 43
Adverbial clauses and phrases, 8–9
Adverbs
   compound, 74–75
   conjunctive, 32–33
   as modifiers of compounds, 73
Advertisements, 315
Age, numbers for, 107
Aggregation signs, 113–114
A.H., 100
A-head, 338
   sample design specification (illus.),
      345

ALA-LC Romanization Tables: Transliteration Schemes for Non-Roman Scripts, 1997 Edition, 150
Align
  copyediting mark, 289
  proofreader mark, 304
Alignment, of table columns, 178–180
Allocation of errors, 304, 309–310
Alphabet. *See* Letters of the alphabet
Alphabetization
  of bibliographies, 230–231
  of index entries, 242, 257–259, 262–263, 265
Alterations, in quotations, 3, 141–144
a.m., 89, 106
American Society of Indexers, 268
Ampersand, 84, 226
An, a, 83
  in table titles, 174
  in titles of works, 264
And, 226
  with equations, 111
  replaced by slash, 34
And/or, 34
Angle brackets, 149. *See also* Guillemets
  in generic tagging, 351
Animal hybrids, 131
Animal names, 39, 59
Annals, 228
Annotated bibliography, 223, 230–231
Anonymous, Anon., 233
Apostrophe, 1–2
  in compound words, 69
  copyediting mark, 286
  in Italian, 159
  and plurals, 58–59, 61, 62, 63
  and possessives, 63–65
  proofreader mark, 306
  in Scandinavian languages, 153–154
  to show omission, 2
Appendixes, 319
Appositives, 4, 9, 13
  in mathematical copy, 111
Arabic
  capitalization in, 169
  transliteration of, 168–169
  word division in, 169
Arabic numerals
  in biology and medical copy, 129
  to designate virus types, 132
  in illustration numbers, 199
  use in documentation, 235
Archaic spelling, in quotations, 143

Archival material
  in bibliographies, 229–230
  in microform, 233
Arrays, 116
Arrow, in chemistry copy, 124
Art. *See* Illustration elements; Illustrations
Art, works of
  permission to use, 321
  titles of, 52, 233
Article titles. *See* Titles of works, articles
Articles
  alphabetization, 258
  indefinite, 83
  in table titles, 174
  in titles of works, 52–53, 264
Ascender, 323
Association names. *See* Organizations, names of
Asterisk, 211
  in mathematical copy, 113, 118
  in physical science copy, 126
  in table references, 183–184
Astronomy, 51, 121
Atomic number, 123
Attribution
  of epigraphs, 144
  of poetry, 145
  of sources within text, 17–18
Attributive position of compounds, 71–74
Author, corporate, 211–212, 218
Author, as indexer, 238
Author, name of
  in bibliographies, 224, 227, 230
  in parenthetical references, 218–220
  in source notes, 211–212, 214
  in subsequent references, 215–216
Author queries (illus.), 276–278
  regarding tables, 186
Author-date system, 218–219
Author-page system, 219–220
Authors, multiple, 218, 224
Author's manuscript checklist, 274–275
Author's revisions
  of copyedited manuscript, 273, 297, 300
  of proofs, 302–303
Awards, 39

B

Back matter, 319
  appendixes, 319

bibliography, 319
  endnotes, 319
  glossary, 319
  index, 319
Back-cover copy, 313
Bar codes, 314
Bar graphs, 189–190
Baseline, 323
Base-to-base measurement, 326
Basis weight, 358
Baskerville (illus.), 331
  legibility of, 335
B.C., 83, 100
B.C.E., 100
Beginning of sentences and phrases,
  36–38
  use of numerals in, 92
Belgian surnames, in indexes, 261
Berne Convention, copyrights and, 319,
  320
Between, used to indicate range, 96
B-head, 338
  sample design specification (illus.),
  345
Bible and biblical books, 50, 84
  documentation of, 5–6, 235
Biblical names, 49, 65
Bibliographies, 207, 223–224, 319
  annotated, 223, 230–231
  author's name in, 224, 227, 229
  books in, 224–227
  copyediting, 279, 295–296
  dates in, 226, 228–229, 231–235,
    236–237
  format, 5–6, 230–231
  in manuscript preparation, 275
  periodical articles in, 227–229
  sample design specification (illus.),
    346
  in science vs. humanities copy,
    223–230
  style sheet notes on, 282–283
  unpublished materials in, 229–230
Billion, 91
Binding, cl, 361–363
  adhesive, 362
  burst, 362
  of endpapers, 361
  hardcover or case, 361
  mechanical, 362
  notch, 362
  of paperbacks, 362
  perfect, 362

plastic-comb, 362
  preparation of signatures for, 361
  saddle, 363
  side-wired, 363
  Smyth sewing used in, 362
  of spine materials, 362
  spiral, 363
  wire, 363
Binomial nomenclature, 50, 88
Binomials, 129
Biology
  Arabic and Roman numerals in, 129
  Greek letters in, 129
  signs and symbols, 127–128, (illus.)
    138
  taxonomic nomenclature, 129–132
Birth name, in indexes, 245, 259
Bitmapping, 349
Black type, 324
Blanks, 315
Block quotations, styling, 30, 139–141
Block-style paragraph, 341
The Bluebook: A Uniform System of Citation,
  234
Bluelines. *See* Blues
Blueprint, 196
Blues, 312, 356
  checklist for proofreading, 312–313
Blurbs, 144–145
Boards, 205
Bodoni (illus.), 331
  x-height of (illus.), 325–326
Body, of table, 178
Bold italic, of vectors, 116, 117
Boldface italic, 324
Boldface type, 324
  copyediting mark, 286
  in endnotes, 211
  general use of, 56–57
  in indexes, 243, 254
  in mathematical copy, 109
  proofreader mark, 304
  of vectors, 116
  of volume numbers, 228
Book blues, 273, 312
Book manufacturing. *See* Typesetting;
    Printing; Binding
Book titles. *See* Titles of works, books
Bookland EAN, 314
Books
  in bibliographies, 224–227
  margins in, 338
  running heads in, 336

Books *(continued)*
  sidebars in, 339–340
  in source notes, 211–213
  in subsequent references, 215–216
Books, parts of
  back matter, 319
  in bibliographies, 225
  front matter, 314–318
  jacket or cover, 313–314
  reference number to, 47, 107
  in source notes, 212
  titles of, 52–53
Bottom of page, proofreading, 311
B.P., 100
Braces
  in computer commands, 133
  in generic tagging, 352, 354–355
  in mathematical copy, 113–114
  in tables, 182
Bracketed serifs, 329
Brackets, 3–4
  in bibliographies, 226, 228, 229
  in chemistry copy, 125
  in citation-sequence system, 220
  with comma, 16
  in computer commands, 133
  copyediting mark, 286
  to mark index entries, 247
  in mathematical copy, 113–114
  with matrices, 116
  with other punctuation, 4
  with parentheses, 3–4
  with period, 27
  in quotations, 142, 143
Brand names, 53–54
Breakout, 340
Breve, use of in Latin, 161
Brightness, of paper, 359
Broadside tables, 185
Broadway (illus.), 328
Built-up form, of fractions, 114
Bulk, of paper, 359
Bulleted lists. *See* Lists
Bullets, 340
  in page design, 339
Burst binding, 362
Business name, in indexes, 261

C

Cabinet ordinance system, of Japanese
  romanization, 171
Caledonia (illus.), 331

Call out
  art, 204, 296
  tables, 172, 187
Callout, 340
Camera-ready art, 296, 300, 309
Cap height, 323
Capital letters, 323
  in mathematical copy, 109
Capitalization, 36–54
  of abbreviations, 38, 81
  of abstractions, 38
  of academic degrees, 38–39
  of animal names, 39
  in Arabic and Hebrew, 169
  of awards and prizes, 39
  at beginnings of sentences and
    phrases, 36–38
  in bibliographies, 225, 227, 228, 229
  of block quotations, 139–140
  of chemical symbol abbreviations, 122
  in Chinese, 170
  of column headings, 177
  in compound words, 45
  of computer commands, 133–134
  of computer terms, 132
  copyediting mark, 285
  of cross-references, 255
  in Czech, 163
  of derivatives of proper names, 39–40
  of drug names, 132
  in Dutch, 153
  for emphasis, 56
  in foreign languages, 148, 149
  in French, 157–158
  of genus names, 129
  of geographical terms, 40–41
  in German, 151–152
  of governmental and political bodies,
    41–43
  following Greek letters, 129
  of historical periods and events, 43–44,
    99–100
  in hyphenated compounds, 45
  in indexes, 253
  in Italian, 159
  in Japanese, 171
  of judicial bodies, 42
  of labels, 56
  in Latin, 161
  of legal material, 45
  of letters representing shapes, 55
  in lists, 102–103
  of medical terms, 45–46
  of military terms, 46

of musical compositions, 53
of numerical designations, 46–47
of organization names, 47
of parenthetical elements, 25, 36
of people, 47–49
of plant names, 39
of poetry, 37
in Portuguese, 160
of prayers, 50
proofreader mark, 304
of proper nouns and adjectives, 38–54, 81
in quotations, 3, 36–37, 139–140, 141–142, 143
of religious terms, 49–50
in Russian, 167–168
in Scandinavian languages, 154
of scientific terms, 50–52
of signs, 56
in source notes, 212, 214, 215
in Spanish, 156
of table titles, 174
of time periods and dates, 52
of titles of works, 52–53
of trademarks, 53–54
of transportation, 54
of viruses, 131–132
of word following colon, 39
Captions, 200
    editing, 204
    in galley proofs, 302
    style sheet notes on, 282
Carbon-copy notations, 6
Caret, 283
    in typemarked mathematical copy, 118
Carryover instructions, in proofreading, 308
Case fractions, 114
Cases in law, 45, 234–235
Case-sensitive text, 134
Caslon, descenders in, 326
Caslon Antique (illus.), 328
Casting off index, 269–270
Castoff, 342–343
Cataloging number, 229
Cataloging-in-Publication Data. *See* CIP data
C.E., 100
Cedilla
    in French, 159
    in Portuguese, 160
Celestial objects, 51
Center, proofreader mark, 304

Centered dot, 115
    in physical science copy, 126
    proofreader mark, 304
    typemarking, 118
Cents, 103–104
Centuries, 99
Century Schoolbook (illus.), 332
    descenders in, 326
Chapter, chap., 235
Chapter number, sample design specification (illus.), 345
Chapter titles, 53
    sample design specification (illus.), 345
Chapter-ending pages, proofreading, 311
Chapter-opening pages, folios and, 337
C-head, 338
    sample design specification (illus.), 345
Chemical elements and compounds, 72, 88
Chemical formulas, 4
Chemical terms, alphabetizing in indexes, 266
Chemistry
    line breaks in chemistry copy, 127
    modifiers in chemistry copy, 127
    names of elements and compounds (illus.), 121–122
    punctuation and relationship in chemistry copy, 124–126
    signs and symbols (illus.), 137–138
    spacing in chemical compounds, 124
    subscripts and superscripts in chemical symbols, 123
Chicago Manual of Style, 208
Chinese
    capitalization in, 170
    names in indexes, 262
    romanization of, 169–170
    word division in, 170
Chronological order, of index entries, 242
Church, 50
Church names, 104
CIP data, 316–317
    in blues, 313
Circumflex accent
    in classical Greek, 165
    in French, 158
    in Portuguese, 160
Citation, of binomial authors, 130
Citations, legal, 45, 234, 245, 266

Citation-sequence system, 220–221
 advantages and disadvantages of, 221
Clarendon (illus.), 332
Class, taxonomic, 131
Classical Greek, 163–164
 transliteration of (illus.), 164–165
 word division in, 165
Classical names, 65
Clauses
 adverbial, 8–9
 with colon, 4–5
 with conjunctive adverbs, 32–33
 elliptical, 33
 main (independent), 7, 32–33
 and parentheses, 23, 25
 restrictive and nonrestrictive, 8–9
 subordinate (dependent), 8–9
Clerical titles, in indexes, 260
Clip art, 203
Clip books, 203
Close-up, 285
Close-up sign, 283–285, 305
Coauthors
 in bibliographies, 224
 in source notes, 211–212
Code of Federal Regulations, 234
Coding, of text elements by author, 274.
 See also Generic tagging; Typemarking
Colon, 4–6
 with appositives, 4
 in biblical references, 5
 in bibliographies, 5–6, 226, 229, 235
 capitalization of word following, 37
 changing to period, 287
 with clauses, 4–5
 with comma, 16
 copyediting mark, 286
 and dash compared, 16, 17
 in dialogue, 141
 in French, 157
 in indented index, 253
 as an introductory mark, 5
 to mark index entries, 246–247
 in paragraph index, 253
 with parentheses, 6
 in parenthetical references, 218–219
 with phrases, 4–5
 with quotation marks, 5, 6, 31
 with quotations, 5, 139
 in ratios, 5–6, 105
 in salutation of letter, 6
 in source notes, 211–215

 spacing of, 6
 in subentry cross-references, 255
 in time expressions, 5–6, 105–106
 in titles, 6
 words followed by in alphabetization,
 258
Color art, 197
 color separation, 197–198
 four-color printing, 357
 two-color printing and color matching,
 198–199, 357
Color key, 357
Color matching systems, 199
Color names, 73–74
Color printing, 357
Color screens, 199
Color separation, 197–198, 357
Column, col., 116
Column graphs, 189–190
Column headings, in tables, 176–178
Columns, 178
 alignment, 178–180
 totals, 180
 of words (illus.), 180–181
Combining forms, 75–78
Comillas, 155
Comma, 6–16
 with addresses, 14
 with appositives, 9, 13
 to avoid ambiguity, 15
 in bibliographies, 225, 226, 230, 235
 binomial nomenclature and, 129
 changing to period, 287
 after chemical expression, 124
 as clause connector, 7–9
 with colon, 16
 with compound predicates, 7–8
 with contrasting expressions, 10–11
 with coordinate modifiers, 12
 copyediting mark, 286
 with dash, 16, 17
 and dash compared, 10, 16
 with dates, 14
 with degrees and titles, 15
 between equations, 111
 with exclamation point, 16, 22
 in index entries, 240, 243, 251, 253
 in international system of units, 120,
 121
 with introductory and interrupting
 elements, 9–10
 and inverted order, 16
 with items in a series, 11–12

with mathematical coordinates, 112
in mathematical copy, 115
with names, 15
with nonrestrictive clauses, 9
with numbers, 14–15, 95
in numbers in tables, 178
omission of, 6, 7, 8–13, 95
with omitted words, 14
with other punctuation, 16
with parenthetical elements, 218–219
with question mark, 16
in questions, 13
with quotation marks, 16, 31
in quotations, 12–14, 140
with restrictive clauses, 8, 13–14
and semicolon, 16, 33–34
with sentence within a sentence, 13, 25
serial, 11–12
in source notes, 211, 213, 214
with subordinate clauses and phrases,
    8–9
in typefaces, 330
words followed by in alphabetization,
    258
Comma fault, 7
Company, Co., 84
Company names, 15, 47, 84
Compass points, 40, 84–85
Compiler, Comp.
in bibliographies, 225
in source notes, 212
Complimentary close, 15, 38
Compositor. *See* Typesetter
Compound adjectives, 70–74
Compound adverbs, 74–75
Compound names, in indexes,
    259–260
Compound nouns, 67–70
Compound predicates, 7–8
Compound verbs, 75
Compound words, 22, 67–68
    abbreviated, 81–82
    capitalization of, 45
    division of in French, 158
    division of in German, 152
    division of in Latin, 161
    division of in Spanish, 156
    hyphenated, 45, 67, 82–83, 95–96
    open, 67
    permanent, 67
    plural, 59–60
    solid, 67
    temporary, 67

Compounds, chemical, 121–122
Computer design, 343
Computer generation
    of bar and column graphs,
        189–190
    of equations, 109–110
    of flowcharts, 192
    of halftones, 194–195
    of line art, 193
    of line graphs, 190
    of pie charts, 188
    of tables, 172
    of typeset material, 348–351
Computer software
    bibliographic compilation using,
        208–209
    documentation of, 236
    indexing programs, 268
    page-layout, 343
Computer terms, 51–52, 88, 236
    acronyms, 133
    capitalization of, 133
    commands, 133–134
Condensed face, 324
Congressional documents and bills,
    documentation of, 233–234
Congressional Record, 234
Conjunctions
    in alphabetization, 258
    capitalization of in titles, 52–53
    coordinating, 7, 32–33
    correlative, 11
    and semicolon, 32–33
Conjunctive adverbs, 32–33
Consistency, as copyediting goal, 276,
    278
Constitutions, documentation of, 234
Contact screens, 194–195
Content notes, 207
Contents. *See* Table of contents
Continued entries, 270
Continued tables, 186
Continuous-tone art (illus.), 193–197
    as line art, 195–196
Contractions, 2, 80
Contracts, indexing, 239
Contrasting expressions, 10–11
Coordinating conjunctions, capitalization
    of, 212
Copy, 272. *See also* Manuscript
Copy editor, 272
    freelance, 276
    for mathematical copy, 108

Copyediting, 275–278
  art and tables, 296
  basic tasks of, 278–280
  copyedited pages (illus.), 298–299
  copyediting marks, 283, 285–290,
    (illus.) 291–293
  cross-references, 294
  electronic editing, 300–301
  extracts, 294–295
  headings, 290
  letterspacing, 327
  lists, 294
  marking the manuscript, 280–281
  notes and bibliographies, 295–296
  style sheet, 281–283, (illus.) 284
  tables, 117, 186–188
  tag (illus.), 276–277
  trafficking the manuscript, 297, 300
  typemarking, 296–297
Copyediting marks, 283, 285–290, (illus.)
    291–293
Copyright, 319–321
  international, 320
  registration of, 320–321
  use of copyrighted material, 321
Copyright line, 316
Copyright notice, need for, 319–320
Copyright page, 316–317
Corporate author, 211–212, 218
Corporate documentation style, 209
Corporate names, 15, 47, 84
  in indexes, 245, 261
Corporate titles, 48–49
Corporation, Corp., 84
Corrections, proofreading, 310
Correspondence, 6, 15
Counter, 324
Country names, 86
Court cases, documentation of, 45,
    234–235
Courtesy titles, 89
  in indexes, 260
Courts, names of, 42
Cover, of book, 313
  types and manufacturing of, 361–363
Cover copy, 313–314
Crafts, documentation of, 232–233
Crash, 361
Crashing, 326
Credit lines, 201
Credits, on copyright page, 317
Crop marks, 205
Cropping, photos, 205–206

Crosshead, 175–176
Cross-references
  copyediting, 279, 294
  in indexes, 244–247, 249
  manuscript preparation of, 275
  proofreading, 310
  punctuation of, 251–252
  style sheet notes on, 283
  styles of, 255–257
  table, 172
CRT typesetting, 349
Cultivar, cv., 131
Cut-in heading, 175–176
Cyrillic alphabet. *See* Russian, translitera-
    tion of
Czech
  capitalization in, 162
  diacritics and special characters in, 162
  punctuation of, 162
  word division in, 162

D

Dagger, 211
  in mathematical copy, 118
  in table references, 183
Dame, 260
Danish. *See* Scandinavian languages
Dash, 10, 16–17
  in captions, 200
  and colon compared, 17
  with comma, 16, 18
  and comma compared, 10, 16, 18
  copyediting marks, 287
  in Czech dialogue, 162
  in Dutch dialogue, 153
  em, 19
  en, 19
  with exclamation point, 18, 21
  in foreign language dialogue, 149
  in French dialogue, 157
  in Italian dialogue, 159
  to mark index entries, 246–247
  with parentheses, 18, 26
  and parentheses compared, 17
  with period, 18
  in Polish dialogue, 161
  and question mark, 18, 28
  with quotation marks, 31
  in Russian dialogue, 167
  in Scandinavian dialogue, 154
  and semicolon, 17, 18

spacing of, 16
in Spanish dialogue, 155
in table numbers, 174
three–em, 19, 230
two–em, 19
Data verification, as copyediting task, 279
Databases, 51–52
Dates, 98–100
  abbreviations in, 85
  A.D. and *B.C.*, 83, 100
  and apostrophe, 99–100
  in bibliographies, 226, 228–229, 231–235, 236–237
  elided, 97
  geological, 100
  inverted styling of, 99
  in military correspondence, 85, 99
  in parenthetical references, 218–219
  punctuation of, 14
  in source notes, 213, 214
  in table columns, 180
Days of the week, capitalization of, 52
  in Czech, 163
  in Dutch, 153
  in foreign languages, 149
  in French, 157
  in Polish, 162
  in Russian, 167
  in Scandinavian languages, 154
  in Spanish, 156
Decades, 99–100
Decimal comma, 120
Decimal fractions, 101–102
  in monetary units, 103–104
  in tables, 179
Decimal points, in tables, 179
Decimals, spacing, 120
Decked head, 175–176
Declination, 121
Decorations, military, 46
Dedication, 318
Definitions, in mathematical copy, 109
Degree sign, in biology and medicine, 128
Degrees, academic, 15, 38–39, 85, 89
Degrees, of arc, 100–101, 121
Degrees, of temperature, 100–101
Delete sign, 283–285
Deletions
  copyediting, 283, 285
  proofreading, 305
Demibold, 324

Demonstrations, in mathematical copy, 109
Dependent clauses. *See* Clauses, subordinate
Derived international system of units (illus.), 119–121
Descender, 323
Design. *See also* Page-design elements
  of indexes, 268–271
  mixing typefaces, 330
  of tables, 173, 177
Design specifications, 273, 323, (illus.) 345–346
  abbreviations used in (illus.), 344
  caption, 200
  checking proofs against, 308–309
  and generic tagging, 352, 353–354
  index (illus.), 271
  mathematical copy, 118
  table, 187
  in typesetting process, 349
  writing, 343–344
Designer, 272
Desktop publishing, 343
Determinants, 116
D-head, 338
  sample design specification (illus.), 345
Diacritics
  in biology and medicine, 128
  in classical Greek, 164–165
  copyediting, 289
  in Czech, 163
  in Dutch, 153
  in foreign languages, 149–150
  in French, 158–159
  in German, 152–153
  in Italian, 160
  in Latin, 161
  in Pinyin, 170
  in Portuguese, 160
  in Russian, 165–167
  in Scandinavian languages, 155
  in Spanish, 156
Diaeresis
  in Dutch, 153
  in French, 159
  in Portuguese, 160
  in Spanish, 156
Diagonal. *See* Slash
Dialogue
  in block quotation, 140–141
  capitalization of, 36–37

Dialogue *(continued)*
    in Dutch, 153
    in English vs. foreign languages, 149
    in French, 157
    in German, 151
    in Italian, 159
    in Polish, 161
    punctuation of, 29
    in Russian, 167
    in Scandinavian languages, 154
    in Spanish, 155–156
Dictionary entry, in author-date refer-
    ences, 219
Die neue deutsche Rechtschreibung, 151
Digital proof, 196
Digraphs, 149
    in Portuguese, 160
Dingbats (illus.), 340
Direct address, 10
Direct question, 14, 27, 30
Direct quotation, 12–14, 28, 143
Directions. *See* Compass points
Directory names, 134
Direct-to-plate process, 195, 349–350, 356
Discography. *See* Sound recordings
Diseases, names of, 45, 132–133
Display equations, 108
Display type, 328
Displayed lists, copyediting, 294. *See also*
    Lists
Dissertations, documentation of, 215,
    229–230
Doctor, Dr., 89
    in index, 260
Document instance, 353
Document type definition (DTD),
    352–353
Documentation, 207–210, 231–237. *See*
    also Endnotes; Footnotes; Parenthet-
    ical references
    of Bible, 235
    citation-sequence system, 220–221
    of classic literary works, 235
    of electronic sources, 236–237
    of government and legal publications,
        233–235
    of nonprint sources, 231–233
    purpose of, 207
    white-copy system, 221–223
Dollar amounts, 103–104
    in tables, 178–179
Dot gain, 357

Dots. *See* Ellipsis points
Dots per inch, 195
Double dagger, 211
Double entry, in indexes, 245
Double numeration, 112
Doubled tables (illus.), 185–186
dpi. *See* Dots per inch
Drop capitals, 341
Drop caps, 341
Drop folios, 337
Drop-out type, 342, 197
Drug names, 45–46, 132
Drum scanner, 195, 198
DTD. *See* Document type definition
DTP. *See* Desktop publishing
Dummy, 273, 342
Dummy boards, 342
Duotone art, 199
Dust jacket. *See* Jacket
Dutch
    capitalization in, 153
    diacritics and special characters in, 153
    punctuation of, 153
    surnames in indexes, 261
    word division in, 153

E

Earth, 51
Editing
    electronic, 300–301
    index entries, 249–250, (illus.) 251
Edition of book, 213, 226
Editor, Ed., 212, 225, 230
Editor queries, 276–278
Editorial insertions, 3–4, 141–144
Editorial production, 272–273
    of art, 203–206
    of tables, 186–188
Editorial revisions, inserting, 281, 283,
    308
Electronic editing, 300–301
Electronic sources, documentation of,
    236–237
Elements, chemical, 88
    names and symbols of (illus.), 121–122
Elision of numbers, 97
Ellipsis points, 19–21
    and comma, 16
    copyediting mark, 287

indicating omission in quotation, 142–143
in mathematical copy, 115
omission of, 20
with other punctuation, 20–21, 142
and period, 20
in poetry, 20, 147
spacing of, 19
in tables, 178
Elliptical clauses, 33
Em dash, 19
in attributions, 144
copyediting mark, 287, 305
proofreader mark, 305
in tables, 178
three-em, 19, 230
two-em, 19
Em quad, 290
defined, 325
Em space
defined, 325
proofreader mark, 305
in table numbers, 174
E-mail, documentation of, 237
Emphasis, styling for, 56, 144
Emulsion, 356
En dash, 19
copyediting mark, 287
with inclusive numbers, 96–97
proofreader mark, 305
En quad, 290
En space, defined, 325
Encyclopedia entry, in author-date references, 219
Endnotes, 209, 210–211, 319. *See also* Documentation; Footnotes; Notes; Parenthetical references
of articles, 214–215
of books, 211–213
copyediting, 295
locators in, 244
manuscript preparation of, 275
numbers in, 210–211
proofreading, 310
subsequent references to books and articles, 215–216
substantive notes, 216–217
of unpublished materials, 215
in white-copy system, 221–223
End-of-line division, 22, 79, 96
in Japanese, 171
Endpapers, 315, 362

Entry-a-line index, 239
Enumerations, 102–103
capitalization in, 102–103
punctuation of, 24, 28, 102–103
Epigraph, 30, 144–145
in front matter, 316, 318
Epithet, personal, 48
Equations
breaking, 110
design specifications (illus.), 118, 345–346
displaying, 110
generating on computer, 109–110
numbering, 112–113
spacing, 112
structure of, 110–112
Era designations, 83, 100
Esquire, Esq., 89
Essay titles, 53
et al., 211, 224
Ex- compounds, 76
Ex parte, 266
Ex rel., 266
Examples
design specification (illus.), 345
in mathematical copy, 109
Exclamation point, 21–22
with comma, 16, 22
copyediting mark, 287
with dash, 18
with ellipsis points, 142
with parentheses, 21, 25
with period, 22
with question mark, 21
with quotation marks, 21, 31
Exclamations, 10, 14, 18
Expanded face, 324
Extended face, 324
Extra bold type, 324
Extracts, 30, 139. *See also* Foreign languages
copyediting, 294–295
permission to use, 321
of poetry, 145–147
and quotation marks, 30
quotations within, 140–141

F

F&G's. *See* Folded and gathered sheets
Facing pages, proofreading, 311

Factorials, 115
Family, taxonomic, 131
Family relationship terms, 48
Federal, capitalization of, 42–43
Federal Register, 234
Fences, 113–114
Field, table, 178
Figure, Fig., 199
    parts of (illus.), 200
Figure caption, sample design specification (illus.), 346
Figures (numerals), 91–95, 98. *See also* Numbers
Filenames, 134
Film, 349, 356
Film proofs, 312
Films, documentation of, 232
Filmsetting. *See* Phototypesetting
Fineline process, 196
Finish, 359
First proofs, 273, 302
    illustrations and, 206
Flap copy, 313
Flat, 356
Flatbed scanner, 195, 198
Flowcharts, 192
Flush left and right, 336
Flush outside, 336
Flush-and-hang indention, 341. *See also* Hanging indention
-fold (suffix), use with numbers, 78
Folded and gathered sheets, 273, 313, 361
Folios, ff., 243, 337
    proofreading, 310–311
Font, 328
Foot line, 336
Footers. *See* Running feet
Footnotes, 209, 210–211. *See also* Documentation; Endnotes; Notes; Parenthetical references
    of articles, 214–215
    of books, 211–213
    copyediting, 295
    in galley proofs, 302
    locators in, 244
    in manuscript preparation, 275
    numbers in, 210–211
    proofreading, 308, 310–311
    in spread-width tables, 186
    subsequent references to books and articles, 215–216
    substantive notes, 216–217

    table, 182–184, 211
    of unpublished materials, 215
Foreign languages. *See also under individual languages*
    capitalization in, 149
    punctuation in, 148–149
    use of diacritics, 149–150
    word division in, 149
Foreign names, in indexes, 261–262
Foreign terms, in indexes, 254
Foreign titles of works, in indexes, 264–265
Foreign words and phrases, 30, 54, 60, 72
Foreword, 318
Format, bibliographic, 230–231
Four-color printing, 197, 357
Four-color process, 197
4-head, 338
    sample design specification (illus.), 345
FPO art, 206
Fractions, 101–102, 114–115
    breaking equations and, 110
    common, 101–102
    decimal. *See* Decimal fractions
    mixed, 101
    spelled-out form, 96, 101
Fraktur, 152
Free sheets, 361
Freelance copy editors, 276
Freelance indexers, 238–239
Freelance proofreaders, 301
French
    capitalization in, 157–158
    diacritics and special characters in, 158–159
    punctuation of, 156–157
    surnames in indexes, 261
    word division in, 158
From, used to indicate range, 96
Front matter, 314–315
    acknowledgments, 318
    blanks and advertisements, 315
    copyright page, 316–317
    dedication, 318
    design specifications and, 344
    endpapers, 315
    foreword and preface, 318
    half-title, 315–316
    lists of illustrations and tables, 318
    table of contents, 318
    title page, 316

Front-cover copy, 313
Frontispiece, 316
ftp, 236
-ful words, plurals of, 62–63

G

Galleries, color, 197
Gallery section, for art, 196
Galley proofs, 273, 302
Garamond (illus.), 332
  x-height of (illus.), 326
General notes
  in continued tables, 186
  in tables, 183
Generic tagging, 351–355
  examples of, 353–355
  of special characters, 354
Genus names, 50–51, 129–130
Geographical terms, 40–41, 85–86
Geological dates, 100
Geological terms, 51
German, 150–151
  capitalization in, 151–152
  diacritics and special characters in,
    152–153
  punctuation of, 151
  surnames in indexes, 261
  word division in, 152
Glossary, 319
  design specification (illus.), 346
gopher, 236
Goudy Old Style (illus.), 333
Government organizations, capitalization
  of in Russian, 168
Government Printing Office, 233
Government publications, 233–234
Governmental bodies, 41–43, 104
GPO. *See* Government Printing Office
Grain, of paper, 358–359
Graphic Artists Guild Handbook: Pricing &
  Ethical Guidelines, 202
Graphic design. *See* Design
Graphics
  bitmapped, 349
  object-oriented or vector, 349
Graphs, 188
  bar and column graphs,189–190
  flowcharts, 192
  line graphs, 190–192
  in manuscript preparation, 275
  pie charts, 188

Grave accent
  in biology and medical copy, 128
  in classical Greek, 164–165
  in French, 158
  in Italian, 160
  in Pinyin, 170
Gravure printing, 355
Grayscale art, 193
Greek. *See* Classical Greek
Greek letters (illus.), 117
  in biology and medical copy, 129
  copyediting, 289
Gregg Reference Manual, 208
Groundwood, 360
Guillemets, 149
  in Czech, 162
  in French, 156–157
  in German, 151
  in Italian, 159
  in Polish, 161
  in Portuguese, 160
  in Russian, 167
  in Scandinavian languages, 154
  in Spanish, 155
Gutter margin, 338

H

Haček
  in Czech, 163
  in Pinyin, 170
Hair space
  copyediting mark, 286
  defined, 325
  proofreader mark, 306
Hairline serifs, 329
Half-title, 315–316
Half-title page, 315
Halftone screens, 198
Halftones, 193–197
A Handbook for Scholars, 221
Hanging indention, 319, 341. *See also*
  Indention
Headband, 361
Headers. *See* Running heads
Headings. *See also* Running heads
  in bibliographies, 230
  checking, 279
  column, 176–178
  copyediting, 290, 294
  in indexes, 240–241, 247
  letterspacing of, 327

Headings *(continued)*
  in memorandum, 6, 38
  page design and, 338
  proofreading, 306
  in stubs, 175–176
  typemarking, 296–297
Headline-style capitalization
  in book titles, 225
  in column headings, 177
  in table titles, 174
Headnote, 174
Heads, 338
Hebrew
  capitalization in, 169
  transliteration of, 168–169
  word division in, 169
Helvetica (illus.), 333
  leading in, 325–326
  x-height of (illus.), 325–326
Hepburn system, of Japanese romanization, 171
High-contrast reproduction, 195–196
Highway numbers, 98
Historical periods and events, 43–44
Hole, 342
Holidays and holy days, 52
Homonyms, in indexes, 247, 258–259
Honorable, Hon., 89
Honorific titles, 89, 260
Hook, in Polish, 162
Horticultural varieties, 131
House of Representatives, H.R., H., 233–234
HTML (HyperText Markup Language), 353
http, 133, 236
Humanities copy
  author-page system use in, 219–220
  bibliographic entries in, 208, 223, 230
  parenthetical reference use in, 209, 217, 219–220
Hundred, 91
Hybrids, 131
Hypertext transfer protocol. See *http*
Hyphen, 22–23
  with abbreviations, 23, 182–183
  in addresses, 98
  in alphabetization, 257–258
  in compound names or words, 45, 67–78
  copyediting mark, 287
  with numbers, 95–96
  in physical science copy, 125–126
  with prefixes and suffixes, 22, 75–78

  proofreader mark, 305
  in ratios, 105
Hyphenated compounds, capitalization of, 212

I

Ibid., 215–216
Identifications, in captions, 200
Illustration, illus., ill., 244
Illustration elements
  captions, 200, 204–205
  credit and permission lines, 201
  labels, 201–202
  numbers, 199
Illustration proofs, 206
Illustrations. *See also* Illustration elements
  in blues, 312
  color art, 197–199
  continuous-tone art and halftones, 193–197
  copyediting, 279, 296
  editorial production of, 203–206
  folios and, 337
  in galley proofs, 302
  illustration elements, 199–202
  as index entries, 265
  labels for, 56
  in layout, 342
  line art, 193
  lists of, 318
  locators for, 243
  manuscript preparation of, 275
  obtaining, 202–203
  in page proofs, 310
  proofreading, 308, 310
Imagesetter, 195, 349
Imperfect character, proofreader mark, 305
Imposition, 356
Imprint name, in bibliographies, 226
in press, 226
In re, 266
Inclusive numbers, 96–97
  in article source notes, 214–215
  in book source notes, 213
  with dash, 19
  elided forms, 97
  in indexes, 243
  with percentages, 105
Incorporated, Inc., 15, 84
Indefinite articles, 83

Indefinite pronouns, 65, 83
Indented index, 239–240
  continued entries in, 270
  cross-reference style, 256–257
  indention of, 254
  punctuation of, 252–253
Indention
  of bibliographies, 230
  copyediting marks, 289–290
  of displayed equations, 110
  of extracts, 30, 141, 145, 146, 294–295
  hanging, in glossary, 319
  of indexes, 252–253, 254–255, 270
  in page design, 341
  of quotations, 139–141
Independent clauses. *See* Clauses, main
Index cards, use in indexing (illus.),
  252
Index design specifications (illus.),
  270–271
Index entries
  compiling, 247, 249–251
  cross-references, 244–246
  editing, 249–250, (illus.) 251
  main headings, 240–241
  page references and other locators,
    243–244
  sorting, 250, (illus.) 251
  styling, 251–255
  subheadings, 241–242
Index preparation
  alphabetizing, 257–259
  compiling entries, 247, (illus.) 249–251
  marking page proofs, 246–247, (illus.)
    248
  phrasing headings, 247
  producing final copy, 266–268
  proofreading, 271
  sorting by computer, 267
  styling cross-references, 255–257
  styling entries, 251–255
Indexer, freelance, 238
Indexes, 172–173, 319. *See also* Index
  entries; Index preparation; Indexing
  problems
  computer programs for, 267–268
  design and typesetting, 268–271
  types and formats, 239–240
Indexing problems
  abbreviations, 265
  legal citations, 266
  numbers, 265–266
  personal names, 259–263

  place-names, 263–264
  titles of works, 264–265
Indirect discourse, 13–14
Indirect question, 13–14, 27–28
Indirect quotation, 13, 24, 28
Individual possession, 66–67
Inflected forms of verbs, 2, 23
In-house editor, 272
  tables and, 187
Initials
  in bibliographies, 223
  of company names, 83–84
  in personal names, 26, 88, 263
Ink, 357–358
In-line form, 113
  of fractions, 114
Input, 133–134
Insertions
  editorial, 3–4, 141–144
  of editorial revisions, 281, 283
  lengthy, in proofreading, 308
  proofreader mark, 305
Inserts, art, 196
Inside margin, 338
Integral sign, 115–116
Interjections, 10, 21
International copyright, 320
International Standard Book Number.
  See ISBN
International Standard Serial Number.
  See ISSN
International system of units (illus.),
  119–121
  derived units (illus.), 119–121
Internet. *See* On-line sources
Interpolations, 143
Interrogative elements and sentences,
  27–28
Interrupted speech, 17, 21
Interrupting elements, 9–10, 23–24
Introductory elements in sentences, 8,
  9–10, 33
Inverted punctuation marks, 155
Inverted quotation marks, 149
Ionic charge, 123
ISBN, 317
Isotope, 123
ISSN, 317
Italian
  capitalization in, 159
  diacritics and special characters in,
    160
  punctuation of, 159

Italian *(continued)*
   surnames in indexes, 261
   word division in, 159–160
Italic type, 54–56, 324
Italicization
   in annotated bibliographies, 230–231
   of artworks, 232–233
   in attributions, 144
   in bibliographies, 223, 225, 228
   of binomials, 129–130
   copyediting mark, 286
   of court cases, 234–235
   for emphasis, 55, 144
   of films and videotapes, 232
   of foreign words and phrases, 54
   of government publications, 233–234
   in indexes, 241, 243, 254
   of legal case titles, 45, 234–235
   of letters of the alphabet, 55
   of letters referred to as letters, 30
   in lists, 102
   in mathematical copy, 109, 113, 117
   of medical terms, 45
   of musical compositions, 53
   of numerals, 55
   of on-line sources, 236–237
   in physical science copy, 125–126
   and plural forms, 61
   and possessive endings, 65
   proofreader mark, 305
   punctuation following, 55–56
   in source notes, 212, 214
   of speakers' names in dialogue, 141
   of subspecies, 130
   of titles, 52–53, 231–233
   of words referred to as words, 29, 55
   of words suggesting sounds, 29, 55

J

Jacket, of book, 313–314
   printing of, 363
Jacket copy, 313–314
Japanese
   capitalization in, 171
   names in indexes, 262
   romanization of, 170–171
   word division in, 171
Joint possession, 66–67
Journal title. *See* Titles of works, periodicals
Judicial bodies, 42, 104

Junior, Jr., 15, 88, 89
Justified line, 327
Justified margins, 338

K

Kerning, 327
Keyword, 240
Kunreishiki, 171

L

Labels
   for graphs, 192
   in illustrations, 201–202
Labor unions, 104
Lady, 260
Lake, in indexes, 263
Languages, names of, 48
   in Czech, 163
   in French, 157
   in Italian, 159
LaTeX, 109
Latin
   capitalization in, 161
   diacritics and special characters in, 161
   punctuation of, 161
   word division in, 161
Latin abbreviations, 86–87, 211, 215–216
Latin names (biology), 50–51
Latin phrases, 243
Latitude, 87
Law cases, in indexes, 254
Law firm, documentation style, 209
Laws, documentation of, 234
Layout, page, 342–343
Leaders, 181–182
Leading, 326–327
   legibility and, 335
Lecture titles, 53
Legal citations, 45, 234–235
   in indexes, 245, 266
Legal publications, documentation of, 234–235
Legibility, of typefaces, 330, 335–336
Legislation, 38, 44
Legislative bodies, 41–42
Lemmas, 109
Letter-by-letter alphabetization, 257
Letterpress printing, 355

Letters. *See* Correspondence
Letters of the alphabet
  within compound words, 70
  in lists and outlines, 24, 26, 102–103
  plurals of, 61
  referred to as letters, 30, 55
  representing shapes, 55, 80
  typeface characteristics, 323
Letterspacing, 327
lf. *See* Lightface type
Library of Congress
  copyrights and, 316–318, 320–321
  romanization and, 150
  system of Russian transliteration, 166
Life sciences copy, bibliographic style,
    208. *See also* Science copy
Liftout, 340
Lightface type, 324
line, l., 235
Line art, 193
  dingbats as, 340
Line breaks
  and abbreviations, 79
  in chemistry copy, 127
  in mathematical copy, 114
  and numbers, 96
  symbol for, 285, 290, 294, 305, 306
Line editing, 275–276
Line graphs, 190–192
Line length, legibility and, 330, 335
Line spacing (illus.), 326–327
Line-break symbols, in mathematical
    copy, 118
Lines per inch, resolution, 195
Lists, 102–103
  bulleted, 103
  copyediting, 279, 294
  design specification (illus.), 346
  of illustrations and tables, 318
  page design and, 339
  run-in, 102
  typemarking, 296–297
  vertical, 102–103
Lists of references, 207–210
  and bibliographies compared, 223
  and parenthetical references, 220–221
Literary Market Place, 202
Literary works, documentation of, 235
Loc. cit., 216
Locants, hyphens and, 126
Locator maps, 192
Locators, in indexes, 243–244
Long dash. *See* Em dash; En dash

Longitude, 87
Loose-leaf binding, 362
Lord, 260
Lowercase letters, 323
  copyediting mark, 285
  proofreader mark, 305
lpi. *See* Lines per inch

M

M', alphabetizing names beginning with,
    262
Mac, alphabetizing names beginning
    with, 262
Macron
  in Japanese, 171
  in Latin, 161
  in Pinyin, 170
Magazines
  margins in, 338
  pullquotes in, 340
  running feet in, 336
  sidebars in, 339–340
  titles of, 53, 214, 228, 237
  use of dingbats, 340
Mailing lists, documentation of, 237
Main clauses. *See* Clauses, main
*Manual for Writers of Term Papers, Theses,
    and Dissertations*, 208
Manuscript, 272, 274–275. *See also* Copy-
    editing; Proofreading; Typemarking
Manuscript preparation, 274–275. *See also*
    Generic tagging
  of tables, 172, 275
Map, 244
Maps, 192
  numbering, 199
Margin heads, 339
Margin width, page design and, 337–338
Marine, capitalization of, 46
Markup
  electronic, 350
  of indexes, 268–271
Married name, in indexes, 245, 259
Mass number, 123
Master file, 350
Master proof, 273, 302
Mathematics, 4
  aggregation signs, 113–114
  arrays, 116
  copyediting, 289
  ellipsis points, 11, 287

Mathematics *(continued)*
    footnotes in mathematics tables, 183
    functions, 114–115
    generating equations on computer,
        109–110
    Greek letters in, 117
    integral, summation, and product
        signs, 115–116
    multiplication expressions, 115
    numbering equations, 112–113
    reference symbols in, 295
    signs and symbols in, 108, (illus.)
        134–136
    structuring equations, 110–112
    subscripts and superscripts in, 113
    type styles, 109
    typemarking mathematical copy,
        117–119
    vectors and tensors, 116–117
Matrices, 116
Matrix notation, 109
Maxims. *See* Mottoes and maxims
Mc, alphabetizing names beginning with,
    262
M.D., 89
    in indexes, 260
Measurement, units of, 106–107
    abbreviated, 90, 107
    with slash, 35
    of type, 325–326
Mechanical binding, 362
Medicine
    Arabic and roman numerals in, 129
    Greek letters in, 129
    names of drugs and diseases, 45–46,
        132
    signs and symbols, 127–128, (illus.)
        138
    taxonomic nomenclature, 129–132
    terms in, 45–46
Memorandum heading, 6, 38
Merriam-Webster's Biographical Dictionary,
    261
Messrs., 89
Meteorological phenomena, 51
Metric units, 119
    abbreviated, 82, 90
Microforms, 233
Military terms, 46, 87, 99
    dates, 85, 99
    decorations, 46
    ranks, 46, 87, 260
    time, 106

Million, 100, 104
Minus sign, in table columns, 180. *See
    also* Operation signs
Minutes
    capitalization in, 38
    dialogue in, 141
Miss, 89
    in index, 260
*MLA Handbook for Writers of Research
    Papers*, 208, 219
Model releases, 203
Modifiers
    in chemical formulas, 127
    coordinate, 12, 71
    punctuation of, 12
Monetary amounts, 103–104
Months, names of, 52, 85
    abbreviation in bibliographies, 228
    abbreviation in source notes, 214
    in Czech, 163
    in Dutch, 153
    in foreign languages, 149
    in French, 157
    in Latin, 161
    in Polish, 162
    in Russian, 167
    in Scandinavian languages, 154
    in Spanish, 156
Moon, 51
Mottoes and maxims, 36–37, 54
    punctuation of, 13, 29
Mount, in indexes, 263
Move left or right, proofreader mark,
    305
Movie titles, 52
Mr., Mrs., Ms., 89
    in indexes, 260
Multiple authorship, 218, 224
Multiple indexes, vs. single index, 239
Multiplication expressions, 115
Multiplication sign, 115
    in plant hybrids, 131
    typemarking, 118
Multivolume work, 212–213, 226
Musical compositions, 53

N

NA, n.a., 6
Name of series
    in bibliographies, 225–226
    in source notes, 212–213

Names, personal. *See* Nicknames; Personal names
Names, proper. *See* Proper names
Name-year system, 218–219
National, capitalization of, 42–43
Natural sciences copy
　bibliographic style, 208. *See also* Science copy
　parenthetical reference use in, 209, 217
Naval, capitalization of, 46
Negatives, 356
New Latin names, 50–51
Newsgroup postings, documentation of, 237
Newspapers. *See* Titles of works, newspapers
Nicknames, 48
no date, n.d., 213, 226
no pagination, n. pag., 213
no place, n.p., 213, 226
no publisher, n.p., 213, 226
Nobility names, in indexes, 260–261
Nonfiction, bibliographic references in, 207
Nonprint sources, documentation of, 231–233
Nonrestrictive clauses and phrases, 9, 13
Nontext references, locators for in indexes, 243–244
Norwegian. *See* Scandinavian languages
Not applicable. See *NA*
Notch binding, 362
Note, n., 244
Notes, 207–211. *See also* Endnotes; Footnotes
　copyediting, 295–296
　first reference, 210
　numbering, 210–211
　parenthetical. *See* Parenthetical references
　proofreading, 310
　subsequent reference to, 211, 215–216
　style sheet notes on, 282–283
Nouns
　adjectival use, 71–72
　capitalization of in German, 151
　compound, 67–70
　plural forms, 58–63
　possessive case, 63–65
　proper. *See* Proper names; Proper nouns
Novellas, 53

Number, No., 87
Number of atoms, 123
Number sign, 211
Number system, 220–221
Numbered lists. *See* Lists
Numbering
　equations, 112–113
　tables, 172, 173–174
Numbers, 91–107. *See also* Dates; Fractions
　in addresses, 98
　adjacent or paired, 92–93, 96–97
　at beginning of sentence, 92
　in citations, 234, 235
　columns of, 177
　and comma, 14–15, 95, 99
　within compound words, 74, 77, 78
　with enumerations, 24, 26–27, 102
　in footnotes and endnotes, 210–211
　with hyphen, 22, 95–96
　for illustrations, 199
　inclusive. *See* Inclusive numbers
　in indexes, 243, 265–266
　in lists, 102–103
　omission of, 2
　ordinal. *See* Ordinal numbers
　plural forms of, 2, 61, 105
　possessive forms of, 66
　punctuation of, 14–15, 95–97
　referred to as numerals, 55
　Roman numerals, 94–95, 103, 234, 235, 274–275, 314
　round, 93
　serial, 96
　in series, 92–93
　with slash, 34, 35
　style sheet notes on, 282
　with suffixes, 78
　with units of measurement, 106–107
　whole, 91, 95
　as words or figures, 91–95

O

Object-oriented-graphics, 349
O'clock, 105–106
OCR system, 350
Offset lithography, 355, 356
Ogonek, 162
Old English (illus.), 328
Old Towne (illus.), 328
Old-style numerals, 337

Omission
   of articles in table titles, 174
   of comma in large numbers, 95
   of comma in sentence, 7–12
   of letters, 2
   of numerals, 2
   in poetry extracts, 147
   within quotation, 19–21, 141–143
   of words, and slash, 34
   of words and phrases, 14
One (number), in addresses, 98
1-head, 338
   sample design specification (illus.),
     345
On-line sources, documentation of,
   236–237
On-screen editing, vs. paper, 300–301
Op. cit., 216
Opacity, 359
Opaquing, 356
Open compounds, 67. *See also*
   Compound words
Operation signs
   breaking equations and, 110
   of vectors, 117
Optical character recognition (OCR)
   system, 350
Optima (illus.), 333
Or, with equations, 111
Order, taxonomic, 131
Ordinal numbers, 93
   in addresses, 98
   in dates, 99
   with personal names, 93
   in spelled-out fractions, 101
Organizations, names of, 47, 83–84, 104
   in Chinese, 170
   in Czech, 163
   in Dutch, 153
   in French, 158
   in indexes, 261
   in Japanese, 171
   in Polish, 162
   in Russian, 168
   in Scandinavian languages, 154
   in Spanish, 156
Ornaments, in page design (illus.), 340
Outlines, 37, 103

P

page, p., 213, 214
   in author-date references, 219

Page design, mixing typefaces in, 330
Page numbers
   in bibliographies, 227, 229
   colon with, 5
   elided, 97
   inclusive. *See* Inclusive numbers
   in manuscripts, 274–275, 280
   in parenthetical references, 218–220,
     222
   as Roman numerals, 94, 166, 274–275,
     314
   in source notes, 213, 214
   in tables, 186–187
Page proofs, 273, 309–311
   marking for index, 246–247, (illus.)
     248
   tables, 187–188
Page references, in indexes, 243–244
Page-design elements
   layout, 342–343
   running heads, running feet, and
     folios, 336–337
   text block, 337–342
Page-layout software, 343
Pages
   bottom, 311
   chapter-ending, 311
   copyedited (illus.), 298–299
   facing, 311
   numbering text, 274–275, 280
   proofread (illus.), 307
   top, 311
pages, pp., 213, 214
   in author-date references, 219
Palatino (illus.), 334
Pantone Matching System, 199
Paper, 358–360
   acid-free, 360
   basis weight, 358
   brightness, 359
   bulk, 358–359
   calendering, 359
   color, 359
   finish, 359
   free sheets, 360
   grade and quality, 360
   grain, 357
   groundwood, 360
   and ink, 357
   offset, 360
   opacity, 359
   in printing process, 356
   recycled, 360
Paper editing, vs. on-screen, 300–301

Paragraph endings, proofreading, 306
Paragraph index, 239–240
  continued entries in, 270
  cross-reference style, 256–257
  indention of, 255
  punctuation of, 253
Paragraph references, in indexes, 243
Paragraph symbol, 211, 289–290, 305
Parallel constructions, 11
Parallels, 211
Parentheses, 23–26
  with abbreviations, 24
  with attributions, 144
  in bibliographies, 235
  with binomial nomenclature, 129–130
  in chemistry copy, 125
  with colon, 6
  in column items, 179–180
  with comma, 16
  and comma compared, 10, 23
  copyediting mark, 287
  in cross-references, 255, 256
  with dash, 18
  and dash compared, 16
  in double numeration, 112
  and exclamation point, 21, 25
  for explanatory material. *See* Parenthet-
    ical elements
  with index locators, 244
  with lists, 102
  in mathematical copy, 4, 113–114, 118
  with matrices, 116
  and monetary amounts, 104
  as multiplication sign, 115
  with nicknames and epithets, 48
  with numbers, 24–25
  within parentheses, 26
  and period, 25, 27
  proprietary drug names and, 132
  and question mark, 25, 28
  with quotations, 25
  and semicolon, 25, 34
  in source notes, 213, 214, 220
Parenthetical elements, 23–24
  capitalization of, 25
  punctuation of, 10, 17–18, 25–26
Parenthetical references, 209, 217–218
  advantages of, 217–218
  author-date system, 218–219
  author-page system, 219–220
  in humanities copy, 217–218, 219
  placement of, 217
  in quotations, 144
  in science copy, 217, 218, 220

Park Avenue (illus.), 328
Participles, 69
Particles, 69–70, 75, 122
  in personal names, 47–48, 253, 261
Parties, political, 43
Parts of a book. *See* Book, parts of
Passim, 243
Peignot (illus.), 328
Pen-editing system, 300–301
Peoples, words pertaining to, 48
  in Czech, 163
  in Dutch, 153
  in French, 157
  in Italian, 159
  in Polish, 162
  in Russian, 167
  in Scandinavian languages, 154
  in Spanish, 156
Per
  in biological and medical copy,
    127–128
  slash used for, 34
Percent, percentage, 104–105
Percent sign, in biology and medicine,
  128
Percentages, 128
  in table columns, 180
Perfect binding, 362
Period, 26–27
  with abbreviations, 26, 79–80
  in bibliographies, 224, 226, 229, 230,
    235
  with brackets, 27
  in captions, 200
  after chemical expression, 124
  copyediting mark, 287
  with dash, 18
  in dialogue, 141
  and ellipsis points, 20, 142
  equations at end of sentence, 111
  with exclamation point, 22
  in index entries, 251
  with names, spacing of, 26
  with numerals, 26–27
  with parentheses, 25, 27
  in parenthetical references, 217,
    220
  in polite requests, 27
  with quotation marks, 27, 31
  with quotations, 139
  and semicolon compared, 32
  in source notes, 213
  spacing of, 26
  in table numbers, 174

Periodical articles. *See* Titles of works, periodicals
Periodical number
  in bibliographies, 228–229
  in source notes, 214
Periodical volume
  in bibliographies, 228–229
  in source notes, 214
Periodicals
  citing on-line, 237
  running heads in, 336
Permission lines, in figures, 201
Permissions, 166, 322
  art, 203, 205, 296
  reviewing, 280
  tables, 183
Personal asides, 24
Personal communications, documentation of, 231
Personal names, 15, 26, 47–48, 88, 94
  in Chinese, 170
  in German, 151
  in indexes, 259–263
Personifications, 38
Photo archives, 202
  permission to use, 321
Photoprint, 196
Photos, 196
  cropping and sizing, 205–206
  obtaining, 202
Phototypesetting, 349
Phrases
  absolute, 9
  adverbial, 8–9
  with colon, 4–5
  foreign, 30, 54, 60, 72. *See also* Foreign languages
  introductory, 8, 9–10
  Latin, abbreviations of, 86–87, 211, 215–216, 234
  nonrestrictive, 9
  with parentheses, 23
  plural forms, 60, 61
  possessive forms, 66
  restrictive, 8
Phylum, taxonomic, 131
Physical sciences
  astronomy, 121
  bibliographic style, 208. *See also* Science copy
  chemistry and physics, 121–127
  international system of units (illus.), 119–121

Physics
  names of particles (illus.), 122–123
  punctuation and relationship in physics copy, 124–126
  signs and symbols (illus.), 137–138
  subscripts and superscripts in physics copy, 123
Pica, defined, 325
Pica rule, 325
Pie charts, 188
Piece fractions, 114
Pigment, 357
Pinyin, 169–170
Pixels, 195
Place-names
  in Chinese, 169–170
  in indexes, 263–264
Plant hybrids, 131
Plant names, 39
Plastic-comb binding, 362
Platemaking, 348, 355–356
  direct-to-plate system, 349–350, 356
Plays
  acts of, 94–95
  attribution lines for, 145
  dialogue in, 141
  documentation of, 235
  titles of, 52
Plurals, 58–63
  of abbreviations, 58–59, 81–82
  of animal names, 59
  with apostrophe, 2, 58–59, 61, 62, 63
  of compounds and phrases, 59–60
  of foreign words, 60
  irregular, 60–61
  of italic elements, 61
  of letters, 61
  of nouns, 58–63
  of numbers, 61, 105
  possessive forms, 63–65
  of proper nouns, 62
  of quoted elements, 62
  of symbols, 62
  of words ending in *-ay, -ey,* and *-oy,* 62
  of words ending in *-ful,* 62–63
  of words ending in *-o,* 63
  of words used as words, 63
Plus sign, in table columns, 180. *See also* Operation signs
p.m., 89, 106
PMS. *See* Pantone Matching System
Poetry
  attribution lines for, 145

capitalization of, 37
and ellipsis points, 20
indexing lines of, 264
permission to use, 321
and quotation marks, 30
quotations, 139, 145–147
slash as line divider, 30, 35
in source notes, 212
titles of, 52, 53
Point, defined, 325
Point size, of rules, 341
Polish
capitalization in, 162
diacritics and special characters in, 162
punctuation of, 161
word division in, 162
Polite requests, 27
Political maps, 192
Political organizations, 43
Popes, in indexes, 260–261
Portuguese
capitalization in, 160
diacritics and special characters in, 160
punctuation of, 160
word division in, 160
Possession, individual and joint, 66–67
Possessive, 63–65, 82
of abbreviations, 66
of common nouns, 63–64
of numerals, 66
of phrases, 66
of plurals, 63, 64, 65
of pronouns, 65
of proper names, 64–65
of words in quotation marks, 66
Possessive pronouns, 65
PostScript, 343, 349
Pound sign, 211
Prayers, 50
Predicate, compound, 7–8
Preface, 318
Prefixes, 75–78
with abbreviations, 82–83
capitalization of, 45
with hyphen, 22, 75–78
in international system of units (illus.),
119–120
in physical science copy, 125
Prepositions
capitalization of, 212
within compounds, 60, 69
in index alphabetization, 258
in titles of works, 264

Prepress. *See* Platemaking; Typesetting
President, 49
Press proof, 357
Prime, 113
Printer's errors, 304
Printers' proofs, 312–313
Printing, 348, 356–357
color, 357
gravure, 355
ink and, 357–358
letterpress, 355
offset, 355, 356
Printing line, 317
Printing plate, 348, 349, 355
in color printing, 357
making of, 356
in offset lithography, 356
Printing press, 356, 357
Proceedings, 228
Product sign, 115–116
Professional name, 245, 259
Professional ratings, 85
Professional titles, 48–49, 89, 260
Professor, in index, 260
Pronouns
capitalization of in Italian, 159
indefinite, 65
possessive, 65
Proofread text (illus.), 307
Proofreader, 272
freelance, 301
Proofreader's checklist, 303, 310–311,
312–313
Proofreader's queries, 303, 304
Proofreading, 301
author's revisions, 302–303
checking proofs against design specifications, 308–309
first or galley proofs, 302
indexes, 271
letterspacing, 327
printers' proofs, 312–313
proofread text (illus.), 307
proofreader's duties and marks,
303–306, 308
second or page proofs, 309–311
tables, 187–188
Proofreading marks, 291–293, 304–306,
308
Proofs, 109, 273
art, 198
checking against design specifications,
308–309

Proofs *(continued)*
  color, 196, 357
  first or galley, 302
  illustration, 206
  printers', 312–313, 356
  second or page, 309–311
Proper adjectives, 38–54
  capitalization of in Latin, 161
Proper names, 64–65, 72. *See also*
    Personal names; Proper nouns
  derivatives of, 39–40
  in French, 157
  in German, 151
  in Latin, 161
  with numbers, 94
  possessive forms, 64–65
  in Russian, 167
  used in names of diseases, 132
Proper nouns
  capitalization of, 38–54, 81
  capitalization of in Arabic and Hebrew,
    169
  in indexes, 246
  plural forms of, 62
Proportional spacing, 326
Prose quotations, assessing length,
    139
Pseudonym, in indexes, 245, 259
*Publication Manual of the American Psycho-
    logical Association*, 208, 219
Publishing data
  in bibliographies, 226–227
  in source notes, 213
Pullquotes, 340
Punctuation, 1–35. *See also individual
    marks of punctuation*
  of abbreviations, 79–80
  of addresses, 14
  to avoid ambiguity, 15
  of biblical references, 5–6, 84
  in bibliographies, 223–231
  of block quotations, 139–140
  changes by proofreader, 304
  copyediting marks for, 286–288
  in Czech, 162
  in direct quotations, 143
  with ellipsis points, 142–143
  of equations, 110–112
  in foreign languages, 148–149
  in French, 156–157
  in German, 151
  in index entries, 251–252
  in Italian, 159
  in Latin, 161

  noting in style sheet, 278
  of numbers, 2, 4, 95–97
  with parenthetical references, 217–220
  in physical science copy, 124–127
  of poetry extracts, 145–147
  in Portuguese, 160
  purposes of, 1
  in Russian, 167
  in Scandinavian languages, 153–154
  in source notes, 211–216
  in Spanish, 155–156

Q

Quanta (illus.), 122–123
Queries
  author, 276–278
  editor, 276–277
  proofreader's, 303
Question mark, 13, 27–28
  with comma, 16
  copyediting mark, 287
  with dash, 18, 28
  with ellipsis points, 142
  with exclamation point, 21
  and parentheses, 25, 28
  and period, 27
  proofreader mark, 305
  with quotation marks, 28, 31
  in typefaces, 330
Questions, 13–14, 27–28. *See also* Ques-
    tion mark
  direct, 27, 30
  indirect, 13–14, 27–28
  and quotation marks, 30
Quotation marks, 28–32
  article titles and, 214
  author-page references and,
    219–220
  in bibliographies, 223, 225, 227, 229,
    232, 236
  in blurbs, 145
  British usage, 31–32
  with colon, 6, 31
  with comma, 16, 31
  copyediting mark, 288
  with dash, 31
  with exclamation point, 21, 31
  with extracts, 30, 140–141
  in Italian, 159
  and italics, 29, 30
  marking, 306
  omission of, 29

with parentheses, 25
parenthetical references and, 217
with period, 27, 31
in poetry extracts, 146–147
with possessive, 66
with question mark, 28, 31
in Scandinavian dialogue, 154
with semicolon, 31, 34
with single quotation marks, 16–17, 140
in source notes, 214
in typefaces, 330
unpublished material titles and, 215, 229
Quotations, 28–32
alphabetizing, 257
assessing length, 139
and attribution of sources, 17–18
with brackets, 3
capitalization of, 3, 25, 36–37, 139, 141–142
colon introducing, 5
and comma, 12–14
copyediting, 294–295
direct, 12–14, 28, 144
editorial insertions in, 3, 141–144
within extract, 140–141
indirect, 14, 24, 28
omissions in, 19–20, 141–144
in parentheses, 24
parenthetical references and, 217
of poetry. *See* Poetry
within quotations, 31–32
within quotations in German, 151
run in, 139
in running text, 5
Quoted elements
compounds, 72
plural forms, 62
possessive forms, 66

R

Race name, 130
Radicals, 114–115
Radio programs, 53, 231–232
Ragged-right margins, 338
Raised dot, in classical Greek, 164
Range of numbers. *See* Inclusive numbers
Raster image processor (RIP) and raster-izing, 349
Ratios, 5–6, 34, 105
Ream, 359
Recto pages, 318

folios and, 337
running heads and, 336
Reduction percentages, 206
Reduplication compounds, 70
Reference list. *See* Bibliographies; Lists of references
Reference number, in books, 47
Reference symbols, 211, 289
in mathematical copy, 118
in tables, 183–184
References, 209. *See also* Endnotes; Documentation; Footnotes, Parenthetical references
Registration, in color proofs, 198
Regulations, documentation of, 234
Religious groups, 50, 104
Religious terms, 49–50
Representative, 89
Reprints
in bibliographies, 227
in source notes, 213
Reproduction (repro) proofs, 273, 312–313, 350
Requests, polite, 27
Rescreening, 196
Resolution, 195
Resolved, 38
Restrictive appositive, 9
Restrictive clauses and phrases, 8
Reverend, Rev., 89
Reverse indention, 341. *See also* Hanging indention
Reverse type, 342
Revisions, author's, 273, 297, 302–303
Rich Text Format (RTF), 352
Right ascension, 121
Right-hand margins, in indexes, 270
Right-justified line, 327
RIP. *See* Raster image processor
Road maps, 192
Roman numerals, 94–95
in biology and medical copy, 129
in constitutional articles and amend-ments, 94–95, 234
in front matter pages, 274–275, 314
in outlines, 103
as oxidation numbers, 125
of personal names in indexes, 260
in plays, 235
in proper names, 94
in table columns, 180
Roman type, 324
copyediting mark, 286
legibility of, 335

Roman type *(continued)*
  in mathematical copy, 109
  proofreader mark, 305
Romanization, 150
  of Chinese, 169–170
  of Japanese, 170–171
Round numbers, 93
  in monetary amounts, 103–104
RTF. *See* Rich Text Format
Rulers' names, 94
Rules
  in page design, 341
  in tables, 181
Run-in, copyediting mark, 288
Run-in index, 239
Run-in lists. *See* Lists
Run-in text, heads and, 338
Running feet, 336
Running heads, 336
  in endnotes, 211, 319
  proofreading, 310–311
  in white-copy system, 223
Run-on index, 239
Russian
  capitalization in, 167–168
  punctuation of, 167
  transliteration of (illus.), 165–167
  word division in, 168

S

Sacred works, 50
Saddle binding, 363
Saint, St., 88
  alphabetizing, 263
Saints, 49, 260
Salutation of letter, 6, 15, 38
Sample pages, 273
  of design specifications, 344
Sans-serif faces, 329
Scandinavian languages
  capitalization in, 154
  diacritics and special characters in, 155
  punctuation of, 153–154
  word division in, 154
Scanner, 357. *See also* Optical character recognition system
Scanning resolution, 195
Scatter diagram, 192
Scattergraph, 192
Scene, sc., 235

Science copy
  bibliographic entries in, 208, 223, 224–230
  parenthetical reference use in, 209, 217
Scientific indexes, boldface type in, 254
Scientific journals, use of citation-sequence system, 220
Scientific Style and Format: The CBE Manual for Authors, Editors, and Publishers, 208
Scientific terms, 45, 50–52, 88, 100–101
Scores, 229
Screens, 196–197
Seasons, capitalization of, 52
Second, 2nd, 2d, 94
Second proofs, 273, 309–311
  illustrations and, 206
Section mark, 211
See also references, 245–246
See also under references, 255
See references, 244–245
See under references, 255
Self- compounds, 76
Semicolon, 32–34
  author-page references and, 220
  changing to period, 287
  after chemical expression, 124
  in classical Greek, 164
  between clauses, 10, 32–33
  with comma, 16
  and comma compared, 32–33
  and conjunctions, 32–33
  with conjunctive adverbs, 32–33
  copyediting mark, 288
  with dash, 18
  in French, 157
  in index entries, 252, 253, 255
  within parentheses, 25
  parenthetical references and, 217
  and period compared, 32
  with phrases, 32
  with quotation marks, 31, 34
  in a series, 33–34
  with *so* and *yet,* 33
  in source notes, 213
Senate, S., 233–234
Senator, 89
Senior, Sr., 15, 88, 89
Sentence fragments, 23, 36
Sentences
  beginnings of, 36–38, 92
  interrogative, 27
  parallelism in, 7

within sentences, 11, 25, 36–37
suspension of structure, 16–17
Sentence-style capitalization
  in book titles, 225
  in column headings, 177
  in table titles, 174
Serial comma, 11–12
Serial numbers, 96
Series
  interrogative, 28
  of main clauses, 11–12
  numbered, 24, 28
  of numbers, 92–93
  of percentages, 105
  punctuation of, 11–12, 28, 33–34
  of questions, 28
Serifs, 323, 329
Sexual bias, removing, 280
SGML (Standardized Generalized
    Markup Language), 352–353
Shapes, indicated by letters, 55
Short story, documentation of, 212
Shot down, 205
SI. *See* International system of units
sic., 143
Sidebars, 339–340
  sample design specification (illus.),
    340
Side-wired books, 363
Signature, 355
  in binding process, 361
  with color art, 357
  order, 312
Signs, in capital letters, 56
Signs (symbols)
  in biology and medicine, 127–128,
    (illus.) 138
  in chemistry and physics (illus.),
    137–138
  in mathematics, 108, (illus.) 134–136
Simple indexes, 239
Single index, vs. multiple indexes, 239
Single quotation marks, 31–32
  in Dutch, 153
  in German, 151
Sink, 347
Sinkage, 347
Sir, 260
Sizing, photos, 205–206
Slash, 34–35
  with abbreviations, 34, 80
  in biology and medicine, 128
  copyediting mark, 288

in dates, 35, 99
in generic tags, 352
to indicate lowercase letter, 285
in in-line equations, 114
to mark index entries, 247
in poetry, 30, 35, 145
proofreader mark, 305
in ratios, 34, 105
spacing of, 34, 35
used in deletions, 285, 287, 305
Slavists' system, of Russian transliteration,
    166
Slug, 309–310
Small capitals, 325
  in attributions, 144
  in computer commands, 134
  copyediting mark, 285
  with dates, 100
  general use of, 56
  in mathematical copy, 109
  proofreader mark, 306
  with speakers' names in dialogue, 141
  in table titles, 174
Smyth sewing, 362
So, as conjunction, 33
Social science copy
  author-date system use in, 218
  bibliographic style, 208. *See also*
    Science copy
  parenthetical reference use in, 209,
    217
Software. *See* Computer software
Solidus. *See* Slash
Sound recordings, documentation of,
    232
Sounds, representations of, 29, 55
Source notes, 216–217
  in tables, 183
Sources. *See* Documentation
Space symbol, 285, 306
Spacecraft names, 54
Spaces, inserting, 286, 306
Spacing
  changing in second proofs, 311
  of equations, 112
  of letters, 327
  line (illus.), 326–327
  in manuscript preparation, 274
  in physical science copy, 124
Spanish
  capitalization in, 156
  diacritics and special characters in, 156
  punctuation of, 155–156

Spanish *(continued)*
  surnames in indexes, 262
  word division in, 156
Spanner head, 177
Special characters, 354–355. *See also*
    Foreign Languages; Mathematics
Specialized maps, 192
Species, sp., spp., 130
Species names, 50–51, 129–130
Specific names. *See* Species names
Specific notes, in tables, 183
Specs, 273
Speech. *See* Dialogue
Speeches, documentation of, 231
Spell out
  copyediting mark, 288
  proofreader mark, 306
Spine copy, 313
Split fractions, 114
Split-level quotation marks, 151
  in Czech, 162
  in Dutch, 153
Spot color, 199
Spreads, 342
Spread-width tables, 186
Square serifs, 329
Stacked heads, 177–178
Standardized Generalized Markup
    Language (SGML), 352–353
State names, 14, 24, 85–86
  in indexes, 265
  in source notes, 213
Stet, 288, 306
Stick-on letters, 202
Stock-market quotations, 107
Story titles, 53
Street names. *See* Addresses, street
Strip, 361
Stripping, 356
Stroke, 323
Stub, 174–176
Style sheet, 281–283, (illus.) 284
  for indexes, 239
Subatomic particles (illus.), 122–123
Subentry, 241
  cross-reference to, 255
Subheadings, in indexes, 241–242
Subject headings, 38
Subordinate clauses and phrases,
    8–9
Subscript
  in chemistry copy, 123
  copyediting mark, 289

fractions as, 114
  in mathematical copy, 113
  proofreader mark, 306
  of summation and product signs,
    115–116
  of vectors, 117
Subsection references, in indexes,
    243
Subsequent bibliographic entries,
    230
Subspecies names, 50, 130
Substantive notes, 207, 216–217
  copyediting, 295
Substitutions, editorial, 283
Sub-subentry, 241–242
Subtitle, 6, 212, 225
Suffixes, 78
  with abbreviations, 80, 82–83
  with hyphen, 22
  with numbers, 78
Summation sign, 115–116
Sun, 51
Super, 361
Superscript
  in chemistry copy, 123
  copyediting mark, 289
  fractions as, 114
  in mathematical copy, 113
  numbers in footnotes and endnotes,
    210–211
  proofreader mark, 306
  reference symbols, 211, 295
  of summation and product signs,
    115–116
  in table footnotes, 183–184
  of vectors, 117
Supplementary clauses and phrases,
    16–18, 23
Supreme being, references to, 49
Suspension points, 155
  in French, 157
Swedish. *See* Scandinavian languages
Symbols
  in biology and medicine, 127–128,
    (illus.) 138
  for chemical elements (illus.),
    121–122
  in chemistry and physics (illus.),
    137
  with inclusive numbers, 96–97
  in mathematical copy, 108, (illus.)
    134–136
  plural forms of, 62

for subatomic particles and quanta (illus.), 122–123
of units of measurement, 107

T

Table, 244
Table design, 173
Table elements (illus.), 176
  braces, 182
  column headings, 176–178
  columns, 178–181
  footnotes, 182–184
  leaders, 181–182
  rules, 181
  stub, 174–176
  table number, 173–174
  title, 174
Table footnotes, 182, 211
Table length, 184–186
Table of cases, 239
Table of contents, 318
Table size, reducing, 184–185
Table spanner, 175–176
Table width, 184–186
Tables, 172–173. *See also* Table elements
  copyediting, 186–187, 279, 296
  design specification (illus.), 346
  folios and, 337
  in galley proofs, 302
  length and width, 184–186
  lists of, 318
  locators for, 243
  manuscript preparation of, 172–173, 275
  proofreading, 187–188, 306, 310
Tagging. *See* Generic tagging
Tags, copyediting, 276–277, 304
Taxonomic nomenclature, 129–132
Television programs, 53, 231–232
telnet, 236
Temporary compound, 67
Tensors, 109, 116–117
Term papers, reference style, 209
TeX, 110
Text block, 337–338, 342, 356
  headings, 338–339
  lists, 339
  ornaments, 340
  pullquotes, 340
  rules, 341

  sidebars, 339–340
Text type, 328
That, replaced by comma, 10
The
  omission of, 214, 228
  in table titles, 174
  in titles of works, 264
Theorems, 109
Theses
  in bibliographies, 229–230
  in source notes, 209, 215
Thick, 323, 329
Thick space, defined, 325
Thin, 323, 329
Thin space, 286
  defined, 325
  in international system of units, 120, 121
  in mathematical copy, 112
Third, 3rd, 3d, 94
Thousand, 91
Three-em dash, 19, 230
Three-em underline, 230
3-head, 338
  sample design specification (illus.), 345
Tilde
  in Portuguese, 160
  in Spanish, 156
Time of day, 5–6, 89, 105–106
Time periods, 52
Time zones, 89
Times Roman (illus.), 334
  descenders in, 326
  leading in, 327
  legibility of, 335
  x-height (illus.), 325–326
Times sign, 115
  typemarking, 118–119
Tipping in, 357
Title page, 316
Titles of persons
  corporate, 48–49
  courtesy, 89, 260
  governmental, 48–49
  honorific, 89, 260
  professional, 48–49, 89, 260
  punctuation of, 15
Titles of works, 52–53
  in Arabic and Hebrew, 169
  art, 52, 232–233
  articles, 53, 214, 227
  books, 52–53, 212, 225

Titles of works *(continued)*
in Czech, 163
in Dutch, 153
in foreign languages, 149
in French, 158
in German, 152
in indexes, 254, 264–265
in Italian, 159
in Japanese, 171
in Latin, 161
musical compositions, 53
newspapers, 52–53, 228
parts of books, 53, 212, 225
periodicals, 37, 52, 53, 228
poetry, 52, 53, 212
in Polish, 162
in Russian, 168
in Scandinavian languages, 154
shortened, in source notes, 215
in Spanish, 156
in subsequent references, 215–216
unpublished materials, 229–230
Titles, table, 174
Top of page, proofreading, 311
Top of the trim, 347
Topographical maps, 192
Topographical terms, 40–41
Totals, in columns, 180
Tracking, 309, 327
Tracks, 309
Trademarks, 53–54
Trafficking copyedited manuscript, 297, 300
Transactions, 228
Transfer letters, 202
Translations, with parentheses, 24
Translator, trans., 212, 225
Transliteration
of Arabic and Hebrew, 168–169
of classical Greek (illus.), 164–165
of Russian (illus.), 165–167
Transparencies, as illustration art, 196
Transposition, 288
Transposition sign
copyediting mark, 288
to mark index entries, 247
proofreader mark, 306
Treaties, 44
Trim, 344
Trim size, 344
TrueType, 343
TruMatch system, 199
Two-color printing, 198–199

Two-em space, between equations, 111
2-head, 338
sample design specification (illus.), 345
Type, units of measure, 325
Type area, 337
Type block, 337
Type family, 328
Type font, 328
Type 1 fonts, 343
Type page, 337
Type size (illus.), 325–326
legibility and, 330, 335
Type styles, 324–325. *See also under individual styles*
Typefaces (illus.), 328–334
distinguishing, 329–330
legibility, 330, 335–336
mixing in page design, 330
visual characteristics, 328–330
Typemarking, 296–297
electronic, 351–354
mathematics, 117–119
of special characters, 353
Typescript, 272. *See also* Manuscript
Typesetter instructions, 280–281
for indexes, 270–271
proofreader's, 310
for tables, 172
Typesetter's errors, 304
Typesetting, 348–355
codes, 350–354
essential elements of, 349
technologies of, 348–350

U

UCC. *See* Universal Copyright Convention
Ultra bold type, 324
Umlaut
in biology and medical copy, 128
in German, 152
in Swedish, 155
Underlining, 56
Underscores, deleting, 285
Unfinished sentences, 17, 20–21
Uniform resource locator. *See* URL
Unit (number) combinations. *See* Inclusive numbers
Unit modifiers, 70–71
United States, U.S., 86

Units of aggregation, breaking equations and, 110
Units of measurement. *See* Measurement, units of
Univers (illus.), 334
Universal Copyright Convention, 320
Universal Product Code, 314
Unpublished materials
  in author-date references, 219
  in bibliographies, 229–230
  in source notes, 215
UPC. *See* Universal Product Code
Uppercase letter, 323
URL, 133, 236
U.S. Board on Geographical Names system, 166
U.S. Government Printing Office *Style Manual*, 168

V

v. (*versus*), 45, 87
Variety, var., 50, 130
Vector graphics, 349
Vectors, 109, 116–117
  typemarking, 118
Vehicle names, 54
Verbs
  with apostrophe, 2
  in compound words, 75
  with hyphen, 23
  inflection, 23
Vernacular forms, of Latin taxonomic names, 131–132
Verse, v., 235
Verso pages, 318
  folios and, 337
  running heads and, 336
versus, vs., 45, 87
Vertical form, of fractions, 114
Vertical lines, determinants and, 116
Vessel names, 54
Vice- compounds, 76
Videotapes, documentation of, 232
Virgule. *See* Slash
Viruses, 132
Volume, vol., vols., 94–95, 107
  in bibliography entries, 226, 228
  in indexes, 254
  in parenthetical references, 219
  in source notes, 213, 214
vs., versus, 45, 87

W

Wade-Giles system, 150
  of Chinese romanization, 169
Wars, names of, 44
Web, 356–357
Whereas, capitalization of, 38
White-copy system, 221–223
Whole numbers, 91, 95
Widow, 311
Wire stitching, 363
Word breaks
  end-of-line, 22, 79, 96, 171, 285
  in indexes, 270
Word division
  in Arabic and Hebrew, 169
  in Chinese, 170
  in classical Greek, 165
  in Czech, 163
  in Dutch, 153
  in foreign languages, 149
  in French, 158
  in German, 152
  in Italian, 159–160
  in Japanese, 171
  in Latin, 161
  in Portuguese, 160
  proofreading, 306
  in Russian, 168
  in Scandinavian languages, 154
  in Spanish, 156
Word spacing, 327
Word tables (illus.), 180–181
Word-by-word alphabetization, of indexes, 257
Word-for-hire contract, 203
Word-processing programs. *See also* Computer software
  bibliographic compilation using, 208–209
  editing using, 300–301
  generating equations on, 109
Words, columns of, 180–181
Words referred to as words, 29
  plural forms of, 63
World Wide Web, photo archives on, 202

X

X-height, 323

Y

Year numbers, 2, 98–100
Year of publication
  in bibliographies, 226–227, 228–229,
    231–235, 236–237
  in source notes, 213, 214
Yet, as conjunction, 33

Z

Zero, 101
  with percent sign, 128
  in table columns, 178–179
  typemarking, 119
Zoological terms, 50–51